An introduction to theories of social change

International Library of Sociology

Founded by Karl Mannheim

Editor: John Rex, University of Aston in Birmingham

Arbor Scientiae
Arbor Vitae

A catalogue of the books available in the **International Library of Sociology** and other series of Social Science books published by Routledge & Kegan Paul will be found at the end of this volume.

An introduction to theories of social change

**Hermann Strasser and
Susan C. Randall**
With special contributions by
Karl Gabriel
Hans Jürgen Krysmanski
and
Karl Hermann Tjaden

Routledge & Kegan Paul
London, Boston and Henley

*First published in 1981
by Routledge & Kegan Paul Ltd
39 Store Street, London WC1E 7DD,
9 Park Street, Boston, Mass. 02108, USA and
Broadway House, Newtown Road,
Henley-on-Thames, Oxon RG9 1EN
Photoset in Great Britain in 10 on 11pt Times by
Kelly Typesetting Ltd, Bradford-on-Avon, Wiltshire
Printed in the United States of America
© Hermann Strasser and Susan C. Randall 1981
No part of this book may be reproduced in
any form without permission from the
publisher, except for the quotation of brief passages in criticism*

British Library Cataloguing in Publication Data

Strasser, Hermann

*An introduction to theories of social change –
(International library of sociology)
1. Social change
I. Title II. Randall, Susan C. III. Series
303.4   HM101   80–42353*

*ISBN 0–7100–0789–2
ISBN 0–7100–0790–6 Pbk*

Contents

Preface and acknowledgments xi

Introduction 1
Susan C. Randall and *Hermann Strasser*

Part I The idea and cause of social change 9

1 Conceptualizing social change: problems of definition, empirical reference, and explanation 11
Susan C. Randall and *Hermann Strasser*

    1.1 What is social change? 11
    1.2 Levels of social change 20
    1.3 Assumptions: the nature of society and the interests of the social scientist 23
    1.4 Causes and processes of social change 26
    Notes 33
    Suggested reading 34

2 Theoretical approaches to the explanation of social change: a survey 36
Susan C. Randall and *Hermann Strasser*

    2.1 The idea of industrial society 36
    2.2 Theories of endogenous social change 40
    2.3 Theories of exogenous social change 73
    Notes 84
    Suggested reading 86

Part II Selected theories of social change: detailed studies   89

3 The historic-materialistic theory of societal development   91
Hans Jürgen Krysmanski and *Karl Hermann Tjaden*
   3.1 Introduction   91
   3.2 The development of human societalization as sequence of economic society formations   96
   3.3 Social development and social change within the capitalist system   106
   3.4 Intersystem-relations within the universal process of societalization   116
   3.5 A general critique of historic-materialistic theory of societal development   125
   Notes   127
   Suggested reading   128

4 The structural-functional theory of social change   130
Hermann Strasser
   4.1 Prologue to a functional analysis of change   130
   4.2 The logic of functionalism   132
   4.3 Functionalism and social change   151
   Notes   181
   Suggested reading   189

Part III Analysis of change on different levels of society   193

5 Levels of sociological analysis: four theories of change   195
Susan C. Randall and *Hermann Strasser*

6 Change of the social system, social groups, and social relationships   199
Susan C. Randall and *Hermann Strasser*
   6.1 Macrolevel analysis: Barrington Moore's theory of societal change   199
   6.2 Structural strain and group reaction: Neil J. Smelser's theory of collective behavior   220
   6.3 Individual reactions to status inconsistency: theories about social status and change of social relationships   245

6.4	Summary and comparison of the three theoretical approaches	266
Notes		272
Suggested reading		274

7 Organizations and social change   276
Karl Gabriel

7.1	Introduction	276
7.2	Social change and organizational development	277
7.3	Social change in organizations	286
7.4	Organizational change as a process	297
7.5	Outlook: from bureaucracy to Ad-Hocracy?	301
Notes		303
Suggested reading		305

Select bibliography   308

Index   331

Figures

3.1 Developmental characteristics of the theory of Marx
    and Engels   93
4.1 Exchange relations between primary subsystem of
    society (AGIL-scheme)   188

Tables

1.1	Empirical levels and theoretical perspectives of social change	31
1.2	Causes of social change	33
4.1	Types of change explained by functionalist theory	176
4.2	The AGIL-scheme differentiated according to the control hierarchy of action systems, social subsystems, structural components, primary functions, and aspects of social change	186
6.1	Levels of specificity of the components of social action	226
6.2	Right-wing extremism by low and high status consistency, controlled for status differences in occupation, income, and education	257
6.3	Responses to status disequilibrium	259
7.1	Several approaches to stages of organizational change	298

Preface and acknowledgments

This study is addressed especially to students of the social sciences who are interested in exploring the possibilities of conceptually coming to grips with, and theoretically explaining, phenomena of change on different levels of society. The authors hope that the text will satisfy the systematic, comprehensive, and illustrative claims that are connected with it.

We would like to express our gratitude to Friedrich Fürstenberg for his intellectual impulses and moral support in launching this adventure. Without numerous discussions with Werner Stark about the explanatory potential of sociological theories, the topics dealt with in this volume would have hardly been mastered. We would also like to thank Peter Hopkins for his encouragement and almost unending patience – patience, it seems, that only publishers are capable of mustering. Maria Nowakowska, Anthony D. Smith, Werner Stark, David Whitney, and Charles Wright have read parts of the work at different stages and their comments were always helpful. Christel Quasigroh, Renate Voigt, Brigitte Brück and Peter Wichmann should be given credit for their conscientious work in helping to prepare the finished typescript.

Hermann Strasser
Susan C. Randall
Duisburg/Dallas,

Introduction

Susan C. Randall and *Hermann Strasser*

Historical development or what we usually call history is one thing; the idea of coming and going, and hence also the theory of the past of human society, is yet another thing. However, such a theory is itself always in the process of development – a development of which the concepts and explanatory schemes that we are going to present here give ample proof. Theoretical ideas about the change of society are in the process of development (1) because society and its history are the result of the *dialectic* relation of purposive actions of society's members and their institutional objectivations; (2) because social reality is, on the one hand, perceived through the lenses of varying value preferences and *interest situations* of individuals and groups and, on the other hand, differently interpreted on the basis of the connection between human interests and social science knowledge; (3) because, as time goes by, the *subject* of study will be a different one, and its theoretical as well as methodical seizure will also change in the wake of adjustments of competing systems of knowledge.

Concepts like evolution, development, transformation, differentiation, industrialization, and adaptation not only reveal a multiplicity of competing meaning systems, but also point to their origin in different phases of social analysis. For example, sociologists of the nineteenth century lived and worked in a world in which the Industrial Revolution was under way, and therefore saw in social change the major problem to be tackled by their society. Their goal, to analyze society, was identical with the study of social change. However, they had to deal with a Newtonian world which believed in an ordered nature of things and which was determined by an omnipresent, invariable, and immanent cause. This 'causal idea' reflected a universal striving for an ideal in human civilization

INTRODUCTION

ranging from Hegel's 'freedom of spirit,' Marx's revolt of modern forces of production against outmoded relations of production, to Sumner's 'what worked best' (cf. Zimmerman, 1961: 4). The result was the classical theory of social evolution which we shall deal with in greater detail in Chapter 2.

For sociology, the analysis of social change did not always constitute the primary subject matter. Particularly, the negative effects of the Industrial Revolution, wars, and war-like struggles in terms of anomie, disintegration, poverty, class conflict, alienation, fragmentation, and bureaucratization brought about a shift in scientific focus from the study of society over time to the analysis of forms, structures, and mechanisms of society. This perspective reached its peak with the structural-functional theory in the late 1940s and 1950s. As discussed in Chapters 2 and 4, the study of social change did not, of course, vanish; it was only restrained and furnished with specific accents. If it is correct that society means, above all, action, formation and change of structure, then sociological theories should be distinguished not by whether they explain change but by *what kind of* change they explain.

It is a common experience that our everyday life, organized as it is in some form, is characterized by orderly persistence as much as by change. As man's biological life cycle (from childhood to old age) and various forms of conflict in political, economic, and social life (e.g., strikes, legal suits, demonstrations) and their implications for change suggest, small-scale changes may be considered as an important aspect of stability and persistence on a larger scale. Thus, changing patterns of social life seem to provide as much predictable continuity to societal organization as fixed patterns do. There are also those events such as social and political revolutions, massive immigration, war, conquest, bad harvest, technological and medical inventions, etc., that bring about basic changes on all levels of society. One is tempted to say that life *is* change, or that the only thing that does not change is the variability of all things. Some social scientists dare to mention those factors that are epochal for more than just parts of 'a' society, that is, indicative of, and producing, change. To name a few: Jacques Ellul (1964) writes about the 'technological society,' Vance Packard (1972) describes the 'restless society,' Helmut Klages (1974) speaks of the 'mobile society,' Warren G. Bennis and Philip E. Slater (1969) – but also Alvin Toffler (1970) – of the 'temporary society,' Burton Clarke (1962) discusses the 'expert society,' while still others envision the 'educated society' or the 'service society' as in the case of Viktor Fuchs (1968), Alan Gartner and Frank Riessman (1974), as well as Jean Fourastié (1949). Finally, Daniel Bell (1973), Alain Touraine

(1971), and also Helmut Schelsky (1975) conjure the dawning of 'post-industrial society,' in which scientists, technicians, and academics in general exert the real power on the basis of their function as producers and disseminators of information and meaning.

International organizations such as the OECD (1975) are not content with these labeling attempts, proposing instead trends of change that refer to specific areas in social life: (1) occupational structure: rapid growth of the tertiary or service sector; decrease of self-employed members in the labor force; increasing importance of certain groups with employment problems (youth, women, older people, unskilled laborers, aliens); (2) economic area: increasing share and importance of public enterprises and state functions; low growth rates of the net national product per capita; change of the labor and recreational system (work organization, technology, system of transportation and communication); increasing socialization of risks and costs; increase of transfer income (subsidized prices, tax exempted goods and services); (3) social, political, and demographic factors: decreasing birth rates and increasing life expectancy; decreasing proportion of the active labor force as compared with the total population; changes of functions in family, school, and peer group; increasing pressure toward integration and interdependence; increasing bureaucratization in state agencies and economic corporations; increasing number of decision makers on the local, regional, national, and international level.

And yet most people believe unshakeably in the *constancy* of central aspects of their lives, be that their occupation, the organization in which they work, values they cherish, or the intellectual subject matter we study scientifically. In his recent book, *Beyond the Stable State*, Donald A. Schon (1971) has aptly shown that the belief in stability is a device to maintain stability, or at least the illusion of it, hence protecting the believer from apprehension of the various threats inherent in change. Those who do not sustain belief in the stable state of one's affairs, inescapably face what Alvin Toffler (1970) has termed 'future shock,' namely, a social disease inflicted upon people who are unable to cope with the strain of permanent novelty in times when traditional patterns of behavior are too often inappropriate or dysfunctional.

Such existential orientation toward stability corresponds, it seems, with a likewise strong desire for an interpretation of history – in all men, not only in those whose business is to interpret the past and the future. This desire apparently originates in everybody's need for a constructive view into the future. What would be more suggestive than to recur to the events of yesterday and today (cf.

Powicke, 1956: 177). The satisfaction of this need, however, hits upon practical as well as scientific limitations which are closely related to the unintended consequences of human action as the following quotation from Norbert Elias's *Über den Prozeß der Zivilisation* (1976, vol. 2: 221) demonstrates:

> [out of] the interweaving of innumerable individual interests and intentions – be they compatible, or opposed and inimical – something eventually emerges that, as it turns out, has neither been planned nor intended by any single individual. And yet it has been brought about by the intentions and actions of many individuals. And this is actually the whole secret of social interweaving – of its compellingness, its regularity, its structure, its processual nature, and its development; this is the secret of sociogenesis and social dynamics.

Every theory of society has a built-in stability-change dimension. Some sociological theories take change in a social item (e.g., industrial*ization*, bureaucratization) as the phenomenon to be explained. To other theories stability or the re-establishment of some stable state of a social item (e.g., industrial*ism*, structure of social inequality) is the phenomenon to be explained. In the latter case, change is simply taken as a transition from one state of a social item to another. If all theories address themselves, in one way or another, to questions of stability and change, the crux of the matter is not which theoretical scheme deals with the change dimension, but rather which one explains more effectively social change, its origins, forms, and directions. Therefore, the talk about sociology or certain theoretical approaches as being able to explain only the structure of interhuman relations and of whole social systems but not its change, is as senseless as stating that one could explain a bird only in the state of rest and not in the state of flight (Martindale, 1964: xii).

These remarks should have made clear that sociological analysis of social change is characterized by the following axes: (1) on the one hand, the interest of members of society in stable states faces a nearly infinite variability of society on all levels; (2) on the other hand, there is the unceasing effort of men to possess knowledge about the past and certainty about the future that faces the impotence of the social sciences to explain history comprehensively and to predict the events of only the next decade, the more distant future notwithstanding. The conceptual and theoretical discussions that we are going to undertake in the following chapters are therefore primarily meant to order a number of different facts and experiences under alternative scientific aspects. Depending on the perspective, change will be understood as change on a small scale (e.g., the formation of a leadership role in a group), as cyclical process (e.g., in the organic sense of growth and decline), or as fundamental change (e.g., change of an aspect of a social system which is constitutive for the system such as the market economy, the parliamentary system or the value pluralism of British or US society). These definitions of social change may be referred to as short-term and long-term changes (e.g., in the labor market and the employment structures) as well as to continuous and discontinuous change (e.g., bureaucratization *vs* invention). What we are saying is that the respective vocabulary for explaining social change(s) directs the attention of the social analyst to *certain* problems and subsequently to *relevant* data that have to be analytically refined.

The present volume is intended to introduce the student into the area of social change by discussing central questions and dimensions of phenomena of social change and by systematically presenting important theoretical approaches to change analysis. Accordingly, the book is divided into three parts. In Part I (Chapters 1 and 2) the assumptions underlying any analysis of change and the dimensions of social change are explicated and the most important theories are surveyed; in Part II (Chapters 3 and 4) two theoretical approaches, namely, the historic-materialistic theory of societal development and the functionalist theory of social change, are dealt with in great detail; Part III (Chapters 5, 6, and 7), finally, is devoted to case studies of change phenomena on different levels of society.

Chapter 1 starts with an attempt to draw the student's attention to the assumptions on which any analysis of social change is based and which concern the character of society and man's position in it. As we shall see, these assumptions have a considerable influence on the conceptualization, definition, and description as well as subsequently on the explanation of cause and process of change. In Chapter 2, theoretical positions, considered to be of central importance by most sociologists, are presented, not least with the intention of acquainting the reader with methodological and substantive problems encountered when studying social change, as well as dealing with the conceptual and analytical differences that are closely connected with the basic orientation of how to go about studying the subject matter in the first place. In that we begin with the idea of industrial society, an attempt is made to distinguish theories of social change in terms of whether they focus on endogenous or exogenous causes of change.

In Chapters 3 and 4, studies of those theoretical approaches are offered which, considering their pervasive use in the discipline, merit detailed elaboration. Hans Jürgen Krysmanski and Karl

INTRODUCTION

Hermann Tjaden deal with the historic-materialistic theory of societal development in which characteristically not the concept of change but those of transformation and development are used. The authors aim at a systematic presentation of problems and propositions central to historic-materialistic social theory as is possible on the basis of today's state of knowledge. The various Neo-Marxisms that have dominated Marxist debates in West Germany, France, Great Britain, and the United States over the last two decades (e.g., Critical Theory, state monopoly capitalism), will be considered only to the extent that they are directly related to the analysis of social development. Hermann Strasser scrutinizes in Chapter 4 the explanatory potential of the structural-functional theory of social change. At first, its logic will be discussed and assumptions, postulates, concepts, and hypotheses of functional analysis examined. By comparing the merits and shortcomings of this approach, conclusions will be derived with respect to the scientific value of a social theory that is based upon functionalist postulates. As in the case of the historic-materialistic theory, functionalist theory is distinguished from non-functionalist approaches in that it poses different research questions.

Because this book aims at making the reader confident with problems and perspectives of the sociological study of change in society, the material in Parts I and II is largely geared toward the kind of change analysis which, historically speaking, has been predominant in the sociological discipline, namely, the macrosociological analysis. If such an emphasis may be justified in a study like this one, we do believe, however, that it neglects an important trend in recent literature which considers, besides social changes on a system level, also changes on other levels of society. Therefore, in Chapters 5, 6, and 7 we deal with various problems and aspects of change analysis on different levels of society.

Chapter 5 purports to introduce briefly the levels on which human action and changes in social relationships may be studied. In Chapters 6 and 7 we draw on four explanatory schemes that are currently used in analysis of change on various levels of society. We selected those approaches because of their illustrative character as they refer to clearly distinct, though partly complementary, levels in the analysis of factors that are associated with the causation and process of change. The first explanatory scheme to be offered in Chapter 6 has been formulated by Barrington Moore in his study of *Social Origins of Dictatorship and Democracy*. It is a societal analysis of change that focuses, above all, on the sources and mechanisms of the transformation of a society with feudal principles of organization to one with industrial principles. The second theory, as contained in Neil J. Smelser's *Theory of Collective Behavior*, refers to social action on the group level directed toward partial or fundamental changes of the social order. The third explanatory scheme is oriented toward the level of social relationships, including various studies on the relations between social status of individuals and their activities and attitudes directed toward change. Finally, Karl Gabriel deals with the dimensions and possibilities of explaining social change on the level of complex organizations.

We do not intend to emphasize the explanatory power of one analytical level or perspective as compared with others. Rather, we would like to point to the great and small differences that we shall encounter on our journey through the various ways of analyzing social change – depending upon, as in the present case, whether we are concerned with the whole society, the group, the organization, or interhuman relationships. Points of contact and complementary aspects of these theoretical approaches will also be considered. In Chapter 6, for example, we have added the same test case, namely, the rise of National Socialism in the Weimar Republic, to the presentation of the theories of Moore, Smelser, and status inconsistency, respectively, in order to compare directly the descriptive and explanatory power of these approaches.

Finally, we should mention the intended functions of the various chapters: the aim of Chapters 1, 2, and 5 is primarily to introduce the subject matter and to provide an overview of relevant theories; the function of Chapters 3, 4, 6, and 7 is to offer to the student a detailed look into select theoretical approaches and specific levels of change analysis; sections 1.4 and 6.4 serve to present systematic and comparative summaries in order to structure the state of knowledge and to stimulate further study. The latter purpose has also been on our mind when we complemented each chapter (except Chapter 5) with 'suggested reading' divided into 'introductory' and 'further reading,' the latter, in turn, split into 'general' and 'problem-related' readings.

Part I The idea and cause of social change

1 Conceptualizing social change: problems of definition, empirical reference, and explanation

Susan C. Randall and *Hermann Strasser*

1.1 What is social change?

1.1.1 Defining change

The question as to what social change actually is is perhaps the most difficult one within the scientific study of change. It involves the often neglected query of what *kind* and *degree* of change in *what* is to be considered social change. Most analysts of change deal with this question implicitly somewhere in their theoretical system or in the context of the latter's application to some empirical case. For the present purpose it should suffice to examine definitions that are frequently used to conceptualize change, in terms of differences and similarities, and subsequently to explore some of the problems and implications of these concepts.

Theorists of social change, be they of the conflict or functionalist, evolutionary or cyclical or whatever school, agree that, in the most concrete sense of the word 'change,' every social system is changing all the time. The composition of the population changes through the life cycle and thus the occupancy of roles changes; the members of society undergo physiological changes; the continuing interactions among members modify attitudes and expectations; new knowledge is constantly being gained and transmitted. On the other hand, many of the social structures within which these changes occur show hardly any traces of change. Robert A. Nisbet (1970: 306) illustrates with the example of the family structure in Western society:

> Consider only the number of undoubted role tensions, not to say domestic squabbles and hatreds, in the history of the family in the West during the past 2,000 years. But the number of changes of

structure of the family and changes of dominant roles in the family have been few. Most are directly related to events outside the family, in other spheres of society, which proved to have substantial impact upon the family. Deviations from the norm of monogamous marriage have always been present in the form of evasions – some of which have been sanctioned evasions, some not. But the norm of monogamy, like the structure of monogamy with its roles and statuses, goes on century after century.

We therefore cannot regard such things as social interactions, changes in the population or in role occupancy, or the conflicts, tensions, and strains of roles, status, and norms as 'change.' Neither can we 'seek to derive change – its sources, mechanisms, continuities or discontinuities, and alleged directions – from the elements of social structure – role, status, norm, and so on' (Nisbet, 1970: 303–4). However, Wilbert E. Moore (1963: Chapter 3) points out the problem of disregarding the aggregate effects of seemingly insignificant, day-to-day alterations. For example, a long-term change in either the birth or death rate of a society can have enormous consequences for the economic system, stratification system, educational, political, and military institutions, etc. Even a change of the occupant of a role, especially if the role is that of a king, prime minister, dictator, president, military commander, etc., can have far-reaching effects.

How, then, can we distinguish between that which is, in a sense, continuously 'changing' (and which, in another sense, remains relatively unchanged) and that which constitutes 'change'? Although there is little agreement on the subject, some distinctions have been developed which may be useful if only to illuminate the state of confusion surrounding the issue at present. Perhaps the most widespread distinction that is currently made between kinds of change is that developed by Talcott Parsons (1951: 480–2) in his analysis of change *within* and change *of* the system, i.e., the orderly processes of ongoing change within the boundaries of a system, as opposed to the processes resulting in changes of the structure of the system under consideration. Many proponents of the functionalist view (and some of its opponents) have adopted or modified Parsons's categorization.

It is correct, however, as Lewis A. Coser (1967: 27) points out, that the distinction between change *within* and change *of* systems is a relative one:

> There is always some sort of continuity between a past and a present, or a present and a future social system; societies do not die the way biological organisms do, for it is difficult to assign

precise points of birth or death to societies as we do with biological organisms. One may claim that all that can be observed is a change of the organization of social relations; but from one perspective such change may be considered re-establishment of equilibrium whereas from another it may be seen as the formation of a new system.

Although this appears to be a useful analytical distinction, conflict theorists, for instance, draw our attention to the fact that the cumulative effect of changes *within* the system may result in a change *of* the system.[1]

> It is precisely Marx's contention that the change from feudalism to a different type of social system can be understood only through an investigation of the stresses and strains *within* the system . . . conflict leads not only to ever-changing relations within the existing social structure, but the total social system undergoes transformation through conflict (Coser, 1967: 25–6).

Although we may distinguish between these two types of change, they should not be seen as empirically unrelated. If we ignore the strains, tensions, and conflicts among elements of the social system as possible sources or mechanisms of change, we are bound to develop a one-sided and utterly incomplete view of the nature of social change. For example, Harry M. Johnson (1960: 630) thinks that it is not necessary to count strain and alteration within a structure as 'change' because 'if it is sociologically important, [it] will bring about changes in values or in institutional patterns' that can then be considered as changes *of* a structure.

In those theories that are based on the assumption that a social system (or a group or a relationship) is a relatively persistent, stable (or at least changing in a smooth, continuous manner) and well-integrated structure of elements (i.e., evolutionary and equilibrium theories), changes within the system are seen as 'normal' processes within the pattern of the social structure – processes that operate in terms of adaptations within the boundaries of that structure. Other common (but not as specific) formulations of the components of structural changes include 'those changes of type, or form, or pattern of behavior' (Nisbet, 1970: 310) or changes in 'the size of a society, the composition or balance of its parts or the type of its organization' (Ginsberg, 1970: 37). Yet, there is still much disagreement as to what degree of alteration in a structure is 'significant' and what type of alterations in which structures should be counted as 'major' or 'minor,' 'central' or 'marginal.'

Whereas among theorists who focus on equilibrium, there is at least some consensus as to what is *not* 'change,' for those who see conflict and change as inherent in social organization (i.e., conflict and 'rise and fall' theories), the subject of social change is even more vague and confusing. Ralf Dahrendorf (1959a: 162) enumerates some of the basic tenets of this view:

1   Every society is at every point subject to processes of change; social change is ubiquitous.
2   Every society displays at every point dissensus and conflict; social conflict is ubiquitous.
3   Every element in a society renders a contribution to its disintegration and change.
4   Every society is based on the coercion of some of its members by others.

For conflict theorists (cf. section 2.2.1) the central argument is contained in the second assumption, that is to say, that antagonisms inhere in every society leading to change via conflict. Even though it is beyond doubt that change is ubiquitous (i.e., operating continuously), conflict theorists also regard some types of change as more important, fundamental or significant than others. At the risk of doing injustice to some conflict theorists, we could assign the label of 'social change' to those types of change that have just been cited as significant ones. We are here referring to changes in power relations or such changes that set up pressures for an alteration in the existing power relations (e.g., for Karl Marx, the development of new forces of production with ensuing changes in the relations of production; cf. Marx, 1964a; Dahrendorf, 1959a: 231ff.; Coser, 1956: 8, 37).

Which changes will be seen as changes in power relations depends, of course, on the theorist's conception of power. For Marx, 'power' meant economic power, but control over (i.e., ownership or disposal of) the means of production also meant political power. The reason for social conflict was seen in divergent interests resulting from the unequal distribution of power between two major groupings: the capitalists or capital realizators who have the power by virtue of their ownership or other legal titles of control over the means of production to rule, exploit, and alienate the non-owners or wage earners (cf. Marx, 1964b: 884–93). For Max Weber, power represented the ability to influence the will of others, i.e., to induce others to act in a way even against their will (Bendix and Lipset, 1966: 8; Weber, 1947: 28).

Regardless of whether we stick with the Marxist tradition by interpreting the power structure as a special case of the property structure or the Weberian conception by considering power differences as universal and property as a special case of the power structure, from a conflict theoretical point of view we are offered the following idea of change: change *within* a system of authority relations (e.g., merger of two companies) and change *of* the system of authority (e.g., through the transfer of power from one social group or class to another – directly via rights of participation in the decision-making process or indirectly via the state's income policy or union actions).

For representatives of the 'rise and fall' theory (cf. section 2.2.3), significant changes are those that mark the transition from one stage or phase of a construed cycle of development to another. Vilfredo Pareto (1966: 265ff.), for example, saw in the closing of the ranks by the governing elite to the non-elite 'foxes' the onset of the former's decline, and this may be said to represent a 'significant' change.

Along the same line we may designate as 'significant' those changes that evolutionary theorists (cf. section 2.2.2) associate with the movement of social forms or a whole society from a 'less advanced' state toward a terminal 'advanced' state or from one level or epoch to another. This is exemplified by Marx's idea that the slavery epoch is replaced by feudalism which, in turn, gives way to capitalism and the latter eventually to socialism. For Auguste Comte, the world of thoughts is characterized by a sequence of theological, metaphysical, and positive epochs in correspondence with respective stages in the development of dominant principles of societal organization: the military, the juridical, and the industrial epoch. Emile Durkheim, finally, envisions societies to follow a process of development that runs from a primitive, pre-industrial stage with 'mechanical solidarity' as the dominant principle of societal organization to ever-increasing complexity and interdependence based on 'organic solidarity.'[2]

So far the discussion of the question of what in effect constitutes change, gives rise only to an admittedly unsatisfactory answer. Those changes in a society that are considered 'significant,' apparently depend on the aspect of society or the segment of social reality that is of strategic importance to the social analyst for the realization of his cognitive interests (cf. section 1.3). Already a first look at the notions that have been traditionally linked with the idea of change is, to some extent at least, indicative: development, progress, evolution, revolution, process, movement, transition, transformation, modernization, industrialization, secularization, urbanization, bureaucratization. They clearly indicate criteria of selection with respect to the analysis of change referring mainly to its scope, time span, direction, and speed. In this case, if we speak of change, we have in mind something that comes into being after some time; that is to say, we are dealing with a difference between what can be observed before that point in time and what we see after that point in time (cf. sections 1.1.2 and 1.2). In order to be able to state differences, the unit of analysis must preserve a minimum of identity – in spite of change over time (Swanson, 1971: 5).

1.1.2 Describing change

Some of the attributes most frequently used in describing change are: magnitude of change, time span, direction, rate of change, amount of violence involved. These dimensions should not be taken as 'either/or' attributes but rather as varying along a continuum from one extreme to another (e.g., revolutionary *vs* evolutionary, small-scale *vs* large-scale).

In order to recognize the *magnitude*, scope or simply extent of change, it is useful to introduce the distinction between small-scale and large-scale changes. This categorization is designed to reflect the 'size and centrality (or strategic character) of the units affected [and] the degree of alteration involved by the change' (Appelbaum, 1970: 8). The types of change that are referred to here range from those that 'are so regular in their recurrence that they are a major component of predictable order, and scarcely to be regarded as change in the sense of altered roles, rules, or conditions of action' (Moore and Cook, 1967: 81) to the other extreme in the magnitude of change 'when all major structural relations, basic institutions, and prevailing value systems have been transformed' (Coser, 1967: 18). Generally, the theorists operating out of an equilibrium model do not regard the first types of change mentioned as comprising small-scale *social* change:

> so long as the process is accompanied by not *significant changes in the group* – that is, by no alterations in the person's positions and their relations and thus in the performances they are expected to play, in rules of conduct, or the results of the system as it continues to operate (Moore, 1963: 46).

As to where the line is to be drawn between small-scale and large-scale changes, the criteria that have been offered are somewhat vague. Kingsley Davis (1950: 622) used the terms 'social change' *vs* 'cultural change' in discussing this dimension:

> By 'social change' is meant only such alterations as occur in social organization – that is, the structure and functions of society. Social change thus forms only a part of what is essentially a broader category called 'cultural change'. The latter embraces all

changes occurring in any branch of culture, including art, science, technology, philosophy, etc. as well as changes in the forms and rules of social organization.

Another distinction offered is that small-scale change 'refers to changes within groups and organizations rather than societies, cultures or civilizations' (Moore and Cook, 1967: 81). Wilbert E. Moore (1963: 46–7), in his book *Social Change*, writes:

> By small-scale changes we shall mean changes in the characteristics of social structures that, though comprised within the general system identifiable as a society, do not have any immediate and major consequences for the generalized structure (society) as such.

Moore (1963: 47) admits that 'the qualifier "major" is possibly evasive, unless some measure of magnitude is available and some meaningful "critical minimum" is accepted as constituting a major effect.' However, he neglects to establish any such measure. A further distinction can be derived from Lewis A. Coser's analysis of social conflict in which small-scale changes may be seen as social conflicts which 'lead to inner adjustments of social systems' and large-scale ones as those which result in 'the breakup of existing social orders and the emergence of a new set of social relations within a new social structure' (Coser, 1967: 18).

A fundamental problem with all of these attempts to conceptualize the magnitude of change (other than their obvious vagueness) involves the next attribute of change to be discussed, namely, the *time span*. That is to say, a change that may be classified as 'small-scale' from a short-term perspective may turn out to have 'large-scale' consequences when viewed over a long period of time, as the decreasing birth rate since the middle of the 1960s in such Western countries as the Federal Republic of Germany exemplifies. Although these descriptions of magnitude may make it possible to classify the effects of an historically 'completed' event, it is difficult to apply them to actual or hypothetical cases of change.

The specification of a time span over which change is to be studied is especially important but lacking in many theories. Moore (1963: 31) suggests that:

> Before propositions about short-term and long-term effects can be objectively tested, the time interval must be specified and the future when 'long-term' effects 'will' display themselves must not be so distant as to be meaningless. For we are reminded of the acerbic comment, attributed to the great economist Lord Keynes. 'In the long run we are all dead.'

Yet, such a specification in terms of months, years, or decades of what will from now on constitute short-term and long-term change in all theories would be utterly unwise. It is always relative in reference to the subject under consideration. Surely the study of the short-term and long-term effects of an economic depression necessitates the use of a different temporal unit than the study of the short-range and long-range effects of the Industrial Revolution.

Not only statisticians but also sociologists know how much the impression of a rapid or slow development of some sort (e.g., economic growth, birth and death rates, attitudes toward sex, moral principles, consumption, leisure) is dependent upon the periodization of change indicating, in turn, the close relationship between periodization and (the perception of) the rate of change. The speed or *rate* at which change takes place may be represented on a continuum from gradual to abrupt, from slow to rapid. In order to be useful this distinction must be accompanied by a specification of the time span and the point in time toward which change is directed, that is, a goal state toward which the changing phenomenon is headed slowly or rapidly, continuously or suddenly. The capacity to assess the significance of change presupposes to some extent an idea of its direction. Similar to Marshall McLuhan's principle that 'The medium is the message,' the rate of change may turn out to be *the* determining factor of its direction. Alvin Toffler (1970) demonstrates precisely this when he describes the future shock as disease of change that results from a widening gap between the rapidity by which our environment changes, and the limited speed at which man proceeds to react to these conditions. By referring to the throw-away society he purports to show where a society is moving in which permanence of social institutions and human bonds have become absent – i.e., a society dominated by an 'economy of impermanence' with wedding gowns made of paper, with rentals and portables in all spheres of life, with furniture and houses in stable structures but exchangeable elements, with temporary needs and rapidly changing preferences for products (cf. Toffler, 1970: Chapter 4).

The fourth attribute of social change is that of its *directionality*. Whether change is viewed as progress or regression ultimately depends on the cognitive interest of the analyst. The guiding interest of cognition may be oriented either toward knowledge about objectified social structures and processes in that patterned relationships between variables are stated, or toward knowing and subsequently abolishing the antagonisms in society. In the first case we have to do with a social–technological or conservative interest of cognition which aims at the production of nomological knowledge for the purpose of extending instrumental, success-controlled action, while in the second case we are dealing with a social–emancipatory or progressive interest of cognition that purports to conceptualize unbearable states of society in order to change them (cf. Strasser, 1976: Chapter 1; Baier, 1969). Under social–emancipatory premises change analysis may, for example, pose the question whether or not the expansion of state activities will, in the long run, contribute to more distributive justice. The affirmative case would then be considered progress. Less profane would be the query whether the change in a religion from three gods into another with one god would necessarily mean progress. Under Christian premises the question would have to be answered positively. If, however, one could look into the future and see that the ultimate result of the development of religion in that society 'is going to be a belief in six gods, a change from a belief in three to a belief in one is not speed at all but retrogression' (Davis, 1950: 627). The same conclusion might be reached if the observer had no insight into the future but were a proponent of polytheism rather than of Christianity. Undoubtedly such a development could also be part of a general movement toward the top – similar to the perspective of historians who believe that time and again peaks besides temporary regresses have been observed in the history of mankind (e.g., Greco-Roman civilization, Renaissance, Industrial Revolution) and of economists for whom the business cycles of the capitalistic economy also represent temporary setbacks in a general trend toward increasing welfare (cf. Moore, 1963: 35–7).

The directions of change usually discerned are cyclical and linear changes, or variations on these two themes. But in order to extrapolate a trend in change we must have a starting point and a terminal point within which change proceeds, as well as some point of reference indicating the direction the change process is taking. One of the main criticisms leveled against all theories that social change, taken as a whole, is 'ultimately' linear or cyclical, is that:

> We cannot know anything about *all* of social change. At best we have reasonably full data concerning a few thousand years of human history, out of millions of past years and no telling how many future ones. Any claim that a mode of change has always persisted and always will persist clearly goes beyond empirical knowledge. The question of what is the ultimate nature of social change is therefore simply a philosophical puzzle that has no place in social science. When we confine ourselves to what is knowable, we find both trends and fluctuations. Indeed, whether a given change is cyclical or linear depends largely on the span of

time under consideration. A decline in business appears as a trend if only a few years are taken, whereas in a larger time context it appears as merely one phase of the business cycle (Davis, 1950: 629).

The last major distinction frequently employed is that between *peaceful* and *violent* change. At times, the attribute 'peaceful' has been considered as practically synonymous with 'gradual,' and 'violent' with 'rapid.' In a certain sense, one can indeed say that rapid change may 'violently' affect the emotions, values, and expectations of those involved. In this case a 'cultural lag' at the institutional as well as social-psychological level occurs, as we have already seen in our discussion of Toffler's 'future shock'. This is true for the occupational sphere as well as for the household sphere. For example, the miner and compositor have become highly specialized technicians; on the other hand, the improvement of the financial situation has brought about a change in the functions of the family, although values and communicative relations are still, to a considerable extent anyway, oriented toward traditional principles or characterized by great insecurity.

In describing change the term 'violence' frequently refers to the threat or use of physical force involved in attaining a given change while 'peaceful' has to do with changes that take place by consent, acceptance, or acquiescence and that are enforced by the usual normative restraints of society. Of course, this distinction ignores the institutional violence often involved in 'usual normative restraints.' Thus, it might be more useful (and more correct) to rephrase this distinction in terms of the degree of violence employed, rather than in terms of its presence or absence.

Other categorizations that have been devised involve the division of changes on the basis of such characteristics as continuous *vs* spasmodic, orderly *vs* erratic, planned *vs* unplanned, and the number of people (or roles) affected by, or involved in, change. Although no hard and fast categories have yet been developed into which we can fit different types of change, the use of the foregoing distinctions, nebulous as they are, may be helpful in clarifying one's conceptualization of any type of change or, at least, they can help one understand the complexities involved in developing a definition of the subject of social change.

1.2 Levels of social change

The second basic question in determining how a sociological theory conceptualizes change involves the scope of the particular theory, i.e., what aspect of human action is being considered 'social' or in what segment of social reality is change presumed to be located. Various theories focus on the individual and group processes which underlie changes in society, while others concentrate on changes on the social system level. Most theories claiming to describe and explain social change are based on one of these perspectives – the psychological (e.g., Freud, Horney), the social–psychological (e.g., Simmel, Mead) or the sociological (e.g., Durkheim, Marx, Parsons). The effect of other theoretical perspectives range from temporary importance, as in the case of Social Darwinism, to insignificant, as is true for geographical and climatic theories. The various levels and scopes of social reality that we have chosen in Chapters 6 and 7 (Part III) for detailed analysis, should also demonstrate how the respective level is suited for describing and explaining change. Obviously, the particular focus of a theory on one or the other level of human action greatly influences its scope as well as its conceptualization of the cause, the impetus, the process, and the effects of change.

In general, most theories that focus on the *individual* personality define the nature of social relations in terms of the fulfillment or repression of various instincts and need-dispositions and with reference to such psychological processes as cognition, emotion, and motivation. Changes are seen as responses to externally produced stimuli; that is, as interchanges between the human organism and his physical and social environment in which man, via the learning process, can obtain information from his environment and thus adapt to it or attempt to adjust the environment to his own needs and goals (cf. Phillips, 1969: 28). Various psychologists have stressed the power of the environment to alter individual behavior (e.g., the stimulus-response theories of Pavlov, Hull, and Skinner), while others emphasize the individual's control over his environment and his problem-solving capacities (e.g., the psychological field theory). In either case, the individual is seen as a goal-oriented creature (regardless of whether these goals are stated in terms of instincts, drives, needs, tension reduction, or whatever) and the social is believed to reside in the interchanges between an individual and his environment, particularly in the psychic response to these interchanges.

Social-psychology principally focuses on the dynamics of *interactions* between individuals. The psychological characteristics and behavior patterns are taken into account as well as the social context within which interaction occurs. Behaviorists such as George Caspar Homans (1967: 31–2) undertake to explain all social behavior in terms of two psychological quasi-laws: that 'the basic units of social behavior are the actions of individual men' and 'that the actions are a function of their [psychological] payoffs [in terms of rewards and costs].' Georg Simmel (1964: 13ff.), who studied such social phenomena as conflict, dyads, gift giving, and strangers, located the social in the interaction among individuals, thus defining it as an interhuman reality, while 'Meadian psychology not only sees the social level as residing in the relations among men, but sees the human personality as arising virtually entirely from human interaction' (Appelbaum, 1970: 3; cf. Mead, 1964: 199). Phenomenological sociologists such as Peter L. Berger (1967: Chapter 1) and symbolic interactionists such as Herbert Blumer (1969: Chapter 1) view society as a dialectical phenomenon that is a human product which, however, feeds back to its producers. Society is made of human meaning, externalized in its institutions through social action and as reality continually reconstructed in interpretative processes of interaction.

Those theorists who stress the psychological aspect of interaction generally single out the role of the individual in changing the 'character' of the group. By contrast, those stressing the social context in which behavior occurs focus on the effect that changes in the group structure or the social structure have on the individual's behavior or attitudes.

The sociologist also studies human interactions but is concerned with the interaction process itself (i.e., with what occurs *between* individuals) rather than the psychological processes *within* individuals. However, sociologists have mainly emphasized the group as the unit of analysis (with individuals seen only as *members* of groups and role carriers) and the relationships between the various groups that comprise the social system. The elements of the social system (e.g., society as a whole or an organization within it) are seen as interdependent so that changes in one part will produce pressures for change in other parts of the system. Within this perspective, or in combination with the social–psychological perspective, a sociological theory may thematize changes of different scopes, that is, on the level of roles, role occupants, role performance, role content, social relationships, complex social structures (identifiable patterns of roles organized around the fulfilment of some function or activity), social institutions (sets of related social structures), the social system (comprising interrelated social institutions), values and norms.

Such an analysis of social change that varies in terms of level (and consequently in terms of unit of analysis) will be presented in Chapters 6 and 7 by means of four theoretical case studies: one referring to the level of society as a whole; the second to that of the group; the third to the level of social relationships; and the fourth to the organizational level. Before we deal with the question of the causes and processes of social change, by considering the level of the changing segment of society, we turn to the assumptions that underlie any theory of change as well as any social theory in general. As we shall see, assumptions, on the one hand, have to do with the perception and conceptualization of social reality and, on the other hand, with pre-scientifically acquired interests of cognition that guide the work of the social scientist.

1.3 Assumptions: the nature of society and the interests of the social scientist

The inquiry into the assumptions about the nature of society is of fundamental importance, if one bears in mind that the explicit and implicit assumptions about man and the social body determine how the phenomenon of change will be conceptualized and eventually explained. If we wish to understand social change, that is, 'the alteration of a social structure over time' (Dreitzel, 1967b: 456), we must be aware of its double character: i.e., on the one hand, we are dealing with a *product* of human actions rendered independent within temporal limits and, on the other, with actions of society's members producing history. Since society is made by men and constituted by the goals they strive for, history must, at first, be understood as a condensed development of goal-oriented actions and only in second place as a manifestation and consequence of the dynamic of groupings and institutions in society. If the morphogenetic, i.e., structure-building society is the subject matter of sociology, nay, of all social sciences, it follows that every theory of society implies a theory of social *stability* as well as one of social *change* (cf. Wallace, 1969: 54–5; Dreitzel, 1967b: 459, 463; Buckley, 1967).

Constructing social theories means, first of all, to consider the following dimensions of social phenomena: (1) the homeostatic–synchronic dimension pointing to the problem of societal organization and stability; (2) the genetic–diachronic dimension referring to the problem of the formation and change of social structures; (3) the autonomic dimension with reference to the problem of exchange relations between the elements of society; and (4) the communicative–constructive dimension pointing to the interpretative and voluntaristic nature of social reality. It goes almost without saying that social theorists do not systematically and in a well-balanced manner deal with these dimensions. At best, the sociological discipline is presented as a multiparadigmatic science (cf. Ritzer,

1975; Strasser, 1977); that is, different manifestations of the research guiding interest and the vocabulary of social explanation are combined into alternative systems of social knowledge production resulting in paradigmatic types of sociological theory. In conjunction with the guiding interest of cognition,[3] the vocabulary of explanation that consists of concepts, propositions, and their logical implications, renders problematic the object of study in specific terms by drawing the scientist's attention to some *segment* of social reality. However, not social reality as such is uncovered by means of concepts but only the scope of empirical data which is recognized as important *through* the lens of the guiding interest of cognition and the vocabulary of explanation. These data, as we know, are then refined by means of various methodological steps such as deduction, operationalization, observation, measurement, and generalization (cf. Strasser, 1976: 9ff.).

In other words, the guiding research interest and the explanatory vocabulary serves to impress upon the given scope of study a selective stamp in the sense that a general image of the major characteristics of the subject matter is produced which, in turn, makes it possible to derive specific hypotheses and to generate theories of different ranges. Such a cognitive image of social reality varies according to the aforementioned aspects of problematization. A sociologist who views society as a functionally integrated system held together by common values as well as recurrent processes of socialization and mechanisms of social control, analyzes change primarily in terms of the differentiation of the system, i.e., the functional specialization of systemic parts, and the (re-)integration of newly formed elements (e.g., the role of teacher differentiating into various roles of special instructor) or deviating elements (e.g., criminals are resocialized). The question of how society is held together, i.e., organized, is central and not the question of what drives it on, i.e., how social structures are formed. In accordance with Isaac Newton we could reformulate the question in the direction of driving force and force of gravity, or simply force and inertia: Is what makes a ball roll the same as what keeps it rolling (cf. Dahrendorf, 1964: 101; Wallace, 1969: 53)? For a sociologist who looks at society from a processual and genetic angle the question of what drives society on and how it changes will be of primary importance: society is seen to manifest itself in the formation and change of its structural elements, that is, in the capacity to solve the problem of social development.

Thus far, we have offered above all two sociological solutions to the problem of social development. The *microsociological* strategy focuses on the continuous formation and reconstruction of social reality by members of society, brought about by their negotiations of the rules of interaction and the interpretation of the situation. In modern action theories that link elements of the tradition of historicism with that of the *verstehende* and dialectical sociology, the idea is stressed that the social is continuously produced, appropriated, affirmed, and, in a specific sense, transformed (cf. e.g., Blumer, 1969). The interpretative re-enactment of the *uniqueness* of historical situations is central to this perspective. Since, as it is held, the meaningfulness of social phenomena defies causal explanation, the question arises as to whether change may, in this sense, be understood and analyzed. We hesitate to answer in the negative and intend not to extend our discussion on the microsociological strategy beyond what we have said here and what we are going to present in section 6.3 and Chapter 7 (cf. also Wiswede and Kutsch, 1978: 39–42, 176–203). The second theoretical strategy is *macrosociological*, which deals mainly with the homeostatic–synchronic and the genetic–diachronic aspects of social institutions and structural relationships (cf. e.g., Parsons, 1951; Dahrendorf, 1959a). It is the Marxist and non-Marxist versions of the conflict-theoretical approach, on the one hand, and the structural-functional theory of society, on the other, which are of particular importance here and which will be our main concern in Chapters 2, 3, 4, 6, and 7.

We may therefore conclude that sociological theories differ, among other things, in what they consider to be *the* primary *explanandum*: societal organization or societal development. It is this decision that largely determines what a sociologist 'looks for, what he sees, and what he does with his observations by way of fitting them, along with other facts, into a larger scheme of explanation' (Inkeles, 1964: 28). It seems that beside the *basic* distinction between theories that derive their change analysis from a problematization of societal organization, and those for which the change perspective results from rendering problematic societal development, sociological theories may be further differentiated on the ground of a *specific* change aspect on which they focus. Some theories purport to identify the changes of a specific *aspect* of society (e.g., the educational system, the function of the family or of urban centers); others are geared toward the explanation of a specific *sequence* of events or social structures within temporal–spatial limits or the change of various *levels* of society (e.g., interaction, organization, society); and a third group of theoretical approaches intends to study change in a *short-term* or *long-term* perspective.

The aspects of rendering problematic stability and development of society become indeed part of the construction of theories about social change. Four types of change theory are usually distinguished, each of which is based upon a specific set of assumptions of different complexity. For example, Richard Appelbaum (1970: 9) differentiates:

> Evolutionary theories, characterized primarily by assumptions of smooth, cumulative change, often in a linear fashion, and always in the direction of increasing complexity and adaptability; equilibrium theory, characterized by the concept of homeostasis, and focusing on conditions tending towards stability as a consequence; conflict theory, characterized by the assumption that change is endemic to all social organisms and focusing on conditions that tend towards instability as a consequence; and rise and fall' theories, characterized by the assumption that societies, cultures, or civilizations regress as well as grow.

The first two types of change theory are similar in their implications for viewing change, for both focus on the 'working out' of strains and conflicts through adjustments and adaptations in the system. The other two are similar in that both see conflict and change as inherent and continuous properties of societal organization.

As we shall see in Chapters 2–5, knowing which kind of assumptions are made in actual research or in the construction of an abstract theory, represents a requisite as to how the resolution of strains, conflicts, and antagonism of any kind will be dealt with cognitively, that is, in theoretical terms: by recurring (1) to adaptive mechanisms, or (2) to the abolition of antagonistic interests (be that indirectly through their suppression or directly through their abolition) in the synthesis of a new form of societal organization.

1.4 Causes and processes of social change

In this section we would like to deal with two questions that are central to most theories of social change. On the one hand, there is the question concerning the causal agents, that is, the conditions that produce change; and, on the other hand, we are going to be concerned with the question of the processes or mechanisms through which change takes place. A sociological explanation of change refers not only to the structure that changes but also to the factors that effect such a change. As with the problem of definition, there is little consensus among the representatives of the major theoretical positions on the sources and processes underlying change.

The concepts of source and process are far from being unambiguous; in fact, they have been used in various ways. In the course of this study, the source of change will be taken to mean the primary or ultimate 'cause' or 'driving force' behind an episode of change. Cause will be defined here as a set of related factors which, when taken together, are both sufficient and necessary for the production of a certain effect. As for process, 'in its most frequent use the term means a transition or series of transitions between one social condition and another' (Gould and Kolb, 1964: 538). The principal conditions or factors involved in the movement of a society, or some aspect of it, from some specified state to a different, i.e., 'changed' state, reveal themselves, so to speak, in the process of change. In determining the change process we have to find the factors that produce change and influence its course, the ways in which change becomes manifest, and to delineate the starting and terminal point of change. This is important because the same phenomenon (e.g., the declining size of the family) may have different causes and manifest itself differently at various points in the history of mankind or a society (cf. Wiswede and Kutsch, 1978: 45).

We may therefore subsume under processes underlying all change and indicating its course, all aspects of structure and system *formation* and the preceding mechanisms taking care of the *selection* from all *possible* events and actions (e.g., such generalized expectations as norms and roles, moreover, such media of communication as power, money, love, and truth). In this sense, processes represent structures that order, for instance, the consequences of events; they appear as principles of structuring social life which, in turn, may be understood as something that emerges, proceeds, and unfolds. Thus, change should be seen as a process among other processes characterized by the fact that its source is located *outside* the structure in the narrower sense, i.e., the changing structure that nevertheless must be recognizable in its identity (cf. Swanson, 1971: 7). While such concepts as change, development, and evolution point to *differences* resulting over a given period of time, the concept of process refers to the *transition* from the point in time t_0 to t_1, i.e., to the various manifestations of the course of change.

The factors of change, the units that (may) change, and the direction of change are fused into the idea of the processual form of change indicating above all the dimension and form in which change takes place: secularization, rationalization, scientific development; state and nation building, participation, redistribution; technological transformation, capital accumulation, mass consumption; population explosion, urbanization, increase in communication; achievement motivation, deprivation (cf. Zapf, 1969: 23). This leads to the question concerning the extent of change measured qualitatively by means of the distinction between change within and change of systems and quantitatively in terms of social indicators of welfare, supposedly providing more information about the rate, linearity, progressiveness, regressiveness, as well as the relation of planned and unplanned changes.

The definitional, causal, and processual aspects of social change are of great importance not only in studying past changes but also in investigating *future* developments. The latter can only be explained, that is, its sequence of events can only be predicted, if its significant conditions in the sense of 'structural certainties' are known (e.g., the changes in population during the next five years or the size of some age cohort in elementary school). The *more variable* a given trend has been in the past and the less these trends reach back into the past, the greater is the uncertainty of such predictions. Prediction of future changes whose emergence is neither discernible in the past nor in the present, can at best be made within the framework of futurology. This does not exclude, however, that the outline of alternative futures on the basis of alternative points of departure leads to useful analyses of possible changes. In this case, the problem is, on the one hand, to demonstrate the *practical* relevance of these changes by indicating the probability of their occurrence and, on the other hand, to show the *theoretical* relevance of their analysis by explicating the underlying assumptions. In the case of 'futuristic predictions,' however, the former is hardly possible, while the latter is – because of its claim to 'rational fantasy' – often not desirable (cf. Wiswede and Kutsch, 1978: 53–60).

As in section 1.2, we shall explore the differences between the psychological, social-psychological, and sociological perspectives, with particular emphasis on the causes of change and their explanation. In finding out which level of analysis is being used in a theory, we should keep in mind the type of questions posed by Morris Ginsberg (1970: 37) in his article 'Social Change':

> Is it true that in the last resort changes are to be traced back to desires or purposes or, perhaps, unconscious drives in individual minds? [a] If the real agents are always individuals, what significance is to be attached to the phrase 'social forces'? Are these concatenations of individual desires or volitions as modified by interaction? [b] Or is causal agency to be ascribed to changes in social structure conceived as bringing about other changes? [c]

Psychological theories of change have generally focused on the 'causal role of desires, volitions or unconscious mental drives in the analysis of social changes' (Ginsberg, 1970: 43). Some psychologists have emphasized the primacy of mental processes and internal psychological conflicts of certain personality 'types' as causal factors in change, but most contemporary psychologists view changes in the situation external to the individual as playing an important role in causation (e.g., Horney, 1937; cf. also Merton, 1968: Chapters 6–8). The process by which change takes place is usually seen as the acting out of individual desires, motives, and intentions (e.g., the 'competitive motive,' the desire to optimize gratifications, the release of 'repressed aggressive tendencies'). The individual responds to his physical and social environment with purposive acts designed to achieve certain goals which are determined by his needs, drives, and instincts.

Social-psychological perspectives on change have frequently focused on the conflicts and tensions between the individual (i.e., his interests, needs, drives, desires, motives, interpretations, perceptions) and the collectivity (i.e., groups, institutions, society, system requirements). Causal factors in social change are seen as the 'desires and purposive acts of men which are stimulated and shaped in various ways by factors in the physical and social environment' (Ginsberg, 1970: 63). Whether priority is given to the changes that alterations in social circumstances produce in the individual or vice versa depends on the orientation of the theorist (*social*-psychological *vs* social-*psychological*). But, in either case, both the individual and the social milieu are seen as capable of inducing changes in the other through interaction.

Social-psychological theories place more emphasis on the part played by social factors in evoking individual responses and shaping motives than do psychological theories. Thus, change is often viewed as the result of group rather than individual efforts to achieve ends. The emergence of a 'common purpose' or 'group mind' is often regarded as an integral part of the change process. From a social-psychological perspective, history may therefore be seen as

> a series of groping efforts of men slowly becoming aware of their common needs and the possibilities of harmonious co-operation. The results of their efforts are embodied in social structures which, in turn, react upon the individual concerned, creating new situations and generating new wants and strains which in their turn stimulate new efforts. Social forces thus consist of the energies of men in conscious or unconscious interaction. The individual will may be often powerless, largely because it is thwarted or unaided by other wills, though on occasions, when opposing forces are equally balanced, the contribution of one or

> more determined men may be decisive. Slowly the interrelations enter into consciousness, making a common purpose possible. That conscious purpose plays an increasingly important part in the shaping of events seems to me beyond doubt. But it is limited by the nature of the will and the conditions in which it has to work, including the consequences of its own action (Ginsberg, 1970: 68).

Studies in group dynamics, cognitive dissonance, status and role strains, status inconsistencies and conflicts, partial and differential socialization, collective behavior and similar topics are examples of contemporary theories focusing on the interactive effects of changes on the individual and his social milieu. Hans Toch's *The Social Psychology of Social Movements* (1965) and Hadley Cantril's *The Psychology of Social Movements* (1941) have been important studies on the interaction between personality and social environment in the genesis of various types of movements aimed at effecting changes in society. Moreover, David McClelland's (1961; McClelland *et al.*, 1953) work on the development of the achievement motivation as a causal factor in social change has gained prominence in the area of social-psychological research.

Another type of explanation of the source of change that shows both psychological and social-psychological traits involves the role played by the 'great man' or by elites in initiating and/or effecting social change.

Max Weber, although primarily a historian rather than a social theorist of change, developed the concept of charisma which has been embodied in some subsequent theories of social change. Weber noted the important role that charismatic leaders had played in providing the 'mainspring' for change throughout history. He used the term 'charisma' to designate

> a certain quality of an individual personality by virtue of which he is set apart from ordinary men and treated as endowed with supernatural, superhuman, or at least specifically exceptional powers or qualities. These are such as they are not accessible to the ordinary person, but are regarded as of divine origin or as exemplary, and on the basis of them the individual concerned is treated as a leader (Weber, 1947: 358).

However, it should be noted that Weber did not attribute the ability of charismatic authority to initiate change as resting purely on personality traits but also on social circumstances such as the leader's ability to perform certain functions valued by members and groups of society.

William I. Thomas (1909: 19) was also concerned with the role of the 'superior individual':

> the power of the attention to meet a crisis is primarily an individual matter, or at least the initiative lies with the individual. . . . The relation of the 'great man' to crisis is indeed one of the most important points in the problem of progress. Such men as Moses, Mohammed, Confucius, Christ have stamped the whole character of a civilization.

Finally, Robert A. Nisbet (1970: 320–1), in his theory of social change, depicts a close relationship of 'innovation-minded' individuals and elites to the process of change.

To attribute causal effects to ideas, elites, material forces or tension-producing antagonisms, decisively influences how the theorist views the process and consequences of change, where he employs his theory, and how the theory can be tested. In Table 1.1 analytical and empirical levels, as well as theoretical perspectives of social change to which the remainder of the book is devoted, are surveyed.

When stating that a theory should deal with the cause of change, we do not recommend the specification of a single, ultimate cause from which all changes spring. The various theoretical positions that we are going to discuss in Chapter 2 are meant to explicate further the idea that monocausal schemes of explanation frequently fail on empirical grounds because they usually imply an attempt to explain too much with too little. It is more likely that all change factors that will be hinted at in these theories play some causal role

TABLE 1.1 *Empirical levels and theoretical perspectives of social change*

Profile of change analysis \ Level/unit of analysis	Individual	Interaction	Group/organization/society
1. The social	Interrelationship of individual personality to his environment in which the former takes in information via learning processes and adjusts to the latter accordingly or tries to adapt the environment to his needs and goals = psychological *reactions* of the individual.	Behavior patterns, personality characteristics and social context represent conditions on the basis of which *interactions* take place.	Individuals as members of groups/organizations and the relations between groups/organizations within the *social system*.

TABLE 1.1 *continued*

Profile of change analysis	Level/unit of analysis: Individual	Interaction	Group/organization/society
2. *Change*			
2.1 Manifestation/ process of change	Realization of individual wants and motives (competitive motive, the wish to optimize gratifications, release of repressed aggressions).	The influence of the socio-cultural environment on mutual expectations of the participants in interaction and their interpretations of the respective situation manifests itself in the daily appropriation of social reality in the sense of its affirmation or reformation.	Elements of the social system are considered mutually dependent, so that change in one part (e.g., technological innovation/role) is likely to effect alterations in other parts (e.g., other roles, educational organization).
2.2 Direction of change	*Individual*→group	*Group*→individual behavior (attitudes) *Individual interpretations* of group reality	*Interdependence* of system parts implies linear, accelerating or retarding change in all system parts
2.3 Analytical perspective	Social-*psychological*	*Social*-psychological (or microsociological)	Sociological (or macrosociological)
2.4 Representatives	Freud, Pavlov, Skinner	Mead, Simmel, Homans	Marx, Durkheim, Parsons, Dahrendorf
In the present volume we deal with:			
Chapter 1: Levels/ causes of change	X	X	X
Chapter 2: Survey of theoretical approaches			X
Chapter 3: Historic- materialistic theory			X
Chapter 4: Structural- functional theory			X
Section 6.1: Change of social systems			X
Section 6.2: Change of collective behavior			X
Section 6.3: Status inconsistency		X	X
Chapter 7: Change in organizations		X	X

in *some* changes. Last but not least in pointing to the assumptions and the socio-historical origins of different change conceptions, we hope to make clear that a single cause could hardly explain all change and that the presumption that the different theoretical approaches are partially complementary and in other respects incompatible, has a lot to commend it (cf. Strasser, 1976: Chapter 1; Chodak, 1973).

Most *sociological* explanations of the origins and causes of change may be categorized in terms of whether (1) change is inherent in the given organization of society, or (2) change is seen as a consequence of external impacts. Explanations in the first sense have to do with *endogenous* change, while the second explanation is related to *exogenous* change (cf. Dahrendorf, 1959a: 127; Levy, 1952: 114). Another categorization would be as to whether theories are based on monocausal or multicausal explanations, i.e., to rest one's explanation of change on a single factor or on a multiplicity of factors. The theoretical approaches presented in Chapters 2, 3, and 4 are intended to provide detailed information along these lines. Table 1.2 is an attempt to summarize these principles of structuring the present study.

TABLE 1.2 *Causes of social change*

1 Location of change	Exogenous ↓ Disturbances (Criterion: delineation of system boundaries)	Endogenous ↓ Differentiation/conflict (Criterion: efforts to stabilize and to change lead to endogenously produced adaptations/ alterations)
2 Specificity of the cause	one factor ↓ technological innovation; economic antagonisms/elite interests	more factors ↓ personality, politics, economy, religion, education, socialization

Notes

1 An interesting illustration of what is meant by this hypothesis is provided by Nicholas C. Mullins (1975) in his study of the mechanisms, the scope, and the rate of change in scientific disciplines. However, as Mullins aptly demonstrates, it is the time span that determines whether some alterations turn out to be change within the system or already change of the system. Let us therefore point to section 1.1.2 where the importance of time span and speed for change analysis is explored.

2 Chapter 2 is devoted to the presentation of the most important schemes of explanation in which these questions will be dealt with in some detail.
3 For the definition of the cognitive interest as normative perspective, see pp. 18–19.

Suggested reading

Introductory reading

MOORE, WILBERT E. (1963), *Social Change*, Englewood Cliffs, N.J.: Prentice-Hall.
If one were taken to the task to recommend one particular book for an introduction into the study of social change, it would have to be this one. It is not only lucidly written but also represents a comprehensive study of the problems in conceptualizing change in general (measurement, direction, range, level) and modernization in particular.

MOORE, WILBERT E. and COOK, ROBERT (eds) (1970), *Readings on Social Change*, Englewood Cliffs, N.J.: Prentice-Hall.
This reader supplements the aforementioned textbook, with special chapters on questions of measurement, sources, and processes of change, evolution, and modernization.

TOFFLER, ALVIN (1970), *Future Shock*, New York: Random House.
The author describes what is going to happen to people who are overwhelmed by change. They suffer from a disease called future shock, in that the rate of change becomes manifest as the direction of change. An attempt is made to define change in various areas of social life as precisely as possible and to examine it with respect to this new quality.

GINSBERG, MORRIS (1968), 'Social Change,' pp. 129–61 in GINSBERG, MORRIS, *Essays in Sociological and Social Philosophy*, Harmondsworth, England: Penguin.
Ginsberg tries to explore the concept of social change historically as well as analytically by discussing various ideas about the source and the direction of change and by providing ample illustrations from various specialties and areas of social life.

Further reading

General

NISBET, ROBERT A. (1969), *Social Change and History*, New York: Oxford University Press.
The author attempts to show the difficulties, problems, and questions connected with the use of the concept of development in studying social change. The assumptions underlying the metaphor of development are discussed and their consequences for describing and explaining change critically examined.

LAUER, ROBERT H. (1973), *Perspectives on Social Change*, Boston, Mass.: Allyn & Bacon.

The author combines theoretical approaches with major issues of social change, thus demonstrating how change may be analyzed on different levels of society and how its mechanisms, patterns, and strategies are depicted and explained.

BELL, DANIEL (1973), *The Coming of Post-Industrial Society: A Venture in Social Forecasting*, New York: Basic Books.

Bell does not offer a theory of industrial and post-industrial society but describes in some detail two trends in industrialized societies: the central importance of theoretical knowledge and the tertiary sector.

ASH GARNER, ROBERTA (1977), *Social Change*, Chicago: Rand McNally.

This text is particularly well suited for students who wish to study change on the level of the individual, the organization, and on a larger scale. The author includes not only the relevant literature but also illustrative short readings from various sources and a discussion of the appropriate methods for studying change on the respective level.

Problem-related

SWANSON, GUY (1971), *Social Change*, Glenview, Ill.: Scott, Foresman & Co.

The author discusses problems of conceptualizing change and deals with the most important dimensions of change with respect to complex organizations.

McCLELLAND, DAVID (1961), *The Achieving Society*, New York: Free Press.

Central to this approach is the development of an achievement motivation and its effects upon society, groups, and individuals.

CHIROT, DANIEL (1977), *Social Change in the Twentieth Century*, New York: Harcourt Brace Jovanovich.

In this book social change is studied in its international context by referring to some aspects of Immanuel Wallerstein's world system perspective and focusing on issues of social inequality, the distribution of power, and international relations.

RODGERS, HARRELL R., jr and BULLOCK, CHARLES S. III (1972), *Law and Social Change: Civil Rights Laws and Their Consequences*, New York: McGraw-Hill.

The book is intended to lay bare the factors associated with successes and failures in civil rights and hence presents a chapter in the recent history and the extent of change in American society.

2 Theoretical approaches to the explanation of social change: a survey

Susan C. Randall and *Hermann Strasser*

2.1 The idea of industrial society

At the beginning of theories of endogenous change there is the empirical development and conceptual representation of industrial society. Already Henri de Saint-Simon regarded industry and science as the most progressive spheres of society guiding industrial action and system formation in the future (Strasser, 1976: 64–76). He separated the 'industrial,' i.e., the diligent and ambitious worker from the idler as did Thorstein Veblen (1899) later. After the Second World War the concept of industrial society became fashionable in that industry was frequently identified with technology and industrialization with the socio-economic transformation of the nineteenth and the early years of the twentieth century. The works of such sociologists as Raymond Aron, Talcott Parsons, Ralf Dahrendorf, David Lockwood, Daniel Bell and Seymour Martin Lipset testify to the prominence of the idea of industrial society. However, already in the days of Herbert Spencer and Emile Durkheim the theory of industrial society served as an alternative to the Marxist tradition of analyzing capitalism (cf. section 2.3.2).

The fundamental elements of this alternative conception consisted in a classification of societies, a theory of class conflict and societal change, as well as a more or less elaborate idea about classlessness. With their classification of societies into urban and agrarian, traditional and modern, and those that are characterized by mechanic or organic solidarity, representatives of the theory of industrial society have made an attempt to understand change better by narrowing the scope of the development of industrial society. When referring to traditional society they usually meant to include everything that was thrown into the graveyard of social history since the coming of the industrial age: impermeability of social strata because of inherited social status (as against an 'open' system with an allocation of social status on the basis of achievement and talent); emphasis on militaristic principles in creating moral cohesion (as against a peaceful system of industrial order based upon exchange relations); authoritarian *vs* democratic system of politics; coherent *vs* fragmented elites; static *vs* dynamic conception of societal development.

The theory of class conflict includes the proposition that class conflict in the Marxian sense is a temporary phenomenon. Actually, class conflicts became institutionalized in the form of generally accepted rules of collective bargaining. As a consequence, economic struggles were separated from political conflicts. Presently, the *moderate* form of this theory is represented by such authors as Lipset and Dahrendorf, for whom classes do persist and conflict comes to be expressed in terms of competition. In its *radical* form as advocated by Robert A. Nisbet, though not strata, and Talcott Parsons, the idea is put forth that classes and class conflict vanished altogether. A differentiated order such as modern society does not permit those kinds of antagonism. The problem of the twentieth century is organization, not division. Toward the end of the last century, Durkheim (1893/1964) had already referred to the socialist movement as the carrier of such conflicts and changes. Finally, with *The End of Ideology* (1965) Daniel Bell seems to have erected a monument to commemorate this world of imagination.

The third element of the theory of industrial society, namely, the idea of classlessness, refers – not unlike the second element – to tendencies derived from the factual development of modern society: it is said that, on the one hand, authority increasingly replaces property as the decisive source of power and, on the other hand, the meritocratic character of industrial society comes to be expressed through more equality of opportunity and social mobility on the basis of individual talents and achievements.

For the Marxist tradition of thought, by contrast, industrial society appeared only as a phase in the transition from capitalism to socialism. Recently developed concepts like 'late capitalism,' as formulated by the Neo-Marxists Jürgen Habermas (1973) and Claus Offe (1977), or 'post-industrial society,' as offered by non-Marxists of different *couleur* (e.g., Bell, 1973; Touraine, 1971; Schelsky, 1975), have not always contributed to a clarification of the issues involved. The phase of late capitalism is characterized by the fundamental antagonism that continues to exist between the increasing societalization of economic production and the persistent appropriation of its products and surplus value on private grounds. This is so *in spite of* the problems of adaptation resulting from altered market conditions and the functions that have accrued to the state – topics that have been in the foreground of the international Marxist discussion. The idea of a post-industrial society is based either – as in the case of Alain Touraine – on the emphasis on conflicts resulting from the increasing power of technocrats and not from property relations, or – as in the cases of Daniel Bell and Helmut Schelsky – on the assumption that in present Western societies the center of power is found to be no longer located in the economic sector but in the cultural–political sphere. Even a casual examination of the pertinent literature (e.g., Anderson, 1976) shows that the different currents of Marxism may be taken as an opposition to the theory of industrial society. Here are its most important theoretical positions:

1   the theory of the state based upon a critique of (especially capitalistic) forms of domination (e.g., Offe, 1977; Habermas, 1973);
2   the theory of state monopolistic capitalism (e.g., Wirth, 1972);
3   the theory of capitalistic reproduction (Altvater, 1972; Müller and Neusüss, 1970; Hirsch, 1973);
4   the syndicalistic theory (Gorz, 1967);
5   the orthodox theory of historic materialism (Hahn, 1968);
6   the theory of the differentiation of the working class (Poulantzas, 1974; Wright, 1976).

The Marxian position, in contrast with the theory of industrial society, may be summarized as follows:

1   Theorists of industrial society see class conflict institutionalized and channeled into individual competition, while Marxists still stick with the idea that the fundamental contradiction between private appropriation of surplus value and the social nature of production leads to a polarization of interests and to collective conflicts. As a consequence, the former, in contrast to the latter, see strains and changes in parts of society as not necessarily leading to revolutionary situations or even outbreaks.
2   Strains and conflicts are conceived by theorists of industrial society as neutralizing and balancing each other rather than cumulating. For Marxists, this is due to the various agencies of legitimation that operate in capitalist society to mask fundamental contradictions and injustices (e.g., educational system, mass media). Economic contradictions, however, (a)

result in disparities of life chances between those who struggle successfully for the realization of their interests and those who do not have effective lobbies (e.g., the aged, migrant workers, consumers, residents of certain areas); and (b) are shifted to the international level resulting in similar disparities between members of industrialized and developing societies.

3   Theorists of industrial society reject, and present evidence against, the Marxian idea of pauperization. They point to increases in life chances for everybody via economic growth and hence an embourgeoisement of the proletariat. While Marxists admit that temporary improvements of the social and economic lot of the working class were possible, they claim to find ample evidence for a proletarianization of parts of the bourgeoisie.

4   According to Marxists, the class situation of the active labor force of a society is maintained with the concomitant consequences of exploitation and alienation. The achievement principle is as much a political chimera as the idea of a gradual stratification of society is but a surface phenomenon. Less ascription, status achievement, some functionality of social inequalities and more social mobility, they go on to say, could not outweigh the negative consequences of the achievement principle as produced by individual competition and the lasting effects of structured social inequality.

With respect to the analysis of social change the theory of industrial society gives rise to two major conclusions.

1   *Revolutionary* change is treated as a residual category, i.e., as a 'deficient mode of change whose causes, conditions, and consequences may not only be found through empirical studies but apparently directly derived from the . . . positive mode of non-revolutionary society by means of deduction' (Bühl, 1970: 60). Revolution not only means abstract discontinuity but also concrete crisis which disturbs continual, i.e., industrial, change. As the following discussion will show, this thesis has especially entered the functionalist and neo-evolutionary theories of change as well as the various theories of modernization, the classical evolutionary theory, and non-Marxist conflict theory. Central to the Marxist conflict theory of social change, by contrast, is revolution as class struggle, that is, as a definitive act set by the oppressed in the unfree phase of the history of humanity. The first conclusion points to the speed and mode of change.

2   The second conclusion, however, has to do with the direction of change. Changes in the economic, political, and cultural spheres that have come about in the course of industrialization

show a tendency toward standardization of, at least, the industrial world. Some hundred years ago, Herbert Spencer meant to observe such a tendency by pointing to the increasing interdependence of social systems, the emergence of civil liberties, and the expansion of world trade. Although Spencer's progressive optimism was later replaced by an equally strong cultural pessimism of the twentieth century, the tendency toward unification of the industrial world seems to be adequately expressed in the notion of *mass society*. The works of Gustave Le Bon and Oswald Spengler have contributed to such a conception as much as those of Hendrik de Man and José Ortega y Gasset. The concept of mass society includes the tendencies toward mental proletarianization and economic embourgeoisement as well as those toward depersonalization of social life through more forms of bureaucratic organization and less forms of communal life. The pendant in political science to the sociological idea of mass society is that of *convergence*: the idea that on the basis of developments in technology ('increasing differentiation'), politics ('public interest,' 'power legitimized through sovereignty of the people'), and ideology ('increased standard of living'), socialist and capitalist societies become more alike (Kiss, 1973, vol. 2: 276ff.). With respect to the Third World the expectation of convergence of all social developments within national boundaries to a kind of world society is bound to turn out to be *the* Utopia of the Second World (Bühl, 1970: 20). Much of modernization research has integrated the assumption contained in the convergence thesis that certain system constraints and system requisites are universally valid. Moreover, the functionalist theory of change, the culture contact theories, and the conflict theoretical approach of non-Marxist origin have made considerable use of the convergence idea.

In order to delineate the Marxist-oriented conflict theory from its non-Marxist version, we are going to outline briefly the Marxist argumentation in section 2.3.1.1, while in Chapter 3 an attempt is made to present answers to the central empirical and theoretical questions that a historic-materialistic theory of societal development raises.

2.2 Theories of endogenous social change

We now turn to the theoretical approaches that have received significant impulses from taking over, or criticizing, the concept of industrial society and which locate the cause of change in the forces that are generated by society or a given subsystem of society. These are the following:

1. the Marxist and non-Marxist variants of conflict theory;
2. the rise and fall or cyclical theory;
3. the classical evolutionary theory; and
4. the multilinear theory of social evolution and the theory of modernization.

2.2.1 Variants of conflict theory

Common to all conflict theoretical approaches is that they explain change in terms of antagonism or tension-producing elements that inhere in social systems. The causes of such conflicts leading to societal changes are especially sought in those elements of the social structure which, on the one hand, are related to the establishment and sanctioning of social norms and, on the other hand, to the control and allocation of scarce resources such as income, property, prestige, influence, and authority. These theories focus on processes of social life that tend toward instability in, and conflict between, parts of society – or simply the actors concerned. Change is seen as the result of a dialectic relationship between dominant elements of society (central values, ideologies, power relations, distribution of resources, etc.) and those arrangements that compete with, or oppose, the former. Not disharmonies in the normative element (i.e., the role expectations) but a society ordered by *principles of domination* (i.e., above all the bureaucratic organizations in the economy, politics, and culture) constitutes the explanatory focus.

2.2.1.1 The Marxist variant

Karl Marx, one of the earliest exponents of conflict theory, witnessed a revolution whose consequences would prove to set new standards for changes in the environment of modern man and, since then, to represent the central theme in sociology:

> What has become evident since the middle of the 18th century and what makes men slip the seemingly eternal routes of their existence in the second half of the 19th century, is not a political, but an economic revolution – a revolution that is not dependent on changes from outside, i.e., wars, new markets, and areas of raw material, new routes of transportation, above all not dependent on transformations of belief and intellectual systems, but for the first time on a revolution of the labor process itself (Plessner, 1959: 76).

For Marx, this revolution that he described as capitalistic, represented the execution of the dialectic of history in the sense that with the coming of capitalism the hitherto persisting antagonism between human existence and its material *limitation* became removable. Well into the eighteenth century the fact that the people could not experience their own contribution to the shaping of the natural and social world, had to be attributed to the low level of development of the productive forces (i.e., qualification of labor force and technology of production), the division of labor, and, concomitantly, the relations of production (i.e., the specific forms of social exchange). This meant that man experienced himself as dominated by nature and society.

Besides the thesis that the historic significance of capitalism must be sought in the potential abolition of the material limitation of human existence, it is asserted that also for the first time the general interest of mankind was embodied by a historical force, namely, the social class of the proletariat. It is thought of as being able to realize freedom and autonomy and consequently to control the course of history. This enables us to draw two important conclusions for a Marxist analysis of the structure and change of capitalistic society:

1 It is the *relations of production* that determine the position and experience in the process of production and utilization and, as a consequence, the distribution of occupational opportunities and life chances, the influence within the work organization and, eventually, the structure of interests within society.

> Historical materialism, then, proceeds from the assumption that productive forces and relations of production do not vary independently of each other, but rather form structures which (a) internally correspond and (b) produce a finite number of developmental stages homologous in their structure so that (c) the succession of the modes of production reveal a developmental logic (Habermas, 1975: 290).

2 The second conclusion concerns the progressive institutionalization of *democratic* forms of interaction that accompany the improvement of material conditions. The idea is that human evolution proceeds by transmitting knowledge from one generation to the next. In other words, it may be identified with the process of socialization whereby the cultural orientation inculcated in society's members evolves to the extent as the implicated learning processes become conscious and controllable. Learning, just as much as thinking, will be reflexive only if it is subject to discourse. If it is correct that cultural

learning progresses with lasting effect under the condition of rational discourse, it may be presumed that in the evolution of human culture a selective mechanism operates to the effect that the extension of discourse to different areas of life is favored. The extent to which thinking is a social act and social action takes place in a cultural framework, it becomes apparent that social change involves cultural creativity. Here Marx is in agreement with Max Weber as well as with his current epigones (Shapiro, 1976: 10; Fallers, 1973: 14).[1]

Both of these propositions point to directed change, that is, to the direction indicated by the *mode of production* and the *development of culture*. They seem to express the material and immaterial side of the evolutionary process of mankind. The proletariat represents the executioner of these historical processes, while the Marxist theory of society conceives of itself as representing the self-reflection of history inspired by the awareness that the proletariat embodies the driving force toward the realization of true human existence.

Without anticipating Chapter 3 of the present volume, where the theory of historical materialism will be dealt with in detail, we are going to discuss its central theses with respect to Marx's explanation of societal changes.

Thus far, our sketch of fundamental ideas of historical materialism refers to two causes of social conflicts; these are closely related to one another and were emphasized by Marx time and again:
1 structural antagonism; and
2 class contradiction.

1 The structural antagonism refers to the negative consequences of the social division of labor in general and to the connection between forces and relations of production. Marx and Engels (1969a: 32–3) view the division of labor as the reason for practically all social evils because it leads to unequal distribution of work as well as of the products of work; generates antagonism between individual and collective interests; causes alienation; and brings into being the state as an illusionary collectivity. The division of labor and its consequences represent the 'central moments in the historical development thus far.' The conflicts that result from the consequences of the division of labor, were for Marx inevitable as long as the social division of labor and interests persisted. They are even magnified by the specific structural antagonism that takes shape in the form of the development of new productive forces (*Basis*) which make continuously problematic the compatibility of the existing relations of production with their corresponding institutions (*Überbau*). The origin of altered forces of production is really

never explained by Marx, however, and presumably attributed to the human striving for innovation or solving problems – an argument that is hardly plausible. Similar to William F. Ogburn's theory of cultural lag (section 2.2.4.3), the changing forces of production necessitate a steady and compatible adjustment of the social superstructure (i.e., laws, political institutions, forms and contents of education, family structure).[2]

2 Regarding class contradiction, two interdependent processes can be derived from Marx's writings: the class struggle and the emergence of class consciousness. The history of human association is shaped by the conflict between two social groupings, that is, between members of society who control the means of production and those who have no power of control and/or appropriation. Their social position is determined by their potential of control over material and personal means of production and the utilization of products. The consequences of such arrangements are not only cooperative relationships but also a potential for anarchic, spontaneous changes and unpredictability originating in the 'natural' antagonism of interest between groupings which fulfill the basic economic functions of wage labor and capital realization. The idea of latent or even manifest class struggle is central to the Marxist understanding of social changes. As mentioned before, the development of new means of production – through educational qualifications or skills incorporated in technological innovations – generates increasing pressure to initiate adaptive changes in the social superstructure. The driving force of change is seen in the transformation of the relation between the two antagonistic classes. Conflict not only leads to permanently changing social relations within the system, but ultimately also to a breakdown of the existing social structure and to the development of new patterns of social relations resting upon new means of production. The oppressed or deprived class organizes, revolts, and 'eventually bursts open the chains' of the mode of production that have become obsolete within the framework of existing institutions.

For an oppressed class to develop into a successful revolutionary force, another important process must take place: the formation of class consciousness. As is well known, Marx distinguishes between a 'class in itself' and a 'class for itself.' In the first case, a class *exists* because of common economic interests of its members (e.g., owner *vs* non-owner); in the second case, a class is seen *to form* through the awareness of common interests. Class consciousness in the Marxian sense emerges when opportunities of communication and association are available so that the idea of a common distressing condition may be disseminated. However, class consciousness becomes real only by participating in the common struggle *against* another class (cf. Lefèbvre, 1972: Chapters 4 and 5; Strasser, 1980).

The *central thesis* of Marxism therefore says that the structural antagonism located in the relationship between basis and superstructure and the class conflict resulting from the opposition of interests among the incumbents of basic economic functions, represents the driving force as well as the cause of social change. The original significance of this proposition and its concomitant theories of pauperization, surplus value, and alienation has been *relativized* by factual and theoretical developments: (1) factual developments such as the general increase of the standard of living, the embourgeoisement of large parts of the traditional working class, the Russian Revolution, and the drastic increase of white-collar workers with a strong middle-class orientation; and (2) intellectual endeavors such as the recent debate over the rising number of functions carried out by the state within the system of organized capitalism (cf. e.g., Adorno, 1976; Offe, 1977; Parkin, 1971; Giddens, 1973; Poulantzas, 1974; Habermas, 1973).

The structural conflict has been relativized in so far as the *primacy* of the forces of production is no longer strictly maintained, although the fundamental contradiction between social production and private appropriation still persists. This discussion refers, in turn, to two aspects of the development of organized capitalism: (1) to the fact that the logic of capitalistic development is not so unequivocal as orthodox Marxists have us believe; and (2) to the potential of the capitalistic social system continually to control its self-negatory tendencies.

The idea of class contradiction has been relativized above all by the argument that class struggles in Western industrial society tend to diminish in intensity and frequency. However, it is argued, this is not to say that class antagonism has been overcome, except one mistook the form of capitalistic manifestation for the logic of capitalistic development. Marx had already understood capitalism not as a structure of a historical social system but rather as its pattern of development. The continuity of the largely latent class contradiction does not exclude that social-structural elements such as the distribution of income, the occupational structure, or the relationship between political elite and ruling elite are subject to a kind of change in which this conflict is expressed. In other words, the class antagonism has shifted from the (private) sphere of production to the (public) sphere of reproduction. In the latter, it is held, discrepancies in taking care of needs of certain individuals and groups increasingly occur because the labor force and the conditions of life as a whole are not reproduced by individual acts of purchasing but rather collectively (e.g., in the area of health care, education, housing, and traffic), though oriented in quality and quantity toward the prerequisites of capital realization in the production process. The invisibility of such a conflict within the sphere of social reproduction (in contrast with that on the work place), moreover, promotes the individualization of the problems and hence the fragmentation of the conflicts in the sense of controlling and depolitization of the working class (cf. e.g., Offe, 1972; Habermas, 1973; 1976; Gorz, 1967). These tendencies toward rendering relative the structural and class contradictions of capitalism may be presented, oversimplified though, as a systemic problem that is not geared toward the solution of the conflict between groups or classes but toward securing the functional compatibility of the different structural elements in society (cf. Godelier, 1970).

That this theoretical debate has come about, has probably to do with Marx's thesis concerning the transition from feudalism to capitalism and, further on, to socialism. That is to say, the transition from feudal to capitalistic society was characterized by a number of technological changes (especially the shift from manufacture to the factory system), while the development of the capitalistic system into socialism is marked by a change in the control over the process and the outcome of production in terms of efforts at socializing the ownership of the means of production and neutralizing the market principle.[3] In the first case, the oppressed class (i.e., the serfs, tenants, and peasants in aristocratic employment in the countryside) was not identical with the revolutionary class of merchants and craftsmen of the rising bourgeoisie in the towns. In the feudal system, conflicts also arose where the growing economic power of the towns pushed the feudal economy aside and where the urban bourgeoisie and the guilds began, mostly with the help of coalition partners, to compete with the rural aristocracy for political influence. Oddly enough, the process of economic and political modernization progressed farthest in those countries in which agriculture had converted to the bourgeois–capitalistic principle of commercialization. (This topic will be dealt with at great length in section 6.1 of this volume.) In the second case of the transition from a capitalistic to a socialistic system, the seed of conflict must be sought in the direct, i.e., exploitative, relation between the proletariat assumed to be revolutionary and the ruling class of the bourgeoisie, the origin of which, as we have seen, may ultimately be located in the division of labor (cf. Marx, 1962a, vol. 23; 1964a, vol. 13; Giddens, 1973: 85).

The contradiction that appears – on the one hand, between the

Marxian primacy of the development of productive forces and the relations of production that plays a subordinate role in causal analysis and, on the other hand, between the Marxian concept of a revolutionary working class and the variable power constellations in history – constitutes the center of crystallization for the critique leveled against the Marxian approach on the part of non-Marxist conflict theorists, not least with respect to the former's explanation and prediction of societal changes. We shall now turn to the latter's perspectives.

2.2.1.2 Non-Marxist variants of conflict theory

Non-Marxist conflict theory as represented by such authors as Ralf Dahrendorf, Lewis A. Coser, David Lockwood, Raymond Aron, John Rex, and Randall Collins, has retained many elements of the Marxist approach to explain change and conflict phenomena, but has dropped the Utopian idealism of the master. A delineation from Marxism, on the one hand, and from biologically and nationalistically oriented conflict theories, on the other, is only possible by way of exemplification. On one side there are sociologists like C. Wright Mills (1956, 1959) and Alvin W. Gouldner (1970) whose works are to some extent oriented toward a Marxist position but who have also been critical of Marxist social theory. On the other side we see social scientists with a Social-Darwinist orientation who account for social change not in terms of the given social structure but by referring to the conflict between different social systems (cf. Gumplowicz, 1885/1926; Ratzenhofer, 1907). Interestingly enough, the latter theoretical approach is nowadays partly continued in a new perspective which

>1 regards underdevelopment as the consequence of the *relation* between the First and Second World, on the one hand, and the Third World, on the other;
>2 considers underdeveloped as well as developed societies in the light of the *same* characteristics of particularism and achievement motivation; and finally
>3 seeks to understand the modernization of underdeveloped societies on the basis of their *own* history (cf. Chambliss, 1973: Part 6; Bühl, 1970).

In a detailed discussion of Marx's theory of class structure and societal development, Dahrendorf (1959a) takes over the model of a dichotomous class structure and, like Marx, assigns to class theory the task to explain social change. The changes that have occurred since the days of Marx and Engels,[4] indicating an extension of authority as the pervasive principle of social organization and hence also a pluralization of interests, power centers, and class relations, suggest a revision of Marx's identification of private ownership with the potential of power in the sense that private ownership is treated as a special case of legitimate authority. According to Dahrendorf, the exercise of any form of authority always implies a latent conflict of interest between those who have power and those who do not have it, that is, who are subordinated to the authority of the powerful. In a nutshell, Dahrendorf has formulated a theory of conflict *between* interest groups in which change results from the conflict of opposite interests inherent in the various authority relations.

> In every imperatively coordinated group, the carriers of positive and negative dominance roles determine two quasigroups with opposite latent interests. . . . The opposition of interests has here a quite formal meaning, namely, the expectation that an interest in the preservation of the status quo is associated with the positive dominance roles and an interest in the change of the status quo is associated with the negative dominance roles, that is, the members of the opposing quasigroups, organize themselves into groups with manifest interests, unless certain empirically variable conditions (the conditions of organization) intervene. Interest groups, in contrast to quasigroups, are organized entities, such as parties and trade unions; the manifest interests are formulated programs and ideologies. . . . Interest groups which originate in this manner are in constant conflict over the preservation or change of the status quo. The form and the intensity of the conflict are determined by empirically variable conditions (the conditions of conflict). . . . The conflict among interest groups . . . leads to changes in the structure of their social relations, through changes in the dominance relations (Dahrendorf, 1964: 107).

For Dahrendorf, then, this opposition of interests may be seen as the source of change while the formation of, and conflict *between*, interest groups represent the mechanism by virtue of which changes in the dominance relations take place. According to him, the ultimate reason for the aforementioned opposition of interests must be sought in social norms, i.e., behavioral rules of society that are sanctioned by laws, because 'Society means setting up norms requiring domination for their establishment and enforcement' (Dahrendorf, 1967: 327).

It is the authority to define, to establish, *and* to sanction norms that links the analysis of the role structure to the analysis of the social system:

THEORETICAL APPROACHES

For Dahrendorf, societies represent those imperatively co-ordinated associations which make the laws for a territorially limited number of other imperatively coordinated associations. The struggle for the power to legislate, the 'monopoly of legitimate force' as Weber called it, is the most comprehensive social conflict. Societal change is thus operationalized in terms of restructuring or at least refilling those dominance positions which make the laws that bind some territory. However, those who rule do not simply succeed with any kind of law they deem desirable. Conflict and dominance theory also thinks . . . in notions of a system of initiative and resistance, of power and value commitments (Zapf, 1969: 21).

In one of his recent studies, Dahrendorf (1979) claims that the concepts of life changes could be employed to fill these rather formalistic propositions with content. His basic proposition that change is more drastic and rapid the more intense social conflicts are, which, in turn, originate from, and are concerned with, dominance structures, indeed lacks an indication as to the direction of change and the content of social conflict. In contrast with Marx, Dahrendorf does not believe that the potential of human capacities has continually grown through history. Rather, man's position in society is closely associated with his life chances. Social conflicts are concerned with securing more life chances or defending a given level of life chances (Dahrendorf, 1979: 89, 91). He therefore defines life chances as 'opportunities of individual development provided by social structures' (Dahrendorf, 1979: 92), and operationalizes the concept in terms of 'options' and 'ligatures.' Options are then defined as alternative opportunities embedded in social structures, which may independently vary with the ligatures understood as moral commitments that provide meaning to an individual's action (Dahrendorf, 1979: 50–1). In other words, choices are made within meaningful boundaries. The history of human society is thus conceived as a process of trial and error in extending options and destroying as well as reconstructing ligatures, especially in the sense of extending civil liberties and effectively controlling power. It seems as if individuals, groups, and societies are in permanent search for the optimal, i.e., acceptable combination of options and ligatures. In the final analysis, change, for Dahrendorf (1979: 192) as much as for John Rawls (1972), results from the human desire to improve significantly the conditions under which one lives.

Coser (1956) shifts the stress of conflict theory in so far as he sees social change to result from strains which, in turn, arise from competition for the scarce resources of power, wealth, and prestige. There is a constant strain between those with a vested interest in the maintenance of the *status quo* and those who seek to increase their share of authority, income, possessions, and honor. However, these strains do not necessarily lead to conflict because attempts to maintain or to change a given distributive system

> as well as feelings of deprivation are relative to institutionalized expectations and are established through comparison. When social systems have institutionalized goals and values to govern the conduct of component actors, but limit access to these goals for certain members of the society, departures from institutional requirements are to be expected. Similarly, if certain groups within a social system compare their share in power, wealth, and status honor with that of other groups *and* question the legitimacy of this distribution, discontent is likely to ensue. If there exist no institutionalized provisions for the expression of such discontents, departures from what is required by the norms of the social system may occur. These may be limited to 'innovation' [i.e., using illegal or illegitimate means] or they may consist in the rejection of the institutionalized goals (Coser, 1967: 31).

In Coser's (1956: 37–8) explanatory system the degree of *legitimacy* of unequal distribution of rights and opportunities plays a decisive role as to whether hostile feelings between members of hierarchically ordered groups in society develop and subsequently turn into conflict behavior. Social conflicts between negatively and positively privileged groups arise only if the former have become aware that they are indeed negatively privileged, that is, that they are deprived of their due share in social resources. Conflict always takes place in interaction between two or more individuals; it represents a 'transaction,' i.e., a new assessment of the distributive system underlying the given social relationships. Social change is thus generated in that conflict leads to an establishment, or restoration of a system of social relations.

Unlike Dahrendorf, Coser succeeds not only in explaining dominance and its consequences for social change but also in analyzing the further question 'in what way social interests, need dispositions and the power structure of society are interdependently modified, enforced or mutually dependent' (Dreitzel, 1967a: 47). As discussed elsewhere (Strasser, 1976: 190–209), Coser consequently arrives at a typology of social conflicts including 1 international and internal conflicts, conflicts between and within groups, and conflicts varying in accordance with the intensity or the degree of threat or employment of force; 2 conflicts taking place directly (e.g., a strike) or indirectly (e.g., through competition); 3 conflicts which, dependent upon whether they are carried out between causal agents or by including substitute objects ('scapegoats'), appear to be 'realistic' or 'unrealistic'. The history of industrial society is characterized by a variety of conflict forms which, as the example of employer–employee relations shows, were only sporadic but often spontaneous and violent in the beginning, while nowadays they are continuous, ordered, and in general non-violent (Bottomore, 1974: 165–6).

While Marx's theory of societal development predicted that industrial conflicts would extend into the political sphere, non-Marxist conflict theorists, above all Dahrendorf, believed they found sufficient evidence that modern industrial society of Western-capitalistic persuasion had succeeded in settling the economic conflict politically (e.g., by regulating the employer–employee relations, minimum wages, and matters of social security in legal terms) thus limiting it to the economic sphere. Non-Marxist conflict theorists seem to explain the decline and the diminishing effects of class conflicts by pointing out that differences of interest are not as closely related to factual conflict behavior, as, for example, Marx had assumed. It is usually referred to as the pluralization of interests according to social position and life situation (Dahrendorf, 1964; 1959) or to the stabilizing function of criss-crossing conflicts (Coser, 1956). Functionalists, by comparison, would stress that divergent interests between classes had largely vanished as demonstrated by the existence of a multiplicity of social strata and classes whose delineation poses empirical as well as methodological riddles (Lipset and Bendix, 1959). Finally, conflict theorists of Marxist persuasion would argue that Marx's long-term predictions of aggravating class struggles, spreading revolutionary movements, and increasing social misery had not become less plausible in the light of the satellite function of the countries of the Third World in relation to the nations of the industrialized world (Chambliss, 1973).

For Coser, as for Marx before him and Dahrendorf after him, conflict represented not only the source of change but also the medium through which it takes place. The thesis of the Marxist philosophy of history that all social changes are consequences of structural contradictions and antagonisms, would only be tenable if one risked fading to concepts of conflict and if one included such change phenomena as the accumulation of knowledge or the distant effects of technologies. This would mean to approach the notion of strain as employed by functionalists. However, it would be more fruitful, depending on the reference system, to inquire into the positive or negative, the integrative or destructive consequences of conflict, but also to distinguish between conflicts promoting change and conflicts hampering or preventing change (as the cases of destructive competition and international conflicts illustrate).

Aron (1950), in his now classic essay 'Social Structure and the Ruling Class,' discusses the conflicts of interest generated by a pluralistic society but devotes much of his study to a critique of Marx's 'classless society.' He writes: 'In one way a classless society resolves the conflicts found in fully mature capitalistic societies, but the solution involves the reduction of society to obedience rather than general liberation' (Aron, 1950: 134).

The nature of social conflict is thus founded in the relationship between different groups which vie for a share in the national income and which vary in the degree of authority as well as the political and economic means they are able to bring into play. Unequal means to succeed in the competition for shares in the national income, as well as the problem of economic recession experienced by industrializing societies, are seen as the major sources of conflict in modern society. The formation of interest groups and the ensuing struggle between them constitute the media through which change occurs.

Types, causes, and consequences of conflicts may be analyzed on the level of social groups or the social system as a whole just as much as they may be the subject matter of studies on the international level. Aron's (1963) work on peace and war exemplifies well how relevant the conflict–theoretical vocabulary is for an analysis of the relationships between states when he invokes such notions as power, force, system of states, types of war and peace, etc. Thus, Aron sees two alternatives to interpret war as a means to regulate the relationships between states that pursue their own national interest. Both peace through law (e.g., in the form of international agreements or supranational bodies) and peace through dominance (e.g., by establishing an empire or spheres of influence) remind us of

1 the extent of power that the nations concerned have recourse to;
2 the vested interests that are entered by all participants; and
3 the role that these factors play in producing or changing these arrangements.

Together with the earlier statements concerning the integrative function of conflicts (cf. Coser, 1956; Gluckman, 1956) and conflict-prone qualities of norms (cf. Dahrendorf, 1968; Lockwood, 1964), this discussion draws our attention to a central characteristic of all social life: the *consensual* nature of conflict and war as well as the *antagonistic* nature of order and peace. To remain within Aron's picture, this assertion is illustrated by the third alternative to war, namely, peace through equilibrium of power. Such an alternative comes into being through a (though often not avowed) consensus of the superpowers on a minimum of behavioral rules and the limits of spheres of influence, on the one hand, and through an approximate equilibrium of control over deterrent weapons, on the other.

Just as much as minimal agreements channel conflicts and the latter may have positive effects on the persistence of the body politic, so is the history of most societies full of examples that testify to the fact that normatively oriented, apparently harmonious relationships among members of society rest upon much coercion and domination prone to develop, under certain conditions, a great deal of potential for conflict and change.

In sum, conflict theorists of Marxist and non-Marxist orientation locate the source of social antagonisms, conflicts, and changes in the *differential distribution* of power – be it economic, political, or status power or simply the power to define goals and norms. Conflict between those who control the access to scarce and valued resources of society and those who pursue a greater share in these resources, is the basic (if not the only) process through which 'significant' changes take place. Just as much as they explain social structures in terms of modes of behavior stemming from patterns of differential control over social resources, so does social change manifest itself in shifts in that capacity of control which, in turn, result from preceding conflicts (cf. Collins, 1975: 61, 89). Oversimplified, one could therefore think of non-Marxist conflict theorists as being representatives of a 'cyclical conflict theory,' as they regard domination and conflict as universal. Marx and his present-day followers in capitalistic societies seem to favor a 'dynamic-evolutionary conflict theory,' for whom conflicts of the kind that we have just discussed are related to a specific social order and developmental stage of human society. In this sense, conflict is seen as eventually leading to harmony, integration, and stability of a future social system. While non-Marxists speak mainly of *gradual* change as a consequence of conflicts, for Marxists this precursor to ultimate social peace is characterized by *abrupt* changes. However, representatives of both perspectives recognize that whether gradual or abrupt changes occur is also dependent upon the degree of flexibility of the social system in question.

2.2.2 The classical evolutionary theory of society

Classical evolutionary theory was based on the assumption that the history of human societies represented the history of their development from a simple, hardly differentiated, i.e., 'backward,' state to a more complex, i.e., 'advanced,' state. Such a development proceeded in a definitive series of stages corresponding with specific kinds of institutions, ideas, and values which, in turn, were characterized by increasing complexity. The dual theme of organic analogy and progression from the 'primitive' to the developed 'ideal' determined most of the early evolutionary thinking.

> Classical evolutionary theory rests on the notion that a cultural item or complex appears when a given society is 'ripe' for it – that is, when it has reached the appropriate stage of evolution. According to this view, causation is internal to society; even if a backward society were exposed to more advanced technology and customs, this society, proceeding on its evolutionary path, would not be prepared to incorporate them (Smelser, 1967: 704).

To be sure, the metaphor of gradual, cumulative, and directed growth of human societies combines the idea that societies are, like organisms, subject to a cosmic–evolutionary as well as an individual–cyclical process of growth, with the hope for human and social perfectibility stemming from the Enlightenment.

In the seventeenth century, under the influence of Newton's principles, the machine provided the model for man's reflections about God and the world, while in the nineteenth century the organic analogy came to be the intellectual framework for the grand systems of thought about the process of human civilization, as the works of Auguste Comte and Herbert Spencer, Emile Durkheim, and Oswald Spengler demonstrate.[5] Although the source of change was seen by the evolutionary approach to inhere in the evolutionary dynamic of every society, it did not succeed in fully explaining the processes that characterized the transition of a society from one developmental stage to the next.

> Most of the classical evolutionary schools tended, rather, to point out general causes of change (economic, technological, spiritual, etc.) or some general trends (e.g., the trend to complexity) inherent in the development of societies. Very often they confused such general tendencies with the causes of change or assumed that these general tendencies explain concrete instances of change (Eisenstadt, 1970: 13).

One of the earliest theories of social evolution to gain prominence was advanced by Auguste Comte who gave to the sociological discipline its name. He described three major epochs or stages through which he believed all societies were destined to pass on the road toward human perfection. They are:

(1) the theological and military epoch in which supernatural preoccupations dominate the culture, and military conquest and slavery are the major social goals; (2) the metaphysical and juridical epoch, which is a transitional epoch between the first and third; and (3) the scientific and industrial epoch, in which positivism displaces religious speculation and peaceful economic production displaces war-making as the dominant aim of social organization (Smelser, 1967: 699).

In regard to social change, Comte saw it as practically synonymous with the inevitable evolutionary process following the natural law that 'results from the instinctive tendency of the human race to perfect itself' (Comte, 1877, vol. 4: 588). According to Comte, evolution was primarily one of human intelligence moving from fetishism to positivism and the corresponding development of societal organization from human activity directed toward war of man against other men to the struggle of man against nature. For Comte, 'the movement of history . . . is effected by action and reaction between the various segments of the total social reality' (Aron, 1970, vol. 1: 99). Different systems of thought develop in the direction of positivism at differential rates, creating chaos and crisis. 'One of the mechanism of the movement of history is precisely the incoherence, at each stage of history, of various ways of thinking' (Aron, 1970, vol. 1: 97). However, this overt chaos would some day be comprehended as the natural, inevitable, and 'orderly' unfolding of history. The equilibrium of forces, that is, the synchronic coordination of their development, advances to the scientific problem of first order, as demonstrated by Comte and later by Marx and Spencer, with the experience of the destruction of the old agrarian and feudal order as their empirical background. Only an order that builds upon these lines of development is regarded as capable of surviving. It is the sociologist's task to discover and to explicate these tendencies (cf. Smith, 1973: 27; Nisbet, 1969: 10).

As man struggles to master nature through scientific discovery and application of laws governing natural phenomena, differentiation and specialization of functions increase. Differentiation in one institutional sphere sets up pressures on related areas of activity in society to move in the direction of 'progress,' i.e., to increase their control over the environment. Neo-evolutionary functionalism as it is mirrored in Parsons's (1967) notion of 'adaptive upgrading' of social systems or in Luhmann's (1971a) idea of reducing complexity by institutionalizing meaning structures on various levels of social systems, seems to originate in those principles of classical evolutionism (cf. Chapter 4 in this volume). Moreover, important elements of William F. Ogburn's theory of cultural lag are already contained in central passages of Comte's works (cf. section 2.2.4.3 below).

Another prominent theorist in this category is Karl Marx. His conflict approach as presented in section 2.2.1.1 can only be understood – especially with respect to the claim to explain and predict social transformations – if the evolutionary framework in which it is offered is taken into consideration. Marx differs from other classical evolutionists in that he regarded the advancement of societies not as smooth, gradual, and continuous change but rather 'as broken into discrete units, or epochs, within which the mechanism [in the system] resulted in slight change but between which there was a complete change of mechanisms themselves' (Beshers, 1964: 283).

Marx identified four major epochs of human history: slavery, feudalism, capitalism, and socialism (which was supposed in time to culminate in communism as the state 'withered away'). Each epoch was characterized by two major antagonistic classes engaged in a struggle for control over the means of production (cf. section 2.2.1.1 above and Chapter 3 below). What is important for evolutionary theory

> is his belief that there is a logic of development operating independently of human will which inevitably results in changes in the structure of society, its origins lying in the relationship of man to the means of production (i.e., factories, mills and machinery), whilst behind this there are the fundamental limitations set by a dominant mode of production (i.e., manual labor or steam power) (Mitchell, 1968: 5).

Another type of evolutionary theory focused on the movement of societies from one 'ideal type' social structure to another. The different types are usually defined in terms of the basis of social integration while the transition is not necessarily evaluated as one of progress or a move toward perfection. Indeed, as with Tönnies (1887/1963) and Durkheim (1893/1964), we encounter an opposite, though not as culturally pessimistic an assessment as in Spengler (1918/26). In 1861, Sir Henry Maine wrote in his book, *Ancient Law*, that societies progressed through a series of stages in which the basis for social order changed from patriarchal kinship bonds and particularistic status criteria to contractual bonds and universal criteria of achievement, freedom, and equality (Maine, 1907). In 1887 Ferdinand Tönnies published his famous dichotomization of social organizations and interpersonal relationships: *Gemeinschaft* as organizing principle rests upon shared morals and sentimental bonds, while *Gesellschaft* is based upon the criterion of rational self-interest (e.g., friendship relations *vs* seller–buyer relations; family *vs* company).

Durkheim followed this tradition of social analysis by developing polar types of social integration, namely, mechanical and organic solidarity. A society based upon mechanical solidarity is characterized by a shared, all-encompassing system of beliefs and sentiments, i.e., a strong collective conscience. Such a society is usually small, agriculturally oriented and exhibits a high degree of homogeneity among its members. 'The individuals, the members of the same collectivity, resemble each other because they feel the same emotions, cherish the same values, and hold the same things sacred. The society is coherent because the individuals are not yet differentiated' (Aron, 1970, vol. 2: 11). Societal organization is simple, usually based on kinship. By contrast, modern, populous and industrial societies are characterized by organic solidarity, based on the social division of labor among its members. The interdependence that results from differentiation of activities, roles, and institutions, provides the cement for this kind of social solidarity. That is to say, a strong collective conscience is replaced by mutual dependence in ensuring cooperation. Societal organization is thus based upon the performance of differentiated social tasks.

With his ideas Durkheim intended to show, especially in contrast to Marx, that moral requirements, as best documented by laws, not economic factors, played a decisive role in shaping the development of human society. For example, in our highly differentiated society individual claims (e.g., private property, social security) rather than collective interests dominate. These individual claims are protected by the legal system. The social function of taking care of the unfolding of individual chances seems to be the progressing specialization of the individual, thus advancing the development of society *via* the maximal exploitation of talents (Dreitzel, 1967a: 48–9).[6]

As for the cause of change in the form of societal organization, it appears to be essentially the same for these theories of evolution of 'ideal types.' An increase in volume and density of population leads to increased differentiation and specialization of functions and an increase in social interaction (or what Durkheim calls 'moral density'). As a society grows in density, traditional bases for authority start to break down. Larger populations lead to a scarcity of resources and an increase in the division of labor develops in order to utilize the resources efficiently. The common bonds of values, knowledge, and shared beliefs diminish as anonymity and impersonality increase with a growing population and structural complexity. The cause of social change is regarded as an internal, 'inevitable' condition associated with the growth of a society in its numbers and complexity (Durkheim, 1964: 262).

The two most important processes involved in the transition from 'simple' to 'complex' societal organization are

1 increasing *differentiation* and specialization of social functions, and
2 the replacement of ascriptive bases for societal organization by *achievement criteria*.

Differentiation refers to the dissociation of major social functions from one another and their subsequent organization into separate but interdependent institutional spheres. As differentiation progresses, activity becomes increasingly specialized around the fulfillment of some single function. In these theories of evolution from one 'ideal type' of society to another, the

> different levels or stages of differentiation denote the degree to which the major social and cultural activities, as well as certain basic resources – manpower, economic resources, motivational – have been disembedded or freed from kinship, territorial, and other ascriptive units. . . . It is this disembedment of resources and activities from such ascriptive frameworks that constitutes the basis for the transformative capacities of societies. . . . The growing autonomy of the different institutional spheres and the extension of their organizational scope . . . opens up new possibilities for development and creativity – for technological development, expansion of political power or rights, or cultural, religious, philosophical, and personal creativity (Eisenstadt, 1970: 15–16).

In the works of Durkheim, Tönnies, and Max Weber, the ideal types as mentioned by Eisenstadt have been particularly stressed. Other evolutionary theorists such as Herbert Spencer and William Graham Sumner have placed social development in a *cosmic* context and have not been afraid of pointing to various social and political consequences. Not unlike Durkheim, Spencer (1896, vol. 2) envisioned a transition from a 'militaristically' organized 'struggle for survival,' above all characterized by political and religious controls, to an 'industrial' society for the integration of which sympathy and knowledge were considered to be of greater significance than force and conquest. In this conception of industrial society we recognize that the Spencer–Darwinian formula of the 'survival of the fittest' is about to be replaced by the Durkheimian idea of the social division of labor, in that differentiation and specialization of economic activities vested more and more people with a social capacity for survival. Spencer believed that 'social or institutional evolution is part and parcel of cosmic evolution as a whole, and hence cannot be successfully controlled by artificial human intervention and guidance' (Becker and Barnes, 1961, vol. 3: 799). And Sumner (1913: 210), greatly influenced by Spencer, wrote:

> The things that will change it [the world] are the great discoveries and inventions, the new reactions inside the social organism, and the changes in the earth itself on account of changes in the cosmical forces. These causes will make of it just what, in fidelity to them, it ought to be. The men will be carried along with it and be made by it. . . . That is why it is the greatest folly of which a man can be capable, to sit down with a slate and pencil to plan out a new social world.

In sum, representatives of evolutionary theory see changes in the social structure as *inevitable* and as the result of forces endemic to all societies that cannot be abolished or altered by human efforts. Inventions and innovation, population growth and functional differentiation are viewed as those mechanisms that make change appear to be an integral part of any society – the iron law of societal development. However, the degree of generalization – for civilizations as a whole and not concrete social structures, social groupings or social relationships are the dominant subject of analysis – makes it difficult to believe in the scientific value of the evolutionary theorists' statements, and fairly easy for critics to dismiss them altogether.

Despite the barrage of criticism leveled against classical evolutionary theory for its single, universal determinants, vague 'prime movers' of history, lack of empirical proof for 'general laws of history,' etc., the evolutionary perspective is still thriving, albeit in a modified manner, in theories of multilinear evolution and modernization.

2.2.3 Cyclical or rise and fall theories of social change

Social theorists who view social processes as following a cyclical pattern locate the sources of change in the *culture*, i.e., as inherent in the total way of life of a society. Like conflict theorists, they focus on the conditions leading to instability but, in addition, are concerned with the processes whereby societies, cultures, or civilizations move along a pattern of growth, stagnation, and retrogression. In other words, change is manifested in the recurrent themes or patterns of 'cultural types,' often interpreted as analogous to organismic patterns of birth, growth, maturity, decline, and death. The pattern 'is not influenced so much by forces external to the culture as by the implications of the culture itself. The causes of change are built into the basic premises of the culture' (Smelser, 1967: 712).

The idea that each society or each state in the cyclical process contains within it the seeds for its own development and destruction, is closely related to the cultural pessimism spreading within the bourgeoisie since the end of the nineteenth century. The destructive effects of industrialization, urbanization, and bureaucratization in Western societies had contributed their share; however, there had been especially the tendency toward secularization and democratization of the political, economic, and educational spheres which undermined not only the intellectual but also the political hegemony of the bourgeoisie, eventually leading to a gradual replacement of the optimistic–evolutionary philosophy of history by pessimistic–cyclical theories of culture (cf. Dreitzel, 1967a: 73–9; Elias, 1976, vol. 1: xxxvi).

The cyclical model of society is based upon the idea that a cultural theme is adopted, developed, and elaborated upon until it is exhausted, and the opportunities for structurally effective achievements and further growth will be limited. The consequence is, it is held, general discontent with the present society which is accompanied by growing disorder until the old cultural pattern is destroyed and society moves on to the next phase of the cycle. Or as Oswald Spengler (1926: 31) expressed it, by reference to the critical phase of the transition of a 'culture' into a 'civilization':

> Civilizations are the most external and artificial states of which a species of developed humanity is capable. They are a conclusion, the thing-become succeeding the thing-becoming, death following life, rigidity following expansion, intellectual age and the stone-built, petrifying world-city following mother-earth and the spiritual childhood of Doric and Gothic. They are an end, irrevocable, yet by inward necessity reached again and again.

One of the best known rise and fall theories is that by Pitirim A. Sorokin. He described three major cultural themes or fundamental social forms which alternate with each other rhythmically.

1 the 'sensate' system dominated by reason, realism, materialism, ethic of success, and empirical orientation;
2 the 'ideational' system characterized by mysticism, strong beliefs, and symbolism to which an orientation based on sentiment and an ethic of conviction corresponds; and
3 the 'idealistic' system representing a combination of sensate and ideational elements (Sorokin, 1937–41, 4 vols, especially vol. 1: 66–75, vol. 2: 775–7).

Sorokin believed that social systems fluctuate between domination by sensate and ideational themes (with the idealistic period intervening during the shift between the two extremes). While a cultural theme is developing, society flourishes. However, when the culture becomes saturated by this theme, innovation and progress are stifled, that is, opportunities for future developments of the theme are exhausted. When this point of saturation is reached, cultural stagnation and disintegration set in, paving the way for the reversal of cultural values. Thus, unlike the linear evolutionists, Sorokin sees the possibilities for development as limited. 'The basic forms of almost all sociocultural phenomena are limited in their number; hence they inevitably recur in time, in rhythmic fashion, and in the course of their changes do not follow a strictly linear trend' (Sorokin, 1947: 701). Although, for Sorokin, the oscillation of cultural systems between the sensate and the ideational themes was inevitable, he did not mean by this that the implementation or actualization of these themes precluded change in the structure and form of society. 'The dominant form of the direction of sociocultural processes is neither permanently cyclical nor permanently linear, but varyingly recurrent, with incessant modifications of the old themes' (Sorokin, 1947: 703).

Sorokin also described another cycle of increasing and decreasing societal integration that accompanies the cycle of cultural types and helps to explain how change occurs. As complete saturation by sensate or ideational forms develops, opportunities for creative activity are exhausted and social integration declines with resultant dissatisfaction, disorder, and outbreaks of violence.

> We have observed that social organization, differentiation, and stratification grow immanently until they reach their optimum point in a given group; when the optimum point is exceeded, groups generate forces that inhibit further differentiation and stratification. On the other hand, when immobility persists too long, social systems generate forces working for differentiation. If systems do not succeed in regaining their optimum equilibrium, they tend to disintegrate (Sorokin, 1947: 704).[7]

With a great deal of historical and statistical material Sorokin tried to verify the hypothesis that Western industrial society of the present time represented an 'overmature sensate social system,' while Western civilization had already reached its ideational peak in the Middle Ages. As evidence for the idealistic system Sorokin found only two cases: Greece of the fifth century, and the late Middle Ages. Apart from the fact that Sorokin's studies were influenced by his preference of the ideational culture in comparison with the sensate culture, such rough, centuries-spanning explanations of change leave many developments in measurable details unnoticed. This fact and his tendency to use empirical data of human history very selectively in order to support his hypotheses, has become the subject of a number of reproaches from his critics (cf. Timasheff, 1967: 276–8; Bardis, 1962: 187).

Vilfredo Pareto's (1966: §§ 2025ff., 2148ff.) theory of 'the circulation of the elites' has gained doubtful fame in the context of the rise of fascism in Italy. According to this (political) rise and fall theory, social change takes place because the strength of certain residues (i.e., predispositions to certain forms of conduct underlying human behavior) changes over time. However, the social system never really changes as it operates in a state of equilibrium in which change in one residue sets up a compensatory reaction in other residues. 'Change for Pareto . . . maintains the system. The elements whose values alter are the residues and the derivations, but they alter quantitatively' (Mitchell, 1968: 122). Society seen through these lenses consists of two basic groups anchored in the economic and political spheres: the foxes and the lions (Pareto, 1966: §§ 2178ff.).

> In the former, the residues of combination predominate – they are innovators, experimenters, risk-takers, mentally mobile. . . . In the latter, residues of the persistence of aggregates have the upper hand; they are traditionalists, followers of routine, advocates of 'sound methods,' mentally immobile. . . . The most prosperous society is one in which the most important residues are best distributed: the leaders should be strong in residues of combination, thus leading the society to innovate; the followers should be strong in the residues of the persistence of aggregates, thus consolidating all the advantage that may be derived from the new combinations (Becker and Barnes, 1961, vol. 3: 1022).

Pareto argues that at the beginning of a cycle the elite is strong in the residues of combination. They use cunning, deception, and force to carry out and enforce their innovations. However, they soon come to stress order, peace, and loyalty within their ranks to preserve the

THEORETICAL APPROACHES

new order. Thus, residues of the persistence of aggregates become stronger among elite members, while, at the same time, they close their ranks to non-elite members in order to maintain their positions. As a consequence innovations become more difficult and the ruling class becomes stagnant. The elite is now composed of characteristics typical of lions and open to attack by the non-elite foxes who are willing to use new means, including deception and force, to realize their social goals. Then, revolution (or, perhaps more accurately, a *coup d'état*) takes place and the new elite of foxes takes over.

> [2056] By the circulation of elites, the governing elite is in a state of continuous and slow transformation. It flows like a river, and what it is today is different from what it was yesterday. Every so often, there are sudden and violent disturbances. The river floods and breaks its banks. Then, afterwards, the new governing elite resumes again the slow process of self-transformation. The river returns to its bed and once more flows freely on. [2057] Revolution occur because – either through a slowing down in the circulation of elites or from other causes – the upper strata accumulate decadent elements which no longer retain the residues appropriate to the maintenance of power and which shrink from the use of force; while among the lower strata, elements of superior quality are increasing which do possess the residues suitable for governing and are prepared to use force. [2058] In revolutions individuals of the lower strata are generally led by individuals from the upper strata because these latter possess the intellectual qualities needful for devising strategy and tactics; the combative residues they lack are provided by individuals from the lower strata (Pareto, 1966: 250).

Lions and foxes turn out to be two types of elite positions, the former representing the social force of authority, conservation, and interpretation, and the latter the force of innovation, differentiation, and achievement. Because the characteristics of the ruling elite are relevant for social changes, Pareto distinguishes between ruling and non-ruling elites (cf. Aron, 1970, vol. 2: 179–87; Kiss, 1973, vol. 2: 118–21).[8]

Max Weber's (1947) theory of social change combines elements of the conflict, evolutionist, and cyclical approach. Marx conceived of human history as a linear sequence of modes of production advanced by class struggles. In contrast to Marx, Weber was of the opinion that capitalism had such a pervasive effect only because it had developed within the limits of an increasingly *rational* way of life in Western societies (Löwith, 1960: 20). For Weber, and later for Dahrendorf as well, dependence on wage earning and private ownership of the means of production represent only special cases of class situations if one considers that all modern organizations such as companies, unions, political parties, churches, and schools are characterized by constant reproduction of an internal oligarchy, on the one hand, and continued bureaucratization, on the other. On the level of interaction, the general trend toward bureacratization in Western societies corresponds with an increase in purposive rationality orienting individual action. The purposive aspects of social action, especially pervading the economic and political spheres, manifest themselves in calculated market and power chances in the realization of which various types of domination play an important role. With the sequence of traditional, charismatic, and rational domination, Weber points to an evolutionary trend in the sense of increasing rationalization. However, by taking into consideration that charismatic leaders may appear, he envisions a recurrent cycle of breaking open the 'iron cage' of bureaucracy and materialism. A series of examples may be derived from recent history of various societies and their central institutions that testify to the significant role of charismatic leaders in initiating social changes (e.g., Lenin, Hitler, Gandhi, Kennedy, Martin Luther King, Mao, John XXIII). This is not to say that the extent and the kind of initiated and actually effected change does not also depend upon specific personality characteristics of the leaders and their 'routinized' successors, the social circumstances, and the capacity of the charismatic leader to fulfill certain functions valued by society.

Other well-known rise and fall theories have been advanced by Oswald Spengler (1926), Arnold Toynbee (1947), Alfred Weber (1950), and Alfred L. Kroeber (1944), although most of them do not essentially differ from the classical evolutionary theories discussed here, especially as far as the issues of cause and process of change are concerned. The cyclical theories agree in that the source of change is seen as inherent in the limitation of cultural patterns, and the process of change is believed to result from stagnation and become manifest in discontent and aggression.

Apart from the organic analogy as employed by a number of rise and fall theorists, cyclical change theories have refined, though often in philosophical display, such important ideas as differentiation and functional requisites, tension, and power. Later on, these concepts would become central to the explanatory schemes of modern representatives of conflict theory and functionalism.

2.2.4 The neo-evolutionary theory of society

It is quite plausible to say that the only remarkable difference between the classical evolutionists and the present neo-evolutionists exists in relation to the respective subject matter (cf. Nisbet, 1969: 223–39). For the former, mankind, civilization or some institutional ideal type of society represented the primary field of study, while the latter chose the apparent variation of change patterns with respect to certain social groups, regions, or organizations as their major focus of analysis.

2.2.4.1 The theory of multilinear evolution

One neo-evolutionary school of thought that emphasizes multilinear evolution has been developed in the works of Julian Steward, Marshall D. Sahlins, Elman R. Service, and others. The theory of multilinear evolution basically seeks to reconcile the parallel patterns of development, as observed by its representatives in many cultures, with the striking diversities in cultural expression which also exist. Steward's argument

> is summarized in the proposition that 'the facts now accumulated indicate that human culture evolved along a number of different lines; we must think of evolution not as unilinear but multilinear.' The task of the anthropologist is to identify culture types within which distinctive lines of evolution emerge. Thus, one type of culture area produces hunters, another an agricultural civilization. 'Human evolution, then, is not merely a matter of biology, but of the interaction of man's physical and cultural characteristics, each influencing the other' (Appelbaum, 1970: 56–7).

Sahlins and Service elaborate upon this idea and attempt to explain both the diversity and general stages of development by employing the conceptual pair of Specific and General Evolution.

> It appears almost obvious upon stating it that in both its biological and cultural spheres evolution moves simultaneously in two directions. On one side, it creates diversity through adaptive modification; new forms differentiate from old. On the other side, evolution generates progress: higher forms arise from, and surpass, lower. The first of these directions is Specific Evolution, and the second, General Evolution (Sahlins, 1960: 12–13).

The process by which societies evolve, rests on the development of an ever-increasing adaptability, that is, capacity to adjust to environmental conditions, cultural heritage, and achievements borrowed from other cultures. Sahlins and Service identify three steps in the evolutionary process to 'higher' cultural forms. The first two involve (1) the production of greater energy transformation, and (2) an increase in societal integration.

> It seems to us that progress is the total transformation of energy involved in the creation and perpetuation of a cultural organization. . . . Cultures that transform more energy have more parts and subsystems, more specialization of parts, and more effective means of integration of the whole (Sahlins, 1960: 35–6).

A highly energized, to remain within the picture, and integrated societal organization leads to the third aspect of progress, namely, (3) the greater adaptability to the exigencies imposed by the physical and social environment. The similarity with Spencer's propositions in his *Principles of Sociology* (1898–9, 3 vols) is at times blatant.

As with the classical evolutionists, today's multilinear evolutionists envision the development of societies to proceed in the general direction of progress toward 'higher forms' although, unlike their classical colleagues, they hold that societies may develop along *different* paths as they progress. Also, unlike earlier evolutionary theories, *external* sources of change are recognized and seen as accounting for some cultural variations in development. This indicates that representatives of multilinear evolutionism have adopted a number of important insights from diffusion theory and research (which we will deal with in section 2.4.1). For example, Service (1960; 1971; 1975) formulates the 'law of evolutionary potential' in which the rejection of a linear evolutionist concept is expressed. He argues that in the socio-cultural sphere progress occurs in a manner depending upon its place of origin (Service, 1960: 97). Dreitzel (1967a: 82–3) summarizes Service's arguments well:

> Each stage of development – he does not think so much in terms of whole social systems like Parsons but rather in terms of the development of single cultural elements such as tools – is characterized by a given degree of saturation, which is reached within a group or society. If the adaptation is too good, that is, the development proceeded in too special a manner, it may end up in a dead-end street and does not continue at all or continues only in some spatial and/or temporal distance. If a cultural element proves useful in a given stage of development, it will be imitated and disseminated by way of cultural contact. The evolutionary potential is especially great if the element is so general that the

attempt of being taken over by another society or culture will hardly be met by resistance. It turns out to be particularly prone of development, if it will be integrated into an alien cultural environment and mixed with the latter's elements and traditions.

2.2.4.2 *Theories of modernization*

Modernization theories may be distinguished from the various theoretical approaches of multilinear evolution of socio-cultural phenomena in that the latter mostly refer to primitive or historical societies and examine the origin and development of certain elements of these societies (e.g., technologies or the state) with respect to their multilinearity (cf. e.g., Service, 1975). Modernization theories, by comparison, are mostly concerned with certain aspects of industrialization in the First and Second World (e.g., Flora, 1974). In other words, they focus on the analysis of transformations that societies undergo during industrialization. Although some of the recent modernization literature has dropped the evolutionary emphasis, the heritage of evolutionary thought is apparent in many of these theories which see the patterns of development as essentially the same for all societies undergoing industrialization and the result of this 'progress' – modernized society – as being quite similar.

Marion Levy's (1967: 89) view of modernization is that:

> We are confronted – whether for good or for bad – with a universal social solvent. The patterns of the relatively modernized societies, once developed, have shown a universal tendency to penetrate any social context whose participants have come in contact with them. . . . The patterns always penetrate; once the penetration has begun, the previous indigenous patterns always change; and they always change in the direction of some of the patterns of the relatively modernized societies.

Wilbert E. Moore (1963: 89) defines modernization as 'the "total" transformation of a traditional or pre-modern society into the types of technology and associated social organization that characterize the "advanced," economically prosperous, and relatively politically stable nations of the Western World'. And finally, Neil J. Smelser (1966: 111) says that the term modernization 'refers to the fact that technical, economic, and ecological change ramify through the whole social and cultural fabric.'

The source of technical and economic change is seen as mainly endogenous innovation, although societies that begin the process of industrialization later than others may borrow certain inventions and knowledge items, enabling them to develop more rapidly than by independent invention alone. Social and cultural institutions presumably change as a direct result of alterations in technology and the means of production. At this point it should be clear how heavily modernization theory is obligated to Durkheim's ideas. The increasing differentiation and specialization of functions lead to heightened 'moral density' (the number of people engaged in social interaction) and a breakdown in traditional social relationships. Heterogeneity of beliefs and interests results, as well as disorganization and destruction of pre-industrial social life.

The two most important, interrelated processes of change involved in modernization are *industrialization* and structural *differentiation*. In traditional or 'pre-modern' society, social needs are met by a single unit or a small number of social units. For example, the kinship system or extended family serves as the center for socialization, religious, educational, and economic activities and, sometimes, political functions. Thus, the major social functions are fused into a single institution. Differentiation of these functions takes place during modernization, at the end of which each function is served by a separate, specialized social structure. For the process of industrialization structural differentiation is central as the former presupposes the differentiated formation of productive processes and the structural independence of production and exchange.

As already mentioned, the processes of differentiation and specialization in pre-modern society disintegrate traditional social structures (e.g., traditional values, norms, role definitions, and other integrative mechanisms). New mechanisms of integration arise only gradually which are themselves differentiated and specialized (e.g., labor unions, interest groups, political parties, other voluntary associations). S. N. Eisenstadt (1964a) points out that differentiation and innovation do not necessarily lead to (re-) integration and the corresponding institutionalization of new norms and roles. Similar to Service, Eisenstadt regards the concepts of differentiation and of development stages as 'important guides for identifying the crucial breakthroughs' (Eisenstadt, 1964a: 386) rather than adequate descriptions and sound explanations of actual changes.

In this context several authors, Eisenstadt among them, have proposed to include the formation and activity of different elites into the analysis of the interplay of the various differentiation processes in order 'to explain systematically the possibilities for institutionalization of such different integrative principles and concrete structures' (Eisenstadt, 1964a: 386; cf. also Shils, 1960; Kerr *et al.*, 1960; Gerschenkron, 1962). Although not enough is known about the rise of new elites and their relationships with other groups, Eisenstadt makes us aware of the significance of active groups with particular 'entrepreneurial qualities' in some segments of society; they try to find solutions for old and new problems and hence determine the speed and direction of social changes. For example, specific enclaves such as monasteries, sects, scientific associations, or political cliques have always played a major role in forming and recruiting elites. For Shils (1963), the scope of variation of institutions in modern, or at least modernizing, societies is mainly explained in terms of the composition and orientation of the dominating elites. He distinguishes between five types of elites as they shape the political system: political democracy, guardian democracy, modernizing oligarchy, totalitarian oligarchy, and traditional oligarchy.

Modernization theories share the emphasis on the tendency to consider solutions of social problems as exchangeable even if they are found within a society defined by state boundaries. From here, it is not far to the idea that all societal developments – on the dimension of East–West as well as North–South – converge. In many cases modern industrial society of the West is offered as the model to be emulated. As with Parsons's functionalist neo-evolutionism, externally induced change is in danger of being dissolved in the schematism of internal paths of development mostly conceived in long-range terms. The ideological potential of such a theory is, of course, no substitute for empirical research, in much the same way as the idea of a technically manageable modernization does not produce identical results of such a development (Bühl, 1970: 19–20).

2.2.4.3 The theory of 'cultural lag'

Another, most interesting theory of endogenous change that came into existence in response to classical evolutionism and may be reckoned among theories of modernization, is William F. Ogburn's theory of cultural lag. Although Ogburn was fascinated by Charles Darwin's explanation of biological evolution, especially as far as its explanatory power is concerned, he soon was convinced by anthropological findings that the development of society is independent from the progress of biological evolution of man. This also meant that the extent to which man inherited his intellectual capacities is independent from the state of development of culture in which man is embedded (Ogburn, 1966: 61–6; Jaffe, 1968: 278). Ogburn criticizes therefore the undue generalizations of evolutionists about inevitable stages of societal development, if we consider that social evolution does not imply biological evolution. Rather, he differentiates between 'the biological foundations of society' and 'the culture,' thus transforming 'social evolution [. . . into] cultural evolution' (Ogburn, 1966: 377).

Ogburn (1966: 377ff.) mentions four factors that decisively influenced cultural development: invention, accumulation, exchange, and adjustment. The factor of *invention* from which the other variables are derived, is of fundamental importance, although all factors do indeed influence each other. These mutual influences should be understood as a multifaceted process of adjustment whose point of departure represents an invention originating in one of the segments of culture and, for example, put to use because of an existing need. The resulting chains of alteration appear as processes in a temporal sequence, meaning that a change in one cultural segment does not simultaneously effect a change in another segment. As these changes are not synchronic but diachronic, *lags* ensue. Such adaptive protractions are defined by Ogburn as 'cultural lag' or 'adjustment of one part of culture to another' (O. D. Duncan's introduction to Ogburn, 1964: xv).

In his extensive studies of change phenomena, Ogburn separated two aspects of the activities of society's members: the material and socio-cultural aspects. He believed that the material culture unfolds and changes according to the principle of accumulation, which simply means that new discoveries and inventions build upon past ones. However, this principle does not apply to other aspects of culture such as values, religious beliefs, art, law, traditions and education, which do not develop cumulatively but rather are replaced by new ones. His central *hypothesis* therefore is 'that changes in material culture proceed at a faster rate than changes in adaptive culture – customs, beliefs, philosophies, laws and governments – and the result is continuous maladjustment between the two types of culture' (Smelser, 1967: 703). The more rapid rate of development in material culture causes social maladjustments and pressures for change in the adaptive structures.

For Ogburn, material innovation represented the most important single cause of change. He demonstrates that in an example:

> I shall begin with a definition. A cultural lag occurs when one of two parts of culture which are correlated changes before or in greater degree than the other part does, thereby causing less adjustment between the two parts than existed previously.
>
> An illustration is the lag in the construction of highways for automobile traffic. The two parts in this illustration are the automobile and the highways. These two parts of culture were in good adjustment in, say, 1910, when the automobile was slow and

the highways were narrow country roads with curves and bends over which had been laid a hard surface. The automobile traveled at not a great rate of speed and could take the turns without too much trouble or danger. It was essentially for local transportation. But as time went on, this first part, the automobile, which is called an independent variable, underwent many changes, particularly the engine, which developed speeds capable of sixty, seventy, eighty miles an hour, with brakes that could stop the car relatively quickly. But the narrow highways with sharp bends did not change as soon as did the automobile. On these roads the driver must slow up or have accidents. A decade or more later we are building a few broad highways with no sharp curves, which will make the automobile a vehicle for long-distance travel. The old highways, the dependent variable, are not adapted to the new automobiles, so that there is a maladjustment between the highways and the automobile. The adjustment, as measured by speeds, was better for local travel around 1910 than it is for long-distance travel on these roads at present. The adjustment will be better on the new express highways. Since the adjustment is made by the dependent variable, it is that part of culture which adapts and is called adaptive culture (Ogburn, 1964: 86–7).

This illustration could easily be supplemented by scores of similar examples such as: What consequences followed from shifting production out of the household into factories and business firms for the social position of women? When and in what way are legal rules adjusted to accidents at work and in traffic, in using medical instruments, and in atomic energy plants?

Ogburn stressed three factors that determine the process of innovations: (1) mental capacities, (2) demand, and (3) the existing knowledge. The first factor refers to the question as to which reservoir of talents is available in a society. The demand variable has to do with the needs that can arise in a society to such a degree that resources must be withdrawn from other places in order to meet them (e.g., to be able to train scientists and technicians for the development of a national defense system). Existing knowledge is relevant for the promotion of inventions as it provides the basis upon which they can be developed. The broader the knowledge foundation, the more numerous and varied the inventions in a society, so that modern societies are continually accumulating new material culture with the consequence that the adaptive culture cannot adjust itself as rapidly, which, as pointed out, leads to social maladjustments (cf. Ogburn, 1946; 1947). To illustrate, let us point to the example of the long-term effects of American educational efforts in the wake of the Sputnik shock or of the expansion of the West German system of secondary and higher education after 1965.

These examples help us to reconstruct Ogburn's analytical steps:

1 At least two variables will be determined.
2 The proof will be made that these variables are adjusted to each other.
3 Stating the fact that a variable changes while another remains unchanged, or that one variable changes at a greater rate than the other.
4 A comparison of the situation in t_0 with that in t_1 (as described in steps 1 and 3) shows that a poorer adjustment of the two variables exists in t_1 than in t_0 (Ogburn, 1964: 89).

In one of his last essays, Ogburn (1964) explicitly states that the independent variable may not only be of technical and economic nature, but also political and ideological. Taking into consideration suggestions by some of his critics, he no longer upheld the idea of the *causal* primacy of technological and economic changes. He generalized his thesis in so far as he now asserted that the cultural lag were independent from the kind of preceding and lagging cultural element, of course presupposing that both elements stood to each other in an adaptive relation (Ogburn, 1964: 91). In this general version, the theory's scope of application depends on how closely related the cultural elements under study are. In any case, the cultural lag is characterized by the differing time spans in which change proceeds.

Ogburn's distinction between material and immaterial culture as well as the primacy that he attributes to technological change, reminds us at times of the Marxian concepts of productive forces and relations of production, economic basis and ideological superstructure. It is not surprising, therefore, that Ogburn's central thesis may already be looked up in Marx's Preface to *A Contribution to the Critique of Political Economy* (Marx, 1964c: 7–11). Marx and Ogburn differ primarily in that the former conceived of social change only in terms of radical transformations. Accordingly, a theory of change must be identical with the theory of revolution, for all other changes are only the reflection of reformistic actions or revisionistic attitudes, of sham fights and betrayal of the working class. Ogburn, by contrast, aimed at the analysis of small-scale changes, especially in terms of interrelated variables whereby one triggers and advances change while the other lags behind thus causing adaptive problems and eventually certain kinds of alterations. Ogburn starts with the idea that cultural lags had to occur wherever integrated and complex societies undergo rapid change. In that he emphasizes the technological aspects of change, he comes close to the assumption of monocausality with which Marx has often been reproached. Ogburn's fundamental idea can also be found in Parsons's AGIL scheme in which change is seen as primarily originating in the economic and technological subsystem (A), while the subsystem concerned with education and socialization (L) which is devoted to structural maintenance, changes the least and hence is apt to define what society is all about. Here we are also faced with a kind of monocausality as we shall argue in Chapter 4. Thus, we arrive at the perhaps surprising conclusion that so different social analysts as Marx, Ogburn, and Parsons do show a number of similarities as far as their methodologies are concerned, although they set their normative, conceptual, and explanatory accents differently.

In sum, endogenous sources of change as outlined by these theories usually stem from one or another kind of inadequacy of the existing society to cope with the various forces that are engendered by the socio-cultural system itself. The processes in which the change of societies becomes manifest are ultimately seen as the 'working out' of contradictions between the old and the new.

2.3 Theories of exogenous social change

Theoretical approaches concerned with exogenous sources of social change generally view society as a basically stable, well-integrated system that is disrupted or altered only by the impact of forces external to the system (e.g., world situation, wars, famine, natural disasters) or by new factors introduced into the system from other societies. For example, technological transfer and brain drain, political, cultural, and consumptive imperialism may lead to the diffusion of cultural traits beyond the limits of single societies. In the following sections, we shall not only deal with the classical diffusion and culture contact theory and explanatory schemes that focus on the influence of crises and events, but also with the equilibrium or functionalist theory of social change.

It is correct, though, that for equilibrium theorists change results from problems of adjustment of, and tensions between, new and old system units. As elaborated upon in Chapter 4, equilibrium theorists presently use a (neo-) evolutionary frame of reference in which change appears as a quality of the social system and not simply a deviation from, or external disturbance of, some state of the system. Central to the functionalist approach are the ideas of differentiation and equilibrium by means of which the evolutionary unfolding of the system's potential is empirically, conceptually, and analytically grasped. This has triggered the reproach that structural-functional theory could only predict change 'which leads the system back to stability' (Wiswede and Kutsch, 1978: 85). According to this critique, change is something that happens automatically, proceeding gradually and continually. Surprises seem to be excluded. In the event that they do occur, they will be attributed to the largely unexplained mainspring of change, namely, differentiation or external impulses. The direction of change seems to be clear: adaptive upgrading of the system. This means that change is understood in evolutionary terms manifesting itself in an increasing capacity of the given system to master its relationships to the environing systems more effectively and more successfully. Regardless of whether we deal with a society as a whole or less complex action systems such as a firm, family, or club, it is always an open question where the impulse to the aforementioned processes of differentiation comes from. At any rate, on the one hand, we deal with requirements of the environing systems and, on the other, with exchange relations between them and the system under consideration. This suggests that in the final analysis *externally* induced changes play a decisive role within the functionalist–neo-evolutionary framework. Such a negative delineation in the sense of mostly non-explicated, and often not even presumed, external influences justifies the classification of equilibrium theory as a theory of exogenous change. Equally good, especially traditional reasons could be cited for a positive delineation in the sense of an endogenous change theory. (Students of the functional theory of change who are looking for an extensive presentation rather than a short overview are advised to ignore section 2.3.3 and pass over to Chapter 4.)

2.3.1 *The classical diffusion and culture contact theory*

Cultural diffusion will be understood as the spread of cultural traits from one society to another. The idea that cultural *diffusion* is perhaps the major source of social change, arose largely in protest against the immanent, self-generating view of change offered by evolutionists. The diffusionists attempted to demonstrate that few, if any, cultural items emerged through independent invention but rather were borrowed from other cultures. The presence of certain cultural traits in a society cannot be regarded as evidence that this society has evolved independently up to the given stage, but rather that it has come into contact with other, more advanced cultures. Thus, one society may evolve to a certain stage in a fraction of the time it took for other societies, simply by the process of borrowing. Representatives of diffusion and culture contact theory basically argue that not a rigid sequence of stages but a series of civilizational stages, varying in number and time span, is the rule. An examination of technology transfer in countries of the Third World, and their efforts toward industrialization, clearly shows that, say, the manufacture stage does not necessarily come into existence between the stage of tribal organization in hunting, gathering, and agricultural societies and that of industrial organization.

The question of whether diffusion or (independent) invention is the most important source of change is therefore essentially pointless. According to Kingsley Davis (1950), social history has demonstrated that inventions are not the result of a single event or one man's work. Rather, they arise from the ideas, contributions, and products of many men. Furthermore, the same invention is often made in different places, at different times, by different men, independently of each other. Following Bronislaw Malinowski (1945), Davis maintains that an invention must not be taken as a single event to be ascribed to a single person, if its nature is not to be completely misconceived.

> In the same way 'diffusion' turns out to be a complex abstraction, not a separate entity. No idea, no practice, no technique ever passed from one society to another without some modification being added to it. The borrowed culture trait must be somehow modified and adapted so as to fit into the existing cultural context. It follows that diffusion and invention are always inseparably mixed. To oppose them as if they were mutually exclusive is to raise a false issue (Davis, 1950: 631).

As a source of change *culture contact* is closely related to diffusion. However, unlike diffusion theory, contact theory focuses primarily on the challenges that extensive and intimate culture contact poses for the existing culture.

> More important than borrowing is the discovery that there is a vantage point from which one's own values no longer appear unquestionable axioms but merely one among alternative systems of values. Thus it is not so much the particular culture with which culture contact takes place as it is the *attitude* toward one's culture that is induced by any serious culture contact. . . . Culture contact gives rise not only to borrowing but to new ideas concerning the necessity for change in the established order and the directions in which such change should go (Turner and Killian, 1957: 520).

Thus, not only are new cultural items *introduced* which may effect changes in the mode of subsistence and technology but also values, norms, role expectations, and goal definitions are *relativized*, generating a situation not conductive to a static social order.[9]

The process by which cultural and social traits are transmitted from one society to another involves, of course, some type of communication or contact. W. E. Moore (1963: 86) lists the following modes of contact and ranks them according to frequency and the number of people involved:

1 Imperialism as colonization and indirect domination;
2 Other wars, conquests, and military occupations;
3 Cultural imperialism in the guise of missionary religions;
4 Mass migration (e.g., Eurasian migration);
5 Individual migration (e.g., transatlantic migration);
6 Economic trade;
7 Tourism;
8 Transferred labor (e.g., slavery, indenture, migrant workers);
9 Transfer of knowledge;
10 Diplomacy, indirect contacts, formal communications.

He also summarizes some of the major factors that have been proposed by various writers to be correlated with the borrowing and acceptance of cultural items:

1 Their simplicity;
2 Consistency with existing values;
3 Prestige of the bearers of novelties;
4 An already changing situation in the receiving culture;
5 Lack of close 'integration' of the receiving system, as exemplified by the importance of disaffected members of society who withdraw from it;
6 The extent and continuity of contact.

Finally, Alvin L. Bertrand (1967: 125–6) presents several factors that he sees as affecting the change process in diffusion and contact situations:

1 The form of culture – normally material items are diffused faster than ideas or ideologies;
2 Degree of coercion – a conquered people must submit to the wishes of their masters, and to the extent one cultural group has power over another group it can force the group to accept its ways;
3 Intensity of cultural contact – when communication is facile

and continuous, diffusion is usually faster than when contacts are difficult and accomplished only on occasion;
4   Amount of cultural inertia – many individuals and groups resist cultural change for a variety of reasons;
5   The presence of a crisis situation.

From this sketchy discussion of social processes underlying diffusion and innovation, several conclusions may be derived despite rather divergent research findings (cf. e.g., Berelson and Steiner, 1964: 613–19, 643–56; Kushner *et al.*, 1962). The query central to diffusion and culture contact theory is whether and how innovations will be effectively transmitted, i.e., accepted. In this context, members of society as role incumbents, i.e., as members of groups and organizations, as men in these membership roles, control varying degrees of influence, power, and money, resulting in differences of interest, and capacity to accept innovations and subsequently to produce change. In the receiving system we will always find willingness to accept and to integrate innovations in varying degrees (cf. Ridder, 1974). The acceptance or rejection of an innovation *may*, first, depend upon congruence conditions. An innovation is congruent if it shows some similarity to the existing cultural elements with which the public is confident. Secondly, the acceptance may depend upon the condition of compatibility that is met if the innovation fits into the new social context without incurring destructive consequences. These conditions have been discussed time and again with respect to innovations in the area of agricultural technology, plant breeding, medicine and, currently, especially in the area of technology transfer from industrial to developing nations (cf. e.g., Barnett, 1953; Mead, 1953; Coleman *et al.*, 1966; Rothman, 1974; Spicer, 1952; Rogers, 1962; Hoselitz and Merrill, 1969).

Let us keep in mind that the diffusionists and culture contact theorists, in contrast to evolutionists, assert that the uniformity of tools, rites, and certain institutions in different societies may be traced to the dissemination, that is, diffusion of customs and inventions of one cultural sphere to another culture by way of *imitation*. One of the most important research questions is therefore devoted to the promoting and impeding conditions of such a diffusion, especially in the receiving system which may be a group, a firm, an office, or a national society. The idea of diffusion can also be applied to the relationships of subsystems within society. Within society, for example, family and company secrets, sexual and religious taboos may constitute major impediments for the diffusion of certain innovations. Perhaps the most important manifestation of this kind of exogenous change are economic exchange, cultural diffusion, as well as conquest and migration which entail quite different consequences for transmission (e.g., assimilation, race conflict, educational and economic reforms). Besides diffusion and culture contact, there are other exogenous factors, namely, the effects of events and crises; it is to these we now turn.

2.3.2 The impact of crises and events

The role of crises or catastrophes brought on by the physical environment (e.g., earthquakes, floods, epidemics), is hardly dealt with in current theories of social change. The reason may be seen in their unpredictability and the difficulty of making generalizations and predictions about their consequences. They do get mentioned in a few studies, though, as by Karl Wittfogel (1957), who formulated the much debated hypothesis that the social and political structures of a number of ancient empires (e.g., Egypt and Mesopotamia) had been determined by the tasks that resulted from the control of the floods and the management of water supplies. However, most geographic and climatic explanations of societal organization and social change have been disproven or discarded.

Small-scale studies of natural disasters have generally shown that neither the event itself, nor the temporary social organizations that arise to deal with emergency, directly change or challenge the social order. However, natural disasters may indirectly provide a background for change. For example, a famine may spark existing discontent with the political order or a widespread disaster may so weaken a country that it is left vulnerable to possible rebellion or invasion (cf. e.g., Erikson, 1976).

Crises of a social nature are more often treated as potential sources of social change. However, as Ralph Turner and Lewis Killian pointed out, well-institutionalized policies for dealing with critical situations often reduce the pressures for change that might arise.

> Catastrophe may be envisioned within the existing social order so that the populace are prepared to accept its inconveniences without doubting the basic adequacy of the established system. Such is generally the case in modern wars. Each nation prepares its populace to accept and deal with a considerable amount of bombing, and results indicate that intensive bombing over an extended period of time does not necessarily break confidence in the existing order. . . . But when catastrophe is of long duration, widespread, and contradicts the assumptions of the established

order, pressures multiply for a change in the system. Thus, when bombing can no longer be accepted as a necessary condition to be tolerated . . . collective opposition to the established order may develop (Turner and Killian, 1957: 521).

Robert A. Nisbet makes crises his central explanatory principle in analyzing the cause of social change. In speaking of what he calls the 'crisis-born nature of change,' Nisbet (1970: 316) asserts: 'The first point to be made about change is that wherever it exists in substantial degree, it is associated with some form of crisis.' A crisis arises when control over one's environment is threatened by the introduction of some new element into the environment or when conventional behavior or thought is found to be inadequate or ineffective. According to Nisbet, crises never arise from strains or conflicts within a social structure. Rather, they are the product of 'events.'

> An event is not a change, though it may be closely related to change. An event is a happening, an *occurrence*; it takes place in time and, of course, in setting. . . . A single event may, by virtue of its crucial impact, alter one's whole career of life. A major event can also alter the character of an entire nation or culture. . . . An event is external and does not grow out of the structure (Nisbet, 1970: 322–3).

Events that create crisis conditions (i.e., that threaten control or which make conventional behavior inadequate) are the ultimate *source* of change. Apart from 'those impacts and intrusions we call events . . . from which modern economic, political, and social history is formed, no understanding of the structural changes so obvious today in the social organizations of peoples on all continents would be possible' (Nisbet, 1970: 324–5). 'Events are by their nature unpredictable, fortuitous, and more or less random' (Nisbet, 1970: 323). In other words, the exact cause of a particular social change cannot be predicted. We cannot generalize about where, when, and how changes may occur or what effects they will have. 'But, wish as we might, we cannot understand social change apart from consideration of events – even if our consideration must always be retrospective and historical rather than analytical or systematic' (Nisbet, 1970: 323).

Nisbet finally discusses what he thinks to be the four major processes of change. Although he sees them as recurrently involved in change throughout history, they are not gradual, continuous processes. This view of change as intermittent, discontinuous, and uneven stems from his conception of the nature of the occurrence of unpredictable, crisis-producing events as the cause of change.

The first major process of change is *individualization*, by which I mean the release of individuals from the constraining ties of long-fixed, traditional social codes or authorities. The second is *innovation* – the circumstances involved in cultural efflorescence of high or distinctive order. Third is the process of *politicization* in which the assertion of power, whether individual or collective, succeeds the ordinary processes of custom and tradition. The fourth is *secularization* – the passage of sacred norms into secular, the replacement of a social order largely governed by religious values by one in which utilitarian or secular values are dominant (Nisbet, 1970: 370).

In his elaboration upon the first three processes, Nisbet draws heavily on insights and data produced by classical evolutionism and modernization research; the fourth is analogous to Max Weber's concept of routinization.

Even if we recognize a great deal of unpredictability and abrupt quality in events, which constitute the empirical foundation for the crisis theory, these events do in fact form a twofold pattern. On the one hand, as Nisbet (1969: 240–1) remarks, every people, state, class, group, and institution has a history of its own. Through their mutual linkages and their anchoring in the past, on the other hand, episodes form that clearly show systemic boundaries.[10]

2.3.3 The equilibrium theory of social change

Probably the best known theoretical approach in present sociology that views exogenous forces as the source of *major* changes in society, though rarely explicitly stated so, is that of functionalism. The early functionalists were impressed, like classical ethnologists, by the variety of socio-cultural phenomena and, like classical diffusionists, by the uniformity of certain characteristics of the various societies. This led them to the idea that cultural manifestations and social institutions were closely related to the satisfaction of basic human needs (cf. Radcliffe-Brown, 1957; Malinowski, 1969). If it is true, it was asked, that needs had largely not changed but the societal organization to meet them had been variable, then social change can only be understood as change of the institutional arrangements available to take care of those needs and/or as change of the manifest and latent functions of these institutions.

The most important assumption on which the functionalist view of society was then based is that of *equilibrium*, at least if we believe in what one of its most prominent representatives proclaimed. Kingsley Davis (1950: 634), following Joseph A. Schumpeter,

Vilfredo Pareto, and Talcott Parsons, states: 'The functional-structural approach to sociological analysis is basically an equilibrium theory.' According to Davis (1950: 634; emphasis added), equilibrium means 'that *in the absence of outside interference* a society will manifest a trend in a direction determined by the state of the socio-cultural variables at a given moment. Furthermore this equilibrium is in part self-restoring: It resists deflection.' Or, as a critic of equilibrium theory says:

> In the most general terms, a system is said to be in equilibrium when its component parts are so compatible with each other that, *barring an outside disturbance*, none of them will change its position or relation to the others in any significant way. . . . A theory of social equilibrium is a theory that seeks to uncover the general condition for the maintenance of a society in stable equilibrium, and to specify the mechanisms by which that stability is preserved or re-established after the occurrence of *outside disturbances* (Guessous, 1967: 23–4; emphasis added).

It does not come as a surprise if early equilibrium theorists have often been criticized for their emphasis on how order and stability is maintained while neglecting how change occurs. The model of a stable equilibrium in particular leaves only 'one point of view from which the problem of structural change can be analyzed – by relating it to the *influence of powerful exogenous forces*' (Guessous, 1967: 27; emphasis in original). Parsons (1961: 70) expresses this idea in system-theoretical terms:

> The process of structural change may be considered the obverse of equilibrating process; the distinction is made in terms of boundary-maintenance. Boundary implies both that there is a difference of state between phenomena internal and external to the system; and that the type of process tending to maintain that difference of state is different from the type tending to break it down.

Besides the concept of equilibrium there is another idea central to the functional approach. It is the idea of *differentiation* that links classical evolutionism with neo-evolutionary functionalism. Differentiation understood as the formation of specialized social structures has been used by the latter to explain the causes as well as to describe the processes of change. In other words, change is explained in terms of the evolutionary potential inherent in a society or one of its elements or units and manifesting itself in varying degrees and forms of differentiation. For example, the kinship system differentiates into occupational and family roles, of the old household community into institutions of consumption, socialization, education, and production. We observe one role and institution as it differentiates over time into two or more roles and institutions embedded in various activities and collective units: in the area of kinship and in that of economic production.

The first condition that must be fulfilled if change is to occur, concerns the separation of the new structural pattern from the old one. This is only likely to happen if the actor is motivated to effect the changes as exemplified by new opportunities for work which had not been available within the framework of the old social structure. Secondly, negative reactions against the forces of change must not overcome the positive tendencies which ultimately requires an effective degree of institutionalized tolerance for the novel and negative sanctions for going along with the old structural pattern. Thirdly, a positive model or ideology must be developed that is apt to demonstrate the advantages of the new system or structural element (e.g., new opportunities to gain access to certain social positions and their rewards). The fourth presupposition, then, refers to the justification of the new model in terms of relevant values. For example, the way in which striving for profit legitimated in England by the Protestant ethic in times when the factory system had not yet been institutionalized, prepared the ground for corresponding changes (cf. Parsons, 1961: 72–4).

Why differentiation does occur often remains unclear or is explained in terms of requirements of the environing systems (e.g., motivation based upon the personality system or the requisite of adjusting to altered conditions of the physical environment). This indicates the direction of functionally explained change: increased adaptive capacity of the system under consideration (cf. Parsons, 1967; 1971). The production system of the factory is, at least under the aspect of productivity, more successful than manufacture and homework. Differentiating the system of production leads to an improvement of the production sector as well as the capacities of the entire social system to deal with the environing systems more effectively (personality, culture, other societies, etc.). In this sense, change can only proceed gradually and in a continuous fashion. Generally speaking, changing requirements of the environment lead to efforts in the system to secure its persistence, that is, to maintain existing social arrangements on various levels of the system. System theory properly understood therefore suggests that the impulse toward adaptive change comes from *outside* the system; moreover, change that implies alteration of the structure or system boundaries, is only conceivable as resulting from external influences threatening the state of the system (cf. Münch, 1973:

168–9). This also means that the system's capacity to survive depends upon the formation of certain institutional mechanisms. The greater and more diverse the requirements of the environment on the system, the greater the extent of that dependency. Parsons (1967), for example, stresses six mechanisms closely linked with the development of Western societies: achieved criteria of status allocation, generalized forms of legitimation, bureaucratic organizations, market and money system, universal legal system, and democratic institutions.

According to the Parsonian version of functionalism, change may be expected to occur most likely, most visibly and directly as well as with the most far-reaching consequences in the area of the economic subsystem of society, i.e. the enterprises (as compared with the political, legal–integrative, and socializational–educational subsystems). Why? Because the economic system is responsible for solving the adaptive problems of society, that is, it directly confronts the physical environment through its organization of production. Although the other subsystems are also related to environing systems, thus facing their own adaptive problems, the economic system is particularly geared toward mastering external requirements on the basis of its *function* within the entire system. Technological innovations and contacts with other societies *via* economic interests may serve as illustrative examples.

Already Durkheim recognized that differentiation is always connected with the problem of reintegration of the existing structure with newly developed parts of the system. This, of course, means that strains in terms of role conflict, normative inconsistency, differential socialization, 'unjustified' inequalities, etc. are generated. At any rate, *strain* refers to a disturbance of the expectational system, that is, mostly the coordination of institutionalized roles and norms. Even if differentiation is viewed as productive of strain, functionalists, however, tend to emphasize the management and subsequent removal of these disharmonies by means of *reintegrative* efforts.

Strains are part and parcel of society as process, because they follow logically and naturally from the various processes of institutionalization, even though they are kept within limits because of the 'automatic' processes of differentiation. They are present everywhere as much as they can always be eliminated, quite similar to sins which are continuously committed and yet forgivable any time.

Especially the works of the American sociologists Wilbert E. Moore and Robert K. Merton contributed to a modification of the equilibrium concept of society, enabling the student to explain a wider range of social changes than traditional structural-functionalism does. Moore's (1963: 10) concept of 'society as a tension-management system' as well as Merton's (1968: Chapters 3, 6, and 7) analysis of the consequences of 'dysfunctional' behavior for change as derived from his five types of role adaptation to the normative structure of a society, do not go as far as the different versions of conflict theory that attribute conflict and change not to the disharmony of normative elements but to the principle of domination pervading the social world.

Notes

1 It follows that a 'radical sociology' in this sense will exist so long as there are fundamental conflicts between major groupings in society. A non-harmonious society – be it factually experienced or only perceived as such – as a kind of existential and interest background generates its 'radical' or 'progressive' sociology time and again (cf. Bottomore, 1974: 14).

2 We consider Jürgen Habermas's most significant contribution to a historic-materialistic social theory to be his argument against the Marxian thesis of the primacy of the development of productive forces. In other words, not the forms of instrumental, i.e., purposive-rational action underlying the development of these forces, but the normative elements constituted by communicative–moral competencies of actors represents, for Habermas, the pace-maker for social evolution. However, he also says that culture is a phenomenon of the ideological superstructure of society and one that ultimately makes possible the use of new productive forces (Habermas, 1975; 1976).

3 This can also mean – and there is some evidence for it – that interdependence between economic–technological basis and political–ideological superstructure becomes stronger in the following sense: (1) that the transfer process of innovations with respect to productive forces (machines, tools, 'modes of production', etc.) has become considerably shorter – in some industries, comparatively speaking, many times over (cf. Richta et al., 1971: Chapter 1; Spiegel-Rösing, 1973: 115; Buckingham, 1961: 1); (2) that, given the shortened transfer process, many small, hardly noticeable innovations accumulate over time to large-scale technological transformations (such notions as automation, electronic or computer revolution may illustrate this point); and (3) that the linkage between economic structure and public policy has become stronger in so far as the state took over new tasks with the mounting problems of controlling organized capitalism, especially in the area of promoting investments, education, research and development, the planning of infrastructures on all societal levels, and the control of social consequences resulting from economic growth, the introduction of new technologies and forms of economic organization (e.g., ecological protection, retraining of unemployed workers, control of multinational companies). Cf. Habermas, 1973; O'Connor, 1973; Rödel, 1972.

4 According to Dahrendorf (1959a), the most important changes that at the same time indicate the transformation of capitalism are the following: (1) the decomposition of capital as demonstrated by the differentiation of the roles of the owner and the manager of the means of production; (2) the decomposition of labor revealed in terms of a diversification of the working class, especially in the sense that the increasing mechanization of production leads to a reduction of unskilled workers and an expansion of semi-skilled and skilled workers; in addition to the internal differentiation of the initial capitalist and working classes, Dahrendorf observes (3) a remarkable increase of the 'new middle class' of white-collar workers which is associated with the expansion of administrative and non-manual occupations; (4) the increase in social mobility through changing mechanisms of recruitment, not only contributing to a blurring of class barriers but also increasingly transforming potential conflicts between groups into competition between individuals; (5) the realization of civil liberties as expressed in universal suffrage and welfare and social security laws for the mass of the population; and (6) the institutionalization of class conflicts in the form of commonly accepted procedures of collective bargaining; this and the attainment of civil liberties had the effect that in present capitalist societies economic conflicts are not likely to be extended to class conflicts that would undermine the whole social order but rather are limited to, and resolved in, the economic sector (cf. also Giddens, 1973; 55–6).

5 As discussed in greater detail in Chapter 4 of the present volume, positivistic organicism has to be considered as the most important precursor of functionalism; furthermore, great significance must be attributed to the development of a holistic perspective which has become characteristic for science *per se* since the beginning of the twentieth century.

6 What is here hinted at on the level of individuals and social roles, should later become the central theme in Parsons's neo-evolutionary change theory on a systematic level in which he entertains the idea of an increasing adaptive capacity of society (cf. Chapter 4 of this volume).

7 An informative discussion is offered by Ralph Turner and Lewis Killian (1957: 517–18) as well as Sorokin (1966: Chapters 5–11, 17).

8 A similar argument has been brought forward by José Ortega y Gasset (1951; 1978) in his search for an explanation of the not only decades, but centuries, enduring fiasco of Spanish politics. His historical studies led him to believe that Spain suffered from a 'lack of the best' ever since its inhabitants had come into contact with the corrupt people of the Westgots. The lack of elites had the effect that Spain, in contrast to England, had to leave its colonies to the ordinary people, which subsequently led to their decay. The instability of Spanish society and politics in the twentieth century is only another consequence of these circumstances. A mature society, according to Ortega y Gasset, is only possible where obedient majorities subject themselves to the influence of minorities with the capacity to rule.

9 An eloquent discussion of the topic can be found in Peter L. Berger (1963: Chapters 2 and 3).
10 In this idea we believe to detect a macrosociological parallel to the ethnomethodological approach as the latter focuses on imponderable events and episodes in the microsocial cosmos, though with more emphasis on endogenous–interpretative elements. We are quite sure that Nisbet would reject such a supposition.

Suggested reading

Introductory reading

ALLEN, FRANCIS R. (1971), *Socio-Cultural Dynamics: An Introduction to Social Change*, New York: Macmillan.
In this introductory text, major theories and their applications in the study of social change are reviewed.

BERGER, PETER L., BERGER, BRIGITTE, and KELLNER, HANSFRIED (1974), *The Homeless Mind: Modernization and Consciousness*, New York: Vintage Books.
This book approaches the problem of modernity and its impact on individual consciousness from the theoretical framework of the sociology of knowledge. At its center is the idea of diffusion of modern consciousness in the Third World and the problems raised by modernity in industrial societies.

SCHNEIDER, LOUIS (1976), *Classical Theories of Social Change*, Morristown, N.J.: General Learning Press.
Here is a review of the major classical theories of change with a focus on three concerns: the dialectic nature of social life, the role assigned to human choice in social change, and the explanatory significance of technological, economic, and cultural factors.

COSER, LEWIS A. (1967), 'Social Conflict and the Theory of Social Change,' pp. 17–35 in COSER, LEWIS A., *Continuities in the Study of Social Conflict*, New York: Free Press.
Using Karl Marx's conflict and change theory as a point of departure, the author elaborates upon the relationship between social conflict and changes in and of social systems.

NISBET, ROBERT A. (1970), *The Social Bond: An Introduction to the Study of Society*, New York: Alfred A. Knopf: Part III.
In Part III of this introduction, several aspects of the concept of change are dealt with and a conception of social change as crisis and event is developed and typical processes of change discussed.

Further reading

General

MOORE, WILBERT E. (1970), 'Reconsideration of Theories of Social Change,' pp. 123–39 in EISENSTADT, S. N. (ed.), *Readings in Social Evolution and Development*, Oxford: Pergamon Press.

Moore attempts to render change in its major dimensions a valuable object of analysis within the framework of structural functionalism.

DAHRENDORF, RALF (1968), 'Out of Utopia: Toward a New Orientation of Sociological Analysis,' pp. 107–28 in DAHRENDORF, RALF, *Essays in the Theory of Society*, Stanford, Cal.: Stanford University Press.

This essay represents a statement against the static bias and the failure of the structural-functional theory to deal with problems of social change adequately. The author advocates instead a conflict–theoretical orientation in the analysis of social phenomena.

CHODAK, SZYMON (1973), *Societal Development: Five Approaches with Conclusions from Comparative Analysis*, New York: Oxford University Press.

The author dwells on the concept of development, which he sees as implying processes of differentiation and of imposing interdependencies, draws on findings from comparative studies, and offers a multidimensional synthesizing perspective on change.

ELIAS, NORBERT (1976), *Über den Prozeß der Zivilisation: Sozio-genetische und psychogenetische Untersuchungen*, 2 vols, Frankfurt a.M.: Suhrkamp.

The author presents an empirically grounded theory of social processes and societal development which is derived from insights about changes in behavioral patterns of secular upper classes of the West and about mechanisms of feudalization as well as the emergence of the state.

Problem-related

OGBURN, WILLIAM F. (1957), 'Cultural Lag as Theory,' *Sociology and Social Research*, 41: 167–74 (reprinted in OGBURN, WILLIAM F., *Culture and Social Change*, Chicago: University of Chicago Press, 1964).

By using illustrative examples, the author discusses the merits of his theory of cultural lag, especially its theoretical underpinnings and empirical applications.

REX, JOHN (1961), *Key Problems of Sociological Theory*, London: Routledge & Kegan Paul: Chapter 7.

In this chapter, Rex presents a systematic survey of conflict theory of social change, especially its non-Marxist variation (Coser, Weber, Mannheim, Myrdal, Dahrendorf).

BARNETT, H. G. (1953), *Innovation: The Basis of Cultural Change*, New York: McGraw-Hill.

This now classical text in innovation research offers a systematic introduction into the presuppositions, incentives, processes, and other conditions for adopting or rejecting innovations in different areas of social and cultural life.

EISENSTADT, S. N. (1964), 'Social Change, Differentiation and Evolution,' *American Sociological Review*, 29: 375–86.

This article presents the central concepts of a neo-evolutionary theory of change and discusses them with respect to their applicability to describing and explaining societal changes.

Part II Selected theories of social change: detailed studies

3 The historic-materialistic theory of societal development

Hans Jürgen Krysmanski and
Karl Hermann Tjaden

3.1 Introduction*

Historical materialism is no theory of social change in the usual sense of the word; *it is a theory designed actively to change social conditions*. It offers an all-embracing theory of the development of human societalization, of formative changes of societies as well as of the inner movements of social systems. Its aim is to grasp the causes of misery, starvation, servitude and degradation in actual social life in order to assist in their elimination. The academic meaning of the concept of social change therefore is but an *aspect* of this point of view. The characteristics of this approach as well as volume and complexity of historical-materialistic research defy attempts at a short, comprehensive introduction: a theory that consciously aims at social change as social praxis and that is designed to comprehend all of social history, cannot be reduced to simple formulas. We therefore confine ourselves to short discussions of assumptions and selected problem areas.

Marx and Engels, in opposition to the classical tradition of social theory (that is being carried on in the positivistic trends of modern bourgeois sociology), conceived of a theory of society that did not stop at the description, analysis, understanding and, at best, piecemeal improvement of social reality. Instead, the constitutive interest of historical materialism has always been to change social reality in the sense of practically transforming the capitalist mode of production. In pursuing this aim, the theory attempts to absorb and to express the experiences of that social class that is the under-

---

* The authors have outlined this chapter together; sections 3.1 and 3.3 is a collective product while section 3.2 is authored by K. H. Tjaden and section 3.4 by H. J. Krysmanski.

pinning of the capitalist mode of production as well as its object of exploitation: the wage-dependent laboring class. Obviously, the practical interests of this class cannot be separated from the performances of a theory that comprehends society in terms of a developing and changeable reality. Adequate theoretical reproduction of the social potential for change is the essential precondition for realizing those class interests, just as reflection on the practical role of social theory is a condition for realizing its theoretical insights.

3.1.1 Epistemological intention and mode of perception

The fact that historical materialism regards itself as being embedded into a *praxis*-theory relation has frequently been misunderstood by its opponents as reducing theory to a political program. The practical interest constitutive of this theory, though, does not so much represent a necessary element but rather one of the preconditions of theoretical development in general. In other words, this theory has been brought forth by certain social problems; historical materialism, in turn, is a reflection upon social activities that could lead to the solution of these problems. Apart from its specific grasp of the social context, historical materialism is characterized by special research strategies.[1]

Marx and Engels began by relating the empirical variety of the real world to those highly abstract structures that classical bourgeois social theory (especially political economy and the philosophy of history) had perceived of: the basic labor and power relations between people on one side and relations between human and non-human nature on the other. The critical expositions of bourgeois theory and the empirical examination of the real development of society forced Marx and Engels to go beyond what would be mere reduction of reality to abstract categories. Adequate scientific procedure in understanding society was possible only by elaborating a system of differentiated categories capable of grasping the general and basic human relations in view of their distinct historical forms and developments and by simultaneously reproducing reality on the basis of the practical experience of social actors, thereby producing the unifying frame for that multitude of definitions.

Figure 3.1 illustrates some of the interrelationships between the critical, empirical–practical, and categorial–systematic aspects of the development of Marxist theory.

Historical materialism as an expression of social praxis is nothing but the theory for developing this praxis: theory of the general

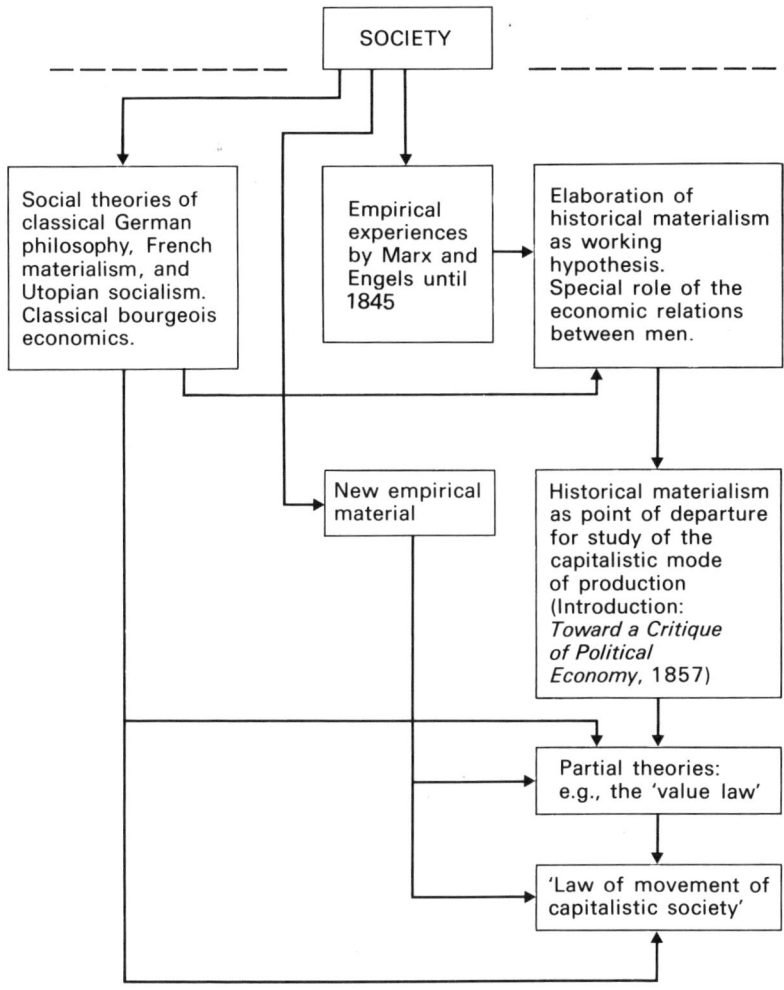

Source: R. Hickel in Marx, 1971: 891.

FIGURE 3.1 *Developmental characteristics of the theory of Marx and Engels*

process of societalization. By attempting to uncover the laws that govern development, structural change and internal movement of society, this theory aims at achieving a higher degree of consciousness and capacity of self-control on the part of everybody involved in the societalization process. Accordingly, historical materialism regards social change not as a scientific theme among many others, but as *the* central problem of its cognitive activity on several levels of social reality: the level of general social development, the level of the development of particular societies, and the level of specific developments in a given society. On all these levels the central point of reference is constituted by the system of material reproduction and production that, to historical materialism, is identical with economic society formations, once the stage of a self-reproducing system of human societalization has been reached.

The category of the economic society formation determines the general object and problem of historical materialism, as well as its approach and mode of perception. The historical-materialistic theory of development pertains to concrete economic society formations in history, i.e., to macro-systems comprising more than mere individual or collective phenomena. Bourgeois theories of social change tend to dwell on these individual and collective levels of behavior. In contrast, historical materialism regards social process (like action and behavior patterns of individuals or groups) as well as phenomena of technological progress or cultural change as manifestations and implementations of the general process of societalization which constitutes social reality. Explaining social change or social conflict on the basis of social activities or by referring to the constraints of accommodation or adjustment would be regarded as merely secondary steps in the theoretical explanation of the movements of social reality (cf. Krysmanski, 1971; Tjaden, 1972). The historical-materialistic theory of development is committed to one crucial assumption: that the essence of man, and consequently the nature of individual and collective activities, must be sought in the fact that man's social existence is identical with the 'ensemble of social relations and conditions,' that he represents as a concrete human being (cf. Marx, 1969a: 6). Consequently, the process of societalization cannot be explained in terms of particular activities and particular phenomena, but only in terms and in the context of a given economic society formation.

3.1.2 Approach and object of study

The main questions asked by the historical-materialistic theory of development derive from theoretical needs and practical necessities. First, there is the analysis of the origins and conditions of the development of the human societalization process in general that was initiated by Marx and Engels in works like *the German Ideology* (Marx and Engels, 1969a). Then, in the *Communist Manifesto*, the general notion emerges that all known history has been the history of class struggles (Marx and Engels, 1969b). Finally, the analysis of the economic system of the capitalist mode of production, especially in the *Capital*, provides the foundations for a theory of the genesis and development of specific society formations (Marx, 1962–4; cf. Marx, 1953; 1961; 1964c). In addition, the necessity to assess political movements in a number of non-European countries is conducive to an extension of the scope of historical materialism, leading Marx and Engels to various attempts to understand the nature and development of pre-capitalist society formations (cf. Marx, 1953: 375–413; Engels, 1962).

Later on, the practical and theoretical development of historical materialism, intrinsically tied to the organizational progress of the labor movement, has concentrated upon problems connected with the unfolding of the internal and external conditions of the capitalist mode of production. Before the First World War, interest was centered on the reproduction problems of the system that have led to the rise of monopolistic and imperialistic structures (cf. Hilferding, 1968; Luxemburg, 1913; Lenin, 1971b). This line of analysis has continued during the 1920s and after the Second World War, adding the problem of capitalistic crisis management by means of scientific–technological innovations and political–administrative control of the economic progress.[2] Lately, there have been mounting attempts to integrate these various approaches into a more general concept of present-day capitalism: the concepts of 'monopoly capitalism,' 'late capitalism' and 'state monopoly capitalism' evolved (cf. Baran and Sweezy, 1968; Mandel, 1972; Gündel *et al.*, 1967; Boccara *et al.*, 1972).

In addition, the development of a socialist mode of production, following the Russian October Revolution of 1917, induced theoretical work on the development problems of socialist societies (cf. e.g., Dobb, 1948; Lange and Taylor, 1948). First concepts of a theory of economic growth, geared to the needs of socialist economies, appear at a relatively early date (Feldmann, 1969). The rise of other socialist societies after the Second World War has led to a tremendous increase in research activities regarding the development of socialist modes of production. Furthermore, the recent history of socialist societies rendered possible differentiated theoretical systematizations of what could be called self-reflection of this kind of society formation (e.g., Zagalow *et al.*, 1970).

The political and national liberation movements in the colonies and quasi-colonies of the capitalist world were productive – even in the 1920s – of discussions of pre-capitalist modes of production. Especially, what had been in the Soviet Union during the 1930s a dogmatically narrowed discussion of the Marxist concept of the Asiatic mode of production was taken up again internationally during the 1960s.[3] This applies to the discussion of other pre-capitalist forms of class society, too; advances in archaeological and ethnological research led to further examination of primitive forms of the social organization of labor (e.g., Childe, 1951; Sellnow, 1961; Godelier, 1973).

It should be noted, too, that the problem of theoretically enlightening the universal development of human forms of societalization, including their interdependent relations, has been the subject of intense international discussions that are still going on.[4] Related to these efforts are all those various methodological and epistemological attempts to examine the category of social and historical law (cf. e.g., Bollhagen, 1967).

It is obvious that the following presentation can only touch a few of these subjects on a rather general level. Essentially we are going to dwell upon three aspects: the problem of the development of human societalization on the basis of economic society formations in general, the problem of social development and social change within the capitalist society formation, and the problem of intersystemic relations within the global process of societalization. Although these aspects are at the center of scientific and political controversy, we will not be able to explicate them fully.

3.2 The development of human societalization as a sequence of economic society formations[5]

Basic concepts and pronouncements of historical-materialistic theory of development refer to 'economic society formations.' The concept denotes macro-social systems constituting specific problem-solving activities, namely, those pertaining to the collective and productive mediation of the material exchange between human and non-human nature. The specifically human way of maintaining existence is to use labor power and to appropriate natural conditions in a socially organized way. Thus, economic society formations are systems of collective and eventually specialized production, distribution, and use of a social product, designed to bring about the problematic exchange between 'man' and 'nature' by means of productive action of human forces upon the non-human forces of nature. They therefore can also be called systems of social production.[6]

Extension of the productive activities of the system is marked by the increase in quantity and performance of socially committed labor power and by an increase of the realm and exploitation of socially appropriated natural conditions, that is, by an increase in the general potential of labor power against its natural conditions. Systems of social *production may therefore be regarded as develop-*

ment forms of the relationship between human and non-human nature. Developing this relationship requires, among other things, the existence of a controlled balance between the use of labor power and its natural conditions, as well as between the task and aspiration of the actors involved. This order of social production is mainly affected by a specific distribution of labor performances and means of production among the members of the social system. The relations of production resulting from this process, serving as the structural basis for social production, will under certain conditions permit an opening of new fields for labor and an increase in surplus labor time (measured in terms of the reproduction requirements of the system), thus leading to an extension of the volume of production. By realizing the potential of productive power and of the control of nature on the basis of certain relations of production, systems of social production can be characterized by certain modes of production. Such a mode of production is the carrier of system activity as a whole and determines to a large extent seemingly unrelated actions and behavior patterns in the social, technical, cultural, or political fields of social praxis.

The establishment of a fixed distribution of labor performances and means of production within the conditions of production may lead to programed crises in system reproduction in the sense that system *stability* can *only be secured* by a *permanent improvement in the relationship between labor investment and labor produce*. In addition, long range tensions in the reproduction of the system are likely to arise, pointing to a mismatch between the relations of production and the heightened level of social reproduction needs. Finally, such insufficient societal distribution of labor performance and means of production will require a transformation of the system of social production itself, i.e., the installation of a mode of production that opens better ways to develop the productive powers and the control of nature. The mode of production and society formation having shown its 'obsolescence' will, then, in the interest of further development of the human productive forces, be replaced by a new formation whose economic structure includes a larger problem-solving potential. The forces of social production, the control of nature, and the social division and relations of labor develop accordingly in such a succession of society formations (cf. especially, Marx 1964c: 8–9).

3.2.1 Social development as progress in societalization

The basis for social development lies in the social, i.e., cooperative and eventually specialized, organization of these productive activities themselves. The fact that the activities of a single human being are always elements of a coordinated social praxis *per se* is an indicator of the flexibility and effectiveness of those practical problem-solving processes constituting the exchange between man and nature. Human activity as a coordinated social practice is the precondition for specializing and unifying social labor as a whole, which historically arose first in the division of labor among the sexes with respect to hunting and protection, on the one hand, and gathering and household maintenance, on the other. Social organization of labor and of the division of labor then became the basis for addressing mental and physical forces to activities that transgressed the immediate control of nature and assurance of subsistence. This facilitated the production of the 'means of development'[7] designed to advance social labor, and especially the application of labor tools and the passing on of labor experience were even in prehistoric times instrumental in expanding the effectiveness of social production.

By accumulating physical methods, and by passing on mental 'means of development,' this expansion of the forces of social production and the control of nature becomes a process that reinforces itself permanently. In particular, it engenders the production, distribution and use of a social *gross product* G which visibly surpasses the requirements for necessary *consumption* on the part of the labor powers and for *reproduction* of the means of production R. The social gross product G begins to incorporate a *surplus product* S, which surpasses the needs of the population as a whole (including the non-working part) and which can be applied for a further increase of social production activities.[8] Of course, this sort of increase depends on converting part of the surplus product S into additional and improved means of reproduction of labor powers and into further production of means of production. The application of specialized labor to socialized labor itself will be of particular importance for the increment of social labor, i.e., the production of tools and machines for the production of labor instruments, and the accumulation of experience for the sake of the application of labor experience (cf. Sellnow, 1961: 113). The economic effects of using part of the surplus product for extending and improving the nourishment for the labor population and for extending and improving the production of the means of production consist of an increase in the social gross product G. This gross product in particular makes an increase in the surplus product S possible because of improvement in the productivity of social production.

In the final analysis we mean by social development an increase in forces of social production and control of nature that man has achieved during his history. The concept of social development always implies this tremendous growth of the societal forces of men and of the societal control over nature and, in one way or another, it has to account for the conditions of this growth. If we define this increase in forces of social production and control over nature in terms of an ongoing societalization process, we try to express the fact that the relationship between human and non-human forces of nature is increasingly mediated, regulated, and controlled by goal-directed social labor and that the social organization of labor itself is becoming more extensive and complex (cf. Marx, 1962a: 192ff.). The task for a theory of social development then is to understand and explain this progress in human societalization, i.e., the progressive increase in the problem-solving potential of human societies.

The development of human societalization may be regarded as the essence, the universal element of world history that begins with the natural history of human life and leads to a global system of human society. In this respect the actual diversity of world history can be interpreted as the realization of a line of development which justifies speaking of social history as a single global process. This global societalization process bears the marks of the history of mankind as well as of natural history. The process of a continuous renewal and extension of social production justifies the old saying that human beings are distinct in that they permanently reproduce themselves and their own history. At the same time, this process must be understood as the realization of a relation of forces put forth by natural history in which human and non-human forces of nature develop in a certain relationship.

The development of human societalization – this is one of the basic assumptions of historical materialism – has progressed in an unsteady, uneven way. This development, based as it is on systems of social production, is shaped by different society formations and will always experience certain impediments or advancements. This formative impregnation of the development of social labor cannot be separated from the general level of the productive forces and control over nature: the dominance of the mallet as the most important 'means of development' does not permit the development of the capitalist mode of production. Therefore, global development of social labor is tied to certain stages which, on the one hand, depend upon the historically specific state of social labor; on the other hand, these stages arise from characteristic objective requirements. For example, the transformation of learning processes stemming from an extended hunting and gathering economy into activities leading to animal breeding and plant cultivation is unthinkable without producing technological instruments suitable for this type of activity.

Such specific requirements of labor development legitimize the assumption that the productive force and control over nature in societies develop in certain stages which account for changes in social forms and society formations. The two turning points in history that have to be considered are the transition to agriculture and machine production of goods, i.e., the agrarian revolution of the neolithic period and the Industrial Revolution of the recent past. In both these technical revolutions the relation between human labor and belabored nature has been shifted decisively in favor of the human side: first by gaining continuous control over natural resources via agrarian production (Childe, 1952: 71ff.; Feustel, 1973b: 75ff.), then by systematically replacing human labor by machines in industrial production (Marx, 1962a: 391ff.). Both revolutions have decisively shaped the forms of human societalization. The agrarian transition, initiated in the neolithic forms of a common weal economy, led to a fixed relation between the mode of production and territorial integrity, causing the substitution of 'natural' relations of production based on kinship systems by 'politically' controlled relationships: the first form of a long series of class-antagonistic systems of social production. The industrial transition, executed within the frame of the capitalist mode of production, has led to a relative mobility of both labor power and the means of production (by changing them into commodities); the mobility of commodities, in turn, has become the precondition for abandoning the constraints of production and for moving toward a politically planned and controlled social economy. This global process of development from pre-antagonistic via class-antagonistic to post-antagonistic societies has been brought about by a number of rather different modes of production and society formations.

3.2.2 *Economic necessity, historical chance and formative laws within the global societalization process*

Economic society formations within the global process of societalization – from early classless society to class-antagonistic societies and finally to the beginnings of modern forms of non-antagonistic societalization – are frequently seen as occurring in a definite sequence, this perspective claiming to be of universal historical validity. A well-known example is the apodictic notion that history has known five basic types of society: primitive society, slave society, feudalism, capitalism, and socialism (Stalin, 1955:

749). Theoretical discussion has largely disproven such assumptions but has also pointed to the importance of clarifying the theoretical issue in order to arrive at propositions on the historical sequence of economic formations according to certain laws. The concept of historical law in formative society development will therefore dominate in the following considerations.[9]

The concept of historical law in social development refers to the global sequence of economic society formations as well as to the movement of a single formation. The concept does not refer to a deterministic succession of types of society or stages of development or an inevitable pattern of development within a formation. Socio-historical laws signify nothing but the cooperation of economic necessity and historical change in view of historical events that have happened or can be anticipated.

First of all, in regard to the development of human societalization in general, one can speak of the succession of distinct systems according to historical laws. Development of society formations in this sense denotes a succession of systems of social production that serves to extend the volume and to increase the effectiveness of social labor step by step. The economic necessity of such a development is demonstrated by the fact that certain steps of progressing societalization are conditions for realizing a comprehensive and regulated economic system. Necessity in this sense, then, is present in certain internal differentiations of stages of social development ranging from pre-antagonistic to antagonistic and post-antagonistic society formations. This refers to the transition from kinship patterns to agrarian community patterns within the primitive (commonweal ownership) mode of production;[10] it also refers to the transition from feudal master and servant relations to the relation between capital-augmentation and wage labor within class-antagonistic modes of production, indicating an organization of labor power and means of production along increasingly collectivistic lines.[11] Historical chance in the global development of labor productivity comes into the picture in the guise of natural changes of geographical milieu, especially climatic conditions, e.g., the influence of the post-glacial climate upon the origins of agrarian modes of production (cf. Childe, 1952: 71ff.). Historical chance is also present in those individual factors that influence development by means of the cultural and political activities in social systems.

Within these relations between economic necessity and historical chance, the various systems of social production advance the global societalization process by increasing its problem-solving potential. However, this does not imply that the physical basis of a concrete society – its territory, labor power, means of production – will necessarily be incorporated into 'higher' economic formations or even, that these elements will pass through definite stages starting with primitive society and ending in a socialist system. Rather, it probably constitutes an exception within world history if the complete physical basis of a concrete society formation is taken over into another stage. Neither can it be said that the logic of development of the interplay between economic necessity and historical chance is capable of constituting a definite sequence of formation. On the contrary, master–servant relations based on land ownership, for example, lead to quite different economic modes of production and society formations: to class societies based upon the relation between slave labor and slave ownership, or based upon the relation between community labor and despotism, or based upon the relation between serf labor and feudal landed property. These society formations are characterized by antagonistic relations between agrarian production and appropriation of the surplus product enforced by quite distinct non-economic means (cf. Marx, 1964b; 798ff.; Töpfer, 1967, 1971; Introduction to Hobsbawn, 1964). Finally, there can be no doubt that such a diversity of *possible* society formations pertaining to the basic type of master–servant relations based on land ownership, would not permit the constitution of any stable time sequence – especially, since a historical coexistence of these formations has been observed frequently enough.

Nevertheless, laws of historical succession of certain society formations can be formulated. They pertain to those economic society formations that have succeeded in realizing definite stages in the development of forces of social production, societal control over nature, and the division of labor. Historically isolated and stagnant forms of social production would not warrant to be put into some 'lawful' order of development. However, Marx did point to the developmental stages of the Asiatic, ancient, feudal and modern bourgeois modes of production (Marx, 1964c: 9) – to be supplemented by the primitive and socialist modes of production – that constitute a historically specific and economically necessary succession of modes of production that has been the motor of the historical progress in the process of societalization (cf. Engelberg, 1974: 149).

This is evident because the movement of specific society formations themselves proceeds according to specific laws of development. The way in which production of a social product B and – in antagonistic societies – the appropriation of the surplus product S is accomplished and the manner in which labor power and the means of production are related to each other constitutes the basic law of economic formations. Laws of this kind express the basic distribu-

THE HISTORIC-MATERIALISTIC THEORY

tion according to the contribution of labor, on the one hand, and the owners of the means of production, on the other; thus, in turn, reflecting the basic modes of producing and appropriating the social product. These laws therefore cover structural–genetic regularities (cf. Zelený, 1973; 19ff.; Bollhagen, 1967: 123ff.). From these laws propositions concerning the formation-specific relation between the elements of the social product may be derived which at the same time express goal functions of the activity of social production. Primitive modes of production serve to sustain $(C + S)$ or, on a higher stage, to increase the social gross product $(G = C + R + S)$ in relation to the reproduction needs of labour (C), R indicating physical capital. Class-antagonistic modes of production, on the other hand, aim at increasing a surplus product (S) in relation to certain 'expenses'. The definition of these expenses varies in the succession of Asiatic, ancient, feudal, and capitalist modes of production in such a way that one can speak of a gradual increase in efficiency orientation in defining the goals of social production. Thus, at the end of this sequence, the capitalist process of social production is geared toward the increase of S (surplus) in relation to the sum of $R + C$ (invested capital as a whole) – of course, under the control of the general rate of profit. The socialist mode of production, in turn, takes the social net product $(C + S)$ or, more advanced, the gross product $(R + C + S)$ as the goal of social production, leading, at the same time, to a decrease in the amount of actual and reified labor expended in the generation of this product.

This sequence of goal functions in activities of social production, simultaneously representing a series of formation-specific laws of development, demonstrates the kind of developmental logic of society formations that Marx stood for. The sequence of primitive, Asiatic, ancient, feudal, capitalist, and socialist modes of production indicates the sort of progressive increase in the problem-solving potential of human society which, at the same time, signifies global progress in the societalization process.

This process derives its continuity from the discontinuity of the process of formations: advances in productive forces and control over nature that have been achieved within a formation of this sequence cannot be further promoted by means of its economic structure, which, in turn, leads to reproduction problems of the system. Further development of the productivity of social labor is possible only by revolutionizing the mode of production, i.e., by realizing a more effective economic structure. This necessity, though, must be followed up by a praxis that is actually effecting social change. Social development according to historical laws, therefore, has nothing to do with any automatism of the historical process. What is meant, in the final analysis, pertains to establishing the conditions – mediated by the relation between necessity and chance – that permit the practical construction of a better social mode of existence. Consequently, transition to such a new mode of production, and thus the practical construction of a more potent economic structure, constitutes a breach within the process of global societalization; by taking over accumulated elements of productive power, of nature control, and of the political and cultural superstructure this process demonstrates a continuity that establishes a cohesive line in the development of real history.

3.2.3 The sequence of pre-socialist modes of production in the process of universal history

The sequence of primitive, Asiatic, ancient, feudal, and capitalist modes of production constitutes progressive stages in the process of global societalization. For a long time, historical materialism has discussed the problem of how this sequence of formations is related to the totality of the historical process – the two obviously not being identical.

By confronting a sequence of formations according to historical laws with what can be called the process of universal history, first of all, a tension between social history as a unified process and as a manifold process may be observed. This relation has been – quite ambiguously – discussed as the alternative of 'unilinear' *vs* 'multilinear' development. However, this formula does not appear to be plausible (cf. Engelberg, 1974: 149–50; Semjonow, 1974: 160). It implies a given basis of social history that is apt to produce either a single line or many lines of development simultaneously. Such a basis of social history, though, is indiscernible. Social history must be regarded, instead, as the internal movement and the external relationship of society formations that realizes, as time goes by, the superimposition of natural history by universal history. There is hardly any sense in using the concepts of multilinearity and unilinearity in reference to the variety of historical concretizations of different society formations. The uneven and unsteady development of human societies suggests the conception of concrete historical society formations that have contributed to the stages of this development; but it also points to concrete formations, like primitive societies of today, that have contributed little or nothing. It would even be inappropriate to regard this relation between unity and variety of history in terms of a 'dialectic of the "unilinear" and the "multilinear" ' (Engelberg, 1974: 150), because the major developments consist of progressing relations between concrete society formations. The real unity of the process of human societalization manifests itself in the global process of social–practical relations between human beings and non-human nature.

In addition, the confrontation between a 'lawful' sequence of formations and the process of universal history may be conceived as tension between social history as development according to historical laws and social history as a real process. This relation has been formulated – ambiguously again – as the alternative of 'dogmatic' *vs* 'empirical' approaches to history. In reality, the attempt to uncover the basic lines of social history in development does not interfere with attempts to examine empirical reality. Description of actual events and explanation in terms of historical laws generate aspects of scientific knowledge that have to be combined. This means that the laws of the process of human societalization and the actual phenomena of the process of universal history are not identical. Hence, it is the task of social science to deal with this 'stretch ratio' between law and reality. Society formations, from primitive communities to antagonistic societies and socialism, constitute a line of development as well as, according to their own laws, evolutionary processes that have been realized at different places and at different times in different forms. The relation between constitution according to laws and realization according to historical–empirical acts should in no way be understood as something like the relation between a given pattern and an ensuing realization. The mode of production as the constitutive structure and the constitutive process of a formation cannot exist without those various real activities in which men engage themselves in their social and physical relations.[12]

This empirical–historical reality of the mode of production and of society formations is reflected in a wide variety of spatial and temporal modes connected with differentiations in the level of development of the productive forces, of control over nature, and of the political and cultural superstructure (Guhr, 1969b: 63ff.). Greece and Rome, England and Japan, the Soviet Union and Vietnam may serve as geographical catchwords for the variety of a social reality that corresponds with the same societal laws. The simultaneous existence of concrete societies, corresponding to different modes of production, and the diversity of relations between these societies as well as the superimposition by dominant societies further complicate the picture. European feudalism and Asiatic modes of production, American capitalism, and American–Indian kinship systems are illustrative examples for the interdependence and coexistence of different society formations. Historical materialism, in no way prepared to negate this diversity and variety, is taken to task to understand and explain this variety.

3.3 Social development and social change within the capitalist system

The following discussion will take up the question of general laws of the capitalist society formation; in addition, changes pertaining to the productive forces, to production, class relations, and superstructures will be considered; finally, an attempt is made to distinguish between different stages in the development of the capitalist mode of production.

3.3.1 The law of movement within the capitalist society formation

The social process of production within the capitalist mode of production develops in terms of the relation between labor and capital.[13] The process of labor, combining human labor power and the objective means of production, mediates – as in all other modes of production – the relations between human and non-human nature via the production of goods. In this particular mode of production, though, labor power and means of production function as partial embodiments of productive capital; essentially, they serve to produce surplus-value which in turn is used to extend the amount of productive capital. This process of 'self-augmentation' of capital – forcing people who possess little more than their labor power to produce values under the control of people owning the means of production – not only mediates all production activities in a specific way, but also defines the general relations between human beings in capitalism.

Within the process of self-augmentation of capital, labor power is sold to entrepreneurs like any other commodity, producing a class of wage dependants; the owners of the means of production are able to appropriate the value product of labor power including surplus-value, i.e., the difference between the value product (net product) and the reproduction costs of labor power (variable capital). Thus human and non-human factors of the labor process constitute elements of productive (self-augmenting) capital in the hands of private owners, producing surplus-value and being augmented through surplus-value (i.e., capital accumulation). The process of increasing societalization on the production side (by means of a differentiation of labor relations) leads to conflict with the process of private appropriation of unrewarded surplus-labor on the basis of private ownership of the means of production. This antagonism between labor and capital constitutes the basic structure of the economic society formation of capitalism. The basic economic relation between surplus-value production and capital accumulation defines the social relations between the major classes within the population, i.e., between the working class and the capitalist class. This socio-economic system as a whole must be seen as the characteristic pattern of development for the production relation between human and non-human nature as well as for the social relations within the capitalist society formation. Social production within this context cannot proceed but in the guise of self-augmentation of capital. At the same time, however, this structural context contains the roots for further development of this society formation: the development of the exchange process between man and nature as well as the progress of the societalization of human labor which constitutes the precondition for conscious control of social circumstances and the abolishment of class rule. Therefore, the capitalist society formation prepares for the content of post-capitalist society formations.

The relation between surplus-value production and capital-augmentation is necessarily a dynamic one (cf. Grossmann, 1969): production under capitalist premises not only reproduces given capital elements and given class relations, it also serves to extend productive capital by converting profits into additional wage capital (variable capital) and into constant capital (value of all means of production employed for productive purposes). *Systematic* exploitation of the fact that human labor power is capable of producing more value than is needed for its reproduction represents what has caused the tremendously rapid development of productive forces and control over nature under capitalism. Acceleration has also accentuated the limits and contradictions of this development. The socio-economic antagonism between surplus-value producing wage labor and surplus-value investing capital-augmentation leads to an opposition between the material labor process (being the content) and the economic augmentation process (being the form) that cannot be dealt with within the capitalist society formation.[14]

Social labor, constituting a system of cooperative and specialized relations that link human and non-human nature, tends to develop as a comprehensive and coordinated system of productive forces. Capitalist value-augmentation aims at optimizing capital earnings through the use of human and non-human factors of production in the guise of capital, thus fostering the process of social production in the interest of private ownership only. Particular increases in productivity within capitalist enterprises may thus lead to aggregated and accelerated increases in productivity on a universal social scale, but only in the sense that market competition will force single enterprises to improve rentability by externalizing costs without regard to the general and long-run effects upon the socio-economic system. This is what Marx (1965: 80) has termed the 'most secret reason for crises' within the capitalist labor and augmentation process, as the development principle of the capitalist mode of production generates a tremendous increase in the productivity of social labor while, at the same time, pressing this process into the narrow-minded limits of private profit economy.

The form, the pattern into which the increase of labor productivity is pressed under capitalism, therefore constitutes the key for explaining the specifically capitalist mode of economic growth. This mode is characterized by recurring crises within the process of surplus-value production and capital accumulation. Increases in the productivity of actual labor by installing more and better means of production happen only if curtailment on the part of wage capital (variable capital) outweighs the investment of additional constant capital. The measuring rod for extending capitalist production never derives from minimizing labor time or labor intensity, or from increasing labor productivity in general. It exclusively derives from minimizing the cost price of a commodity. Typically, the development of labor productivity progresses by promoting technological progress through the curtailment of variable capital in favor of constant capital, i.e., increasing the 'organic composition of capital' (cf. Mender, 1975: 44ff.). This economic law has social consequences: a growing polarization between capital owners controlling an increasing amount of capitalized means of production on one side and wage laborers constantly threatened by being released from the means of production on the other. During economic crises this polarization shows itself in the antagonism between the concentrated power of capital and jobless wage dependants. These crises are, in turn, based upon the particular development of the relations between the various elements of capital as a whole and the social value product, resulting from the growing organic composition of capital (cf. Schmiede, 1973: 117ff., 163ff.).

Capitalist development of the productive forces and control over nature as consisting of capital accumulation and production of surplus-value is characterized by the fact (1) that a society's capital is growing faster than the production of new value, and (2) that the value of productive labor power (variable capital) is decreasing in relation to the surplus-value it produces.[15] Therefore, the process of capital accumulation and surplus-value production comprises the tendency that surplus-value (profit) as part of the new value decreases in relation to the total capital engaged in production, and

THE HISTORIC-MATERIALISTIC THEORY

that capitalist production surpasses the possibilities of value realization inherent in the social system as a whole (downward trend of the average rate of profit on the basis of a limitation in consumption power). The capitalist growth of social labor productivity (by means of substituting actual labor power through material means of production) therefore leads to recurring crises in the self-augmentation of capital; it also leads to long-term reproduction difficulties, i.e., perennial tendencies of economic depression.

Marx (1964b: 221–77) has described the process that systematically combines the downward trend of the rate of profit with the mobilization of *contra-active* tendencies. All economic causes slowing the growth in the organic composition of capital or increasing surplus-value in relation to the amount of variable capital are factors that oppose the downward trend in the rate of profit. They appear mainly during periodically recurring crises when failing enterprises and the release of labor power eventually lead to a decrease in fixed assets and wage quotas as the basis of a beginning recovery. In addition, such occurrences tend to be followed by measures to economize on the amount of labor, again with positive effects and on the rate of profit. In this way the classical type of crisis creates all the conditions for a profitable rise in capitalist production on a higher level of technology.

The downward trend of the rate of profit, though, not only appears in short-term variations but also generates long-term or secular reproduction problems. Its basic tendency has been strengthened since industrialization came about, since the amount of capitalist fixed assets has concentrated on the investment goods industry, and since the economic interests of the working class have been organized in unions. This again has caused counter-movements in the interest of extending the capitalist labor and augmentation process.[16] That is, scientification of the labor process through technological research and development and through rationalization of the use of labor power, on the one hand, and nationalization of certain aspects of production and circulation, especially state investments into infrastructure and state demand for armaments, on the other.[17] At the same time, the process of capitalist production and augmentation itself has led to an ever-increasing concentration of industrial operations and entrepreneurial capital, providing the basis for monopolistic economic units that enhance the power to control capitalist conditions of production and circulation (cf. Baran and Sweezy, 1968: 23ff.; Wygodski, 1972: 15–227). Every one of these factors has contributed to mobilizing the societal potential designed to counteract the secular reproduction problems of the capitalist system. In some way, this amounts to 'the abolishment of the capitalist mode of production within the capitalist mode of production itself' (Marx, 1964b: 454). But mobilization of these counter-tendencies against the periodically effective and secularly reinforced trend of the rate of profit has neither changed the antagonistic form nor the crisis-prone development of the capitalist production and augmentation process. These tendencies merely serve to prolong the progression of the fundamental relation between surplus-value production and capital accumulation.

It should also be stressed that competition between the different economic units remains the essential motor, even on this level of development: not only competition between individual capitals dependent on an increase of productivity for the sake of self-augmentation, but also competition between owners of labor power whose jobs are threatened by the increased organic composition of capital. Competition also exists between the owners of the means of production and the owners of labor power, in so far as they appear on the labor market. Capitalist society evolves as a full-fledged 'competitive society' where the laws of competition govern the actions and the behavioral patterns of all its members.

3.3.2 *The development of the productive forces and the relations of production, class struggle, and superstructure*

The level of technological progress, especially of machine equipment, usually serves as the external indicator for the developmental stage of the productive forces. But these systems of reified labor are activated by actual labor and therefore, in the final analysis, productive force within capitalism presents itself in the form of differentiated and integrated mass labor power. However, labor power within the capitalist mode of production also functions as an element of productive capital, thereby subjecting itself to the constraints of competition that require a constant increase in the production of surplus-value. Increase in productivity in this sense, though, is possible only by increasing the ratio of constant capital and total capital engaged, i.e., by extending and intensifying the use of the means of production while cutting back the use of labor power by further releasing actual labor. This takes place by substituting human skills by means of respective machines and tools and eventually by introducing automatic controls into the production process.[18]

The present stage in the development of the productive forces can be characterized by complex mechanization, partial automatization, and methods of cybernetic control in production; in addition, the technical and scientific qualification of labor power increased, especially in the field of planning and management. At the same time, this process, aiming at 'scientification' of production,[19] causes the dequalification of large portions of the labor force. For productive capital is not interested in the long-run development of man as a productive force, which, in turn, is often opposed to interests of short-term augmentation. Nevertheless, concentration and centralization of capital in the monopolistic process of integration has led to forms of social planning and organization, proving that a level of societalization has been reached within the capitalist process of production which is utterly incompatible with the principle of private appropriation. The growing importance of the comprehensive organization of surplus-value production and capital accumulation is thus beginning to affect relations of capitalist ownership themselves.

As a consequence, the basic antagonistic relationship between wage-dependent labor and capital-augmenting private ownership of the means of production develops in two dimensions: laterally by incorporating more and more units of the non-industrial fields of agriculture, trade, commerce, and services; gradually by increasing the degree of societalization of the forms of property.

This high degree of societalization indicates a tendency of the capitalist conditions of production to develop beyond their own limits, proving the notion that society formations always embrace moments of past and future developments. Ownership of the means of production is subjected to qualitative changes mainly in regard to (monopolistic) capital-holding companies and in regard to state ownership. (1) Monopolistic economic units tend to foster forms of 'collective private ownership' that keep some portions of the capitalist class from exercising organizational control over the production process. By separating capital ownership and capital function this portion of the capitalist class is pushed into a parasitic role. On the other hand, private wealth becomes concentrated in fewer and fewer hands. This economically potent part of the capitalist class, embedded in a wide net of management structures, obviously constitutes the power center of the capitalist system. (2) Simultaneously, state ownership within capitalism becomes an instrument for the economic management and planning in terms of general social interests, while the interests of the ruling class prevail, defining the character of economic development in spite of diverging needs of society.

Yet the forms of basic class antagonism are changing. The differentiation process of dispositional roles and positions in administration and technology is changing the composition of wage labor. On the side of capital-augmentation the picture is further complicated by the growing role of managerial positions in exercising the tasks of entrepreneurial organization and representation. In addition, there is a growing conflict potential between the various types of ownership, especially between the monopolies and non-monopolistic sectors of capitalist economy. Class theory has to take into account these changes with respect to two problems.

The first problem refers to the role of the scientific–technical intelligentsia (cf. Kievenheim and Leisewitz, 1973: 111ff.). This group of scientifically trained functionaries of the capitalist production process stands for the ambivalent nature of this process – the social character of labor and the private character of augmentation. Their class behavior testifies to a definite wage-dependent status on the one hand, while showing certain tendencies to identify with capitalist enterprise, on the other hand, thus leading to wavering attitudes in actual class conflicts. Their degree of class consciousness is dependent upon the degree of insight into the antagonistic interdependence between capitalist restrictions and repressions here and long-term perspectives of organization and planning there. The second problem refers to the group of non-capitalist small property holders and non-capitalist commodity producers (cf. Tjaden-Steinhauer and Tjaden, 1973: 32–3, 138ff., 192ff.). In the capitalist societalization process the majority of this group is pressed into the ranks of wage-dependants, while, as petty bourgeoisie, it is also susceptible to such ideologies as private property and simple commodity exchange which, for example, may provide the mass basis for the development of fascism.

In general, the quality of class conflict today is determined by the stage of development of planning and organization within the system of social production. In other words, wage labor and capital-augmentation are related on the basis of highly societalized capitalist conditions of production. On the capitalist side, changes in industrial management and control as well as scientifically refined strategies of social policy have altered the movements of class conflict. On the labor side, advances in organizational ability, in strategic planning on the basis of a higher degree of differentiation and integration of mass labor, constitute a qualitative leap over nineteenth-century conditions. Apart from the role of socialist countries and national liberation movements, labor strategies have adopted complex, long-term goals capable of advancing the contradiction between the development of the productive forces and the development of the conditions of production within the context of day-to-day policies in the capitalist system. This entails changes in the forms of class conflict, for example, in strike techniques and bargaining behavior and, last but not least, in the role of international organizations responding to the global development of capital.

Finally, the increasing degree of societalization in the development of the production process is expressed in the relation between the mode of production (basis) and its superstructures. It is here that changes in the activities of the modern capitalist state command the center of interest.[20] During the transition from feudalism to capitalism, the central state was already carrying out important functions in advancing the new mode of production: (1) by safeguarding the basic ownership relations, (2) by providing legal sanctions for contractual relations between the owners of capital and the owners of labor power, and (3) by supporting trade and transportation activities. Then, during an interim period, these state activities were dimmed by the enormous energy and dynamics of the private capitalist augmentation process itself.

After basic reproduction problems of the capitalist labor and augmentation process became evident during the depressions of the late nineteenth century, economic interventions on the part of the state stepped up dramatically, aiming especially at influencing commodity production and circulation. Thereby, theoretically speaking, an element of the superstructure began to partake in the development of social production by mitigating the effects of economic crises and by putting the process of capitalist self-augmentation on a long-term basis. In the final analysis, though, no state activity in capitalist economy could hope to elude the laws of capitalism. Accordingly, the modern state is evolving within a system of contradictions: (1) pursuing long-term goals in safeguarding and developing the capitalist mode of production, and (2) trying to mend short-term reproduction problems by means of *ad hoc* support. Consequently, the state as the central element of the superstructure is gaining stature in direct economic conflicts while losing its former role of (relative) independence.

3.3.3 *Stages in the development of the capitalist mode of production*

The structure of problem-solving activities within the capitalist system derives from class-antagonistic conditions of production. The various activities of the social system can only be understood by relating them to the structure of antagonistic reproduction and production processes. Assuming the constitutive nature of these economic structures, though, in no way implies the immutability of the system. Economic and social structures unfold as a historical process. This progress of the structures of problem-solving activities must be seen as being related to the constitutive conditions that are governed by the laws of that particular mode of production (cf. Bollhagen, 1967).

We have tried to show that the concept of structural and processual laws governing economic society formations is essential for historical materialism. These laws have to be uncovered by analyzing the social history of the economic formations in order to demonstrate the unity of categorial–structural and historical–processual analysis. Marx has succeeded in exemplifying this method by analyzing the emergence of capitalism and by following up with an analysis of the unfolding of capitalism. Historical materialism has not yet succeeded in giving an equally convincing explanation of the subsequent development of the capitalist mode of production; but there is agreement on a more general level that capitalism of free competition during the last quarter of the nineteenth century has been transformed into another stage of capitalism. This stage is characterized by a new level in the concentration of industrial labor and entrepreneurial capital, leading to the formation of the modern monopoly and of imperialism. In addition, the emergence of scientific production technology combined with state interventions is generally accepted as a specific trait of 'late capitalism' (cf. Tjaden–Steinhauer and Tjaden, 1973: 36–75). This late phase in the movement of capitalism will now be examined from a theoretical point of view.

Stages in societal development are characterized by specific modifications within the mode of production that enable the social system to react to new problems by developing new capacities for problem solving. These modifications within the structure of the system occur in the context of its history of problems and performances. Thus, social systems are similar to ultra-stable systems in the sense that their mode of production, in the case of disturbances, is capable of immediate readjustments in the interest of keeping up reproduction and extending production – without changing the principles of the mode of production. Such occurrences may be termed changes in systemic strategy. Already in the stage preceding competitive capitalism, impending exhaustion of productive resources, especially labor power, caused tensions that necessitated the progress toward the production of relative surplus-value as an innovative structure of problem solution. Marx described this step in the field of labor organization and technology, generated by innovation activities of competing capitals, as historical progress of the capitalist mode of production that revealed the inner essence of the capitalist mode of production. By generalizing the production of commodities, productive activities in capitalist society aim at the production of exchange-values, especially surplus-value. This enhanced the tendency to decrease the labor time necessary for producing a commodity below the social average (Marx, 1964b: 888) and to increase productivity of social labor by means of technological and organizational measures. The development of mechanized and rationalized production under competitive capitalism therefore constitutes a stage in the general development of capitalism where a structure that corresponds to the principles of the capitalist mode of production and its place in universal history is finally enforced (cf. Marx, 1964b: 269). This 'structure of adequacy' of the capitalist mode of production appearing during the period of competitive capitalism represents the basic pattern to which the further discussion of the development of capitalism converges.[21]

The tremendous development of social productive forces and control over nature, mediated by the principle of competition, was the cause of severe disturbances within the production process of capitalist societies toward the end of the nineteenth century. There are two aspects to the development of labor productivity: large investments of constant capital (because of the heavily capitalized technological progress connected with economic fixation of durable capital goods in industries producing means of production), on the one hand, and progressive unfolding of actual labor power by means of higher qualification (brought about by technological and organizational means connected with the political organization of the working class within the labor movement), on the other. These internal developments are finally supplemented by external ones: in addition to economic and political competition between the imperialist powers, the emergence of a non-capitalist, socialist sector of the world economy and of national liberation movements in capitalist colonies *is beginning to limit the elbow-room of capitalist problem-solving activities*. These specific internal and external changes incite problem- and performance-oriented modifications in the problem-solving structure of the capitalist mode of production that prove to be distinct from the adequacy structure of competitive capitalism. All this must be seen within the context of the genesis and development of a perennial reproduction crisis brought about essentially by an intensification of the downward trend of the rate of profit, as well as within the context of exploring and reinforcing secular reproduction potentials which are capable of counteracting the negative trend of the rate of profit.[22]

Therefore, this stage in the development of problem and performance structures of capitalism, called 'late capitalism,' may be seen in terms of a general reproduction crisis combined with crisis management activities. This does not imply any capacities for unlimited reproduction or sufficient control potential. It only points to the fact that the capitalist system is reacting with a change in the strategies within a basically antagonistic set-up. The essential elements of this strategy have been mentioned already: (1) organizing internal conditions of production and circulation, at least partly along monopolistic lines; (2) securing external conditions of production and circulation by attempting imperialistic control over foreign territory; (3) exploiting the potential of science for creating capital-saving technologies; and (4) exploiting the potential of the state for investments supporting production and hence the realization of surplus-value.

This general problem-solving strategy may be regarded as a structural modification of the capitalist mode of production that has reacted to the perennial crisis of the system in such a way that had undoubtedly stabilizing effects on a secular level. However, the basic reproduction crisis of capitalism had not been eliminated. The persistence of the cycle of periods of crisis and prosperity provides ample proof. In the final analysis, these structural modifications are not capable of realizing those structures of societalized production that would be adequate to the further development of productive force and control over nature. Instead, there is an inflation of substitute solutions which, in contrast to the adequacy of competitive capitalism, must be regarded as 'equivalence structures.' The solutions offered seem to be inadequate to actual reproduction problems; moreover, they lead to their aggravation. Something like a systematic repression of the reproduction problem seems to be taking place, assuring its outbreak in unexpected places in exacerbated forms (cf. Krysmanski, 1971: 32). The scientification of the productive forces, for example, is leading – by means of raising the capital minimum required for investments – to an extension of state interventionism into the conditions of reproduction. By means of infra-structural improvement of productivity, the scientification thus promotes the chances for over-accumulation of capital in relation to the attainable profit. In the final analysis, only the transformation of the problem-solving structures constitutive of the capitalist system, leading to a socialist mode of production, would be adequate to meet the requirement of a systematic development of the forces of social production and control over nature.

3.4 Intersystem-relations within the universal process of societalization

Social systems are subject to historical development. Their

structure is the result of interactive processes between subjective and objective factors. In other words, they constitute the results of human problem-solving activities. Accordingly, relations between social systems are determined by specific types of problem solution derived from system-specific ways of handling the problems implicated by the relation between society and nature as well as by the relationships between men themselves. Problem-solving activities, therefore, are not only capable of producing the internal network of social systems, but also provide the basis for meaningful, goal-oriented relations between systems. During a period of history that is characterized by self-limitation of capitalist development, processes of self-determination within the Third World, and growing competition between the capitalist and socialist systems, this notion of intersystem relations pertains to the fact that international relations not only contribute to further dominance, oppression, dependence, exploitation, and threat, but, by testing various problem solutions, also serves to promote a process of trans-system societalization.

We are convinced that sociology, in view of present knowledge, cannot neglect the idea that social systems are part of a universal constitution process involving social and natural history (Tjaden, 1972: 273ff.). Social praxis, therefore, is not exhausted by dominance activities. Increasingly, social praxis, even on the intersystem level, must be understood as a test of various types of problem-solving activity that are carried out in the interest of majorities or the system as a whole. Intersystem relations in this sense serve as a testing ground for large-scale solutions on different system levels, preferably the most general level.

3.4.1 *Problem-solving activities*

As a concept, problem-solving activity takes social praxis in terms of an interrelation of 'socially produced objects or situations of a challenging nature' (problems) and socially organizable, 'practical procedures of solution' (performances). Social praxis, in this sense, pertains to the labor process itself in so far as it mediates between actual labor (labor power) and reified labor (means of production); it also pertains to the fact that social activities are mediated by communicative and decision-making activities that are central for system theory. In addition, the concept of problem-solving activity – by emphasizing the importance of successful solution structures within the institutionalization process – serves to identify the historical and genetic relationships between problems 'solved once and for all' and solution practices that may be transmitted because they have been unquestionably successful. In other words, social praxis in terms of a development of problem-solving activities can be seen as a context of more or less urgent and complicated problems, on the one hand, and of more or less current and complex performances, on the other.[23]

The central theoretical problem arising in this connection has to do with the relation between reproduction and production. In order to characterize the nature of social praxis on an abstract level, the concept of reproduction may be applied to activities designed to secure and stabilize existing conditions. The concept of production or of the extension of production applies to activities intended to expand social reality. In other words, the stage of development that a social system has reached may be defined in terms of the relations between its 'minimal' (reproduction) and 'maximal' (production) problem-solving activities. All system activities, then, would have to be regarded as occurring within the scope of reproduction and the extension of production, and they would have to be explained in terms of their role in mediating between the 'survival' and the 'growth' of the system. In concrete historical perspective then, activities of a social system such as the capitalist system (e.g., use of force, contract formation, control and communication measures, use of science and technology, in addition to reproductive and productive activities themselves) not only constitute a genetic, sequential structure (a history of problem solutions) but also a hierarchical structure (a system of problem-solving activities).

Finally, these structural properties must be related to a dimension where these problem-solving activities directed at production and reproduction are checked – under the dialectics of 'survival' and 'growth' – against the actual actors realizing them, i.e., social groups and classes. 'Social classes derive from the socio-economic functions, which are intertwined in social reproduction and production such as surplus-value production and capital accumulation in the capitalist system. Social classes represent the central formations of social reproduction; their members personify those economic functions' (Tjaden, 1972: 283–4). Social groups and classes, accordingly, are defined by their functions within the complex system of problem-solving activities, and by their general or specific potential for solving certain types of problem. It may be assumed that there is some correspondence between the basic system-problems resulting from 'survival' and 'growth' and problem-solving activities related to groups and classes.[24]

There is, for example, a 'channeling' of problem-solving activities toward the stabilization of existing social structures by means of successfully institutionalized problem solutions. Thus, problems of distribution connected with the institution of private property may be 'solved' by attempting a more even distribution of private property. Problem-solving activities may also attack historically successful structures of solution because of their inherent contradictions, thus attempting to solve problems according to the state of socially organized opportunities for expansion of reality. Problems of distribution linked with the institution of private property might be solved by abolishing private property of the means of production. This second type of problem-solving activities – which could be called *adequate* in terms of the level that the problem-solving potential of the system as a whole has reached – converges with the activity of groups and classes close to the productive labor process. The first type of problem-solving activities – which could be termed *equivalent* to what has been proven successful in the past – converges with the activity of groups and classes close to processes of decision making, short-term planning, and day-to-day management of affairs.

The antagonism between 'opportunity-expanding' and 'opportunity-controlling' groups (for example, between surplus-value production and capital accumulation) tends to become more severe if the basic functions of reproduction and of extension of production can no longer be mediated through existing solution patterns, especially if the social system is forced to increase its engagement in the processes of intersystem or trans-system societalization. In this case, the original social function of 'opportunity-controlling' groups, namely, to secure the survival of the system as a whole, degenerates into the function of safeguarding the survival of that group itself. The function of safeguarding the survival of the system as a whole will converge with the necessity to expand production on the basis of innovative problem-solving activities and solution structures. With regard to intersystem relations, then, these antagonistic groups gain relevance according to their long-range, intra-system functions: *productive* classes will be able to use intersystem relations in terms of realizing the continuity of the process of societalization beyond actual system-limits; *controlling* classes, by contrast, will merely be able to make use of intersystem relations in terms of a strategy for their own survival. Accordingly, the first group will deal with the cooperative, and the second group with the conflictual, side of intersystem relations.

Here, cooperation and conflict reach a general level of systemic and trans-systemic relevance that is removed from everyday phenomena of cooperation and conflict. On the intra-system level cooperation and conflict may, to a certain extent, be related to the various social classes and their specific problem-solving activities, i.e., along interactionist lines. Conflict, for example, might be understood as an indifferent form of interaction that matches various actors who are characterized by being engaged in similar but competing problem-solving activities. Conflict, in this sense, could be defined, without reference to any specific class, as a type of interaction testing the adequacy of various performances in relation to a given problem, or testing the adequacy of various problems in relation to a given performance. Cooperation, correspondingly, would be that type of interaction in which problem-solving activities reinforce each other. For the sake of comparison between systems, these interactionist concepts of cooperation and conflict may serve to identify characteristic problem-solving activities and to illustrate basic differences in the general system of solution structures. However, on the level of intersystem relations, the importance of a concept of cooperation-prone and conflict-prone social classes, based upon the inherent difference between reproduction- and production-related activities, becomes self-evident. For the process of trans-systemic societalization obviously is no deterministic process, but a process constituting its own subject along the way.

3.4.2 Problem-solving structures

Societal systems, in so far as they constitute a system of historically successful, institutionalized solution structures, do not develop in a random way; they are subject to general and specific laws of development. In order to address itself to the problems of the genesis and relevance of social structures, sociological theory has to draw upon the insights of the philosophy of history and upon the results of various sciences. Social praxis, the persistence of certain historically evolved solution structures, and the force of structural revolutions, could not be understood any other way. It is precisely its capability to integrate the most diverse scientific insights into a unifying theoretical framework that sets historical materialism apart as a superior activity directed at theoretical problem solving. Political economy and approaches based upon its assumptions have succeeded in uncovering the specific historical laws of the capitalist system.

A model designed to explore the structural basis of intersystem relations should draw upon these insights. In other words, there is little use in adding another taxonomic model of the structure of social systems were it not for the sake of summing up the basic results of historical materialism. Therefore, our model of a system of solution structures and problem-solving activities refers to that set of socio-economic activities, structures, and laws that have been expounded in the earlier sections of this chapter.

Solution structures may be regarded as socially organized strategies to solve socially evolved problems. They constitute action patterns for dealing with problematical objects and object constellations. The historical-materialistic analysis of capitalism draws attention to a number of 'capitalist' solution structures dealing with such social problems as rapid expansion of the productive forces, extension of production in view of rapid population growth, and social organization of the exploitation of nature. Capitalism reacted to these problems by institutionalizing a number of solution structures that have increased the societalization potential of capitalism itself. Among the solution structures inherent in the capitalist mode of production the following stand out: (1) production of goods as production of commodities by free wage laborers under the control of free owners of the means of production; (2) universal exchange of commodities connected with circulation of money; (3) capital accumulation based upon surplus-value production; (4) relative and/or absolute expansion of the means of production in connection with relative and/or absolute release of labor power in the course of the development of the productive forces; (5) concentration of labor and capital and the emergence of monopolies; (6) growing social organization of capitalist production; and (7) societalization of the production of commodities by means of increasing state control. On the basis of these predominantly economic solution structures a number of secondary social, political, and psychological structures and processes have evolved that are frequently central to non-materialistic social science. This has led to valuable insights into the operation of the superstructure, but it has also led to many substitutions of the essential by the superficial.

In order to analyze intersystem relations on a global level, pertaining to the trans-systemic process of societalization involving both capitalist and socialist systems, the specific nature of 'socialist' solution structures within a highly socialized system free from class antagonism has to be explored as well. One thing should be evident by now: 'Socialist' solution structures, whether economic or social, must have developed in the bowels of capitalism – on foreign territory, so to speak. The agent of this development, operating within the capitalist system for 'socialization' against 'privatization,' is identical with the labor movement in the widest sense. In addition, the October Revolution, the Second World War, and the liberation movements in the Third World have produced a number of socialist states that are pushing for a more or less exclusive realization of socialist problem-solving activities, although, of course, 'capitalist' solution structures tend to persist, to some extent, there. The fact that today capitalist *and* socialist problem-solving activities proceed under state protection and on the basis of territorial integrity have undoubtedly speeded up the exhaustion of the potential of capitalist solution structures. Only fifty years of socialist development sufficed to melt away the 200-year time-lead of capitalism. Yet, there is no way of telling when and how this growing entanglement of capitalist and socialist solution structures will be transformed into a trans-systemic process of societalization.

Our model, though, will have to address the question of how to conceive of the unity and diversity of solution structures of different historical maturity in terms of the relation between different social systems. Obviously, the type of thinking that might be called strategic is of little use, conceiving, as it does, of intersystem relations in terms of territorial integrity and in terms of symmetry between national actors moving in an ahistorical world. Thus, intersystem relations should be seen in terms of complex social relations and asymmetrical interactions, one side appearing as a moment in the development of the other side. Consequently, capitalism would have to be regarded as a stage in the development toward socialism or socialism would have to be viewed as some sort of historical aberration from the all-embracing development of capitalist–industrial society. Both of these asymmetric models would permit to explore various phenomena of international cooperation (integration, incorporation, reinforcement of existing structures, etc.) and of international conflict (crisis, instances of dominance and demarcation, etc.).

Sociological theory does offer a generous supply of concepts to feed the idea 'socialism as a temporary aberration from capitalist–industrial society.' The development of functionalist system theory in particular must be understood as an attempt to expand the activity patterns of the capitalist system within the framework of a world society. Functionalist system theory, at the same time, has denounced socialist problem-solving activities as 'collective behavior' stemming from the fringes of social existence. Socialist societies and structures, in this perspective, would necessarily become the object of processes of convergence and absorption into the 'main stream.' Finally, this approach seems to ignore the very notion of intersystem relations, except on an abstract level, because the 'other side' is perceived as the source of moves and countermoves in a strategic game, but not as the point of departure for alternative historical solution structures. In the final analysis, this represents a type of imperialist thinking, attractive in some ways, but incapable of grasping the real content of intersystem relations of conflict and cooperation. It is a type of thinking that stood behind the development of the disastrous American Vietnam policy and that is still a major element in the development of imperialist strategies, especially if the complexities of the ongoing process of trans-systemic societalization are negated.

On the other hand, there are advantages in attempting the construction of a model that perceives of the relation between the capitalist and the socialist society formations in terms of contradictory, interrelated stages in the development of distinct solution structures. First of all, both sides could be taken 'seriously' in such a model; they could be subjected to a historical examination of their respective merits from the point of view of the general process of societalization. Achievements of both sides could be put into a genetic and historical perspective without suppressing successful solutions of the past or excluding promising solutions of the future. Finally, such a model would be capable of expressing the fact that our historical experience regarding socialist solution structures is limited indeed – compared to what capitalism has taught us already about its capabilities, both good and bad.

3.4.3 Intersystem relations

From a sociological point of view, intersystem relations must be regarded in terms of a trans-systemic process of societalization that proceeds in a dialectic manner and is based on corresponding processes of societalization within the respective social system. These processes of societalization may be understood in terms of the development of problem-solving activities and in terms of the formation and historical examination of solution structures. Accordingly, two levels of intersystem relations may be distinguished: (1) the relation between the more or less successful problem-solving activities and solution structures of the social system in question, and (2) the historical relation between the social systems according to their status in the sequence of society formations.

This approach to intersystem relations sets itself apart from approaches that were of a *strategic* and *cataclysmic* kind (Rapoport, 1968). The strategic approach to intersystem relations is akin to the outlook of those actors within the system of international relations who define the guidelines of policy without regard to the socio-cultural context or legitimacy, i.e., in a socio-technological way. The strategic approach, then, is rational in the sense of permitting the calculation of the action potential of the other side within the framework of the theoretical possibilities inherent in one's own system; in this sense it is a hegemonial, imperialistic approach catering to the limited rationality of one's own system, detached from the general process of history. This approach naïvely presumes that there are rules of universal validity (like in chess) without being able to account for the historical emergence of social rules and laws in the context of the general development of societies. In the final analysis, this approach will conceive of international relations in terms of a game between power elites employing their 'social resources' like chips in a game of roulette. This imposition of the perspective of the ruling classes upon the social sciences inevitably leads to a regression in social relevance, since social relevance obviously must be defined to include the interests of the ruled classes as well.

The cataclysmic approach tends to view history in terms of catastrophes not amenable to rational analysis; it would introduce moralistic categories of fatalism and compassion, etc. into the study of intersystem relations. Obviously, such an approach could gain only subtle influence on scientific analysis, but even so it can be detected as an undercurrent in many strategic theories of international relations, especially in the guise of Social Darwinism. Irrationalisms of this type had been the forerunner of fascism in the past; it holds a certain attraction for those groups of policy-makers that represent classes which have lost the capability to legitimize their problem-solving activities within the general process of societalization.

Systemic and trans-systemic processes of societalization, naturally, do not develop without conflict. Within the capitalist system, what is developing as the principle of the societalization of production by means of capital-augmentation constitutes the exact contradiction of what is developing, simultaneously, as the principle of private capital accumulation. This contradiction, in spite of all attempts of state control over the perennial crises of reproduction, defines the basic structure of the system as a whole. At the same time, it is entirely feasible to distinguish between antagonistic and non-antagonistic conflicts, i.e., between conflicts capable of revolutionizing the social structure in its totality and conflicts that may be integrated into the system as it exists. This distinction, though, should be freed from superfluous ideological weight: even the pursuit and resolution of *antagonistic* conflicts is something that must be regarded as a necessary element in the general process of social development and that, by no means, in the case of transforming one society formation into another, must lead to disruption and violence. In fact, concerning highly differentiated society formations such as capitalism and socialism, antagonistic conflicts in violent form should be the exception. In addition, many highly socialized problem-solving activities (e.g., in the field of

THE HISTORIC-MATERIALISTIC THEORY

ecology) already demand trans-systemic forms of cooperation. This is the point where the role of the state, and especially the role of inter-state relations, is gaining importance. Within the development of the relations between capitalist and socialist systems, this aspect of the connection between the level of state activities and the level of social activities in general is becoming increasingly significant and would have to be included into a theory of inter-system relations and trans-systemic processes of societalization. A discussion of this question, though, would be beyond the scope of this introduction.

3.5 A general critique of historic-materialistic theory of societal development

Historic-materialistic theory of societal development aims at understanding human societalization, in order to comprehend the concrete history of past and present societies and to influence in practice the ongoing history of present-day societies. Obviously, this far-reaching goal has been attained only imperfectly. Some of the successes and some of the shortcomings will be listed here.

3.5.1 Its merits: what it does

Historic-materialistic theory of societal development is based upon a concept of the relations between societies, human beings, and non-human nature; the concept corresponds with the results of modern natural science. For this reason reciprocal relations between the theory of evolution in the natural sciences and the theory of development in the social sciences may be established, promoting the dialogue between the natural and social sciences, for example, in the field of ecology. Accordingly, historic-materialistic theory is able to tear down traditional boundaries between these disciplines without disowning the relative uniqueness of the respective object areas and their ensuing specific contents and methods.

Historic-materialistic theory of societal development has been able to formulate an intelligible and useful approach to understanding world history by comprehending historical change in terms of a step-by-step development of the 'metabolic' exchange between man and his natural surroundings. This concept indicates the basic line of historical development without reducing all historical phenomena to this general trend. The assumption that history is based upon a succession of specific formations dealing with the exchange between man and his natural surroundings makes it possible to do away with the dubious construct of 'social evolution' and the methodological problems it raises. Accordingly, it becomes feasible to account for all the variations in form and problem-solving capacities within a unified theoretical framework. Thus, the main fallacy of old and modern sociological concepts of evolution could be avoided: the reduction of a complex reality to an abstract logic of evolution. The notion of a succession of society formations within a general process of societalization, finally, provides an adequate framework for answering the question as to how obsolete and innovative societal forms articulate in their coexistence.

3.5.2 Its shortcomings: what it does not do

Although historic-materialistic theory of social development aims at understanding history in terms of a succession of societal formations representing ever-increasing problem-solving capacities, some of these societal formations have not yet been fully understood. In addition, the exact sequence of these formations is still a matter of debate. As a result, large portions and periods of factually known world history have not yet been interpreted in terms of formation theory. Historic-materialistic theory is systemic social theory and does not claim to be empirical historiography; still, much more historical research has to be done before known historical reality will be comprehensively explained in theoretical terms.

Although historic-materialistic theory sees itself as a science designed to uncover social and historical laws, it has succeeded only in regard to certain societal formations in formulating the laws governing their specific processes of societalization. Obviously, the analysis of the capitalist system has progressed farthest. But even here additional theoretical effort will be needed to elaborate upon the general genetic–structural laws of capitalist development in a way that will permit to link insights into partial structures and processes with the more general notions of the development of this mode of production.

Finally, in spite of the fact that historic-materialistic theory of development conceives of itself as a science pertaining to the whole social reality, its pronouncements focus on certain aspects and leave other aspects of a given societal formation in the dark. This is true, for example, with respect to the change in certain patterns of the kinship and family system or the functions of cultural superstructures within the general development of the social system; this also pertains to the territorial aspects of social development. These fields require further effort in order to increase the explanatory potential of historic-materialistic theory of societal development.

Notes

1 For the research methods of historical materialism, see in particular different articles in Schmidt (1969), as well as Zelený (1973) and Ritsert (1973).
2 Examples are: Grossmann (1929), Varga (1934), Dobb (1937), Moszkowska (1943), Sweezy (1956), Gillman (1968), Mattick (1971), Wygodski (1972).
3 Cf. the detailed analysis by Sofri (1969) and more recently Hindess and Hirst (1975: 178–9).
4 Cf. in particular the debates in the following periodicals: *Marxism Today*, 1961/2; *La Pensée*, 1964ff.; *Ethnographisch-Archäologische Zeitschrift*, 1967 and 1968; *Zeitschrift für Geschichtswissenschaft*, 1968 and 1969.
5 Section 3.2 summarizes parts of Chapter 3 of Tjaden (1977).
6 Cf. the epilogue in Tjaden, 1971: 437ff. The importance of this category for historic-materialistic theory of development has been emphasized by Lenin (1971a: 131).
7 Cf. Engels, 1968b: 656; also Engels, 1968a; Feustel, 1973a.
8 Concerning the issue of the extent of the social surplus in early prehistoric modes of production, cf. Mandel (1969: 24–5) on the one hand, and Godelier (1973: 53–4), on the other.
9 See Bollhagen (1967) and Griese (1971) on the concept of historical law.
10 Cf. Marx, 1962b: 388–9. For a discussion of this transition and of the transition to early class society, cf. Guhr (1969a) and Hoffmann (1972).
11 This transition was comprehensively analyzed and explained by Marx (cf. Marx, 1962a: 741ff. and Dobb, 1963).
12 Cf. in this context Tjaden, 1973: 49–72, especially 63ff.
13 The following chapter is based on Marx's and Engels's theoretical analyses of capitalism, particularly in *Das Kapital* (Marx, 1962–4). For an introduction, see Sweezy, 1956.
14 Grossmann, 1969; regarding the role of use value, see Rosdolsky, 1969: 68ff.
15 The downward trend of the profit rate is discussed by Freiburghaus and Müller (1973: 166ff.); cf. also Rolshausen, 1970.
16 By contrast, many authors tend to explain perennial reproduction problems of modern capitalism in terms of the outcome of the First World War and the October Revolution in Russia. Cf. Institut für Weltwirtschaft und internationale Beziehungen der Akademie der Wissenschaften der UdSSR, 1972: 14. Cf. also Tjaden-Steinhauer and Tjaden, 1973: 38–75.
17 Cf., for instance, Mandel, 1978: 101ff., 171ff., 230ff.; Boccara et al., 1972: 38ff., 486ff., 526ff. For an introduction, see Mender, 1975: 77–115.
18 For a theory of the development of productive forces, see Marx, 1962a: 331ff.
19 For the problem of scientification of production, see Autorenkollektiv, 1972; Stölting, 1974.

20 For a theory of the superstructure of the state in capitalism, cf. Hirsch, 1973.
21 For the concept of adequacy structure and the corresponding concept of equivalence structure, cf. Krysmanski, 1971: 27ff.
22 Cf. Hirsch, 1973: 199ff., 217ff; Tjaden-Steinhauer and Tjaden, 1973: 38ff.; and section 3.3.1 above.
23 This relation is explicated in a table showing levels of achievement and sequences of problems, in Krysmanski, 1971: 27–9.
24 The distinction between equivalent and adequate problem-solving activities can be considered to be relevant for groups or classes simultaneously (Krysmanski, 1971: 27–36).

Suggested reading

Introductory reading

MARX, KARL and ENGELS, FREDERICK (1969), 'Die deutsche Ideologie,' pp. 9–567 in *Marx-Engels-Werke*, vol. 3, Berlin: Dietz.
Here Marx and Engels develop the basic categories and assumptions of historical materialism by dealing with liberal ideology.

MARX, KARL (1969), 'Zur Kritik der politischen Ökonomie,' pp. 3–160 in *Marx-Engels-Werke*, vol. 13, Berlin: Dietz.
The author outlines the ruling principles of the capitalist mode of production.

ENGELS, FREDERICK (1962), 'Der Ursprung der Familie, des Privateigentums und des Staates,' pp. 25–173 in *Marx-Engels-Werke*, vol. 21, Berlin: Dietz.
Engels applies historical-materialistic theory to an analysis of prehistoric conditions.

DOBB, MAURICE (1963), *Studies in the Development of Capitalism*, New York: International Publ.
This book represents a historical analysis of the rise and development of capitalist societies.

WYGODSKI, S. L. (1972), *Der gegenwärtige Kapitalismus*, Cologne: Pahl-Rugenstein.
This is a theoretical analysis of modern capitalism.

Further reading

General

BOLLHAGEN, PETER (1967), *Gesetzmäßigkeiten und Gesellschaft*, Berlin: Deutscher Verlag der Wissenschaften.
In this study, central categories of historical-materialistic analysis as a systematic science are expounded.

ENGELBERG, ERNST (1974), 'Probleme der gesetzmäßigen Abfolge der Gesellschaftsformationen,' *Zeitschrift für Geschichtswissenschaft*, 2: 145–73.

The author explicates basic problems and elaborates upon the ruling principles of a theory of society formations.

GODELIER, MAURICE (1973), *Ökonomische Anthropologie*, Reinbek: Rowohlt.

The author lays the foundations, and comes up with important results, of historical-materialistic theory about prehistoric and early antagonistic societies.

HAHN, ERICH (1968), *Historischer Materialismus und marxistische Soziologie*, Berlin: Dietz.

Hahn points to basic theoretical problems of historical-materialistic social research.

TOMBERG, FRIEDRICH (1974), *Basis und Überbau*, Darmstadt: Luchterhand.

The analysis of the relation of social, political, and intellectual processes and the corresponding mode of production is of central concern.

Problem-related

CHILDE, V. GORDON (1951), *Social Evolution*, New York: Schuman.

The author delivers a historical-materialistic interpretation of empirical trends of pre- and early history.

INSTITUT FÜR WELTWIRTSCHAFT UND INTERNATIONALE BEZIEHUNGEN DER AKADEMIE DER WISSENSCHAFTEN DER UdSSR (1972), *Politische Ökonomie des heutigen Monopolkapitalismus*, Frankfurt a.M.: Verlag Marxistischer Blätter.

Empirical trends in present capitalism are described and interpreted in great detail.

MANDEL, ERNEST (1978), *Late Capitalism*, London: NLB.

A detailed description and interpretation of empirical trends in present capitalism is presented.

MARX, KARL (1968), 'Das Kapital,' *Marx-Engels-Werke*, vols 23–5, Berlin: Dietz.

This is the breviary of any Marxist oriented analysis of the economic system of capitalist societies.

SELLNOW, IRMGARD (1961), *Grundprinzipien der Periodisierung der Urgeschichte*, Berlin: Akademie-Verlag.

The author attempts a systematic theory of prehistoric development.

SOFRI, GIANNI (1969), *Über asiatische Produktionsweise*, Frankfurt a.M.: Europäische Verlagsanstalt.

This study gives a detailed account of the discussion on pre-capitalist class societies in general and the Asian mode of production in particular.

SWEEZY, PAUL M. (1956), *The Theory of Capitalist Development*, New York: Monthly Review.

This is perhaps the most systematic explanation of the Marxist theory of the capitalist mode of production.

4 The structural-functional theory of social change

Hermann Strasser

4.1 Prologue to a functional analysis of change

We consider the structural-functional approach to the study of social change the most prominent one with respect to its dissemination among sociologists and social anthropologists as well as the empirical and theoretical results that it produced.[1] Its ascent to prominence has been accompanied by normative and methodological considerations, on the one hand, and conceptual refinements, on the other.

Most social theorists at the turn of the century developed their conceptual and analytical schemes out of an experience of a national culture as the examples of Spencer, Durkheim, Weber, Pareto, Tönnies, Spengler, Radcliffe-Brown and others demonstrate. As a consequence, they often ignored relevant intellectual developments in other countries. However, they all seem to have tacitly attributed great importance to the facts of change in the sense that only a theory of society that was capable of explaining large-scale transformation and movement as well as small-scale variation and change in social life could claim to be scientifically adequate. Moreover, they were convinced that it was possible to order the array of observable changes in history into a single, i.e., coherent, conceptual framework and to provide a unified theory of all social change (cf. Smith, 1973: 1).

The only internationally effective social theory then was Marxism, which offered such a theory of social *development* by picturing 'the modern world system' (Wallerstein, 1974) of capitalism as carrying the seeds of its own destruction. In that Marxists conceived of social reality as process they aimed at understanding, explaining *and* producing social development. The key to

THE STRUCTURAL-FUNCTIONAL THEORY

their dynamic conception of the 'unity of theory and practice' was the notion of social class. Moreover, the Russian Revolution heightened the anxieties in Europe and North America, and with the Great Depression of the 1930s the popularity of Marxist social theory rose among intellectuals and ordinary people on both sides of the Atlantic.

Especially in the US, therefore, the pressure mounted to develop theoretical alternatives to Marxism (cf. Parsons, 1970). However, it was reserved to Talcott Parsons (1) to assimilate the thus far nationally fragmented outlines of European social theory within the framework of an American structure of sentiments and assumptions (cf. Gouldner, 1970: 148); and (2) to oppose materialistic determinism and the Marxist emphasis on the variability of property and power arrangements in generating further development of society. In this double effort, Parsons's thesis of the convergent drift toward a voluntaristic social theory was also meant to provide an answer to the social disorganization and demoralization caused by the Great Depression (cf. Strasser, 1976: Chapter 6.2).[2] Beyond that, Parsonian functionalism must be considered the heir of a tradition of studies on social change that assumed the feasibility and desirability of a single theory of change (Parsons, 1961). Although Parsons, as we shall try to demonstrate in later sections, does admit that change is ubiquitous, he tends to relegate – as a consequence of the kind of questions he considered to be central to sociological inquiry[3] – the study of change to a minor sociological preoccupation (cf. Parsons, 1951: Chapter 11; 1954a). As functional analysis differs from non-functional analyses in the kind of questions it raises (cf. Kingsley Davis's Introduction to Goode, 1951: 17), it is not surprising that 'Most primary theoretical and methodological debates in post war social science have centered on functionalism and alternatives to it' (Martindale, 1965: ix).

In line with the main purpose of this volume to introduce the reader to the functional theory of social change, we shall be less concerned with the differences between variations of the functionalist approach (e.g., cf. Sztompka, 1974; Demerath and Peterson, 1967). Rather, the functional analysis of social change is taken as a more or less single theoretical stance in that we concentrate, though by far not exclusively, on the theoretical position of its most outstanding representative, Talcott Parsons. Such a procedure permits us to survey and evaluate the functionalist approach in its entirety and to familiarize the student with a comprehensive system of describing and explaining social change.

In order to render the structural-functional approach to change phenomena a worthwhile learning experience, we suggest to test the following *working hypothesis*: A social theory based on the concepts of order, equilibrium, and integration is unrealistic; two facts make it so: conflict and change. This statement seems to imply three distinct, though interrelated, questions: (1) What are the elements of an order vocabulary of social explanation upon which a theory of society may be based? (2) How does such a theory of society deal with conflict and change? (3) What are the criteria according to which sociological concepts are judged as adequate or inadequate, realistic or unrealistic?

In order to get to the core of the matter, we will first present a detailed account of the assumptions, postulates, concepts, and hypotheses, which constitute functional analysis. The concept of order will be used to refer to an image of society as a system of action unified by a shared culture or common value system and as a functionally integrated *system*, which is held in equilibrium by certain recurrent processes. The notion of functional analysis will be taken as focusing on society as 'a systemic whole with constituent parts in search of a mutually adjusted equilibrium' (Demerath and Peterson, 1967: 2). In the context of this study, therefore, the order or integration vocabulary of social explanation will be regarded as a substantive requisite for functional analysis and as synonymous with equilibrium theory with respect to the study of change phenomena.

4.2 The logic of functionalism

The aim of the present section is to define the concepts of order, integration, and differentiation, to discuss their role within the vocabulary of social explanation considered central to functional analysis, and, finally, to provide a methodo-logical base for the assessment of their heuristic value in subsequent sections. As suggested before, functionalism should be regarded as a theory and research strategy that is guided by certain heuristic maxims or working hypotheses which guide actual research by asking distinctive questions.

A model or vocabulary of explanation is usually considered as consisting of a set of propositions which are logically connected with one another. These propositions are not assumed to be reflecting the facts within an area of inquiry; rather, they are assumed 'because they refer to facts which are considered similar to those studied within an area of discourse' (Isajiw, 1968: 115). May Brodbeck (1959: 374) has termed the similarity between the elements of the model and the elements of that area of knowledge of which it is a model as isomorphism. In the study of social phenomena, the isomorphism of laws (e.g., in physiology and sociology) is not at all a symmetrical one; that is, most of the models of society were taken over from the natural sciences, from areas about which there was already a good deal known. Since grounded knowledge in sociology has always been scarce, it is not surprising therefore that it has witnessed an influx of speculative models or guesses about isomorphisms. These analogical as well as other 'domain assumptions'[4] largely make up scientific models of society and provide a 'general image of the main outline of some major phenomenon, including certain leading ideas about the nature of the units involved and the patterns of their relations' (Inkeles, 1964: 28).

4.2.1 The use of the organismic model and its consequences

Historically speaking, the concept of order is derived from an organic analogy. Its most important manifestation can be seen in the interrelated concepts of structure and function, which figure prominently in the works of Spencer, Durkheim, Malinowski, Radcliffe-Brown, and Parsons and his followers.

As we shall see later in this study, it is the idea of an 'organismic' system assumed by functionalism that makes it distinct from other forms of explanation in sociology. Social science literature has come up with two outstanding types of theoretical explanation, that of methodological individualism and that of methodological collectivism such as functionalism (cf. Nagel, 1961: 520ff.). The former places the focus of determinacy, that is the area in which a proper *explanans* of some *explanadum* can be found, in the social-psychological realm as theories of social behaviorism and symbolic interactionism do. Functionalism, by contrast, attempts to place the focus of determinacy in the attributes of collectivities. Not only is the focus of determinacy placed in the attributes of collective entities rather than individuals, but a functional explanation also implies the assumption that systems of relations between human actors, in their own right, are capable of exercising a determining influence upon their behavior (cf. Isajiw, 1968: 6). It is this form of holism derived from physiology that became central to the structural-functional approach.

Alfred R. Radcliffe-Brown (1952: 178–9) explicitly invoked the analogy between organism and society by tracing their main points of similarity in that both

1   represent an integrated whole;
2   maintain a certain structural continuity in the face of transformations at the level of their parts; and
3   imply internal processes that fulfill specific functions.

Each one of these properties of organic life corresponds to a particular concept that is also at the center of traditional functionalism:

1   *interdependence* referring to the linkages among social actors and social relations that make up a social structure;
2   *equilibrium* referring to the continued attempt to preserve social-structural stability through such self-regulatory mechanisms as socialization and social control; and
3   *differentiation* referring to the process and the outcome of the institutionalization of social roles and organizations performing certain functions in society.

Radcliffe-Brown (1935: 396) clearly states:

> To turn from organic life to social life, if we examine such a community as an African or Australian tribe we can recognize the existence of a social structure. Individual human beings, the essential units in this instance, are connected by a definite set of social relations into an integrated whole. The continuity of the social structure, like that of an organic structure, is not destroyed by changes in the units. Individuals may leave the society, by death or otherwise; others may enter it. The continuity of structure is maintained by the process of social life, which consists of the activities and interactions of the individual human beings and of the organized groups into which they are united. The social life of the community is here defined as the functioning of the social structure. The functions of any recurrent activity, such as the punishment of a crime, or a funeral ceremony, is the part it plays in the social life as a whole and therefore the contribution it makes to the maintenance of the structural continuity.

Accordingly, the analysis of the functions of various behavior patterns or cultural items in relation to the total social system to which they belong should yield two crucial tasks of a science of society, namely, to show how social systems *perpetuate* themselves by maintaining their structural form, and how social systems *change* by adjusting their structure (Radcliffe-Brown, 1957: Part 2; cf. also Nagel, 1961: 520–2). Radcliffe-Brown holds that any activity or cultural item may be regarded as explained when it is demonstrated that it has the effect of maintaining the social structure. Moreover, he says, while in animal organisms the organic structure can be observed to some extent independently of its operation, 'in human society the social structure as a whole can only be observed in its functioning' (Radcliffe-Brown, 1952: 180). Whereas in biology the study of evolution can build upon structural analysis, social structure can often only be recognized after an analysis of the change of structural forms has been carried out (cf. Dahrendorf, 1959a: 127; Rex, 1961: 63–5). Thus, the social structure is defined in terms of activities and the effect of these activities on such units as individuals and groups. At this point it is important to mention another element in biological organisms that is not in a one-to-one correspondence with social organisms. While in healthy biological organisms the activities of the organs and units are practically identical with those which have the effect of maintaining the life of the organism, in social organisms people do things invoking the cooperation or opposition of other people, although these activities do not necessarily maintain the social structure. The organismic model is therefore at best useful in explanations of *some* human actions.

In other words, an uncritical use of the organic analogy may be detrimental to the explanatory purpose in social science.

1 As Sztompka (1974: 50–2) correctly notes, the first danger is that of *reification* when the methodological purpose of comparing society to an organism (as a guide for further inquiry) is turned into an ontological claim that society *is* an organism (cf. also Collins, 1975: 93; Beattie, 1964: 56).

2 A second, more subtle danger consists in stressing only points of (relative) convergence between organic and social systems at the expense of recognizing fundamental differences and dissimilarities. (a) First of all, the *properties* of the respective elements or elementary processes are fundamentally different as demonstrated by a comparison of organic cells with people, respiration with economic production, or blood with money. (b) The same is true with respect to the *structural* characteristics of organism as compared with society: The elements of an organic structure are as strongly integrated as their specialization is pronounced; by contrast, social systems are less integrated and their specialization of elements and processes is less marked. (c) Neither have the latter a central *control* agency as organisms do.

3 A third dissimilarity refers to the course of dynamic *changes* an organism takes as opposed to society: While an organism may undergo only internal changes such as growth, metabolism, or adaptation a society experiences more or less radical changes, be they of intra-systemic or extra-systemic origin.

These possible misapplications of organic analogy may also be taken as the major reason why a number of sociologists have reproached functionalism with having a static bias (e.g., Dahrendorf, 1968; Homans, 1971; Lockwood, 1964).

SELECTED THEORIES OF SOCIAL CHANGE

As pointed out earlier, theories of social change that are based on organic analogy – especially classic evolutionism and neo-evolutionism as well as tendencies within functionalism – have always tended to emphasize the human attempt to maximize control over a more or less adverse environment through the means of self-development and self-adjustment. That is to say, society as well as mankind is seen as evolving through the stages of increasing control over, and adjustment to, the environment, both physical and social.[5] Two points should be emphasized here. On the one hand, common premises such as immanent sources of change, differentiation, and genetic continuity testify to the affinity between organicism and functionalism with respect to the analysis of *both* structure and change. On the other hand, these considerations must not blur one's view of the fact that organic changes have a cyclical character whose starting and terminal points can easily be specified, while social changes do have a directive and, to a considerable extent, irreversible character which mostly lack any definite beginning as well as any conceivable end (Sztompka, 1974: 52). Undoubtedly, the neglect of this fundamental difference has led to the factual and alleged *ahistoric* bias of some trends of contemporary functionalism (e.g., Dahrendorf, 1968: 107).

As stated earlier, the term function is used by Radcliffe-Brown to signify the contributions an item makes toward the maintenance of a certain state of the social system. This meaning of function points to the crucial problem of *survival* or paramount purpose of the organism which has given rise to an elaborate discussion on the 'functional prerequisites of a society' (e.g., Aberle *et al.*, 1950; Parsons, 1961; Parsons and Smelser, 1956; Merton, 1968). However, Radcliffe-Brown himself recognized that the endeavor in sociology to prove that certain processes were necessary for societal survival was doubtful, even though such a demonstration was possible in biology. He made it clear that societies do not cease to exist as physical organisms do; rather, they become different societies, i.e., they change their structural type. Thus, the concept of function takes on a problematic significance. If it cannot demonstrate the fact of structural change as clearly as the facts of death or illness, it would be difficult to assign to it any significance with respect to 'survival value' or 'vital importance.'[6] This not only forecasts a shadow on Parsons's and others' 'functional prerequisites,' but also questions the distinction between 'normal change' and 'structural change' (cf. Parsons, 1951: 480ff.; Parsons, 1961: 70ff.).

Early functionalists such as Radcliffe-Brown and Bronislaw Malinowski shared the notion of social change as change of structures and functions. In the case of Malinowski (1969) this meant that institutions change while they take care of unchanging needs. Just as function is seen as fulfillment of needs, so new cultural elements may lead to 'positive' social developments and social disorganizations to 'negative' social changes that result from doing away with old institutions without replacing them by new ones, thus leaving certain 'basic needs' unfulfilled.

Both Malinowski (who traced functions to natural human needs) and Radcliffe-Brown (who distinguished between functions and functional prerequisites and saw functions as elements of an integrated system whose parts are interdependent) were taken to task by Robert K. Merton (1968: 79–91) who was able to show that the postulates of 'universal functionalism,' 'functional unity' and 'indispensability' of each element for the social whole only deflects (functional) analysis from taking into consideration the relationships among the elements of social action. To put it differently: Since it is assumed that some higher unit of reference exists, the analysis of conflict and change on all levels of societal organization is obstructed (Touraine, 1974: 38; Hempel, 1959). However, these classic functionalists seem to suggest a distinction between *social* change that refers to altering structural elements (Radcliffe-Brown) and *societal* change that implies changing functional prerequisites (Malinowski). Both authors work with the idea of some state of equilibrium for the maintenance of which each element of the system has specifiable functions. Elements are considered to be exchangeable so long as the new element has the same function. On the one hand, a system whose elements are always related to the same functions presupposes permanent change (cf. Luhmann's (1972) equivalence functionalism). On the other hand, the system remains identical with itself so long as the functions in the system must be preserved (cf. Parsons's (1961) functional imperativism). Here, change is automatic; it lies within the system, i.e., inseparable from the idea of the system as defined by its interdependent parts – the very interdependence that produces change.

In the light of various community studies this also calls for a reassessment of the concept of dysfunctionality. From studies such as those by Frank and Ruth Young (1962) about patterns of community growth, by Edward Spicer (1952) on the impact of technology on primitive communities, and Robert Redfield's (1930) and Oscar Lewis's (1951) study of the Mexican village Tepoztlán, to name a few, we can infer that whenever certain traditional activities have been displaced because of contact with more articulated structures, their displacement has led to a period of rapid change and extensive instability in these and other areas. Assuming that the particular social system was in fact stable in the pre-contact period, we may even speak of the displaced activities 'as having had a function in promoting the survival of the earlier structural type' (Rex, 1961: 71). Obviously, it would not make much sense to regard such a change in the pattern of social actions as necessarily dysfunctional. Dysfunctional for whom? Too often, social scientists, anthropologists in particular, have seen change negatively by contrasting the new social pattern with the old one – the traditional pattern representing the 'healthy' social organism.

Merton (1968: 106) also insists that some concept of the needs of the system is vital to sociological analysis, and he is at great pains to establish such needs objectively. As John Rex (1961: 73) has remarked, Merton's actual cases of 'latent functions' seem 'to refer quite definitely not to the needs of the system but to the purpose of groups of individuals.'[7]

The point is that functional statements can be regarded as appropriate only in connection with systems possessing self-maintaining mechanisms for certain of their traits. They seem to be pointless or even misleading, particularly in view of a general theory of change, 'when used with reference to systems lacking such self-regulatory devices' (Nagel, 1956: 251–2). The systemic model of society turns out to be the core of functionalism on which the use of the organic analogy had important methodological, conceptual, and ideological bearings. However, this is not to deny that as early functional analysis was applied to isolated, often regionally limited, mostly primitive communities, the organic analogy worked well in spite of its static, ahistoric, and at times teleological, bias.

4.2.2 Dynamic analysis

We have seen that social scientists who used the organic analogy were led to posit a structural and processual similarity between society and an exemplar of a system, the biological organism. By assuming that the function of any *recurrent* (physiological/social) process implies a correspondence between it and the needs (i.e., the necessary conditions for existence) of the (organic/social) system under consideration (Radcliffe-Brown, 1952: 179), these authors attributed to its elements 'survival value' for the particular system. To put it differently: As systems change through time, relevant patterns of action or forms of social organization are selected and persist, while dysfunctional patterns are dropped. Only in the sense that such a selective process of functionalization was conceived of taking place over a considerable period of time, this type of functional theory became a dynamic one (Moore, 1963: 9). As

THE STRUCTURAL-FUNCTIONAL THEORY

indicated above, the idea of survival led functionalism to an elaborate attempt to identify the 'functional prerequisites' of any society (Aberle *et al.*, 1950; Parsons, 1951; Parsons and Smelser, 1956; Levy, 1952). They will be further discussed later in this chapter.

All types of functional analysis agree to treat 'the *consequences* of some behavior or social arrangement' as 'essential elements of the *causes* of that behavior' (Stinchcombe, 1968: 80). Since social phenomena tend to exhibit the characteristic of 'equifinality' (Heider, 1958), namely, that there is usually a number of means rather than only one by which to reach the same end, we concur with Stinchcombe (1968: 80; emphasis in the original) that, 'Whenever we find *uniformity of the consequences* of action but *great variety of the behavior causing those consequences*, a functional explanation in which the consequence serves as a cause is suggested.'

The postulate to treat social phenomena as dynamically *interdependent* variables, which Parsons referred to in his discussion of the 'dynamic interest of theory' that would result in 'dynamic knowledge,' directs our attention to the central concern of functionalism:

> The essential feature of dynamic analysis in the fullest sense is the treatment of a body of *interdependent* phenomena simultaneously, in the mathematical sense. The simplest case is the analysis of the effect of variation in one antecedent factor, but this ignores the reciprocal effect of these changes on this factor (Parsons, 1954a: 215–16; emphasis in the original).

Functionalism's foremost representatives, Parsons and Merton, seem to agree that in the present state of the sociological discipline 'dynamic analysis in the fullest sense' could not be realized and that structural-functional theory is the best substitute for dynamic analysis (cf. Parsons, 1954a: 216–17; 1951: 20; Merton, 1968: 75–6). Merton (1968: 75) notes that the ideal, dynamic, conception has been expressed in a more extended but also less precise form by such notions as 'functional interdependence,' 'mutually dependent variations,' and 'functional relations.' However, Parsons's major concern with functional theory lies on an analytical level different from that of Merton. As indicated, he offers an analysis that views all social phenomena as variables of one all-inclusive (and empirical) system. Merton (1968: 55ff.), on the other hand, is preoccupied with specifications of functional analysis in order to employ it in empirical research. He focuses on 'the practice of interpreting data by establishing their consequences for larger structures in which they are implicated' (Merton, 1968: 101).

Despite Merton's exercised theoretical restraint with respect to *systemic* assumptions, his theoretical position is no less questionable.

For Parsons, who stresses the systemic reference point and hence the explanatory power of systemically imposed imperatives, it is the most essential condition of successful dynamic analysis to refer continually and systematically 'every problem to the state of the system as a whole' (Parsons, 1954a: 216). Parsons constructs his alternative to the ideal of dynamic analysis in terms of three analytical steps. First, one treats groups of interrelated variables as *structural* categories, that is, as constants, in order to reduce the complexity of interdependent factors (e.g., the institutionalized order of norms and values). In other words, these categories are not derived from other variables, but independently defined, and may thus provide adequate description of the empirical social system, although *stable* structures cannot be proven empirically.

In a second step, once these structural categories are defined they must be linked to the variable elements of the system. This is done by establishing the relevance of the structural categories to the total social system by employing the concept of *function*. Thus, Parsons's concept of function, closely related to that of Radcliffe-Brown, serves to provide a criterion for determining the importance of dynamic factors and processes within a given system. The functional relevance of some socio-cultural item (e.g., event, institution) will be found in the differential consequences for the total social system: maintaining its stability or producing change in it, promoting integration and order or disruption and change of the system in some sense. It is the assessment of systemic relevance from which the notion of functional analysis is derived.

According to Parsons, functional analysis would not be complete if it did not, in a third step, include a set of '*dynamic* functional categories.' They 'must describe processes by which these particular structures are maintained or upset, and the relations of the system to its environment are mediated' (Parsons, 1954a: 218). On this analytical level the problem of explaining social change is supposedly taken care of.[8]

What Parsons's dynamic analysis amounts to is the assumption

1 that some *preferred state* of a given system is defined in terms of a particular configuration of elements and their interrelationships (e.g., a common normative structure that is properly internalized by members of a given society);
2 that this particular structure of the system tends to be preserved by *self-regulatory mechanisms* which, so to speak,

automatically counteract deviations from that structure arising from extra-systemic sources (e.g., socialization and social control operating by means of various types of sanctions).

Of course, it is true that within Parsonian functionalism the tendency to preserve a given structure of the system (or at least to establish and stabilize some normative order) is very generally expressed in the concept of equilibrium' (Parsons and Shils, 1951: 180). It is also important to keep in mind that interdependent relations between the elements of a social system can only be conceptualized if it is assumed that social mechanisms operate to guarantee the systemness and functioning of action systems of any kind. This therefore suggests that the analysis of change *in* and *of* systems cannot be separated from a study of equilibrium states and equilibrating mechanisms, of the integration of roles within personality systems, the formation of consensus within collectivities, and the organization of cultural orientation systems. In short, the reproach against functionalism to focus on equilibrium, stability, and integration at the expense of conflict and change would be justified only if it claimed to be capable of coming to grips with social reality in its totality (Touraine, 1974: 39; Dahrendorf, 1958: 175).

What we have just said does not invalidate another critique, however. In that functional analysis places emphasis on the interdependence of a system's parts and their role in producing change, it seems to have the (desired) effect of excluding the randomness of change sources located outside the system. It thus renders change *automatic* and the idea of the *system* inseparably tied to the idea of *change* produced by its (definitional) property of *interdependency*. In other words, change can be deduced from the properties of *any* system (Smith, 1973: 155; cf. e.g., Parsons, 1951: 177–8). Furthermore, the self-regulating mechanism is said to take effect with respect to the system's (changing) preferred state whenever changes occur in the system's environment or inside the system that alter the relation of the system to its environment. With the assumption of a moving equilibrium or even an eternal disequilibrium, functional analysis comes close to accepting Nisbet's (1969: 236) and Eisenstadt's (1964a: 235) postulate that change is inherent in all social systems 'because of basic problems to which there is no overall continuous solution. These problems include uncertainties of socialization, perennial scarcity of resources relative to individual aspirations, and contrasting types of social organization (e.g., *Gemeinschaft vs Gesellschaft*) within the society' (Eisenstadt, 1964a: 245). It is true that functionalists had more often than not dismissed the research implications of such a postulate as residual – in spite of Parsons's (1951: 552) claim that 'There are serious strains and inconsistencies in the value-implementation of any complex social system.'

In conclusion we may state that the crucial problem with dynamic functional analysis is that it deals with internal disturbances and outside pressures for change in terms of a given system's *response* to them without regard to the transition between equilibrium states or to 'the influences generated by the actual process of readjustment to a new equilibrium state upon the nature of that state' (Smith, 1973: 137). Its central question to be answered does not so much concern the source, the timing, and the intensity of change as the extent to which it penetrates the system, i.e., how change affects the movement of the presupposed equilibrium system and its various components (cf. Dahrendorf, 1958; Rex, 1961: 131–5; Cohen, 1968: 172–207, especially 191–4).

4.2.3 The concepts of system, functional equivalence, and functional autonomy

4.2.3.1 Normative and factual aspects of system analysis

In a now famous presidential address, Kingsley Davis (1959) has gone so far as to deny that functionalism is any *special* methodology or theoretical approach in sociology. He contends that social scientists in general and sociologists in particular use much the same analytical framework. Davis holds that any scientific discipline assumes 'a *system* of reasoning which presumably bears a relation to a corresponding *system* in nature,' and goes on to ask:

> How else can data be interpreted except in relation to the larger structures *in which they are implicated*? How can data on the earth's orbit, for example, be understood except in relation to a system in which they are involved – in this case, the solar system or the earth's climatic system? Since in science some kind of system is being dealt with, an analysis of the effect of one factor must always be made with the possibility in mind of a possible return effect ('feedback') on that factor itself. If, for example, the increase of fish (y) in a pond has the effect of increasing the toxicity (x) of the water, the growth of the fish population (y again) will eventually cease unless other factors intervene. This is not explaining things solely by their consequences, but rather by the way their consequences react upon them (Davis, 1959: 759).

To be sure, all science studies the relation of parts to some systemic whole. However, this does not mean that all science follows the same procedure as functionalism, especially not since there are different *types* of systems.[9] This chapter primarily purports to show that functionalism is not a myth, which will be dispelled with time, as Davis believes, 'but an important though fragmentary approach to social reality' (van den Berghe, 1963: 696).

Let us return for a moment to the divergent conceptions of functionalism in Parsons and Merton. We have documented that Merton's orientation is to interpret data 'by establishing their consequences for larger structures,' while Parsons considers the 'systematic reference of every problem to the state of the system as a whole' to be of central importance. That is to say, Parsons places great emphasis on the notion of 'system,' while Merton directs our attention to 'units' or 'items' and avoids explicit use of the system concept. While Merton adapts a 'strategy of minimal commitment,' Parsons seems to be maximally committed to a system model (Gouldner, 1959: 243). However, the two leading functionalists agree to explain any social pattern or item only in the context it occurs, that is, to analyze it in its relation to other patterns.

In order to understand the analysis of change in functional terms, it is important to keep in mind Parsons's assumption that 'the *whole* system must be conceptually constituted prior to the investigation and analysis of specific patterns' (Gouldner, 1959: 244–5). Traditional functionalism defined the social system in analogical, mostly organic, terms; modern functionalism, on the other hand, uses the method of abstraction in the sense of explicitly stating 'the most generalized dimensions in terms of which systems, formally construed, may vary and then to stipulate the conjunction of formal system dimensions which are to be applied to social behavior' (Gouldner, 1959: 242). The adoption of the systemic frame of reference seems to indicate that 'in the last resort we must think in terms of elements in mutual interaction' (von Bertalanffy, 1968: 45).

Unlike traditional functionalism's imagination of global societies as social organism, modern functionalism uses the system concept not only to describe global societies and less inclusive entities such as social groups and communities, but also to identify networks of social relations such as the economy and the polity or different types of action systems such as culture, society, and personality. Although the distinction between macrofunctionalism and microfunctionalism has been introduced to denote the different reference systems (cf. Martindale, 1960), contemporary functionalism is nevertheless left with the problem of reproach of employing the system concept as an analytical, and often merely as a classificatory, instrument rather than as a theoretical representation of some empirical entity based on theoretically deduced problems and hypothetically formulated explanations. Functionalists have indeed dealt with social systems almost exclusively on an analytical level focusing on variables, relations, roles, statuses, subsystems, etc., rather than in concrete terms such as people, their interactions, collectivities, groups, classes, needs, and the like (Sztompka, 1974: 54).

Thus, functionalists have maneuvered themselves too often into a scientific dilemma by converting the methodological necessity of employing the system concept into a theoretical virtue, supposedly resulting in social knowledge with immediate empirical reference. The failure to distinguish between the analytical and the concrete level in the study of social systems is closely linked with the functionalists' tendency to focus on normative (consensual) elements at the expense of factual (coercive) power elements. Norms and power are not understood as alternative modes of institutionalizing social relationships, but rather society is viewed as consisting of social institutions primarily defined as moral entities, thus resulting in an emphatic emphasis on common value elements in an attempt to explain the integration of social actions.[10] However, Merton did draw attention to the ubiquitous tension between consensual and coercive elements of the social structure as well as to the ever-present possibility of the use of power to maintain institutions and of the deinstitutionalization of power:

> It is not enough to refer to 'the institutions' as though they were all uniformly supported by all groups and strata in the society. Unless systematic consideration is given the *degree* of support of particular 'institutions' by *specific* groups, we shall overlook the important place of power in society. To speak of 'legitimate power' or authority is often to use an elliptical and misleading phrase. Power may be legitimized for *some* without being legitimized for *all* groups in a society. It may, therefore, be misleading to describe non-conformity with *particular* social institutions merely as deviant behavior; it may represent the beginning of a new alternative pattern, with its own distinctive claims to moral validity (Merton, 1968: 176; emphasis in the original).

The postulate inspired by the natural sciences to qualify causally any function as an effect to be effected is obviously linked with the idea that functionalists seek to study invariant relationships between definitive causes and definitive effects where equivalent or at least alternative possibilities to produce functional contributions cannot be excluded (Luhmann, 1971a: 13). Functionalists like

Niklas Luhmann, partially following Merton (1968: 87–8, 106), regard the concept of functional equivalence as

> the key for detaching functionalism from the causal method. Function is not an effect to be effected but a meaning scheme which sets up a scope of comparison for equivalent contributions. It denotes a specific point of view on the basis of which various possibilities may be grasped under a single aspect. From this point of view, then, the various contributions appear to be equivalent, mutually exchangeable, and fungible, while they are not comparable as concrete processes (Luhmann, 1971a: 14).

In other words, this so-called *equivalence functionalism* purports to find the functional equivalence 'of several possible causes under the aspect of a problematic effect' (Luhmann, 1971a: 14). Such a limited scope of comparison depends, of course, upon the definition of the functional point of reference. Not the invariant relationship between a cause *and* an effect is the focal point but rather the invariance of a cause *or* an effect. That is to say, the effect as the problem of reference may be directed to some area of causes as much as the cause whose justification is seen as problematic may be referred to an area of effects. For example, the problem of stabilizing behavioral expectations can be solved in the course of time through recurrent experiences as well as socially through consensus. The expectational consensus, in turn, may be achieved, say, either through institutionalization of role expectations or through leadership. Finally, authoritative leadership may be taken as problematic and achieved in different ways (e.g., through personal prestige, expertise, office). In order to establish functional equivalences, the relation of several causes or several effects, respectively, must be analyzed under the relevant point of reference. The point of reference of Luhmann's equivalence functionalism is no longer the traditional problem of survival or the prerequisites of an action system's existence, but rather it is concerned with those crucial aspects of a given action system where functional equivalences become visible. That is to say, those problem areas are at stake that reveal the possibilities of a system's variation on different levels. Such points of reference as the function of authority and the equivalent possibilities to stabilize authority, of course, do not explain why certain functional contributions do occur. Rather, they point to possibilities of change; to possible paths of historical development, say, of a social system and their feedback effects on the various system levels.

Such a look at the problem does produce intriguing perspectives with respect to the analysis of social change. However, under methodological auspices the question must be raised whether the transformation of the old survival problem into a series of questions is apt to really overcome the functionalist approach as represented by Parsons and Merton. It is true that the latter have usually assumed that a latent causality operates in social life, which is to say that the function of an action, event or institution – defined as effect – feeds back to the initial conditions. However, such an assumption does consider, at least implicitly, functional alternatives. In that Luhmann attempts to operationalize the survival problem, he seems to dislocate it only: The idea of the functional point of reference includes that of the functional prerequisite, even though the empirically given strategy to cope with the problem represents only one of several possibilities to furnish functional contributions. The progress of Parsons and Merton in comparison with the early functionalists consisted precisely in linking the functional reference problems with institutional–cultural solutions *via* the method of comparison of functional alternatives. At any rate, they recanted, in different ways though, the evolutionary principle that all institutions or actions in a society produced functional contributions and were functionally necessary for all parts of the system (cf. Merton, 1968; Parsons, 1951; 1971).

For the present purpose it suffices to say that functionalists have tended to ignore the propensity to social conflict and change that arises from some degree of *functional incompatibility* between institutional patterns (the defining characteristics of relevant parts of a social system) and their factual substructure facilitating social relationships which, if actualized, would threaten the existing institutional order. To put it simply: While the *legitimation* of authority as institutionalized power takes the form of general principles, *acts* of authority are always specific. In the words of Lockwood (1964: 247n.), 'authority is never given, but is always contingent upon its exercise.' Functionalists, in other words, are more concerned with the theme of norms–consensus–order, i.e., the moral aspects of social integration, rather than with the possible lack of fit between the (normative) presence or absence of a claim to legitimacy and the (factual) sentiments of those who are subject to authority and who suggest the theme of power–alienation–conflict as a sociological alternative (cf. Parsons, 1960: 173; Lockwood, 1964: 136; Solloway and Strasser, 1977; Marwedel, 1976).

Undoubtedly, most functionalists have indulged in focusing on the normative mechanism of social integration. Lockwood's (1956) reproach against Parsons that there is no place for the 'factual substratum' of social structures in the latter's systemic model of society is, considering the former's premises, justified. Lockwood's answer to the question of where one finds the *real* authority relations in such a conception is worth mentioning; The cultural system may provide norms that limit the exercise of power; however, in Parsons's view the exercise of power appears as a social mechanism designed to guarantee a minimum of functional harmony (cf. e.g., Parsons, 1961: 60–79). The lack of fit between the normative realm and the factual substratum, between the strategies of social integration and system integration, point to the question of how functional analysis takes into account the antagonistic tendencies prevalent in any society, namely, that its parts strive for autonomy while they must be integrated as well.

4.2.3.2 *System integration and functional autonomy*

As we have seen earlier, the concept of system implies the notion of interdependence, which, in turn, refers to three aspects of the very definition of a social system. To assume systematic interdependence means, first of all, that there are parts of the system engaged in mutual exchanges. Secondly, if each element is interrelated with all the others, no element can in principle exist outside the system (cf. Parsons and Shils, 1951: 107). However, the idea that each element of a social system is related to every other element seems to be the exception rather than the rule. In other words, thirdly, the notion of interdependence implies the principle of reciprocity as the type of interrelation is left unspecified. This leads to the further assumption that the exchanges and interactions among system parts, be they individuals, groups, or institutions, are symmetrical and hence equitable (cf., e.g., Malinowski, 1926: 46; Lenski, 1966: Chapter 3).

There can be no doubt that a certain degree of reciprocity is a precondition of any society's persistence:

> Any one structure is more likely to persist if it is engaged in reciprocally functional interchanges with some others; . . . the less reciprocal the functional interchange between structures, the less likely is either structure, or the patterned relation between them, to persist, . . . *unless compensatory mechanisms are present* (Gouldner, 1959: 249; emphasis in the original).

A number of compensatory mechanisms are conceivable to create social imbalances, for instance, various kinds of social norms that sanction unequal exchanges (cf. Randall and Strasser, 1976a: Chapters 3 and 4) and power arrangements that may compel continued extraction of services for which there is little functional reciprocity (Gouldner, 1959: 249–50). Given the universality of norms and power differentials, we may state that only a part of the relationships and exchange processes in a social system is of a symmetrical nature. Furthermore, in complex social systems there is 'generalized exchange' to a considerable extent, that is, indirect exchange in the sense that A fulfills the needs of B, B those of C and C those of A, etc. Since we cannot assume symmetrical exchange and complete interdependence in social life, functional analysis is confronted with the task of finding out which element is connected with which other element(s) with respect to which function (Bühl, 1975: 24).

The concept of functional reciprocity, nay, of varying degrees of reciprocity and functional autonomy also conveys the idea that it is not sufficient to provide an explanation of the persistence of some social phenomenon in terms of its consequences for the larger structures in which it is implicated. For instance, in his analysis of the latent functions of political machinery in the United States, Merton (1968: 126-36) failed to trace explicitly 'the manner in which the groups or structures, whose needs have been satisfied, in turn "reciprocate" and repay the political machine for the gains it provides them' (Gouldner, 1959: 249). To cite yet another example, a functional analysis of, say, the system of higher education requires, to be complete, to uncover not only the consequences of what universities (A) do for the state, society, or some specific group (B), but also in what way the state (B) reciprocates the university system (A) (e.g., the state grants self-governing mechanisms to universities such as self-recruitment, some degree of financial autonomy, publicity). This shows that functional analysis must not cease before it has attempted to establish empirically the reciprocal functionality; only then it conceives of the parts of the system as existing in and for themselves and not merely in their system character.

We may therefore postulate that the notion of interdependence of the parts of the social system which is so central to the system approach, must be taken as problematic rather than as given. From the principle of reciprocity may be inferred that there are varying degrees of interdependence among the parts of a social system. Consequently, 'if there are degrees of *inter*dependence, there must also be degrees of *in*dependence or functional autonomy' (Gouldner, 1970: 226). Society as an ongoing concern presupposes system parts with relative functional autonomy as much as most system parts need to be integrated, to some extent, into the whole system, if they are likely to realize their objectives. Otherwise there would only be possible annihilation or total structural change.

In the light of the fact that different system parts contribute differently to any (goal) state of the system and hence both to changes and to the stabilization of the system, Parsons's stress on the 'web of interdependence' ('everything influences everything else') within the system comes close to substituting postulation for research. The problem of functional autonomy of the parts, as pointed out earlier, enters into the functional analysis of social systems when strain, tension, contradiction, or discrepancy between the component elements of the social and cultural structure have to be dealt with. Regardless of whether strains are dysfunctional for the existing social system or instrumental in leading to changes in that system, they always exert pressure for change, thus putting to test the more or less effective operation of social mechanisms for keeping these strains within limiting bounds (Merton, 1968: 176).[11]

The notion of functional autonomy, we have said, focuses not primarily on the 'whole' or on relations between parts, but rather on the parts themselves in spite of their relations to each other. However, inasmuch as integrative pressures are exerted by a system part (i.e., by the managerial element that identifies with the system and interprets requirements of the system for integration), these pressures lead not only to integration proper but also to the mobilization of power to maintain some measure of autonomy on the part of the system managers. In other words, these tendencies toward system integration are inherently geared toward *oligarchic* centralization which, in turn, threatens the autonomy of other parts of the system – thus generating opposition, conflict, and continued power reassessments (Gouldner, 1970: 216). By attending to the possibility that the mutual needs of the parts need not be, and most likely are not, symmetrical and that any part may be more *or* less dependent on another part of the social system, the concept of functional autonomy directs sociological analysis to social structures and developments that are productive of tensions.

Finally, there is yet another key element in the system concept that we should mention here. For structural-functional theory to have relevance, says Parsons (1951: 483), 'it must apply to a boundary-maintaining type of system,' that is, to a system in which the coexistence of counteracting forces results in a state of equilibrium. In this sense, Norbert Elias (1976, vol. 1: xxi) is correct when he notes that the Parsonian notion of social change refers to 'a state of transition between two normal states of changelessness produced by disturbances.' However, it is precisely these balanced states of the system(s) that are to be explained. They are explained by dwelling on the assumption that a social system not only tends to maintain its boundaries, but also that its self-regulative forces are apt to restore displaced equilibria (cf. Parsons and Smelser, 1956: 247–8; Merton, 1968: 176). For Parsons, it is the equilibrium assumption, that is to say, the system containing cultural patterns that tend to be maintained and have stabilizing effects on other social phenomena, from which functional analysis advances to the principle of determinacy or causality.[12]

Apart from the critique in terms of asymmetrical interdependence, reciprocation, and functional autonomy, Parsons's alleged multiple causation model, despite its claim that all social and cultural phenomena are generated by many factors rather than one, clearly attributes a paramount place to one variable: shared moral beliefs or value elements institutionalized in the social system and internalized by role players and designed to insure social integration through system equilibrium. In this respect, Parsons followed the tradition of Comte and Durkheim. Similar to Marx, his attention is fixed on establishing that certain elements within the social system have ultimate control over it.[13] The opposing arguments that in any society forces may operate to protect some measure of functional autonomy of system parts *and* to strive for more integration, gave rise to alternative ways of understanding and explaining social change: the functional approach and its more or less radical critiques.

4.2.4 Recapitulation

Before we go on to discuss the question of how a sociological theory based on the concepts of system, order, and integration deals with the problem and facts of social change, we should summarize the basic principles of the functional approach by deriving them from the logical and partly substantive consideration presented thus far:

1 Societies are seen as systems of *interdependent* parts.
2 A system is assumed to be self-maintaining and self-regulating, thus fundamentally in a state of *equilibrium*.
  (a) The different social forces are viewed as parts of a more or less integrated whole and hence explained in relation to the *integration* of the system, that is, as more or less contributing to it.
  (b) Social integration is achieved through *value consensus*, that is, through goals and principles which most members of a given social system agree on; this consensus is implemented through the mechanisms of institutionalization, socialization, and social control.
3 Accordingly, dysfunctions, *strains* and conflicts do exist, but

they tend to resolve 'themselves' or become 'institutionalized' in the long run.
4 Social *change* is generally conceived as occurring in a gradual and adjustive manner through differentiation and adaptation to extra-systemic pressures.

4.3 Functionalism and social change

4.3.1 Change without progress?

Social scientists have always sought to affirm their desires and succeed with their hopes by studying and becoming part of the forces and direction of the development of society up to their own time. In the nineteenth century they closely identified either with one of the rising industrial classes (bourgeoisie and workers) or, as in some cases, with the aristocratic–military elites whose power was steadily to subside. However, in the nineteenth century the bourgeoisie, and later the working class as well, still had *to struggle* for its rise to power which also meant that, to them, development, progress, and a better future represented not only hard facts but also an ideal of great *emotional* importance (Elias, 1976, I: xxxiii; Strasser, 1976: 7). Saint-Simon, Comte, Spencer, and Marx may be mentioned as notable examples of this kind of sociological theorizing.

In the course of the twentieth century, the bourgeois and laboring classes and their representatives have been able to establish themselves institutionally and ideologically as the dominant groups. As a consequence, one's nation, i.e., national consciousness, beside class ideals, began to play an increasing role as an ideal and supreme social value for the bourgeoisie and later also for the labor movement. When sociologists of the eighteenth and nineteenth centuries spoke of society, they meant 'civil society,' a human society that usually transcended all state limits. With the nation, organized within state boundaries, as the supreme value, more often than not replacing class ideals – once fought for, now attained, and to be defended in the future – it is no wonder that many sociologists of the twentieth century no longer envision a 'human society' beyond state boundaries but increasingly refer to the ideal image of a national state (Elias, 1976, I: xxxvi; cf., however, Luhmann, 1975a: 11–12).

Of course, a number of other external factors contributed to these developments in the study of social phenomena, which we cannot discuss here at length. Mention should be made of the fact that in eighteenth- and nineteenth-century sociology the study of social change was closely related to the ideal of progress; that is, in times when social progress was marked, although its pace was still slow and its scope limited. Although today more people seem to profit from the advancements in the sciences, in technology and medicine as well as from a rising standard of living to a much greater extent than ever before, for many people progress is no longer an ideal. One reason for dropping the idea of progress as an ideal and a concept may be seen in recurrent wars, the permanent danger of war, the threat of nuclear weapons, and in the worldwide disaster of technologically induced pollution and fear; another reason is the declining leadership role of the traditional industrial nations of the West along with the continuing population explosion and the persistent gap in material wealth between industrialized and developing countries. Rather, as industrial societies become increasingly complex, we observe a growing demand for functional analyses on organizational as well as societal levels. With the ascent of formal and substantive system analyses to political appreciation, the possibility of sudden and drastic changes has been increasingly swept under the methodological rug (cf. Bühl, 1975: 34; Gouldner, 1970: 362ff., 455ff.; Böhret, 1972). The exploration of functional requirements apparently replaces the scientific concern with progress and development.

4.3.2 The equilibrium theory of change

We have presented a few arguments to support the view that the functional approach 'was developed partly in reaction to the preoccupation of much nineteenth-century social inquiry with questions concerning the origins of social institutions' (Nagel, 1961: 520). There is also reason to believe that modern functionalism is in many ways the twentieth-century legacy of early evolutionary theory, among other things because of its receptiveness of the organic analogy, that is, organism being the paradigmatic case of a system (cf. Appelbaum, 1970: 131; Gouldner, 1959: 241). Functional system theory and evolutionary theory basically agree that social systems change as a consequence of altered requirements on the part of the system's environment, manifested in terms of adaptation of the system to that environment (Münch, 1973: 168; Luhmann, 1971a). The influence of the evolutionary idea in social theorizing about history and change remains considerable (Smith, 1973: Chapter 2). In order to examine further the thesis that the difference between much of modern functionalism and nineteenth-century evolutionism is primarily a matter of emphasis, we should now attend to the question of what the substance of this legacy is and who its heirs are.

4.3.2.1 The evolutionary legacy

According to Comte, Western civilization develops in an evolutionary way, that is to say, it progresses uniformly toward human perfection and thus changes continuously. He simply considered the laws of social change as a 'form of the great principle, which of the two great constituent elements of Positive Sociology – Order and Progress – makes the second the result and consequence of the first, according to the maxim: *Progress is the development of Order*' (Comte, 1875: 152). In his organic view of society, its structure of functional interdependence, and his analysis of the development and consequences of functional differentiation (Comte, 1875: 329ff.), he not only paved the way for Herbert Spencer and Emile Durkheim, but also for system theorists like Parsons and structuralists like Marion Levy.

Because of their emphasis on an ever-increasing societal complexity and interrelatedness, Spencer and Durkheim can be classified as major contributors to the evolutionary legacy. Spencer's (1958: 394) central argument was that both society and living organisms increase, in the course of their life cycle, in mass or size as well as in structural complexity from a few uniform parts to numerous interrelated unlike parts. In other words, growth is accompanied by a substantial increase in complexity. Durkheim (1964) identified social facts (e.g., the division of labor) and established the efficient cause (i.e., increased moral density) and its function (i.e., the need it fulfills in society). We may therefore regard him as the father of modern functionalism (cf. Strasser, 1976: 113–22). For him, increasing moral density, which he defines as the result of an ever-increasing number of people in interaction with each other brought about by population growth, urbanization, and improved means of transportation and communication, determines the nature of social relationships, thus generating the dynamics of social change.

As urbanization and technological developments force previously separated members and groups of society to interact with one another, conflict over scarce resources inevitably ensues as individuals with similar needs and interests can exist harmoniously only in separation from each other (Durkheim, 1964: 267). According to Durkheim, the increasing individuation of man tends to be reflected in a tangle of social pathologies because contemporary man lacks a collectivity with which he can identify. For example, the legal system of a highly differentiated society tends to protect individual rather than collective interests, that is to say, above all, private property (cf. Dreitzel, 1967a: 48–9). In Durkheim's explanatory scheme, the division of labor emerges as the social sheet-anchor against a threatening Hobbesian war of all against all. Indeed, the social division of labor permits more people to survive and coexist than under conditions of universal rivalry in which the opponents would be obliged to fight to a finish (Durkheim, 1964: 266–70).

The awareness of, and approach to, the crisis of his age was typical of Durkheim's preoccupation with the problem of order, that is, with the conditions of French society of his time. Durkheim develops a theory of social change based upon a careful macrosociological analysis of differentiation through strains resulting from greater density of social interaction. However, for him, the division of labor in society is not only a consequence of these developments, but is also a self-regulatory mechanism in the sense that it serves to establish organic solidarity based upon the value of meritocracy and the normative potential of occupational associations. To be sure, Durkheim (1964: 266) sees members of society 'in rivalry everywhere' as they compete for scarce resources. Just as normal forms of the division of labor are the result of, and a solution to, the struggle for existence, so abnormal forms of the division of labor come into being not 'because of a necessity of its own nature,' but rather because of the impact of 'external forces.' Once these abnormal forms take effect in society, attempts at coerced conformity by those with political power and attempts by the oppressed to (re-)establish the 'natural state' of the social system ensue. Durkheim clearly invokes the concepts of equilibrium, differentiation, and strains (cf. e.g., Durkheim, 1964: 372–88).

Unlike Marx, Durkheim believes that in the history of the social division of labor economic factors played a less important role than changes in law, values, and morality. The guaranty that *individual* capacities can develop freely serves to motivate individuals to specialize to the greatest extent possible, thus promoting *societal* development through the exploitation of all talents. Such a social order is characterized by a situation in which one's position is dependent upon skills and in which social inequalities express natural differences. An opposite tendency is viewed by Durkheim as pathological which may cause organic solidarity to break down and be replaced by constraint (Durkheim, 1964: 376).

There can be no doubt that Durkheim did recognize the ubiquity of conflict and the importance of constraint in a society where only imperfect solidarity is possible; but these considerations follow from his fundamental concern for a normative foundation of solidarity.[14] For Durkheim, coerced rather than spontaneous solidarity must result in disaffection among the oppressed groups which will eventually lead to a reorganization of society along more equitable lines. He therefore pins great hopes on occupational decentralization, since the differentiation of society proceeds along occupational lines (Durkheim, 1951: 389–91). That he sought to avert the threat of normlessness through occupational decentralization and organization, must be understood as a consequence of his morphological approach which made him refrain from attributing a reality *sui generis* to antagonistic groups in modern society. In his mind, classes were always antagonistic groupings, whereas occupational associations were not. He preferred to think in terms of the 'whole' and to ignore the struggles between 'parts.'

For Comte, we have seen, sociology primarily purported to formulate a theory of change within patterned behavior and institutional development. Accordingly, change proceeds in a regular, predictable fashion. Change is development or growth in which order can be discerned. Fundamental to this approach is the concept of system that views social phenomena, including change processes, to be of a systemic quality that influences and delineates the direction (and perception) of change; equally important, however, is the concept of equilibrium that helps to account for the growth of a given system in terms of the process of differentiation. Anticipating a proposition to be discussed later, it may be said that the fusion of evolutionism's systemic underpinnings with the equilibrium concept eventually led to the functional approach that, in turn, recurred to an evolutionary frame of reference within which social equilibria are thought to operate and develop (Smith, 1973: 130).

In order to understand fully the close relationship between evolutionism and functionalism the following considerations should be kept in mind. Just as nineteenth-century social scientists, and evolutionists in particular, were puzzled by the far-reaching changes that had taken place in their epoch and respective society, so functionalists, from Malinowski to Parsons, were fascinated by the relative stability and persistence that pervaded social life *in spite of* concomitantly observable changes, strains, conflicts, dissensus, violence, and deviance. For Comte and Spencer, Lewis H. Morgan and Edward B. Tylor, and to some extent also for Marx and Durkheim, the study of these social transformations represented a device for discovering the true foundations of social order (Bock, 1963b: 229). Far from unanimously praising the unending social improvement as the social philosophers of the Enlightenment had done, they were generally distressed by the disruptive consequences of change inducing them to envision ways and means by which the fundamental social order could be restored. Of course, each one of them saw the coming of social redemption in a distinctive way: Comte through a humanitarian religion, Spencer through liberalism perfecting evolution, Marx through communism, and Durkheim through an occupational estate system.

These evolutionists accepted change as a *natural* and hence necessary phenomenon in the sense that the moving force and unilinear direction of change were attributed to the unfolding of what is potential in societies and cultures. If change is an unfolding of a potential, it follows (1) that change is *immanent* in the social phenomenon that changes; (2) that it is *gradual*, continuous, and ubiquitous manifesting itself in sequential stages cumulatively related to each other; (3) that it reveals *directionality* as it points to a process moving from one point in time to another; (4) that, as this directed process shows a characteristic pattern from the homogeneous to the heterogeneous, change in society may be equated with *differentiation*; and (5) that, as change is natural to, necessary for, and immanent in a social entity, it proceeds in a *uniform* manner through time and space (Bock, 1963b: 234; Nisbet, 1969: 212; Spencer, 1899, I: 265–307). When evolutionists did observe developmental discrepancies within the same society or developmental differences between societies, they assumed that these inconsistencies were due to differing stages in a universal and uniform process of growth. Where such an explanation was not possible, variations in the rate of change, including the absence of change, were accounted for by citing extraneous or exceptional circumstances.

Although evolutionism did not include a theory of social persistence, its notion of unfolding the potential of some phenomenon implied some conception of what was being unfolded (Bock, 1963a: Part 1). If we follow the evolutionary postulate that the key to an understanding of change can be found in discovering what society *is*, we enter directly the functionalist domain which stipulates that structural analysis should precede any social inquiry into (evolutionary) change (Bock, 1963b: 231–2; Levy, 1952: 43–5; Parsons, 1951: 483 *et passim*; Moore, 1960: 817).[15] In their critique of classic evolutionism, early functionalists, more than present-day functionalists, stated bluntly that the reason why evolutionists had failed to give an adequate account of social and cultural change was their neglect, and sometimes inability in, describing what society and culture *is*. Perhaps Radcliffe-Brown (1957: 71–89) was correct when he stated most succinctly, and not unlike Comte, that dealing with the 'diachronic' problem of how societies and social systems change their types presupposes that the 'synchronic' problem of classification and persistence of social systems be addressed (cf. also Gluckman, 1968). His distinction between changes *within* a social system and change *of* (the structure of) the social system makes sense only if posited as the problem that a change of the system can also stem from external forces, and that within-changes eventually, but not necessarily, lead to of-changes by way of genetic cumulation (Nisbet, 1969: 232–3).[16]

Nevertheless, functional change analysis has taken over two central elements from classic evolutionism: the first is of a more metatheoretical nature, the second implies important conceptual consequences, though both are rooted in a philosophy of history commonly accepted by evolutionists.

> 1 Common to all evolutionists of the nineteenth century was the concern for the true foundations of social order, having realized that the fabric of their societies had been torn in the wake of the vast transformations generated by the rise of capitalism and that a return to the institutions of *ancien régime* was not possible. From these concerns for what was required to establish a new, integrated, society there was only a small step to what functionalists considered central to any inquiry into what happens in society, namely, to know its *functional requisites* (cf. Comte, 1855: Book VI, Chapters 5 and 6; Aberle *et al.*, 1950; Bock, 1963b: 230).
>
> 2 In finding those fundamentals of society, evolutionists hoped to establish a new, lasting, state of equilibrium that was conceived of, though vaguely, as an equilibrium that vacillated along the continuous path of change prescribed by its sources immanent in the social system. Instead of searching for some evolving potential, functionalists demystified the principle of *immanence* by bashfully attending to the question of why change occurs at all in terms of structural *differentiation* and functional specialization as well as immanent strains and dysfunctions (e.g., imperfect socialization, role conflicts, competition).

However, while these flexibilities and strains appear to tend to change a given social structure, other items are said to maintain or strengthen it. This has been taken to mean either that the balance of those forces is an empirical question suggesting a moving, but precarious, equilibrium (Merton, 1968: 105–7; Moore, 1960) or that the stabilizing and pattern-maintaining tendencies clearly dominate the equilibration process, thus directing attention to tracing the repercussions of given changes within some systemic web of interdependence rather than to discovering initial factors in change processes (Parsons, 1951: 494, 533, 535). 'At the most general levels, there is no difference between processes that serve to maintain a system and those that serve to change it' (Parsons, 1966: 21). Just as evolutionism saw order arising out of (ordered) change, so functionalism may be identified as a theory of change-within-order. As we shall see below, the theory of order becomes a theory of change in that it refers to the forces that threaten to disturb a given equilibrium as well as to those that contribute to preserve it (cf. Smith, 1973: 131).

4.3.2.2 Evolution and differentiation

The evolutionary elements of modern functionalism may also be referring to theories of modernization which are concerned with correlates of industrialization. These theories are said to be diachronic, that is, they tend to infer process from a methodology of comparative statistics; the direction of change is believed to be unilinear in that all societies are supposedly undergoing parallel series of transformations in the course of industrialization (Appelbaum, 1970: 36). As pointed out by neo-evolutionist theorists, modernization is usually defined in terms of technology or viewed as being conceptually and empirically related to economic development (Smelser, 1966: 111; Moore, 1963: 89–92). In that opposing values, pattern variables, and other structures of traditional and present societies are contrasted, industrialization is seen as resulting in a growing societal systemness.

> What results from the changes described in such theories [of industrialization and modernization] is not so much a higher stage but a more complex social structure, containing more structural differentiation and functional specialization, albeit in greater societal interdependence and cohesion (Chodak, 1973: 10).

As social systems modernize, new social structures emerge to fulfill the functions of those that are no longer performing adequately. Smelser (1959a) has shown that modernization may be understood as an uneven process of structural differentiation that creates tensions (e.g., specialization leading to ambiguous role definitions subjecting men to strains of anxiety that result in some episode of collective behavior). Even if the mechanism of social reintegration fails to keep abreast of rapid differentiation within a given time span, new integrative mechanisms will eventually develop (cf. Merton, 1968: 135; Smith, 1973: 97; Smelser, 1959a).[17]

Above we have singled out *differentiation*, i.e., the development of functionally specialized societal structures, as the central concept that links classic evolutionism and (neo-evolutionary) functionalism (Appelbaum, 1970: 54; Parsons, 1967; 1966: 22 *et passim*). It is not only a link in the sense that both approaches emphasize the same explanatory principles (e.g., immanence, continuity, uniformity) but also a sign of cognitive reorientation in the sense that a narrowing of interests from the total society or civilization to a specific social system or culture was to take shape. One no longer speaks of stages of development of societies but instead of tensions and segmental disharmonies within a social system (Nisbet, 1969: 229). The development of Durkheim's work may be cited as the prime example of such a transition in focus. In his first major work *The Division of Labor in Society* (1964), first published in 1893, he described in evolutionary terms the stages according to which social solidarity developed in human society. With the publication of *The Elementary Forms of Religious Life* (1912/47), Durkheim set the stage for modern functionalism by focusing on the forms and elements of social structure and change located *within* the social system. The beginning of his methodological breviary was then to read as follows: 'The first origins of all social processes of any importance should be sought in the internal constitution of the social group' (Durkheim, 1950: 113; italicized in the original). Specifically, in his study of religion he selects the elements of one religion, namely, the cults and rites and prayers of the Australian Aborigines and in doing so he actually treats the elements of *all* religion.

We have seen that the concept of differentiation refers to the source, the way, and the direction of societal change: the source is immanence, the way is adaptation to environmental conditions, and the direction is the movement from homogeneity to heterogeneity. Adaptive differentiation and (re-)integration represent the structural brackets of the evolutionary process toward greater heterogeneity, in Spencer's days just as much as in the bulk of modern functionalism (cf. Schneider, 1976: 1–12; Spencer, 1958: 554; Parsons, 1964a). Contrary to Parsons's (1937/68, I; 3) early intellectual banishment of Spencer, in functional analysis of social change Spencer is not dead. In a more recent publication, Parsons (1966) integrated the adaptive and directive aspects of social change through differentiation into the notion of *adaptive upgrading*:

> If differentiation is to yield a balanced, more evolved system, each newly differentiated substructure (e.g., the producing organization . . .) must have increased adaptive capacity for performing its *primary* function, as compared to the

performance of *that* function in the previous, more diffuse structure. Thus economic production is typically more efficient in factories than in households. We may call this process the *adaptive upgrading* aspect of the evolutionary change cycle (Parsons, 1966: 22; emphasis in the original).

The neo-evolutionary Parsons (1966; 1967) views history as a process that generates more complex and general normative codes. Since these codes consist of societal values and norms (e.g., law) as well as symbols (e.g., language) that function to control man's actions, their differentiation and generalization tends to maximize the cybernetic control over those systems that environ the social system (i.e., organisms, personalities, and cultures). Evolution, in this sense, is the type of process that *changes* (rather than maintains) social structures in the direction of greater effectiveness in controlling the environment or, in Parsons's (1966: 21) words, that leads to 'the enhancement of adaptive capacity.' Not surprisingly, therefore, the (evolutionary) criterion for distinguishing the three main stages of civilization (primitive, intermediate, and modern) that Parsons traces is the use of certain systems of normative codes.[18] Parsons does mention that each stage shows greater institutional variety, but the multilinear path of evolution narrows visibly as we approach modernity. One gets the impression that, although his over-all scheme of evolution may be called multilinear, the routes to *contemporary* (Western) society he envisions were few, possibly only one, that tend(s) to converge or narrow toward the end. Smith (1973: 34,33) summarizes this point well:

> A central 'stem' leads from the primitive stage through the [intermediate] archaic societies of the ancient Near East, through Rome and Islam, and more especially through Greece and Israel, to the modern stage of the West today. Around this central continuity the evolutionary stream radiated adaptively into separate branches, many of which turned out to be adaptive failures. Primitive societies too are treated as 'dead-end' cases. . . . What Parsons seems to be asserting here is that, as the series develops, so evolution becomes more unilinear. Translated into chronological terms, this means that the nearer we come to contemporary society, the greater the number of societies which are 'nonevolutionary survivals' [. . . that] found social 'niches' which allowed them to exist despite the development of more advanced societies around them. . . . These range from the tribes of Papua or East Africa to great imperial civilisations like China, Russia and Islam. . . . However, his interpretation of Weber, and his application of the

scheme of pattern-variables to historical societies, lead him to emphasize the uniqueness of Western development and to treat it as normative for other civilisations.

According to Parsons, then, it is nature's way to generate a complex of structures and associated processes (i.e., 'evolutionary universals') that 'increase the long-run adaptive capacity of living systems,' so 'that only systems that develop the complex can attain certain higher levels of general adaptive capacity' (Parsons, 1967: 493). Organisms have increased their adaptability through eye and brain, while societies evolved due to their incorporation of religion, language, stratification, bureaucratic organization, money and market, and democratic association. Although combinations of universals by and large determine the stage of civilization to which given units belong, the distance of these universals from ascriptive, particularistic bases takes care, so to speak, of the evolutionary fine-tuning. We may now better understand Parsons's account of his emphasis on Western development:

> In development terms, it became clear that, with the exception of the organization of the French state, the fundamental structural contributions of seventeenth-century society were of the associational–pluralistic character, notably ascetic Protestantism, common law, and parliamentarism as well as science and the rapid development of a market economy. In its capitalistic form, the industrial revolution certainly moved society farther in this direction, as did the democratic revolution. From this perspective it became clear, perhaps especially under the influence of Tocqueville, that the modern society emerging in North America was beginning to play a role in the total modern system of the twentieth century somewhat parallel to that of the European northwest corner of the seventeenth. This society owed its primary distinctive features to an associational–pluralistic emphasis and not to the sharpness and rigidity of its class discriminations nor to its especially high bureaucratization. In addition to decentralized governmental democracy, examples would be its federalism and separation of powers, the religious constitution of separation of church and state, denominational pluralism, and the capacity to absorb, in the sense of integration by inclusion, large immigrant religions and ethnic groups, though this absorption is far from being complete (Parsons, 1970: 857).

Like any theory of evolution, that of Parsons also assumes that selection is selection only 'if it is capable of de-realization of the possible' (Luhmann, 1975g: 200). The question arises whether, considering Western civilization, this justifies the conclusion that evolutionary universals appear in the guise of functional prerequisites of modern societies and that their increasing degree of differentiation points to a narrowing of the variability of the path of development of these societies? For Luhmann (1975a: 13–18), the growing complexity, that is, differentiation of the levels of system formation, is connected with a differentiation of interests and perspectives. This increases not only the structural possibilities but also the actual occasions for negations and hence generates more possibilities to vary the given structures. For example, the increased differentiation of interaction systems and the social system entails 'that society will be independent from the conflict mode of its interaction systems' (Luhmann, 1975a: 17). In this context the social system type of organization takes on special significance whose principle of boundary maintenance and self-selection consists in linking the membership with such conditions as subjection to authority in exchange for income.

Without endangering its own continuity society can therefore afford breaking off interaction as strategy for solving conflicts in large measures. Take, for instance, innovations, in the widest sense, on all levels of society which are only possible if social relations can be discontinued and new ones established. In the simplest, archaic tribal societies in which interaction, organization, and society as possible system types are largely identical, such conflicts were either not possible or, if they did occur, they had extremely destructive effects. A society is capable of highest complexity only where the different system types are clearly delineated and fulfill various functions. In such a case society is no longer dependent upon reductions of complexity, that is, upon establishing a difference between the system and the environment, which are then accomplished by the system types of organization and/or interaction. To illustrate, differentiated systems of organization have not – or only to a limited extent – to take into consideration the respective other roles of their members, say, in the family, church, politics, clubs, and neighborhood (Luhmann, 1975a: 14).

We therefore concur with Luhmann that this normalization of conflict behavior entails less *global* conflicts in complex societies but, compared with the frequency of interaction, if they do occur, they are also more threatening to the social order. According to Luhmann (1975e: 124), the future possible shows a greater capacity for complexity, which also means that it is compatible with a larger number of varying states of society. Hence it is only fruitful to think about a history of modern society that defines these conditions of future possibilities and does not imply a linear–teleological conception of the future. Evolution is thus understood 'as a form of changes of systems' consisting in the differentiation of functions of variation, selection, and stabilization.[19] That is to say, these functions will be fulfilled by different mechanisms and then again recombined. 'A theory of cultural and social evolution . . . would have to show in what way social systems are capable of differentiating and recombining these mechanisms' (Luhmann, 1975f: 151).

The reproach of cultural bias against Parsons is therefore justified only on the ground that he readily assumes that not only some general function but also its corresponding evolutionary form or structure is a universal requisite of social development. As a case in point, the family is a necessary condition for further enhancement of societal adaptation, because the functions of socialization are universal; likewise democracy, because societies must take care of the need for freedom under the condition of consensus (Smith, 1973: 36–7).

In *conclusion*, Parsons's neo-evolutionary stance views 'evolution as largely a process by which culture comes to control the social structure, after first gaining autonomy from it' (Smith, 1973: 39). Ever since he has assigned priority to the normative order and its function to organize collectively the life of a population, culture is accorded a central role in determining long-term evolutionary trends just as much as universalism, achievement, and pluralism triumph in the modern stage of Western civilization.

> I believe that, within the social system, the normative elements are more important for social change than the 'material interests' of constitutive units. The longer the time perspective, and the broader the system involved, the greater is the *relative* importance of higher rather than lower factors in the control hierarchy, regardless of whether it is a pattern maintenance or pattern change that requires explanation (Parsons, 1966: 113; emphasis in the original).[20]

4.3.2.3 Changing equilibria: functional requisites and social strains
The preceding discussion was intended to demonstrate, by way of examining the neo-evolutionary aspects of Parsons's change analysis, the importance of the concept of differentiation in linking evolutionism and contemporary functionalism. For Parsons (1961: 44), *differentiation* is 'the master concept for the analysis of social structure.'

However, the concept of differentiation alone, Parsons says, is not sufficient; the principles of 'segmentation' and 'normative specification' are also needed. *Normative specification* refers to the normative culture institutionalized in the social system in which norms are differentiated on the basis of functional specifications of units and subunits. In other words, there is 'a hierarchy of generality of the patterns of normative culture institutionalized in a social system, one that corresponds to the general hierarchical relations of its structural components' (Parsons, 1961: 45). The concept of *segmentation* denotes 'the development of subcollectivities, within a larger collectivity system, in which some of the members of the larger system participate more intimately than in others' (Parsons, 1961: 45). Segmentation, in this sense, is independent of the differentiation of functions among subcollectivities; as the example of the thousands of nuclear families in a society shows, such a social structure is highly segmented but not necessarily highly differentiated. The degree of complexity of a society depends upon which principle *primarily* establishes the differences between system(s) and environment(s). As the environment offers always more possible realities than a social system is capable of working up, the reduction of the relation between system and environment to a structure that is *meaning*ful to system members, requires besides the mechanisms of selection and variation that of stabilization. Modern society is stabilized by the mechanisms of system differentiation (e.g., occupational division of labor), the limits of which, in contrast with variation and selection, may be indicated. The formation of systems opens up future possibilities out of the selection of which history results. Evolution will be indicated in terms of those structural changes that follow from the combined effect of the mechanisms just mentioned (Luhmann, 1975e: 106; 1975f: 151).[21]

In line with his initial definition of function in terms of a given socio-cultural item's relation to the state of the whole social system, Parsons (1961: 60ff.; 1966: 22-4) now renders dynamic the social processes by operationalizing them as, and coupling them with, functional 'input-output-exchanges.' Each differentiated substructure is then conceived as producing goods or services that become resources for other substructures (outputs) and as receiving the exchange products of other units as its own resources (inputs). These processes of generation and utilization of resources are regulated by certain types of exchange media such as money and power.[22] Processes of expanding deviations and of delaying interactions lead to altered exchange movements and in many cases to changes in the social structure. This is so because the structural units of the system, namely, membership roles and their composite products, i.e., institutions, control more or less influence, power,

THE STRUCTURAL-FUNCTIONAL THEORY

and money, resulting in differing capacities to effect innovations and hence to generate change (cf. Ridder, 1974: 9).

These exchanges and normative specifications interlocking the units of a social system also serve to prevent the process of differentiation from leading to the total independence or functional autonomy of some parts. However, as functionalists conceptualize systems in terms of their interdependence, they tend to focus on the whole and the close interrelatedness of its parts, 'the oneness of the whole' (Gouldner, 1970: 215). Differentiated and specified interrelationships between subsystems of society, it is inferred, continuously fulfill requirements institutionalized in order to preserve the social system as an ongoing concern. For Parsons, the processes of socialization and social control play a crucial role in meeting the systemic requirement of minimum integration of individual and collective goals in that the internalization of society's norms and values in its members and their continuous motivational effect on individual action is assured.

> The integration of a set of common value patterns with the internalized need-disposition structure of the constituent personalities is the *core phenomenon* of the dynamics of social systems. That the stability of any social system except the most evanescent interaction process is dependent on a degree of such integration may be said to be the fundamental dynamic theorem of sociology (Parsons, 1951: 42; emphasis added).

In posing the question which structural arrangements or (evolutionary) forms meet those systemic prerequisites of social development and what these imperatives mean in a concrete social context, functionalists are again confronted with the problem of invoking either impermissible tautologies or unwary ethnocentrism by unwarranted identification of the functions of a system of social relationships with the internal requirements of the corresponding social structure (cf. Touraine, 1974: 51; Smith, 1973: 36–7). According to Parsons, however, functional considerations mediate between the exigency of the relative stability of a structure and the exigency of the given environment of the system.

> The functional categories of social system concern, then, those features in terms of which systematically ordered modes of adjustment operate in the changing relations between a given set of patterns of institutionally established structure in the system and a given set of properties of the relevant environing systems (Parsons, 1961: 36–7).

The statement shows that Parsons assumes that functional

requirements remain constant in the sense that they are fixed and that they may be specified without regard to the particular situation in time and space. Although some representatives of modern functionalism have hesitatingly recognized the possible validity of assuming changing requirements (e.g., Levy, 1952: 40), a number of critics have convincingly argued that the attainment of a system's preferred global states is dependent on the changing environment in which the system is situated (Sztompka, 1974: 109–10).

Functionalists deliver a theory of societal persistence which is what their evolutionist colleagues failed to do. Needless to say, the preferred partial states expressed in terms of functional requirements or system needs have been regarded as indispensable for the realization of the preferred global states of the system as a whole (survival, adaptation, structural continuity, etc.). Already Malinowski (1969) presented a detailed catalogue of functional requirements that took the form of 'cultural answers' to particular individual and social needs ranging from 'basic needs' (e.g., food and safety satisfied by the cultural means of nutritive system and weapons, fortifications, and army organization respectively) to 'derived needs' (e.g., transmission of cultural heritage by the cultural means of the educational system or codification and regulation of human behavior through sanctions satisfied by social control mechanisms).

In their study, Parsons and Smelser (1956: 17) demonstrate how 'every social system functions in a situation defined as external to it' and in what way interchanges between system and situation occur. It is assumed that 'process in any social system is subject to four independent functional imperatives or "problems" that must be met adequately if equilibrium and/or continuing existence of the system is to be maintained' (Parsons and Smelser, 1956: 16; cf. also Parsons et al., 1953: Chapters 3 and 5). With respect to the interchange concerning the situation's significance as a source of consummatory interests of the social system, Parsons and Smelser (1956: 17) put forward stability as the criterion for satisfying the prerequisite of (consummatory) goal attainment:

> A goal state, for an individual actor or for a social system, is a *relation* between the system of reference and one or more situational objects which (given the value system and its institutionalization) maximizes the stability of the system. Other things equal, such a state, once present, tends to be maintained, and if absent, tends to be 'sought' by the action of one or more units of the system. The latter case is necessary because only in limiting cases are processes in the situation closely

'synchronized' with processes in the system of action; hence the system must 'seek' goal states by controlling elements of the situation. Goal states may be negative, i.e., noxious situational conditions, or positive, i.e., a maximization of favorable or 'gratifying' conditions.

Furthermore, it is argued that the second, consummatory, imperative of system integration 'is to "maintain solidarity" in the relations between the units in the interest of effective functioning' (Parsons and Smelser, 1956: 18). Note that the criteria of stability and effective functioning on the basis of an integrated whole can be – analogously – treated as a 'uniform state' which is begot or maintained by homeostatic mechanisms. The study of social change clearly proceeds along the line of functional prerequisite analysis:

> Any system of action can be described and its processes analyzed in terms of these four fundamental categories. The aim of analyzing a system is to assess the *effects* of changes in the data of the system, the situation, and the properties of its units, on changes in the *state* of the system and the states of its component units; statements about the effects on the system and its units are framed *in terms of* these four dimensions. For instance, we say a system 'adapts' to certain situational disturbances. Furthermore, if these categories formulate 'directions' in which process can move, certain constraints prevent processes from moving equally in all directions at once, at least unless very specific conditions are fulfilled. Indeed, the idea of system itself implies such constraints (Parsons and Smelser, 1956: 18–19; emphasis added).

In structural analysis, we have seen, Parsons (1964a: 84) regards the 'concept of stability . . . as a defining characteristic of structure . . . equivalent to the more specific concept of stable equilibrium – which in another reference may be either "static" or "moving".' In locating structures in larger systems, he singles out boundary positions where social change unfolds:

> A system . . . is stable or (relatively) in equilibrium when the relation between its structure and the processes which go on within it and between it and its environment are such as to maintain those properties and relations, which for the purposes in hand have been called its structure, relatively unchanged. Very generally, always in 'dynamic' systems, this maintenance is dependent on continuously varying processes, which 'neutralize' either endogenous or exogenous sources of variability which, if they went far enough, would change the structure. A classic

example of equilibrium in this sense is the maintenance of nearly constant body temperature by mammals and birds – in the face of continuing variation in environmental temperature and through mechanisms which operate either to produce heat, including slowing up its loss, or to slow down the rate of heat production or accelerate its dissipation.

Contrasted then with stability or equilibrating processes are those processes which operate to bring about structural change. That such processes exist and that they are of fundamental scientific importance is nowhere in question (Parsons, 1964a: 84).

Parsons seems to suggest a distinction between *substructural* change as part and parcel of the processes productive of structural stability and those processes productive of *structural* change. For him, 'structural change in subsystems is an inevitable part of the equilibrating process in larger systems' (Parsons, 1961: 71). It is thus important to separate processes of equilibration and processes of structural change, since such a difference 'seems inherent in the conception of a social system as cybernetic system of control over behavior' (Parsons, 1961: 71). However, the point is that *structural change* is seen as resulting from *changes in the environment* of the system or from changes within the system that modify the relation of the system to its environment (cf. Parsons, 1964a: 85; Parsons and Smelser, 1956: 16–17; Sztompka, 1974: 95).

Parsons, in other words, does recognize two major sources of structural change: exogenous and endogenous. *Exogenous* sources can be located in tendencies toward change in the environing systems: the organisms, the personalities, and the cultural systems. For example, changes in the genetic components within a population may affect future role performance and the social system's capacity for proper socialization, thus altering individual behavior and its social patterns. Quite naturally, another source of external change is change that originates in other social systems. We mention here only the potential impact of societies with different political orders on each other in addition to exogenous cultural borrowing and diffusion mediated by contacts among societies.

The distinction between structural and substructural change points to the *range* of social change. In this sense, we can speak with W. E. Moore (1963: Chapters 3 and 4) of small-scale and large-scale changes. The separation of endogenous from exogenous change, by contrast, refers to the *cause*, that is, to the focus of determinacy. Endogenously as well as exogenously produced change may, however, be of small-scale or larger scale quality, although this depends, first of all, upon the level of the system concerned (e.g., interaction, organization, society). In the case of the societal system, Parsons and Smelser are correct in assuming that there are two kinds of factors bringing about change: (1) those resulting from cultural diffusion (exogenous), and (2) those that spring from the articulation of roles and norms constituting the social system and leading to conflicts and strains (endogenous).

A social system is always characterized by an institutionalized value system. The social system's first functional imperative is to maintain the integrity of that value system and its institutionalization. This process of maintenance means stabilization against pressures to change the value system, pressures which spring from two primary sources: (1) *Cultural* sources of change. Certain imperatives of cultural consistency may mean that cultural changes taking place *outside* the value system relevant to the social system in question (e.g., changes in the belief system) may generate pressures to change important values *within* the social system. The tendency to stabilize the system in the face of pressures to change institutionalized values through cultural channels may be called the 'pattern maintenance' function. (2) *Motivational* sources of change. Motivational 'tensions,' arising from 'strains' in any part of the social situation or from organic or other intra-personal sources, may threaten individual motivation to conformity with institutionalized role expectations. Stabilization against this potential source of change may be called 'tension management' (Parsons and Smelser, 1956: 16–17; only second and third emphasis in the original).

By introducing the concept of strain that supposedly precedes change, functional analysis, at least that of Parsonian persuasion, relativizes the static implication of the equilibrium assumption. On the one hand, it is postulated that societies respond to the change pressures by adjustments designed to maintain 'a relatively precarious state of moving equilibrium' (Parsons, 1951: 520). On the other hand, strain is understood as being inherent in the various processes of systemic differentiation and reintegration. At this point, significant aspects of the disequilibrium assumption are invoked in that the actual structure of the system is assumed to be 'constantly lagging behind the changing goal states of the system. There is a constant strain between the actual configuration that would be functional for the actual preferred states of the system' (Sztompka, 1974: 158; cf. also Moore, 1963: 18; Eisenstadt, 1964a: 235; Merton, 1968: Chapters 6 and 7). This point must be emphasized since the adjustment postulate entailed by the equilibrium assumption practically precludes the conceptualization of endogenous change, which, in turn, would suggest that all changes had to be initiated *outside* the system. Such a conclusion also follows from the functionalist principle of interdependence according to which all elements of the system depend on each other as well as on the whole system and cannot exist outside the system, which again suggests that a stimulus for internal change is hardly conceivable. Before formulating a conclusion as to the range and direction of change accounted for by strains, we should further elaborate upon the concept of strain that is so central to the study of *endogenous* sources of change.

Strain may be defined as a disturbance of the expectation system of society, the latter being an essential part of relevant actors' articulation of need-dispositions with a set of cultural patterns. To put it in Parsonian terms: 'A strain is a tendency to disequilibrium in the input–output balance between two or more units of the system' (Parsons, 1961: 71). As the case of institutionalizing roles in the social system shows, 'vested interests' in one form or another will always resist change inherent in the institutionalization process (cf. Parsons, 1951: 491–2). Parsons's notion of strain clearly points to a conflict situation generated by, for example, imperfect socialization and ambiguity of role specification in the (established) system of role-expectations. These situations constitute endogenous sources of change; however, as Parsons remarks, 'change is never just "alteration of pattern" but alteration *by the overcoming of resistance*' (Parsons, 1951: 491; emphasis in the original).

However, Parsons tells us only half the story in so far as he sees 'vested interests' involved only in *resisting* change by maintaining the gratifications provided in an established system of role-expectations. For example, once the middle-class American values of egalitarianism, professionalism, and scientism had been successfully translated into material well-being, it became virtually impossible to overcome subsequent class privileges in the face of the political power of their beneficiaries, on the one hand, and of needed change, on the other (cf. Thrall and Starr, 1972). Their vested interests were clearly directed toward keeping the system intact rather than changing it.[23]

In short, the process of *institutionalization* plays a central role in Parsons's attempt to explain at the same time order and stability as well as conflict and change, as it involves the development of a normative bond between actors that regulates their interaction. However, since actors' 'motivational structures' are only imperfectly interlocked, strains within social systems are created with change as the possible result (cf. e.g., Parsons, 1954a: 231).

THE STRUCTURAL-FUNCTIONAL THEORY

According to Parsons (1961: 70–9), the tension that results from a violation of the expectation system will subsequently lead to one or more of three types of action to remove it: (1) resolution, i.e., restoration of full conformity with normative expectations; (2) isolation, i.e., less than normal performance by the deficient units is accepted as other parts assume their residual function; and (3) change in the structure itself. Parsons goes on to describe the conditions under which strain is likely to engender *structural* change rather than alternative (1) or (2). To be sure, 'a change in the structure of a social system is a change in its normative culture,' which is at the most general level 'a change in the paramount value system' (Parsons, 1961: 73). Structural change tends to occur (1) when the forces of control in the lower order of the cybernetic hierarchy fail to contain the strain; (2) when the forces of change succeed in enlisting 'allies' to their cause within the system; (3) when the forces of change develop a full-fledged ideology or model of the new system that change will bring about; (4) when the forces of change can provide sanctions for conformity with their new system; and (5) when the forces of change can overcome the forces of resistance against change (Parsons, 1961: 73).

Our discussion thus far has shown, though at times only implicitly, that the institutionalization of norms, values, and roles contributes not only to social (re-)integration but also, and always, breeds normative ambiguity, opposition of interests, and hence tensions and strains – as there will be always groups and individuals who oppose or reinterpret norms, totally or partially, which had been set up by elites with more or less public consensus. Therefore, we can say that 'the possibility of conflict and potential change is always present, rooted in the very process of crystallization and maintenance of institutional systems. The direction and occurrence of change depend heavily on the nature of this process' (Eisenstadt, 1970: 12).

In conclusion, it may be said that in accounting for social change both orthodox (e.g., Parsons) and unorthodox functionalists (e.g., Eisenstadt and W. E. Moore) focus on internal problems that spring from a social system's attempt *to establish* a normative order (cf. Smith, 1973: 52). Merton's (1968: Chapter 6) discussion of the contradictory relations between approved cultural goals and institutionalized, though for some members of society restricted, means exemplifies particularly well why and in what way a normative means–ends scheme gives rise to a variety of strains that foster change on various levels of the system (e.g., individual role adaptations, educational institutions) and in varying degrees (e.g., cultural goals and/or institutional avenues to attain them).

Specifically, stratification systems may be viewed as continually generating pressure on individuals and groups to deviate systematically from, and eventually to change, the cultural prescriptions of society (cf. Lipset, 1975: 186). Functionalists account for structured social inequality in terms of the need of social systems to fill positions of varying functional importance with qualified personnel. The rewards that men and positions enjoy are a function of the degree to which their qualities, performance, and possessions measure up to the standard allegedly set by their society (cf. Davis and Moore, 1945; Parsons, 1957: 159; Parsons, 1953: 94). By contrast, conflict theorists of different persuasion explain inequality and class conflict by referring to interests of those in power and in control over the means of appropriation and reward that contradict the interests of those who are subject to power and have little control over sanctions. They actually integrate the analysis of inequality into the theory of social conflict and change (cf. Dahrendorf, 1958; 1959a; Mills, 1956; Coser, 1956; 1967; Gouldner, 1970; Wright, 1976).

4.3.2.4 Recapitulation
Before we conclude with a general critique, we shall briefly recapitulate the central elements of the functional analysis of social change.

The structural-functional theory consists of a system of *structural* categories which is held to be logically and substantively adequate for describing the essential elements of relations within a social system. This approach also includes a set of *dynamic* functional categories, which supposedly articulate directly with the structural elements. Functional categories are charged with the task to describe the processes by which social structures are maintained or disrupted, and the relations of the system to its environment. Structures are given, while functions are considered to be problematic in the sense (1) that the sociologist looks for specific functions of those structures, especially with respect to self-regulatory mechanisms or negative feedback effects that serve to equilibrate deviations from, and to secure the maintenance of, the desired state of the system (*structural*-functionalism); (2) that certain conditions are assumed to be given for the system to function normally (positively put) or to prevent the total destruction or the change of structural characteristics of the system (negatively put); functional requisites viewed as universal serve as reference points for phenomena that change over time (*requisite* or imperative functionalism); (3) that alternative structural arrangements are found to be equivalent in fulfilling a given function with respect to the solution of limited social problems (*equivalence functionalism*); and, finally, (4) that the analytical focus on the stabilizing, pattern-maintaining, and boundary-defining processes of social life also reveals structural strains and functional flexibilities inherent in the social system and operating as immanent sources of change; the principles of differentiation, immanence, continuity, and uniformity are designed to unravel the specific forms of the underlying evolutionary tendency toward increasing 'the long-run adaptive capacity' or toward increasing 'the complexity of society' (*evolutionary* functionalism).[24]

The reference points derived from theory and selected under certain aspects are of fundamental importance to functional analysis (Ridder, 1972: 336). While Durkheim referred to societal health, Malinowski to the satisfaction of individual and social needs, Radcliffe-Brown to social integration, Parsons to the realization of a relatively stable structure of the social system through integrative mechanisms, Merton, by contrast, put forth a series of reference points depending on cognitive interests and implying different consequences for individuals, groups, organizations, and society as a whole. Functional analysis can be understood as including structures and processes that are apt to maintain as well as to suspend stability. Thus, the fundamental reference problem of any functional analysis, and hence also that of change, is *stabilization* permitting statements about the identity and limits of social systems and suggesting that structural analysis must precede evolutionary inquiry.[25]

The point is that the identification of conditions of change with those of stability, or more precisely, that preservation and change of a given state of the system do not preclude each other is, at any rate in functional terms, conceivable only if we assume that a *moving equilibrium* is operative in social contexts allowing only for *continuous*, relatively predictable and controllable processes of change (Parsons, 1961: 31; Devereux, 1961: 51–9). Only in this sense (1) social change is regarded as part and parcel of social systems; (2) change processes are imputed with structure-forming and structure-dissolving effects; and (3) change processes are recognized as structured phenomena (cf. Waldmann, 1975: 138).

Of course, by focusing on the specification of mechanisms by which stability is preserved or re-established after social disturbances have occurred functional analysis either ignores or de-emphasizes sources and patterns of social conflict by acknowledging the endemic nature of conflict and/or that it is pathological to the functioning of the social system to be contained by extending social control. Such a position undoubtedly reflects what a number of sociologists have called the *conservative* bias of functionalism (cf. Touraine, 1974: 59; Myrdal *et al.*, 1944, vol. 2: 1055–6; Strasser, 1976: Chapters 1 and 6; in contrast LaPiere, 1938: 55–6; Merton, 1968: 98–100).

4.3.3 A general critique of the equlibrium approach

4.3.3.1 Its merits: what it does

If we were to believe Kingsley Davis and George C. Homans (1950: 450), the pervasive use of equilibrium models, not only in sociology but in practically all social sciences, would speak for themselves, especially for their explanatory value. Davis (1950: 634–5) writes:

> It is only in terms of equilibrium that most sociological concepts make sense. Either tacitly or explicitly anyone who thinks about society tends to use the notion. The functional-structural approach to sociological analysis is basically an equilibrium theory. . . . The various elements which may be employed for sociological purposes turn out to be not single items but whole congeries of variables within themselves – what we might call subequilibria. . . . Since the variables are mutually dependent, an examination of change in one variable will inevitably lead to an examination of changes in other variables. If, for example, one starts with technology one soon finds oneself discussing related economic changes, because business firms either foster or withhold inventions according to which is profitable. Asking how withholding is possible, one next gets involved in the patent laws and hence in the political structure. And so on. In the end, in order to explain the total change in a society, one would have to consider the main variables constituting the social equilibrium.

We have pointed out that the equilibrium approach essentially attempts to reveal the conditions for maintaining a society in a stable equilibrium. In order to do so the mechanisms are determined and specified by means of which relative stability is preserved or restored. In other words, functional explanations are related to systems that maintain and establish their equilibrium *vis-à-vis* their environment. A latent causality is assumed in the sense that within the system there are causes that become effective in the case of disturbances in order to bring the system back into a stable state (cf. Luhmann, 1971a: 11). Thus, such a theory does not describe what actually happens in most societies, but rather outlines 'what society *would be* like *if it were* to function as an equilibrium system' (Guessous, 1967: 24). Because of its stabilization or system-maintenance point of reference, Durkheim's, Parsons's, and others' functionalism that demonstrates the 'interdependence between different elements of social structure came to mean the search for self-equilibrating mechanisms in society' (Moore, 1968: 367).[26]

Concerning causes of social change, the functionalist principle of interdependence seems to suggest a cyclical rather than a multiple causation model by looking upon all variables as being both dependent and independent. Although functionalists in the tradition of Comte, Durkheim, and Parsons claim to assume an amorphous rather than stratified interdependence among system parts, they have always assigned a special role to the variable of shared moral beliefs (cf. Gouldner, 1970: 226–31).[27] Parsons's cybernetic condition-control hierarchy clearly testifies to his preference for this specific variable. Whatever the functionalist position in the debate between single factor, multiple causation, and cyclical causation models, the functional analysis of change has placed particular emphasis on the distinction between exogenous and endogenous sources of change. *Exogenous* changes that stem from such factors as cultural diffusion or genetic influences, are seen as random disturbances of structural arrangements whose definitional criterion is that of system delineation (i.e., physical, psychic, cultural, international system *vs* social system). *Endogenous* change is viewed as being characteristic of social systems and as originating from inherent disturbances of the system that find expression in continuous processes of structural differentiation and normative specification. The criterion of definition is here the built-in tendency toward stabilization (which leads to internal processes of adaptation). Although Parsons (1951: 493) hastens to say that 'strain is not itself a "prime-mover",' but 'a mode of the impingement of other factors on an interaction system,' other functionalists regard the concept of strain, tension, or discrepancy between preferred, culturally defined states of the system and (old) social–structural arrangements as the key notion 'bridging the gap between statics and dynamics in functional theory' (Merton, 1968: 176; cf. also Moore, 1963: 8–21; Sztompka, 1974: 95; Davis, 1950: 634; Eisenstadt, 1964b: 235; Bock, 1963b). As we have seen thus far, the idea that change is built into society in terms of strains leads to a conception of continuous, gradual and timeless change.

We may therefore conclude that the functional theory of change, as discussed here, is, at least logically, capable of explaining three types of change in social life (Table 4.1): (1) *necessary* change; that is to say, functional imperatives make certain changes, adaptations, or adjustments necessary as the realization of social stability is

SELECTED THEORIES OF SOCIAL CHANGE

viewed to depend on their satisfaction (of course, the definition of necessary change is closely connected with the assumption of the so-called prerequisites for survival which, following Luhmann, we have found to be rather problematic); (2) *compatible* change; that is to say, in order to attain optimally and most effectively the diverse goals set by the polity, changes that are consistent with the maintenance of social stability may be effected; (3) *oscillatory* change; that is to say, because of the strains and frictions inherent in the processes of equilibration involving substructural changes, social stability will temporarily, and to a limited extent, vacillate around the equilibrium state of the social system.

TABLE 4.1 *Types of change explained by functionalist theory*

Type of change	Degree of system requirement	Example	Relation between types of change
Necessary change	Shall	Educational reform (e.g., change of curriculum contents and of the number of high scool graduates; new types of educational institutions as a consequence of technological changes affecting employment and occupational structure)	(1) With respect to the *range* of change holds true most of the time: (a) Necessary change > compatible change > oscillatory change. (b) Necessary change can also be structural/compatible change.
Compatible change	Can	Reform of divorce and abortion law (in part as legally sanctioning already existing facts, in part as adjustment to trends in marriage law, family politics, and public morals)	(2) With respect to the focus of determinacy or *causal factors* holds true most of the time: Oscillatory change ('strains') leads to compatible and/or necessary change.
Oscillatory change	Must	Rise and solution of role conflicts (resulting from a shift in role occupancy or from role requirements which, in turn, originate in various processes of differentiation)	

With the preceding discussion in mind, we *hypothesize* that, according to the equilibrium theory of change, a society will maintain or establish stability over a long period of time only when it is capable of undergoing *necessary* changes. These changes in societal components usually proceed in two kinds of pattern. The first involves periodic sequences of structural *differentiation*, by means of which new specialized subunits are built up, supposedly enabling the social system to cope with particular problem areas. We have already dealt extensively with this point. The second major change pattern refers to the occurrence of periodic 'phase-movements' in the sense of *shifting concerns* of a given collectivity with one set of functional problems to another. Under the influence of Robert F. Bales (1950), Parsons came to reformulate the equilibrium laws and problems in terms of phases. Small, face-to-face groups were found to have their interaction processes permanently shifting and not in equilibrium. Thus, Parsons began to point out that no single stage in time and space provides optimal satisfaction to all functional imperatives.[28] In other words, each stage satisfies one imperative more than others, and there is a (revolving) cycle in which only one imperative enjoys its momentum at a given problem point. Rethinking our discussion of the concept of differentiation, it should now be clear that differentiation of (namely, the difference between) system and environment produces not only meaning but also *temporarity*, as not all imperatives can be simultaneously fulfilled, that is, not everything can happen at the same time. The generation of a meaningful relation of system and environment is based upon the effect of various system processes over time. In social life, the production, and particularly the conservation of, meaning is only possible in the course of time (cf. Luhmann, 1975e: 105).

The processes of differentiation and phase-movement underscore the importance of conceiving of the maintenance of social stability as continuous and dynamic and of society as being in a dynamic, rather than static, equilibrium. The social equilibrium is maintained by intra-systemic changes, which makes – but concurring with prominent social analyses of the nineteenth century – the understanding of change a prerequisite of that of the social structure. If change is considered normal, because it is immanent, and continuous, because it is gradual, the problem of (studying) change is one of the source and the speed rather than one of its absence or presence (cf. Lauer, 1973: 4–5).

4.3.3.2   Its shortcomings: what it does not do
In our discussion of the equilibrium model we arrived at the conclusion that on the basis of *its* premises change analysis is capable only of accounting for *some* of the changes and transformations that occur more or less regularly in social life. It does *not* provide a

comprehensive framework for a general theory of change in and of social systems. The point is not that the results, i.e., the kind of change explained, render the functional theory of change questionable, but rather its underlying premises. The functional approach is primarily concerned with the question of how the elements of society are combined into a functioning whole (cf. Lockwood, 1956; Dahrendorf, 1958). The equilibrium model is based on such postulates as stability (in the sense of coordinated processes within the system), functional teleology (cf. Levy, 1952: 52–3; Buckley, 1957: 246–8), and that society rests on the consensus of its members (cf. Merton, 1968: Chapter 3; Dahrendorf, 1958; 1959a: Chapter 5; Moore, 1963: 5–11). Rather, the explanatory potential of the concepts of moving equilibrium, differentiation, and strains is limited to continuous and relatively controllable processes of change. This is precisely the point that Dahrendorf (1958: 175; emphasis added) attempted to get across when he states 'that the criticism of the structural-functional theory for the analysis of conflict is directed only *against a claim of generality* of this theory, but it leaves untouched its competence with respect to the problem of integration.'

If a social system really rested upon a general consensus, it could hardly 'allow' structurally caused conflicts. According to Dahrendorf (1968: 115–16), 'conflict always implies some kind of dissent or disagreement about values;' otherwise, as Rex (1961: 120) remarks, practically only one type of conflict, namely, that of the safety valve, would be admitted and dealt with. In this case, as we know, the actor, faced with a frustrating situation as he is, displaces the goal of his actions, of course, without alleviating the cause of the frustration (cf. Coser, 1956: 156). Parsons hence also arrives at an individualization of social conflict and at the same time gives the impression that conflict is of a pathological nature. Sociology is thus dispersed from the task to deal with conflicts which go beyond the safety-valve type.

What is the scope or range of change phenomena of which the equilibrium model does not or cannot give a reasonably adequate account? Let us, for a moment, consider the class of changes Parsons labels 'structural,' that is to say, changes involving a transformation of the fundamental elements of society. First, he presents his own reasons why his theoretical scheme was not capable of yielding explanations of all processes of change, be they of extra- or intra-systemic origin. 'The reason is very simply that such a theory would imply complete knowledge of the laws of process of the system and this knowledge we do not possess' (Parsons, 1951: 486). In the meantime, he intimates we'd better concentrate on coming to grips with *normal* changes *within* the system which would allow us to formulate a theory of the social system's responses to given disturbances (cf. Guessous, 1967: 31). The pattern of systemic reaction to social disturbances is that of movement to a new position of equilibrium.

Apart from the fact that the notion of equilibrium represents only a partial and normatively infused conception of social life (cf. Strasser, 1976), how does this theory account for a system state in which the range of social equilibrium has been displaced? Numerous examples from the political, economic, and technological spheres could be cited to demonstrate that the movement from the old to the new equilibrium state does not always proceed in terms of an infinitesmal number of steps (cf. Schumpeter, 1951; Pigou, 1935; Spicer, 1952; Brinton, 1965). Since, Parsons would reason, processes within a social system that generate, affect, and are affected by conflict and change, are neither on the factual nor theoretical level transparent, the occurrence of structural change might still be analyzed in terms of powerful *exogenous* forces. There is a wide range of external sources apt to contribute to the transformation of social systems – from biological factors and demographic variables such as immigration and population growth, psychological variables such as motivation and aggressiveness, to cultural ones such as diffusion, acculturation, international subversion, and charismatic leadership (cf. Parsons, 1961: 71ff.; 1951: 486–96).

This is not to say that descriptive–historical, psychological, or change variables were not important. However, if it could be shown that certain types of change stem from *structural arrangements* within the social system whose basis of legitimation is regarded as coercive–problematic rather than consensual-given, then to relegate these sources of change merely to internal inconsistencies and/or to external influences would mean not only to distort reality but also to abdicate analytical responsibility. On the other hand, the question must still be raised whether, assuming that we possessed complete knowledge of the laws of processes operating within a system in equilibrium, this would allow us to explain and predict the occurrence and the repercussions of external disturbances. Is it sufficient and reasonable to explain events and changes such as the French Revolution, the rise of capitalism, the occurrence of a general strike, or the emergence of a revolutionary movement by referring to the motivational states of individuals, diffuse historical developments, the dictates of a 'prime mover,' or other *dei ex machina*? Does not the idea come close to the assertion that sequences of structural change are only abnormal phenomena and thus merely 'exceptions to the smooth course of events postulated by the equilibrium model – exceptions which are brought about by single, individual, nonrepetitive events that may be amenable to historical analysis but not to theoretical generalization?' (Guessous, 1967: 31).

For methodological and theoretical reasons functionalists are not capable of redeeming their claim to offer a unified theory of order *and* change by deriving the mechanisms of change from the same conditions from which they draw those of social order. Societies are delineated by various kinds of boundaries from their environment but not isolated; it is therefore unrealistic to assume that their properties can escape *external* influence. It would be utterly misleading to deny the influence of conquest, migration, war, trade, and cultural borrowing on the development of a given society. The preoccupation with differentiation, strains, and reintegration *limits* their scope of explanation to conditions of normative breakdown, system impairment, and system reintegration.[29] If functionalists were to stick closely with the evolutionary principle that change is by and large the realization of a unit's potentialities, they would have to deny the emergence of novelties altogether (Smith, 1973: 57–8).

In sum, the outline of the structural-functional approach has demonstrated that it includes an elaborate vocabulary of social explanation. It provides an explanatory device for a limited range of determinate changes only, and stops short in explaining radical changes in society and in locating structural origins of persisting social conflicts that generate small-scale or large-scale changes or both. As the central concepts of equilibrium, differentiation, strains, and reintegration ignore important properties of social life, the functional approach to social change must be regarded as, in part at least, unrealistic and, if it claims to offer a general theory of change, false and misleading. Various considerations suggest that functional analysis should *drop* the postulates of value consensus and (perhaps) equilibrium as they depict social structures and processes not as they actually operate but what they would be like if they functioned within a system in equilibrium on a consensual basis. We presented some evidence that there is no necessary relationship between consensus and equilibrium or between conformity with a given moral code and integration. We therefore recommend that functional analysis *integrate* other key concepts such as functional autonomy, functional alternatives, degree of functional reciprocity, and disequilibrium. Most importantly, functionalists should not follow the *evolutionary fallacy* in trying to rescue their analytical framework by arguing that it is applicable in the long run, during the indefinite period of which the system under study will have adjusted to given circumstances. Only in this sense, we suggest, Spencer should be declared dead.

Notes

1 Two recent books on the subject concur with this proposition. Anthony D. Smith (1973: vii; emphasis added) states that 'if America remains the *most dynamic and influential* centre of sociological activity, . . . the functionalist theory of social change . . . represents the single most pervasive and dominant approach to change in America today.'
In a comprehensive analysis of functionalism as a research methodology, Piotr Sztompka (1974: xii, emphasis added) believes that 'the conceptualization of social reality in systemic-functional terms makes up the *most fruitful* approach to both questions that are central for the theory of society: the question of order and persistence, as well as that of conflict and change' (cf. also Merton, 1968: 73; Nisbet, 1969: 228; Gouldner and Sprehe, 1965).
The present author readily acknowledges his great indebtedness to excellent work by Smith (1973) and Sztompka (1974) in preparing what is contained in the present study.
For the following discussion we should distinguish between method and methodology. The former refers to techniques of grasping the scope of reality and data which had been preselected by theory, while the latter focuses upon the logic of some analytical device such as the functionalist approach and is geared toward the goal of explaining observed or imagined effects in some social context. In other words, we shall be concerned here with the methodological aspects of functional analysis.
2 The solution that Parsons offered was a call for cementing moral values. In order to grasp fully the nature of social life, i.e., *its structure*, the nexus between the individual and the social order, and not the course of society over time, i.e., its *historicity*, came to be postulated as the fundamental problem to be solved by a science of society. Sociology turned from a study of society in time to one of the forms and the mechanisms of societal organization that keep it in some state of equilibrium. The individual is accorded a 'status-role set' that places him in various institutions while the mechanism of institutionalization continually provides for the integration of the social system that is surrounded and kept in boundaries by the cultural system, the personality systems, organic systems, and other social systems.
3 Namely, how any sort of equilibrium and stability is achieved *at all* in most societies, most of the time, in view of the fact that each of these societies represents a 'veritable powder keg of conflicting forces' (Devereux, 1961: 33).
4 Gouldner (1970: 29ff.) distinguishes between 'background assumptions,' i.e., explicit and unlabelled postulations, and 'domain assumptions' which are background assumptions applied only to members of a single domain. He states:

Domain assumptions about man and society might include, for example, dispositions to believe that men are rational or irrational; that society is precarious or fundamentally stable; that social problems will correct themselves without planned intervention; that human behavior is unpredictable; that man's true humanity resides in his feelings and sentiments (Gouldner, 1970: 31).

5 Smith, 1973: 146–7; Nisbet, 1969: 211–39. A specific example of how the social character unfolds through the stages of religious evolution is presented by Bellah (1964); a general, grand-scale attempt is made by Parsons (1967; 1966; 1971).

6 For example, as Parsons, following Max Weber (1947) and his own pattern-variables scheme (Parsons, 1951: 58–67, 180–200), emphasizes the uniqueness of Western development and treats it as normative for other civilizations, he orders institutional structures into a hierarchy which is also a sequence and consequently can hardly avoid 'survival' hypotheses (Smith, 1973: 34).

7 The crux of the functionalist position seems to live in the notions of 'adaptation' and 'adjustment' as used by Merton. Merton (1968: 105) defines function as follows: '*Functions* are those observed consequences which make for the adaptation or adjustment of a given system; and *dysfunctions*, those observed consequences which lessen the adaptation of the system.' According to Johan Galtung (1977), this boils down to the question 'Functional for whom?' and Galtung proposes to give the answer in terms of some shared values within a social subsystem. Functionality and dysfunctionality thus depend on the values in the social system or subsystem taken as a point of departure (cf. also Münch, 1973: especially 71–6).

8 In his attempt to counter more effectively the reproach by his critics that the structural-functional theory was not capable of explaining social change, Parsons (1964b) first replaced the concept of function by that of process and then included the evolutionary principle in his theoretical system by construing 'evolutionary universals' that explained the continuity and change of social systems (Parsons, 1967; 1966; Eisenstadt, 1964b; Bellah, 1964). He designates as an evolutionary universal

> any organizational development sufficiently important to further evolution that, rather than emerging only once, it is likely to be 'hit upon' by various systems operating under different conditions ... thus representing a complex of structures and associated processes the development of which so increases the long-run adaptive capacity of living systems in a given class that only systems that develop the complex can attain certain higher levels of general adaptive capacity (Parsons, 1967: 493).

9 Sociological functionalism of this persuasion makes sense only if self-regulatory mechanisms can be discovered that involve the maintenance of a narrow range or goal state of a given variable. Accordingly, the difference between a functional and a non-functional statement

becomes a matter of emphasis that is comparable to the difference between stating that B is the effect of A, and saying that A is the condition or cause of B (Nagel, 1956; 251).
10 We are not concerned here with David Lockwood's (1964) critique of the 'coercion theory of society' and the 'conflict model of society' (cf. Dahrendorf, 1959a: Rex, 1961), i.e. concentrating their intellectual fire on a special version of functionalism, namely, 'normative functionalism.' In doing so, Lockwood holds, they have become overly involved with the problems of 'social integration,' thus ignoring 'what is just as relevant to their central interests in conflict and social change, namely, the problem of "system integration," ' for the solution of which 'general functionalism would still seem to be the most useful instrument. . . . Whereas the problem of social integration focuses attention upon the orderly or conflictful relationships between the *actors*, the problem of system integration focuses on the orderly or conflictful relationships between the *parts* of a social system' (Lockwood, 1964: 244–5).
11 This is to say that social systems tolerating a great deal of role-strains, status-discrepancies, racial tensions, and normative ambiguities, and even basic contradictions over long periods of time, do not necessarily undergo more or less drastic changes. The weakening of social structures or setting up of institutions to deal with these conflicts always implies some sort of intra-systemic adjustments, i.e., re-formation of social relations (even if this only means getting used to less rigidly defined norms, as abortion and pornography laws demonstrate).
12 Cf. Nadel, 1957: 144–5; Isajiw, 1968: 66–7; Gouldner, 1970: 231. To quote Parsons (1951: 482):

> [The] elements of the constancy of pattern must constitute a fundamental point of reference for the analysis of process in the [social] system. From a certain point of view these processes are to be defined as the processes of maintenance of the constant pattern. But of course these are empirical constancies, so we do not assume any inherent reason why they have to be maintained. It is simply a fact that, as described in terms of a given frame of reference, these constancies are often found to exist, and theory can thus be focused on the problems presented by their existence. They may cease to exist, by the dissolution of the distinctive boundary-maintaining system and its assimilation to the environment, or by transformation into other patterns. But the fact that they do exist, at given times and places, still serves as the theoretical focus for analysis.

13 Parsons's 'An Outline of the Social System' (1961: 30–79) is particularly informative with respect to the role of values and norms, of socialization and internalization, in society. See also Parsons (1951); Parsons and Shils (1951); Gouldner (1970: 226ff.); and Strasser (1976: Chapter 6).
14 Durkheim (1964: 377; emphasis added) makes this point perfectly clear:

> Constraint only begins when regulation, no longer corresponding to the *true nature of things*, and, accordingly, no longer having any *basis*

> *in customs*, can only be validated through force. . . . Inversely, we may say that the division of labor *produces solidarity only if it is spontaneous* and in proportion as it is spontaneous. But by spontaneity we must understand not simply the absence of all express violence, but also of everything that can even indirectly shackle the free *unfolding* of the social force that each carries in himself. It supposes, not only that individuals are not relegated to determinate functions by force, but also that no obstacle, of whatever nature, prevents them from occupying the place in the social framework which is compatible with their faculties. In short, *labor is divided spontaneously only if society is constituted in such a way that social inequalities exactly express natural inequalities*. But, for that, it is necessary and sufficient that the latter be neither enhanced nor lowered by some external cause. Perfect spontaneity is . . . a consequence and another form of . . . absolute equality in the external conditions of the conflict. It consists . . . in a subtle organization in which each social value, being neither overestimated nor underestimated by anything foreign to it, would be judged at its true worth.

15 This is what Parsons (1968, I: 450) hinted at when he stated in his first major work that to have a theory of social change 'it is necessary to know what it is that changes.'

16 To put the same point in a later language, we quote Merton (1968: 94–5):

> By focusing on dysfunctions as well as on functions, this mode of analysis can assess not only the bases of social stability but the potential sources of social change. . . . The strains and stresses in a social structure which accumulate as dysfunctional consequences of existing elements . . . will in due course lead to institutional breakdown and basic social change. When this change has passed beyond a given and not easily identifiable point, it is customary to say that a new social system has emerged.

17 See also Smelser's (1962) theory of collective change, as discussed in section 6.1.2 of the present volume.

18 For example, *writing* through language and literacy is seen as crucial for the emergence of the intermediative level as it permits, above all, knowledge to be transmitted and stored more easily. It also means that, specifically, education, contacts, and contracts were facilitated and, generally, culture's influence on society was enhanced. Societies of the intermediate category range from the ancient civilization in Egypt and Mesopotamia to the late-medieval societies in Europe. The modern level did not come into being until a *legal system* had appeared that furthered the independence of norms from the exigencies of political and economic interests. Its organization is highly generalized according to universalistic principles enforced by procedural primacy enabling the system to cope with changing circumstances and various types of cases without prior commitment to specific solutions (Parsons, 1966: 26–7; 1967).

19 The most important mechanism of variation is language. Language not only provides the possibility of negation but strengthens also the conflict capacity of society in that potentials for rejection are generated. At first, language fulfills also the function of *selection*. After the introduction of writing it is supplemented by symbolic media codes such as power/law, truth, love, and property/money, which increase the probability that communication is accepted. Ever since the early civilizations they are regarded as 'indispensable.' The function of *stabilization* is served by differentiation of such systems as politics, science, family, and economy which correspond to the aforementioned media of communication. These subsystems of society that gained their profile especially against religion, made it possible (1) that solutions of problems can be reproduced under changing environment conditions, and (2) that, since the rise of civil society, structural changes in all areas of society proceed at a rate unknown thus far. For Luhmann, the mechanism of stabilization dominant in archaic societies is that of segmental differentiation, while strata differentiation was typical for high cultures and functional differentiation characteristic of modern society. To put it in over-simplified terms: The stability of the society of modern Europe is based upon its capacity for variation and a pronounced mechanism for system differentiation which, in turn, plays a significant role in generating variations, as the present world of a tripolar social order seems to demonstrate (cf. Luhmann, 1975f: 150–4, 170–92).

20 To put it in yet other terms: According to Parsons, the relationship between the various types of action system as well as within the social system are ordered by the principle of cybernetic priority in connection with the primacy of the relevance for the different exchange requirements of the respective subsystem. These relationships are surveyed in Table 4.2. As much as the behavioral organism links the action system with the anatomic–physiological characteristics of the physical organism, so does the personality system represent the control center for the behavioral organism. Whereas the social system controls the personality systems of its members, the cultural system with its apparatus of symbols and value orientations directs the social system (Parsons, 1961: 37–8). Social systems and their subsystems are, in turn, located on a cybernetic condition–control hierarchy, which means that change is expected to occur within the given conditions, on the one hand, and to be governed by the control systems, on the other. The hypothesis is suggested that the more generalized the value or cultural pattern, or the higher a phenomenon located on the hierarchy of control, the less likely it is to change. Change on the cultural level is change *of* the system. The lower structures are located on the control hierarchy, the more readily they will adjust to changing conditions and their environments. However, these changes tend to lose force as they ramify through the system. For instance, changes in the economic sphere, which is highest on the hierarchy of conditions but lowest on controls, are relatively common. Some of these changes will affect the polity, still fewer the societal community, and probably none the

TABLE 4.2 *The AGIL-scheme differentiated according to the control hierarchy of action systems, social subsystems, structural components, primary functions, and aspects of social change*

Control hierarchy of action systems						
	Cybernetic control hierarchy		Subsystem of society/of the social system	Structural element of the social subsystem	Primary function	Aspect of the developmental process
Action system	Change	Stability				
Behavioral organism (A)			Economy (enterprises)	Roles	Adaptation (A)	Adaptive upgrading
Personality (G)			Polity (political organization)	Collectivities	Goal attainment (G)	Differentiation
Society (I)			Societal community (social control agencies)	Norms	Integration (I)	Inclusion
Culture (L)			Education (socialization agencies)	Values	Pattern maintenance (L)	Value generalization

Conditions/Range of change → (Condition hierarchy: A < L)

← Conditions/Sources of stability (Control hierarchy: L > A)

Source: Adapted from Parsons, 1971: 6, 11.

institutionalized cultural patterns. Parsons (1960: 295ff.) confirms this illustration in one of his essays by concluding that those values that integrate American society, i.e., instrumental activism, etc., have not changed in any fundamental way in American history.

21 As mentioned in note 20, segmental differentiation is characteristic of archaic societies, leading to the identity of system and environment. Stratification predominates in high cultures in that equality with respect to rank within the system and inequality with respect to the environment is established. Functional differentiation is typical of modern societies producing functional identity within the system and functional non-identity with respect to the environment.

> Segmental differentiation focuses on small-scale endogenously produced variation and a threatening environment in that identical units (residential communes, families, tribes) which can survive partial annihilation through death or secession, are differentiated. Stratification is geared toward the centralization of resources and control over considerable variation through domination of the *maiores partes*. Functional differentiation makes a social order possible in which stabilization serves, above all, to secure the compatibility of the subsystems in relation to each other and in which media-specific selectors (e.g., maximum profit, reason of state, passionate love, 'curious' research) may operate regardless of stabilization without endangering the persistence of society as a social system (Luhmann, 1975f: 153).

22 In general, systems can only persist by maintaining and selectively controlling processes of exchange with environing systems. Specifically, social systems such as society, a firm or a family, presuppose exchange relations with other societies and subsystems respectively, if the goals of stability and effective functioning should be achieved (which is, by the way, identical with the definition of equilibrium). Figure 4.1 purports to illustrate this statement by drawing attention to the exchange relations among the primary subsystems of society.

23 The question that should be raised is whether institutionalization is 'implemented' by an undefined collectivity such as society in order to bring individuals in line with the 'core' of the value system of society, as Parsons wants to make us believe; or is it 'carried out' by organized groups *against* some individuals and groups and interests and *for* other individuals and groups and interests? As Coser (1956: 121–37) has demonstrated, social conflict may create new norms and promote change of common social norms which is necessary for the readjustment of the relationship between contenders.

24 Cf. Parsons, 1967: 493 and Luhmann, 1971a: 151 respectively. Recent attempts to avoid some of the pitfalls of these functionalisms led to additional types of functional analysis that have not been discussed here in detail, although casual references have been made. Above all, we have in mind historical functionalism (e.g., Ridder, 1972), subjective functionalism (e.g., Luhmann, 1971a), and processual functionalism

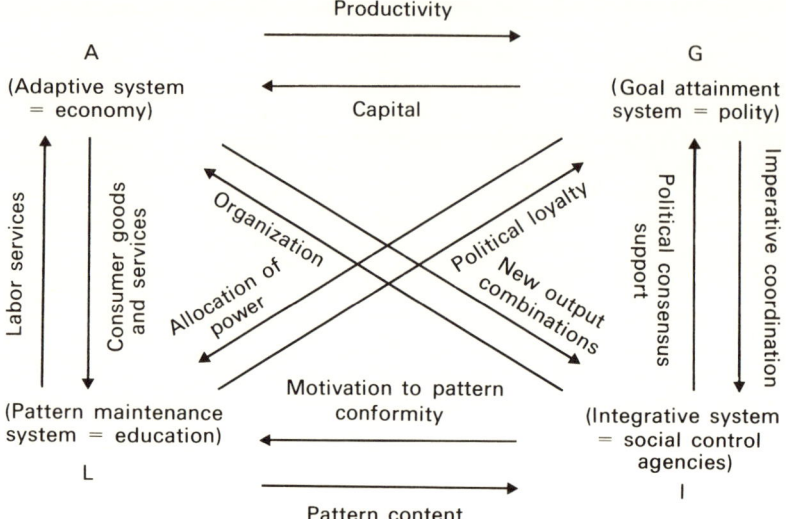

Source: Adapted from Parsons and Smelser, 1956: 68.

FIGURE 4.1 *Exchange relations between primary subsystems of society (AGIL-scheme)*

(e.g., Buckley, 1967). For an excellent survey of these developments, see Bühl, 1975: 9–35.

25 Luhmann (1971a: 27), for example, points out that 'All functional analyses are ultimately conducted in reference to problems of stabilization as guidelines. The functional interpretation of action clearly points to the fact that given the network of alternative possibilities social actions are always in need of stabilization.'

26 For further references, see Homans, 1950: 307–8; Parsons, 1951: 383–4; Hempel, 1959: 293–7. Part of the following discussion draws heavily on Guessous, 1967.

27 The question as to how change occurs in the first place, if a common value system is assumed, hardly embarrasses them. The answer is that change producing strains arise (1) because of socialization deficits due to the life cycle and/or class-specific experiences; (2) because not all members of society feel equally committed to all values and norms (e.g., the value of private property or freedom of press); (3) because of difficulties in synchronizing norms and roles in the wake of system differentiations; and (4) because of the permanent possibility of external influences (be it from other social systems or from non-social systems).

28 For instance, from 9 to 12 a.m. a man works and serves goal attainment and adaptation, neglecting tension management; from 12 to 1 p.m. he may suspend the former and concentrate on tension management; from 1 to 5 p.m. he returns to goal attainment at the expense of tension management; after 5 p.m. he manages tension to the exclusion of goal

attainment. Of course, at no time can he completely forget one need, or prolong the satisfaction of any one over a period of time without jeopardizing others. Although there is no neat delineation possible, it is legitimate to say that a tendency can be found in society to institutionalize these phases (e.g., daily phase with work from 9 to 5 and then relaxation, or weekly phase with work from Monday through Friday and then rest period). From a system perspective, one can easily arrive at a classification of social structures in terms of their respective problem concerns and corresponding phase-movements. For example, the economy and national defense deal with adaptive problems; the state and legal institutions concentrate on integrative difficulties; the family, informal groups, mass media, churches, and education (as an agency transmitting culture) are primarily involved in problems of pattern maintenance and tension management.

29 Parsons, for example, invested considerable effort into analyzing the rise of the Nazi movement in Germany, and in doing so he singled out 'four major broad sets of conditions which must be present if such a movement is to spread widely and gain ascendency in the social system' (Parsons, 1951: 521; cf. also pp. 520–34; 1954c: 104–23). In the last analysis, the seizing of power by the Nazi Party is accounted for in terms of 'the existence of a widespread alienative motivation' as a consequence of a 'rapid process of industrialization,' which, it seems, accidentally met a 'highly unstable . . . power structure in postwar Germany' (Parsons, 1951: 523–4). As an alternative explanation, one could contend that the social cleavages persisting in the Weimar Republic originated in the antagonistic authority relations prevailing after the fall of the German monarchy and resulting in a massive usurpation and redistribution of social and political power by the Nazi regime; and that the fundamental, and eventually self-destructive, conflict was a struggle between groups that emerged from the confrontation of the new authority structure with the traditional, though still effective and spiritually present, power structure of pre-war Germany (cf. e.g., Dahrendorf, 1958; in Chapter 6 of the present volume, we try to compare several theoretical approaches by using the same empirical case, namely, the rise of National Socialism in Germany).

Suggested reading

Introductory reading

MERTON, ROBERT K. (1968), 'Manifest and Latent Functions,' pp. 73–138 in MERTON, ROBERT K., *Social Theory and Social Structure*, enlarged ed., New York: Free Press.
This chapter may be regarded as the functionalist breviary; it is clearly and lucidly written.

PARSONS, TALCOTT (1961), 'An Outline of the Social System,' pp. 30–79 in PARSONS, TALCOTT, SHILS, EDWARD A., NAEGELE, KASPAR, and PITTS, JESSE (eds), *Theories of Society*, New York: Free Press.

In this essay, Parsons first presents the structural-functional categories for analyzing social systems, then develops a theory of social equilibrium, and, finally, discusses the problem of structural change under endogenous and exogenous points of view.

GLUCKMAN, MAX (1968), 'The Utility of the Equilibrium Model in the Study of Social Change,' *American Anthropologist*, 70: 219–37.

In this essay the potential of the equilibrium model for explaining change phenomena of different kinds is critically examined.

PARSONS, TALCOTT (1967), 'Evolutionary Universals in Society,' pp. 490–520 in PARSONS, TALCOTT, *Sociological Theory and Modern Society*, New York: Free Press.

The essay represents one of Parsons's basic works for establishing a functionalist change theory on neo-evolutionist grounds.

Further reading

General

PARSONS, TALCOTT (1966), *Societies: Evolutionary and Comparative Perspectives*, Englewood Cliffs, N.J.: Prentice-Hall.

PARSONS, TALCOTT (1971), *The System of Modern Societies*, Englewood Cliffs, N.J.: Prentice-Hall.

These two volumes deal with the sequence and the characteristics that societies show in the course of their evolution as social systems. Upon examination of anthropological, historical, and sociological material Parsons depicts evolutionary universals and arrives at the distinction between 'primitive,' 'archaic,' 'intermediate' and 'modern' societies.

SMITH, ANTHONY D. (1973), *The Concept of Social Change: A Critique of the Functionalist Theory of Social Change*, London: Routledge & Kegan Paul.

Smith undertakes a detailed discussion of the (neo-)evolutionistically inspired functional theory of change, confronts explanatory reality with claims, and offers proposals as to how to improve this approach.

GOULDNER, ALVIN W. (1959), 'Reciprocity and Autonomy in Functional Theory,' pp. 241–70 in GROSS, LLEWELLYN (ed.), *Symposium on Sociological Theory*, New York: Harper & Row.

Exchange and power relations between the elements of a social system are at the center of a still profound critique of traditional functional analysis.

Problem-related

CANCIAN, FRANCESCA (1961), 'Functional Analysis of Change,' *American Sociological Review*, 25: 818–27.

By drawing upon a number of examples as to how interpersonal relationships are formed and which characteristics they show, the author demonstrates when, where, and to what extent changes of these relationships occur and what kind of research problems may be expected.

LOCKWOOD, DAVID (1976), 'Social Integration and System Integration,' pp.

370–83 in ZOLLSCHAN, GEORGE K. and HIRSCH, WALTER (eds), *Social Change: Explorations, Diagnoses, Conjectures*, Cambridge, Mass.: Schenkman.

In this essay Lockwood examines the critique leveled against functionalism by conflict theory and attempts to construct a synthesis of Marx and Parsons by distinguishing between social integration in the sense of control over behavior and system integration in the sense of cooperation between the representatives of the institutional order and those who control the means of production.

LENSKI, GERHARD (1976), 'History and Social Change,' *American Journal of Sociology*, 82: 548–64.

Lenski defends here the neo-evolutionary approach to the study of social change against charges by Robert A. Nisbet (1969) on methodological and substantive grounds.

PARSONS, TALCOTT and PLATT, GERALD M. (1973), *The American University*, Cambridge, Mass.: Harvard University Press.

The authors attempt to demonstrate the explanatory potential of the structural-functional theory of change with reference to the evolution of the system of higher education in such industrial-capitalistic societies as the US.

Part III Analysis of change on different levels of society

5 Levels of sociological analysis: four theories of change

Susan C. Randall and *Hermann Strasser*

Most types of sociological theory of social change, including those presented in Chapters 2–4, have been traditionally oriented toward finding the causes of large-scale social transformations and to describing the central processes that characterize the transition of societies from one state to another. In recent decades, many change theorists have withdrawn from these general propositions and directed their efforts toward the description of single processes in which changes of a small as well as a larger scale manifest themselves. Attendant with this shift has been a change in focus to include other than societal-level analyses of change. Contemporary theorists have taken considerable notice of the impact of social conditions on groups and individuals as well as the role of individuals in initiating and effecting change. As demonstrated by Wilfred Trotter's *Instincts of the Herd in Peace and War* (1916) and Gustave Le Bon's *The Crowd* (1896/1952), studies on the role of the individual and group in relation to change were frequently done under psychological rather than sociological premises. In section 1.2 we have already elaborated upon that.

However, in their attempt to stick with more specific and testable hypotheses than their precursors, these theorists of the 'middle ranges' have largely shunned such problems as causation. In short, the field of social change is currently characterized by an abundance of theories that deal with either broad, general aspects of change or with more specific details, but rarely with both.

Nevertheless, the absence of 'grand theories' in the field need not necessarily represent a significant deficiency in our knowledge about the subject. The specialization characteristic of many new theories has added greatly to our understanding of social change. Indeed, it might prove more fruitful to combine various theories that deal with different though complementary aspects of change, or with changes on different levels of society, in order to gain an adequate conception of change.

In Part III of this volume, we are going to present theoretical approaches, each of which focuses on a different *level* of society. Moreover, we are going to explore the possibility of using these theories as independent but complementary explanatory schemes. The result is not meant to be a theoretical synthesis explaining all aspects of change and change on all levels of society. In view of the paradigmatic structure of sociology, this is neither possible nor desirable. Each of these theories is limited in its applicability to specific types of change. We will try to show, at best, how the more specific theories can serve to fill in the gaps in the explanation of change which are produced by the broadest theory.

The first theory to be elaborated upon refers to Barrington Moore's *Social Origins of Dictatorship and Democracy* in which factors are analyzed that necessitate change in a social order. His is primarily an historical account of the changes produced in various societies by the introduction of commercialization into the agricultural sphere. This perspective might be employed within a more general framework for studying what occurs when the power relations of an existing social order are challenged by pressures for change. His theory provides an analysis of structural conditions that produce societal change and a formula for predicting the type of change that is likely to occur.

The second theory is Neil J. Smelser's *Theory of Collective Behavior* which differs from Moore's in several respects. Whereas Moore's theoretical statements are drawn from extensive historical reviews of specific episodes of change, Smelser has developed an abstract analytical model of universal determinants which he superimposes on concrete cases. Smelser, as opposed to Moore, focuses more on concrete mechanisms by which change takes place rather than on causes. Moore is interested in long-term developments, while Smelser tends to focus on single, mostly short-term episodes of change. In this respect Smelser's ideas resemble those expressed in the theory of revolution developed by James C. Davies (1962). According to Davies, the emergence of a revolutionary potential against the old regime may be traced to an immediate worsening of circumstances until eventually perceived in optimistic terms. Finally, Moore's theory aims at explaining society-wide changes while Smelser's encompasses both small-scale changes within a society and those on a larger scale.

Most sociological explanations of change, including those of Moore and Smelser, stress the social forces that give rise to change but relegate the question as to why people participate in movements designed to effect changes in society to the realm of implicit assumptions. General laws of social development and social conditions such as economic hardship or social disorganization, to name just two examples, are cited as reasons for the rise of social movements. Little explanation is given for why specific groups or individuals take part in these movements. The third theory, or set of related theories, to be presented deals with this aspect of the change process. The so-called *theory of status inconsistency* represents a social-psychological view of the relationship between the social status of individuals and groups, on the one hand, and their activities and attitudes relative to social change, on the other.

Finally, Chapter 7 is devoted to a fourth theoretical approach: the analysis of *organizations* as social subsystems. The reason for choosing this analytical and empirical level is twofold. On the one hand, organizations, especially bureaucratic and complex organizations in state and economy, are viewed as the result of social transformations that are associated with the rise of modern society, the national state, and democratic revolutions, technological changes in the wake of Industrial Revolution, and the bureaucratization of the economy and the state as well as the secularization of our social life. On the other hand, organizations – as a consequence of the complexity of modern societies – increasingly intervene between the social system as a whole and the innumerous interaction systems. They are characterized by the principles of system boundary maintenance, formation of structures, and structural change in which they differ from social relationships and inclusive social systems as well as such groups as families, peers, strata, and classes. We would like to pay particular attention to which systemic problems in organizations come into existence when, how, and in what kind of processual patterns, and also to which change effects on the environing subsystems and the total system may be expected.

The theories of Barrington Moore and Neil J. Smelser, of status inconsistency, and the change in and through organizations will be discussed here mainly because they represent *different* approaches to the systematic study of social change. We neither claim, of course, that they cover all important aspects of social change, nor, though there is ample evidence for the contrary, that they are necessarily representative of the theoretical approaches to these areas of discourse.

In Moore's approach, explanatory principles of the conflict theory of Marxist as well as non-Marxist persuasion are combined: the political outcome of modernization is seen as resulting, on the one hand, from the ways in which the agrarian ruling class and the exploited classes, particularly the peasantry, react to the introduction of commercial agriculture and, on the other hand, from the power relationships between dominant, rising, and oppressed social groupings. Smelser, by contrast, posits the group, defined as generating actions based on some generalized belief, in the centre of discussion. For him, social groups and patterns of collective behavior represent special cases of a social system characterized by values held in common as its basic frame of reference and ultimate cause of the kind of social action to be expected to occur. Smelser's approach may therefore be taken as an exemplification of the functionalist theory of social change. By focusing on the causes of status discrepancies as well as individual and group strategies to eliminate its stressful effects, the status inconsistency approach includes both macro- (mainly of the functionalist type) and micro-sociological (mainly of the interactionist and behaviorist type) elements of social analysis.

To be sure, the discussion of change in and through organizations occupies a special position in so far as it combines various theoretical elements. There are neo-evolutionist ideas that provide cognitive access to the problem of social change through the emergence and expansion of complex organizations, while propositions along the lines of structural-functionalism, modernization and conflict theory dominate the explications about structure and change of organizations in present-day society. Given the systematic purpose of this chapter and its eclectic realization, we refrain from including it in the comparative analysis to be presented in section 6.4. The point is that change in organizations may be traced to two major causes: (1) the coexistence of contradictory organizational principles in an organization which leads to strains; and (2) the alterations introduced in organizations which themselves give rise to strains and hence to further changes. This clearly shows how much the changes in organizations are reflected on the interaction, group and societal levels.

After presenting summaries of the theories of Moore, Smelser, and status inconsistency, some of their major differences will be discussed and, on the basis of these differences, the possibility of combining them as independent but complementary schemes will be explored. The task of comparing them will be facilitated, as mentioned already, by recurring to the *same* phenomenon, that is, the rise of National Socialism in the Weimar Republic (sections 6.1.4, 6.2.7, and 6.3.4).

6 Change of the social system, social groups, and social relationships

Susan C. Randall and *Hermann Strasser*

6.1 Macrolevel analysis: Barrington Moore's theory of societal change

6.1.1 The thesis

The theory of social change presented by Barrington Moore is an attempt to explain the important structural factors behind the main historical routes that the major nations of the East and West have taken in their transformation from agrarian to modern industrial societies. The three routes to the modern world that he examines are:

1 Democracy, via a bourgeois revolution (e.g., England, France, US);
2 Fascism, via a conservative revolution from above (e.g., Japan, Germany);
3 Communism, via a peasant revolution (e.g., China, Russia).

The *key* to understanding why a country followed a particular historical route to modernization lies, according to Moore, in the ways in which the landed upper classes and the peasants reacted to the challenge of commercial agriculture (Moore, 1966: xvii).

The dominant features of the three basic political configurations that emerged as these nations started on the road to modernization are briefly summarized below:

1 *Democratic capitalism*: The development of an economically independent bourgeoisie which the landed upper classes and peasantry either supported or were destroyed by, via revolution or civil war.

2 *Reactionary capitalism*: A coalition between the older landed elites and the relatively weak rising commercial and industrial class, directed against the lower urban and rural classes. Bourgeois revolution was either non-existent or weak and easily defeated.
3 *Communism*: The maintenance of power by the agrarian bureaucracy and landed nobility which stifled all but the most feeble attempts at commercialization and industrialization, leaving behind a huge peasant population which ultimately revolted against the ruling classes.

For the purpose of analyzing how and why particular political outcomes resulted from certain structural conditions and responses of the landed aristocracy and the peasantry to the pressures of economic modernization, we have isolated several variables that seem to be of major significance in Moore's treatment of the subject. Moore does present an abundance of historical facts about each nation's progress on the road to modernization which serve to tie these variables into specific cases and 'fill the gaps' of explanation. However, since we are concerned with the broad theoretical implications of his work rather than with summarizing his detailed historical accounts, we will discuss only those variables that contributed significantly to his formulation of a general theory of the social origins of democracy, fascism, and communism.

The central *variables* in Moore's analysis are:

1 the 'starting point' (or social setting prior to modernization);
2 persistence or non-persistence of a strong central authority and its relationship with the landed aristocracy;
3 response of landed aristocracy to commercialization and the form which this commercialization takes;
4 conditions of the peasantry resulting from the landed elite's response to the pressures of modernization;
5 strength or weakness of bourgeoisie relative to landed aristocracy;
6 nature of coalitions between classes; and
7 presence or absence and type of revolution.

It is important to point out that we have isolated these variables only for means of analysis and that in specific historical situations they are intimately interrelated.

The plan of this summary will be to describe Moore's major theoretical propositions by sketching the basic configuration of these variables as they relate to democracy, fascism, and communism, and by examining how they operated in the specific historical instances that Moore discusses (England, France, US, Japan, and China) to produce certain political forms.

Moore's point of departure is England which he sees as the ideal-typical example of a bourgeois revolution culminating in parliamentary democracy. France and the US are aberrant variations on the same theme. Rather than positing separate ideal types of fascism and communism, he analyzes them basically in terms of the ways in which they deviate from the model of parliamentary democracy, i.e., he looks at the conditions necessary for parliamentary democracy which were lacking in countries that terminated their route to the modern era in fascism or communism.

6.1.2 The variables

6.1.2.1 The social structure prior to modernization
Although Moore does not examine in detail the history of premodern societies, he does point out that certain structural differences in agrarian societies may have influenced their subsequent development. 'Yet even if the starting point is not decisive in itself, some may be much more favorable to democratic developments than others' (Moore, 1966: 415).

Moore believes that the character of feudalism in Western Europe promoted subsequent democratic developments whereas social arrangements in other parts of Europe and in Asia lacked certain of the ingredients favorable to democratic ideas and institutions. The most important of these elements of Western feudalism were: (1) growth of the notion of the immunity of certain groups and persons from the power of the ruler; (2) the concept of the right to resist unjust authority; and (3) the concept of contract as a mutual engagement freely undertaken by free persons (derived from the feudal relation of vassalage). According to Moore, these ideas led to the delicate balance between too much and too little royal authority which was an essential ingredient for parliamentary democracy. In Russia no such balance was struck, for there was little reciprocal sharing of obligations and power between the ruler and the independent nobility. Bureaucratic China lacked a strong conception of corporate immunity from central authority. Japanese feudalism stressed loyalty to superiors and a divine ruler and lacked the concept of free contract.

Moore emphasizes that, although he sees the role of ideas or cultural themes as important, he does not consider them to be the sole key to historical explanation. (Note that early Prussian society had features similar to those that became the ancestors of parliamentary democracy in other parts of Western Europe.) Rather, he sees them as intervening variables between people and 'objective' situations which greatly influence the response to a situation. Moore does not attempt to explain the historical developments of these countries in terms of their cultural values, but rather seeks to determine out of what conditions and experiences those values and institutions arose, which lent themselves to the development of democracy, fascism, or communism. The following variables that are concerned with the social, political, and economic conditions of the major classes in these societies may serve to clarify the bases of the various cultural themes.

6.1.2.2 Presence or absence of a strong central authority and its relationship with the landed aristocracy

Moore designates the sixteenth and seventeenth centuries, during which time powerful central governments were established in all countries that he examines (except the US), as the beginning of modernization. In general, the development of strong central governments served two main functions in bringing about modernization. First, they checked the power and arbitrary rule of the nobility and, second, they 'rationalized' the political order, that is, they established more or less uniform administrative and legal systems and helped to create an organized military machine. These two tasks were carried out early by the royal absolutist regimes but not until the nineteenth century, after modernization had begun, in the agrarian bureaucracies.

Although strong central authorities developed in all of these countries, the important variable is whether or not pre-industrial royal absolutism or agrarian bureaucracy persisted into modern times and whether or not it sided with the landed aristocracy to form a conservative regime.

In general, the persistence of a nobility economically dependent on the land in alliance with a strong central authority which protects the privileges of the nobility is unfavorable to the development of *democratic capitalism*, as it tends to resist the formation of an independent bourgeoisie. Instead of allowing an independent commercial class to arise, the nobility, aided and protected by the central government, may continue to make its living from what it can extract from the peasants.

In England there was no strong alliance between central authority and landed aristocracy during modernization. Instead, a rough balance of power between crown and nobility emerged. The English Civil War had checked royal absolutism and the landed aristocracy established early a firm, independent economic base, in that they took on commercial traits by participating in trade and commerce.

French social structure lacked this important balance of power between monarch and landed elite. Instead of gaining independence, the leading sector of French nobility 'became a decorative appanage of the king' (Moore, 1966: 40), dependent on him for feudal protection. Moreover, instead of turning to commercialization for income, the nobles continued to extract dues from their peasants. Those independent commercials who did arise were 'co-opted' into the nobility and its conservatizing system of privileges. This fusion of ruler, aristocracy, and entrepreneurial bourgeoisie into a conservative *ancien régime*, dominated by the monarchy, would have been a strong obstacle to the development of parliamentary democracy had the French Revolution not destroyed it.

The United States of America (after the Revolution) did not face the problem of destroying a well-established absolutist regime, and the Southern aristocracy was involved from the very beginning in commercial agriculture. However, the Southern landed elites did not extend their commercial activities past agriculture and their interests were opposed to Northern industrial development. They constituted a force inhibiting modernization which was eventually destroyed by the Civil War.

The *fascist* configuration of this variable involves the persistence of a strong royal bureaucracy closely allied with the landed aristocracy, both of which rely mainly on the extraction of a surplus from the peasants for use and marketing. Commercial and manufacturing interests are allowed to develop but controlled to a great extent by the central government and landed elite. The *communist* variation displays the same relationship between royal bureaucracy and landed aristocracy as fascism, the main difference being that almost all commercial impulses within the elite and peasantry are stifled.

6.1.2.3 The response of landed aristocracy to commercialization and the form that this commercialization takes

One of the greatest impacts of commerce, both locally and internationally, was on the traditional exchange economy. As markets spread, cash economies developed, placing demands for more and more cash on rulers and lords. Rulers responded by levying heavier taxes on the lords, who reacted either by turning to commercial farming themselves or by extracting increased surpluses from the peasants. In general, the former response occurs where there is a fairly independent nobility and the latter is found where the landed elite remains closely tied to a strong central authority which is able to carry out the repressive measures necessary to hold down the labor force on the land.

The English response to commercialization was most favorable to democratic capitalist development. The English aristocracy turned to a form of commercial farming, removing most of its remaining dependence on the crown. They set their peasants free to decide for themselves, thus creating a large potential urban labor force.

The commercial impulse was much weaker in France where the aristocracy generally left the peasants in control of the soil. Where the French nobles did turn toward commerce, they compelled the peasants to turn over a large part of their produce which the nobles then marketed. Thus, in France, peasant society was left largely intact but often economically drained, a situation that might have led to a peasant revolution had the French Revolution not crippled the monarchy and landed elite and, with them, the major resistance to democratic bourgeois development.

The response of the landed elite in the US to commercialization was plantation slavery, a politically and socially repressive system unfavorable to democracy basically because it impedes the development of an independent bourgeoisie and requires a strong, authoritarian political apparatus. Democratic developments were made possible mainly because (1) the landed aristocracy did not control the emerging bourgeoisie in the North and West, and (2) the Civil War destroyed some of the landed elite's repressive hold over the South.

In contrast to the *democratic* route in which an independent bourgeoisie develops and the transition to commercialization is made either with the help or destruction of the landed elite, the *fascist* response to pressures to commercialize is carried out through a labor-repressive system. In this case the landed upper class, in conjunction with the central political authority, uses various political and social levers (as opposed to reliance on a free labor market) to ensure an adequate labor force to work the soil and provide surplus for marketing and consumption. A bourgeois class is allowed to develop but kept under control by the landed aristocracy. A dependent bourgeoisie, coupled with this reliance on serfdom or slavery for agricultural surplus, leaves the conservative alliance of central authority and landed elite in full control and is likely to result in fascism (unless the *ancien régime* is destroyed by revolution, e.g., in the US). Such was the case in Japan and Germany.

One of the major differences between the democratic and fascist routes, on the one hand, and the *communist* route, on the other, has to do with this variable of the response of the upper class to commercial agriculture. 'Where the landed upper class has turned to production for the market in a way that enables commercial influence to permeate rural life, peasant revolutions have been weak affairs' (Moore, 1966: 459). There are several different ways in which this development has taken place. For example: (1) the landed upper class can preserve peasant society in order to extract a surplus (e.g., early Meiji Japan); (2) traditional peasant society can be destroyed, either by breaking its connection with the land (e.g., England) or by intensifying the connection by (re-)introducing serfdom or slavery (e.g., Prussia). However, it is where the commercial impulse within the landed aristocracy is very weak that there is the greatest possibility of a peasant revolution leading to a communist regime. Moore basically attributes this to the failure of the landed upper class to establish reciprocal social and economic ties between itself and the peasantry. Peasant society is left intact but economically drained as nobles extract increasingly larger surpluses from the peasantry without giving them the means for increasing their productivity. Such was the case in eighteenth-century France as well as in China and Russia during the nineteenth and twentieth centuries.

6.1.2.4 Condition of the peasantry resulting from landed elite's response to pressures of modernization

This variable is closely related to the preceding one and has been discussed to some extent in the previous section. Generally speaking, a massive reservoir of peasants persisting into the modern era of industrialization has always been unfavorable to democratic development. The channeling of peasants off the land and into an open labor market seems to be most conducive to the development of *democratic* capitalism. If, instead, they are held on the land by a labor-repressive system, the socio-political climate will not be favorable to the development of democratic institutions as a powerful, repressive government will be required to keep them on the land.

Through the system of enclosures, England was able to eliminate the peasant question, driving them off the land to the cities and the 'new world'. The US also largely avoided the problem of a peasantry because of their relative absence from the country's origin. (Although the slaves could be considered as peasants, they were too weak as a class to present a revolutionary problem.)

France did not escape the problem of a large peasant mass persisting into the modern era. Indeed, Moore attributes the present instability of French democracy partly to this factor. However, the French Revolution, in which the peasants and the bourgeoisie were allied against the French aristocracy and monarchy, served as an alternative way of getting the peasants off the land and paved the way toward institutions favorable to democratic development (Moore, 1966: 426).

A large peasant population surviving into the modern era is characteristic of both the fascist and communist routes. The main difference between the two on this point stems from the different responses of the landed elites to modernization and the resultant differences in the living conditions of the peasant population. As pointed out earlier, in the *fascist* route, the landed elite, in alliance with the central authority, turns to commercial agriculture by keeping the peasants on the land and forcing them to produce a surplus for consumption and marketing. In the *communist* route, the landed elite does not turn to commercialization and does not introduce commercial agricultural techniques into peasant society but continues to squeeze more produce out of them. The former course forces the peasants into modernization by introducing just enough changes in rural society as to insure that the peasants generate a sufficient surplus to allow the landed elite to appropriate and market the goods at a profit. The latter course resists techniques that would increase productivity but continues to demand increased surpluses.

Briefly put, modernization entails the development of markets and the establishment of peace and order over a large territory for the purpose of transporting goods. In countries such as Japan, Germany, and the US, the processes of modernization and labor-repression served to strengthen the ties between lord and serf as well as the control that the lord had over the peasants. The development and maintenance of strong ties between the peasants and local nobles Moore sees as essential to the development of a reactionary reservoir of sentiment among the peasants and hence to the prevention of a peasant revolution. Strong ties between the two groups are basically maintained through a division of functions (mainly protection in return for production) and the creation of what Moore calls 'conservative solidarity' (i.e., cohesion between the two groups is established by tying those with actual and potential grievances into the prevailing social structure by giving even the most impoverished a stake in the system).

In countries that did not turn to commercial agriculture, bonds between the lord and peasant were weakened. The central authorities increased the burden on the peasants in order to militarize, meet the costs of a growing bureaucracy, etc., pushing many peasants below the subsistence level. Furthermore, where the protective function was also taken over by the central authority rather than by local landed elites (e.g., in China), a crucial tie between the upper class and peasantry was dissolved. As opposed to the conservative solidarity characteristic of the peasants tied to the lords, a condition that Moore terms 'radical solidarity' may arise. In radical solidarity the institutional arrangement is such that grievances spread throughout the peasant community and turn it into a solidary group hostile to the landlord, rather than providing an institutionalized means for redress of grievances. Radical solidarity arose in Russia, in response to the generalized land hunger, aligning the richer peasants with the poorer against the landlords. In China, where a certain minimum of property was necessary to be a 'part' of the recognized religious and social system, the Chinese communists were able to create this type of solidarity among those who had been pushed below the minimum property level and no longer had a vested interest in the existing social structure.

6.1.2.5 Strength or weakness of the bourgeoisie relative to the landed aristocracy

According to Moore, the development of a strong bourgeois class that can effectively compete for political power with the landed aristocracy is essential for *democratic* capitalist development.

In England the commercial class was strong, mainly because a large portion of the aristocracy had turned to bourgeois capitalism in response to pressures for commercialization. That is, the landed elite became 'bourgeoisified,' thus strengthening and leading the new commercial interests while simultaneously weakening the hold of the traditional landed nobility. In the US, the Northern industrialists broke the hold of the Southern aristocracy in the Civil War and this asserted their dominance as the nation's primary economic class. In France the bourgeoisie was weak. The nobility absorbed the more powerful peasants who had turned to commercial agriculture by granting them titles and privileges. However, the developing bourgeoisie who had not been thus coopted aligned themselves with the peasants to destroy the resistant elite in the revolution.

Thus, in the development of bourgeois capitalism, the landed elites either became an important part of the capitalistic and democratic trend, as in England, or, if they opposed it, they were destroyed as primary political powers via civil war or revolution.

In the nations that eventuated in *fascist* regimes we find a developing capitalist class in alliance with (rather than in competition with or dominance over) the landed upper class. In this situation, the powerful bourgeoisie is not allowed to develop independently but rather controlled by the landed elite. Commercialization and industrialization are fostered, but the landed elite retains the dominant hand politically. In the cases of Germany and Japan, the 'industrial class . . . is too weak and dependent to take power and rule in its own right and . . . therefore throws itself into the arms of the landed aristocracy and the royal bureaucracy, exchanging the right to rule for the right to make money' (Moore, 1966: 437). For reasons pointed out in the preceding section, the peasantry does not align itself with the bourgeoisie to overthrow the elites, as happened in France.

In China and Russia the bourgeois class was small and politically dependent. In China the imperial bureaucracy stifled the development of a strong commercial class. It absorbed ambitious individuals into the imperial service in an attempt to prevent the rise of an alternative, commercial avenue to legitimacy and social status. In both Russia and China, where commerce did arise, it was heavily taxed and controlled by the rulers for their own profit. After the decay of the Chinese imperial apparatus in the late eighteenth century, commercial and industrial elements turned to the provincial gentry for protection. However, these local officials were able to stifle commercial independence even more effectively than had the imperial bureaucracy. 'Not until 1910 did the Chinese business class begin to show some definite signs of emerging from official influence and domination' (Moore, 1966: 177).

The commercial and industrial classes of Russia were also kept weak under the control of the Tsarist regime as late as 1917. In neither country did they have enough power or wealth to constitute a worthwhile ally either for the peasants (as had been the case in France) or for the nobility (as in Germany and Japan). The route to *communism* was obvious.

6.1.2.6 *The nature of coalitions between classes*

Moore believes that the nature of the relationship between the landed upper classes and the upper stratum of the town dwellers (which he terms bourgeoisie) is one of the most important variables in determining the political outcome of modernization.

The type of coalition most favorable to *democratic* development is an alliance of the aristocracy with a strong bourgeoisie against the crown. This type of coalition occurred in England, further weakening the royal authority and enabling the industrial leaders to gain a firm political and economic hold. It is essential for democratic capitalism's development that the bourgeoisie be the dominant partner in the coalition, i.e., that the urban interests prevail over the rural.

In France and the US the landed aristocracies did not align themselves with the new industrial leaders; rather, they were destroyed by the bourgeoisie which formed temporary coalitions with the peasants (France) and the central government (US). In both cases, the hold of the conservative *ancien régime* was broken, allowing capitalist interests to dominate.

In contrast with the English case, the bourgeois–elite alliance that took place in Japan and Germany was of a *reactionary* nature. The landed aristocracy was the dominant partner and the coalition was directed against the peasants and workers. Thus the old politically and economically powerful aristocracy retained its position and the upper stratum of the bourgeoisie became part of the elite – the opposite of what occurred in England. Although, in the case of a reactionary coalition, the commercial and industrial elements are too weak and dependent to take power and rule themselves, they are strong enough to make a worthwhile political ally for the aristocracy and bureaucracy. Thus industrialization may proceed fairly rapidly although under the protective wing of the landed upper class. Even under this type of coalition, democratic features have developed (e.g., the Weimar Republic, Japan in the 1920s, and Italy under Giolitti). However, these developments have been unstable and shortlived, basically because the landed elite, in the absence of a revolutionary upheaval, retained a large share of the political power. And, with the rural interests holding the balance of power, the fundamental structural changes necessary to modernization were resisted – until a revolution from above imposed such changes upon the society.

Where the commercial and industrial elements are quite weak (e.g., Russia and China), another type of coalition occurs, with quite different results. If the bourgeoisie is perceived as being not strong enough to become a worthwhile ally for the royal bureaucracy or the landed elite and thus is not 'bought off' with a piece of the political and economic power of the regime, the urban leaders may join forces with the peasants, providing direction and leadership for peasant grievances in return for massive support necessary to seize power. However, even after the peasant-powered revolution has crippled the regime, neither liberal nor reactionary capitalist development is likely due to the weakness and underdevelopment of the trading and manufacturing classes.

6.1.2.7 *Presence or absence of a revolutionary upheaval or revolution from above and time in the era of modernization in which the revolution takes place*

Moore sees a revolutionary break with the past as a necessary condition for successful modernization. In general, the earlier in the era of modernization this break takes place, the more favorable it is for the development of *democratic* institutions; the later this break occurs, the more firmly entrenched the power of the landed aristocracy and central government becomes, presenting a solid front of conservative upper-class opposition to bourgeois development and the social reforms necessitated by modernization. The major import of a revolutionary break with the past is to destroy the alliance of big landlords with the central political machinery which inhibits the institution of the fundamental structural changes necessary for the adoption of commercial and industrial enterprises.

The English Civil War checked royal absolutism and gave the landed aristocracy a free hand in developing commercial enterprises early in the modern era. The French Revolution broke the power of the pre-commercial landed elite and royal authority, making it possible for independent commercial groups to develop and gain power. 'In this sense . . . the French Revolution constituted an alternative way of creating institutions eventually favorable to democracy' (Moore, 1966: 426). The American Civil War was the last of the three major bourgeois revolutions, likewise destroying the power of a landed elite which stood in the way of modernization via capitalism.

The next form of modernization was characterized by revolution from above, eventuating in *fascism*. This occurred in those countries in which the power of the landed elite had not been diminished and where commerce and industry had grown up under the protective wing of the conservative regime. In such countries a minimum of social adjustments to modernization had been allowed by the nobility and the necessary structural changes had to be initiated from above as the peasants and workers were unable to make them themselves. Moore's position is that where industrialization and commercialization are accomplished through labor-repressive systems and without revolutionary upheaval, structural modernization will be imposed from above and fascism will be the end result.

Fascism may be seen as an attempt to make conservatism popular and plebeian, that is to say, as a reaction against the upper-class coalition directed against peasants and workers. According to Moore, fascism is the product of the forced entrance of capitalism into the rural economy and of the structural strains arising in the post-competitive phase of capitalist industry. The small peasant suffering under the advance of economic modernization became the key figure in the ideology of the reactionaries. They emphasized a return to the 'simple, uncomplicated, romantic life of the peasant' which the strains of modernization had disrupted. The lack of revolutionary upheaval in response to the strains is partially explained by the appeal of this conservative ideology and further by the ties the peasant had with the lord (conservative solidarity).

The third major type of revolution – *peasant upheavals* – takes place late in the era of modernization. This type is most likely to occur in countries where the commercial and industrial impulses have been stifled and where a large peasant class has survived into the modern era, subject to the strains of a severe labor-repressive system. As under the great agrarian bureaucracies, the close social bonds between the landed upper class and the peasantry are destroyed if the central authority takes over the judicial and protective functions of the lord. An 'agrarian bureaucracy, or a society that depends on a central authority for extracting the surplus, is a type most vulnerable to such outbreaks [i.e., peasant rebellions]' (Moore, 1966: 459).

The breakdown in the ties between lord and serf can lead to the development of what Moore calls 'radical solidarity,' i.e., institutional arrangements that allow grievances to spread throughout the peasant community (rather than upward to the lord) and turn it into a solidary group hostile to the landlord. Such a situation may turn into open rebellion if leadership is provided by the wealthy peasants, local town elites, etc., who have become disenchanted with the existing regime. Moore agrees with Marx here that peasants cannot make a revolution *only* by themselves.

In Russia, radical solidarity arose in response to the general land hunger, turning both rich and poor peasants against the Tsar. In China, the communists were able to mobilize the support of huge numbers of peasants who had been pushed below the minimum level of subsistence. In neither case were the peasants tied into the dominant social structure nor were acceptable channels available for expressing grievances. In both cases direction and support from disenchanted urban leaders was necessary for the discontent to be channeled into revolution.

6.1.3 Summary of the features characteristic of the democratic, fascist and communist routes to the modern world

1 Persistence or non-persistence of a strong central authority and its relationship with the landed aristocracy:
Democratic: Development of a balance of power to avoid (a) too strong a crown (thus avoiding repressive social control apparatus), or (b) too independent a landed aristocracy (thus avoiding

dominance of rural over urban), or (c) a monolithic alliance between crown and nobility (which could prevent development of an independent bourgeoisie).
Fascist: Persistence of a strong royal government in close alliance with the landed aristocracy (able to control emerging commercial interests).
Communist: Same as above except that the landed aristocracy is quite dependent on, and controlled by, the strong agrarian bureaucracy.
2   Response of the landed aristocracy to commercialization:
Democratic: Large segment of the landed aristocracy leads the way in commercial agriculture, becoming economically independent and politically powerful, promoting urban over rural interests.
Fascist: Landed aristocracy responds to pressures to commercialize by establishing a labor-repressive system with the help of the central political authority. Just enough commercial innovations are instituted to insure adequate agricultural surplus. Developing bourgeois class is kept under the control of the aristocracy and central government.
Communist: Nobles respond by extracting increasingly larger surplus from peasants without providing them with the means to increase their productivity. Commercial and industrial impulse among nobility is very weak and is all but stifled among the peasants.
3   Condition of the peasantry resulting from landed elite's response to pressures of modernization:
Democratic: The 'peasant problem' is solved by channeling peasants off the land and into an open urban–rural labor market.
Fascist: Peasants are kept on the land but supplied with modern agricultural techniques to meet demands for increased productivity. Commercial impulse permeates rural society.
Communist: Burden on peasants is increased by pressure to produce more but they are not given technological means to do so.
4   Strength or weakness of bourgeoisie relative to landed aristocracy:
Democratic: Bourgeoisie becomes stronger than traditional landed aristocracy; urban interests dominate over rural interests. Large part of nobility becomes 'bourgeoisified.'
Fascist: Landed aristocracy remains stronger than bourgeoisie. Bourgeois development is controlled by the nobility.
Communist: Bourgeois development is stifled.
5   Nature of coalitions between classes:
Democratic: Coalition with bourgeoisie as dominant partner in alliance with (a) the landed aristocracy and directed against the

crown, e.g., England; (b) the peasantry and directed against the aristocracy and crown, e.g., France; (c) the central government and directed against landed aristocracy, e.g., US.

Fascist: Coalition between landed aristocracy and bourgeoisie (with landed aristocracy as dominant partner) directed against peasants and workers.

Communist: Coalition between urban leaders and peasants against bureaucracy and local nobility.

6   Type of revolution and time in the era of modernization in which the revolution took place:

Democratic: Revolutionary break with the past early in the era of modernization which destroys alliance of landed aristocracy with the central government.

Fascist: No revolution prior to industrialization and commercialization. Labor-repressive system is used to impose commercial techniques without modifying the social structure. Modernization of structure is imposed from above.

Communist: Absence of a commercial revolution in agriculture led by landed elite and absence of a bourgeois revolution. Massive peasant class survives into the modern era but with few bonds between it and the rest of the system.

6.1.4   *Application of Barrington Moore's theory to the Nazi Revolution*

Moore uses Japan as his primary example of the modern route to fascism although he cites Germany as an equally good example and frequently refers to developments in Germany in his analysis of the determinants of a fascist response to the strains of modernization (Moore, 1966: xi, xv, xvii). Our application of his theory to the German case will parallel the discussion of his major points presented in the preceding section.

The *first* condition that Moore deems essential to a fascist route to modernization is the persistence of a powerful landed aristocracy in alliance with a strong central authority. This alliance must be responsive enough to the pressures of modernization to foster the development of commercial and agricultural interests for trade, yet strong enough to stifle the liberation of the peasantry and prevent the development of an independent bourgeoisie which could threaten the power of this conservative autocracy.

As Moore (1966: 435–6) notes:

> In northeastern Germany the manorial reaction of the fifteenth and sixteenth centuries . . . broke off the development toward

the liberation of the peasantry from feudal obligations and the closely connected development of town life. . . . The Prussian nobility expanded its holdings at the expense of the peasantry . . . and reduced them to serfdom. As part of the same process, the nobility reduced the towns to dependence by short-circuiting them with their exports. Afterward, the Hohenzollern rulers managed to destroy the independence of the nobility. . . . The result in the seventeenth and eighteenth centuries was the 'Sparta of the North,' a militarized fusion of royal bureaucracy and landed aristocracy.

Although commerce and industry were allowed, even encouraged, to develop, they were kept under the control of the *ancien régime*. As Moore (1966: 437) again illustrates:

Marx and Engels in their discussion of the abortive 1848 revolution in Germany . . . put their finger on this decisive ingredient: a commercial and industrial class which is too weak and dependent to take power and rule in its own right and which therefore throws itself into the arms of the landed aristocracy and the royal bureaucracy, exchanging the right to rule for the right to make money.

After the Franco-Prussian War of 1870–1 and until the First World War, Germany was united under the strong control of the Kaiser, the Junkers – the powerful land owners – and the army officials. Most of the top government officials and top army officials were members of the landed aristocracy. Even when the Weimar Republic was established in 1918, supposedly replacing the monarchy and Junker aristocracy with democratic rule, these groups (in combination with the new class of wealthy industrialists) constituted the real ruling force in Germany. President von Hindenburg was himself one of the landed nobility and opposed democratic moves to break up the large feudal estates and reduce the power of the rural-based aristocracy. Thus the Weimar ideal of democratic majority rule was rendered a façade by the powerful pressure groups that really controlled Germany: the Junkers, the old military caste, and the large industrialists.

Contrary to what some of Moore's critics think (e.g., Rothman, 1970), however, Moore does not argue that the formation of a reactionary coalition inevitably leads to fascism. 'Where the [reactionary] coalition succeeds in establishing itself, there has followed a prolonged period of conservative and even authoritarian government, which, however, falls far short of fascism' (Moore, 1966: 437). Moore cites the period from the Stein–Hardenberg reforms to the end of the First World War as a crucial period in Germany in which the authoritarian government was tempered by democratic features. However, the democratic institutions were never able to attain enough support or stability to allow the Weimar Republic to cope with the severe economic and political strains of modernization. Some of the reasons that Moore (1966: 441, 444) cites for Germany's inability to maintain its democracy and its subsequent turn to fascism are: (1) a continuing allegiance to royal absolutism; (2) the development of a very powerful, repressive bureaucratic apparatus in the central government, under the control of the reactionary coalition; (3) the maintenance of the peasantry on the land plus the fostering of a reactionary anti-capitalist ideology among the peasantry who blamed the capitalists, rather than the aristocracy, for the strains on peasant life brought about by modernization. As Wiener (1975) points out then, Moore's analysis is obviously not a single-factor or strict economic–determinist one as some critics have charged (e.g., Almond, 1967; Benson, 1972; Lowenthal, 1968; Black, 1967).

The second condition that Moore sees as essential to a fascist route to modernization is the development of a labor-repressive economic system to ensure an adequate labor force. This reliance on serfdom or slavery to produce commercial surplus, coupled with a dependent bourgeoisie, allows the conservative *ancien régime* to control the modernization process while avoiding peasant or bourgeois revolution. As noted above, the Prussian nobility had early reduced the peasantry to serfdom.

The third condition suggested by Moore as important in the development of fascism – the development of conservative solidarity between land owners and peasants – is closely related to the preceding one. Conservative solidarity 'derives its cohesion by tying those with actual and potential grievances into the prevailing social structure' (Moore, 1966: 476). Conservative solidarity provides institutional links between peasant society and the upper classes, thus making peasant revolts either unlikely or easily suppressed. That is, while exploiting the peasants via labor-repressive mechanisms, the ruling classes must establish and maintain bonds based on tradition, ideology and/or mutual needs (e.g., for protection in exchange for production). The result of this conservative solidarity may be, as in the case of Germany, strong conservative, or even reactionary, political sentiments among the peasantry, rendering them if not an ally at least not an enemy of the *ancien régime*.

In Germany the effort to establish a massive conservative base in the countryside long antedates the Nazis. . . . the basic elements of Nazi doctrine appear quite distinctly in the Junker's generally successful efforts, by means of the Agrarian League established in 1894, to win the support of the peasants in non-Junker areas of smaller farms. Führer worship, the idea of a corporative state, militarism, anti-semitism, in a setting closely related to the Nazi distinction between 'predatory' and 'productive' capital, were devices used to appeal to anti-capitalist sentiments among the peasantry. [Later] Nazi propaganda presented the romantic image of an idealized peasant, 'the free man on free land.' The peasant became the key figure in the ideology of the radical right as elaborated by the Nazis (Moore, 1966: 448, 450).

The fourth and fifth conditions in the development of fascism are closely related and will be discussed together. These require that: (a) a 'reactionary coalition' be maintained, i.e., the aristocracy remain allied, as the dominant partner, with the bourgeoisie, and (b) the peasantry remain allied with the aristocracy rather than with the bourgeoisie. The existence of both of these conditions in Germany has been briefly discussed above. However, a few more comments are here in order. First, with regard to relations between the landed aristocracy and capitalist interests, Moore says:

The state aided industrial construction in several important ways. . . . All of these measures at some point involved taking resources or people out of agriculture. Therefore they imposed from time to time a serious strain on the coalition between those sectors of the upper strata in business and in agriculture that was the main feature of the political system. Without the threat of foreign dangers, sometimes real, sometimes perhaps imaginary, sometimes as in the case of Bismarck deliberately manufactured for domestic purposes, the landed interests might well have balked, to the point of endangering the whole process. [However,] material and other rewards . . . were quite substantial for both partners as long as they succeeded in keeping the peasants and industrial labor in place (Moore, 1966: 440–1).

It must be noted that the alliance was becoming rather shaky during the Weimar regime. Some of the wealthy industrial and commercial leaders were 'cooled out' by being absorbed into the nobility but others began to chafe under the rural-orientation and immense power of the Junkers. At the same time, 'the Junkers were becoming more and more frightened of industrialists whose tariff policies were very much at odds with their own' (Cantril, 1941: 255). However, the severe economic and political crises that befell postwar Germany served to create a common concern for these groups which led them to support a similar cause – strong central authority which could stabilize the economy, ward off any threat of left-wing revolution, and reassert Germany's international commercial position.

Essentially fascism protected big agriculture and big industry at the expense of the agricultural laborer, small peasant, and consumer. 'As we look back at fascism and its antecedents, we can see the glorification of the peasantry as a reactionary symptom in both Western and Asiatic civilization at a time when the peasant economy is facing severe difficulties' (Moore, 1966: 452).

With regard to the second point – alliance of the peasantry with the aristocracy rather than the bourgeoisie – the imposition of commercially profitable labor-repressive serfdom and the development of conservative solidarity with the nobility served to prevent a coalition formation between the peasants and the capitalists.

> Plebeian anticapitalism thus appears as the feature that most clearly distinguishes twentieth-century fascism from its predecessors, the nineteenth-century conservative and semiparliamentary regimes. It is a product of both the intrusion of capitalism into the rural economy and of strains arising in the postcompetitive phase of capitalist industry. Hence fascism developed most fully in Germany where capitalist industrial growth had gone the furthest within the framework of a conservative revolution from above (Moore, 1966: 448).

The final condition for the development of fascism has to do with the way in which modernization and the break with tradition are accomplished. In the fascist route to modernization, the break from tradition is incomplete because of the absence of a peasant or bourgeois revolt against the *ancien régime*. Commercialization is imposed from above but, tied to conservative rural interests, the *ancien régime* is unwilling to make the thoroughgoing structural changes required for complete modernization.

> Now, in the course of modernization by a revolution from above, such a government has to carry out many of the same tasks performed elsewhere with the help of a revolution from below. . . . As they proceeded with conservative modernization, these semiparliamentary governments tried to preserve as much of the original social structure as they could, fitting large sections into the new building wherever possible (Moore, 1966: 438).

ANALYSIS OF CHANGE ON DIFFERENT LEVELS OF SOCIETY

In short, the old regime tries to retain its power and privilege within a new socio-economic order. With a few concessions to the capitalists, the nobility attempt to retain, even improve, their favored political and economic position. It is this reluctance to introduce fundamental structural changes (combined, of course, with the other factors we have discussed) that dooms such nations to a fascist solution for, without such basic changes, they are unable to adapt to the changing conditions in the world around them. As Moore (1966: 442) says, Germany was

> trying to solve a problem that was inherently insoluble, to modernize without changing [the] social structures. The only way out of this dilemma was militarism, which united the upper classes. Militarism intensified a climate of international conflict, which in turn made industrial advance all the more imperative. . . . To carry out thoroughgoing structural reforms, i.e., to make the transition to a paying commercial agriculture without the repression of those who worked with soil and to do the same in industry, in a word, to use modern technology rationally for human welfare was beyond the political vision of these governments. Ultimately these systems crashed in an attempt at foreign expansion, but not until they had tried to make reaction popular in the form of fascism.

6.1.5 Summary and critique

In sum, Moore attributes Germany's fascist 'revolution from above' as arising from a particular historical, political, and economic configuration with the following elements: (1) The alliance of the Kaiser (and, later, the President and other important figures) with the Junkers in a very powerful *ancien régime*. (2) The *ancien régime* was willing and able to foster commercial and industrial growth yet retain its dominance over the bourgeoisie. Powerful capitalists were brought into the conservative regime and thus were willing to ally themselves with the Junkers against the proletariat and the peasants. (3) The Junkers were able to reintroduce serfdom successfully and to extract substantial surplus from the peasants, while still retaining the peasants' (at least partial) allegiance and preventing an alliance with the bourgeoisie. (4) The unwillingness of the 'Rye and Iron' alliance to sacrifice their position in order to make needed social and economic changes. Thus the military and economic disasters that beset Germany could not be dealt with by the weak Weimar regime or resolved within the existing structure. By 1932 half of the German population was living on almost a starvation level (Cantril, 1941: 223) and the factionalized governmental structure was incapable of gathering enough support to push through any programs that might ameliorate the ever-worsening conditions.

Moore's thesis, that industrialization is likely to culminate in fascism in the absence of a 'revolution from below' that would destroy the hold of the *ancien régime*, has been criticized by some. For example, Lawrence Stone (1972) and C. E. Black (1967) argue that Moore's view of fascism as the culmination of long historical developments gives too much importance to Germany's 'brief bout' with fascism under Hitler. They cite the development of democratic institutions in post-war Germany as a refutation of a 'fascist culmination' theory of industrialization in Germany. Gordon Levin (1967: 241), however, counters this argument, saying that 'the defeats and occupations of 1945 may be seen as providing in some sense the bourgeois revolutions which Germany and Japan both missed.' And Jonathan Wiener (1975: 313) adds:

> Thus, for Moore, one way or another, the *violent* destruction of the traditional agrarian ruling class is necessary if democracy is to have a chance in a developing society – destruction either through social revolution, or international war; either by the exploited classes, or by foreign powers.

In contradistinction with some of the most recent social science literature on revolution (e.g., Schieder, 1973; Lenk, 1973; Gurr, 1970; von Beyme, 1973), Moore must be credited not merely with having reserved – for political–ideological reasons – the concept of revolution for an analysis of certain transformations of the power distribution among social groupings (e.g., the rise to power by the Nazis), or of revolts of some segments of the population (e.g., not just of peasants and workers), but with bringing the concept to social scientific fruition by sounding the relationship between revolution, society, and history. He also succeeded in describing the different routes of important societies to modernization as a result of the given constellation of dominant (such as the landed aristocracy), rising (such as the bourgeoisie involved in commerce and industry), and oppressed classes (such as the peasantry).

His attempt to explain the three main routes from the pre-industrial to the modern world[1] in terms of the 'ways in which the landed upper classes and the peasants reacted to the challenge of commercial agriculture' (Moore, 1966: xvii) contributed furthermore to the clarification and critique of competing theoretical approaches. Moore (1966: 474–5) revealed not only the psychological reductionism implicit in the theories of 'the revolution of rising expectations' and of 'relative deprivation' which have become so prominent in recent years but also their failure as *general* explanations for why and when changes in the life of some part of a population lead to revolutionary manifestations in what form and to what political end (cf. Marx and Engels, 1961: 397; de Tocqueville, 1856: 214; Runciman, 1966; Gurr, 1970; Davies, 1962; Tanter and Midlarsky, 1967). Interestingly enough, Moore's theses are confirmed by such prominent non-Marxists as Walter W. Rostow (1960) and Edward A. Shils (1963). In his well-known study, Rostow describes the process and stages of economic growth by attributing great significance to the rise of the bourgeoisie for the take-off of the Industrial Revolution. For Shils, social classes, on the basis of their temporary predominance, are the agents of economic and social change. In contradistinction to Rostow and Gunnar Myrdal (1974), for Moore nationalism does not play an important role in stimulating industrialization. The same is true for religion, which is hardly ever mentioned by Moore, except in his analysis of the Indian and Chinese ways to modernity (cf. Moore, 1966: 333–6, 383–4, 503–4). Finally, in contrast with Marx, and not unlike Joseph A. Schumpeter (1927/74), Moore does relativize the function of the working class with respect to the organization and change of society, as he has also attempted to do in his recent study on the German working class from 1848 to 1920 by casting doubt on the Marxist notion of the revolutionary industrial proletariat (Moore, 1978).

6.2 Structural strain and group reaction:
Neil J. Smelser's theory of collective behavior

6.2.1 *The concept of collective behavior*

Smelser's *Theory of Collective Behavior* (1962) is an attempt to explain systematically why episodes of collective behavior occur where they do, when they do, and in the ways they do. He uses, as the defining characteristic of 'group' behavior in general, the kind of belief under which behavior is mobilized. Collective behavior is action based on a generalized belief. These generalized beliefs differ from those that guide other types of behavior in that they involve a belief in the existence of extraordinary forces (threats, conspiracies, etc.) which are at work in the universe. They also involve an assessment of the extraordinary consequences that will follow if the collective attempt to reconstitute social action is successful (or unsuccessful).

In formulating his definition of collective behavior, Smelser lists three characteristics, the combination of which separate it from other types of group phenomena:

1 Collective behavior is *uninstitutionalized* – it is formed as a response to an unstructured situation.
2 Collective behavior is an attempt to *reconstitute* all or a part of the social order – it redefines social action when conventional modes of dealing with a situation are inadequate.
3 It is guided by a *generalized belief* (as defined above).

Thus, his definition of collective behavior is: (1) an uninstitutionalized mobilization (2) to reconstitute a component of social action on the basis of a (3) generalized belief. This definition excludes, as necessary characteristics, distinctive psychological states and patterns of mobilization, for, although they are important, they form no observable unique patterns that are necessary for episodes of collective behavior to occur. As types of collective behavior he excludes crime, audiences, ceremonial behavior, and other group phenomena (often listed under the heading); that is, they are either institutionalized or not oriented toward reconstituting social action.

Having set the outer boundaries of the field, Smelser identifies the major types of collective behavior: the panic, the craze, the hostile outburst, the norm-oriented movement, and the value-oriented movement. In order to uncover the determinants of collective behavior, he introduces two major foci of determinacy:

1 The general determinants – to explain why collective behavior occurs at all.
2 The unique combination of determinants for any collective episode – to explain why one form of collective behavior occurs rather than another.

The concept of the organization of these determinants he borrows from economics; it is that of the value-added process. An example of this process is the conversion of iron ore into a finished automobile by a number of stages of processing like mining, melting, tempering, shaping, and combining the steel with other parts, painting, delivery to a retailer, and selling. Each stage 'adds its value' to the final cost of the product. The main point is that each stage must combine according to a certain pattern before the next stage can contribute its particular value to the finished product. Every stage is therefore a necessary condition for the appropriate and effective addition of value in the next stage. The sufficient condition is the combination of every necessary condition according to a definite pattern. Moreover, each additional stage limits the possible type of outcome. Smelser applies this logic to outbursts of collective behavior, which he considers to be produced by an elaborate sequence of determinants. These determinants must not only be present if collective behavior is to occur, but they must also combine in a definitive pattern. He lists six general determinants, each of which is a necessary condition, and all six, when properly combined, constitute a sufficient condition, which must exist for the generation of every sort of collective behavior. Furthermore, each determinant appears in many varieties, the unique combinations of which determine the type of collective behavior. As the various forms combine, the determination of the kind of episode that will result becomes increasingly specific, ruling out alternative behavioral possibilities.

Smelser's (1962: 12–21) determinants of collective behavior are:

1. structural conduciveness,
2. structural strain,
3. growth and spread of a generalized belief,
4. precipitating factors,
5. mobilization of participants for action, and
6. operation of social controls.

The value-added logic implies a temporal sequence of activating an event or situation as a determinant, but only one analytic sequence of occurrence. In other words, any or all of these determinants may have existed for any length of time, but only when they become activated in a definite pattern do they contribute to the formation of collective behavior.

    1 *Structural conduciveness* is the most general determinant and a necessary condition for the activation of the other five. Structural conduciveness refers to social conditions that are permissive of a given sort of collective behavior (e.g., a large compact, residentially segregated minority population represents a structural feature that is more conducive to race riots than areas with other residential patterns).
    2 *Structural strain* refers to a conflict between components of social action (e.g., between the value of equality and discrimination practices such as the Jim Crow laws). The major types of strain (it will later be shown how they lead to typical episodes of collective behavior) are ambiguity (e.g., normative vagueness), deprivations (e.g., negative privilege), conflicts, and discrepancies. In order for the strain to be a determinant, it must fall within the scope established by the condition of conduciveness. The two must combine, thereby narrowing the range of possible final outcomes.

3 *Growth and spread of a generalized belief.* Before collective action can be taken to reconstitute the situation permitted by structural conduciveness and brought on by strain, this situation must be made meaningful to potential participants. A generalized belief supplies the meaning by (a) identifying the source of strain, (b) attributing certain characteristics to this source, and (c) recommending that certain actions be taken to relieve the strain. For example, the belief may be that (a) the communists are the source of strain, (b) they are conspiring to undermine the moral fiber of our youth, and therefore (c) we ought to get rid of them.

4 *Precipitating factors.* When they occur in the context of, or are interpreted in the light of, the other determinants, they give generalized beliefs concrete, immediate substance, thereby providing a setting toward which collective action can be directed.

5 *Mobilization of participants for action.* Once the preceding determinants have been activated, the only remaining necessary condition is to bring the affected group into action. This point marks the onset of a collective action, be it panic, hostility, agitation for reform, or revolution. In the mobilization process leadership and communications are very important.

6 *Operation of social controls* is really a counter-determinant and it is its relative weakness or effectiveness that makes collective behavior possible or impossible. We know from measures of social control that they are designed to guard against the accumulation of concomitant factors, i.e., to interrupt or prevent their operation. There are two kinds of social control: (a) those social controls that minimize conduciveness and strain, thereby preventing collective behavior, and (b) those that are mobilized after a collective episode has begun. They determine how fast, how far, and in what direction the episode will develop.

The value-added logic of these determinants assumes a continuity of *substance*; i.e., the six determinants of collective behavior are parts of one process. They are multiple determinants of *some* single outcome. There is also a continuity of *locus* implied, for the determinants must be communicated to persons of similar enough experience so that these conditions will be interpreted in a like manner.

Now we shall examine the ways in which the value-added explanation of the various determinants may be analyzed in relation to the components of social action which they are activated to reconstitute. Through this analytical framework of social action we may trace the course and type of collective behavior that will result as the determinants accumulate.

6.2.2 The components of social action

One of Smelser's main theses is that collective behavior can be classified and analyzed under the same conceptual framework as all social behavior. That is, even though the extremes of social behavior differ like collective behavior and conventional behavior, they have essential similarities. That is to say, both face situations imposed by social life (e.g., both must be legitimized by values, both involve an assessment of the situation in which they occur). Because of these characteristics common to all social behavior, Smelser introduces an analytical framework to describe the components of action at the social level. It is a 'flow chart' of the paths along which social action moves. He uses this chart to investigate what happens to these components of social action when institutionalized ways of reacting fail in the face of unstructured situations. *One major set of reactions to this failure constitutes the major types of collective behavior.* Such behavior is hence to be understood as an attempt to reconstruct a disturbed social order or parts of it.

Smelser has designed his theoretical construct of the components of social action to operate at the social-system level. It analyzes the relations among actors rather than individual personalities. The units of analysis are *roles* (e.g., husband, physician, citizen) and *organizations* (e.g., political parties, firms, families). He uses the term 'social system' to refer to interaction not only at the societal level, but on down to even informal interaction among two persons.

Smelser's (1962: Chapter 2) four basic components of social action are:

1 values,
2 norms,
3 mobilization of individual motivation for organized action, and
4 situational facilities.

1 *Values* refer to the generalized ends that provide the broadest guide to purposive social behavior. Values are the most general component; they do not specify kinds of norms, organizations, or facilities which are required to realize these ends. For example, countries in which the value of democracy constitutes the core of legitimacy for their political systems do not necessarily have the

CHANGE OF THE SOCIAL SYSTEM, GROUPS AND RELATIONSHIPS

same principles of representation or the same elective systems. These differences do not lie at the value level, but rather involve various ways of implementing the political value of democracy. Values, then, are the most general statements of legitimate ends that guide social action.

2   *Norms* are more specific than general values, for they specify certain regulatory principles which are necessary if these values are to be realized. For example, the value of democracy provides only criteria for judging the legitimacy or illegitimacy of whole classes of behavior. Norms must be established to indicate how democracy may be realized (e.g., rules for elections, public administration). Norms range from formal, explicit regulations to informal, even unconscious, understandings.

3   *Mobilization of motivation into organized action* determines the form of organization of human actions. It specifies who the agents in pursuit of the valued ends will be, how the actions of these agents will be structured into concrete roles and organizations, and what the system of rewards will be. This component includes what is commonly called social organization or social structure (e.g., families, churches, government agencies, business firms, associations).

4   *Situational facilities* – the final component – involves the means and obstacles that facilitate or hinder the attainment of concrete goals in the role or organizational context. Situational facilities refer to the actor's knowledge of the environment, his ability to predict consequences, his tools and skills. This knowledge is relative to the possibility of realizing a goal which is part of his role or organized membership. For example, a businessman employs various facilities in making a decision in the market by referring to information about market conditions, knowledge of investment, and ability to finance the enterprise. In other words, facilities are the means used in the agent's assessment of the situation.

6.2.3   *The structure of the components of social action and their relations among them*

The four components of social action stand in a *hierarchical relation* to one another: values–norms–mobilization into organized role behavior–situational facilities (cf. Table 6.1). This rank order placing values on top and situational resources in lowest position reminds us of Parsons's AGIL-scheme which is also organized in terms of a condition–control hierarchy.[2] The *dimensions* that characterize Smelser's rank order of action components testify to that fact. (a) As we move from top to bottom, the concrete details of involved action receive increasingly more specific definition. (b) Any redefinition of a component of social action necessarily makes for a readjustment in those components below it, but not necessarily in those above it. For example, changes in fundamental values such as the principle of equality incur changes in the definition of norms (e.g., the legal regulation of labor contracts), the mobilization of motivation (e.g., the recruitment of social positions), and the resources in the situation (e.g., politics of the labor market).

TABLE 6.1 *Levels of specificity of the components of social action*

Level	Values	Norms	Mobilization of motivation for organized action	Situational facilities
1	Societal values	General conformity	Socialized motivation	Preconceptions concerning causality
2	Legitimization of values for institutionalized sectors	Specification of norms according to institutional sectors	Generalized performance capacity	Codification of knowledge
3	Legitimization of rewards	Specification of norms according to types of roles and organizations	Trained capacity	Technology, or specification of knowledge in situational terms
4	Legitimization of individual commitment	Specification of requirements for individual observation of norms	Transition to adult role-assumption	Procurement of wealth, power, or prestige to activate Level 3
5	Legitimization of competing values	Specification of norms of competing institutional sectors	Allocation to sector of society	Allocation of effective technology to sector of society
6	Legitimization of values for realizing organizational goals	Specification of rules of co-operation and coordination within organizations	Allocation to specific roles or organizations	Allocation of effective technology to roles or organizations
7	Legitimization of values for expenditure of effort	Specification of schedules and programs to regulate activity	Allocation to roles and tasks within organization	Allocation of facilities within organization to attain concrete goals

More specific →

Source: Smelser, 1962: 68.

However, the same is not true with respect to the opposite direction if, say, a company alters its production technique; in this case, the principles of the economic order of a country (e.g., those of a market economy) need not necessarily change as well.

Each component of social action possesses an internal organization which involves seven levels of specification. These divisions within a component successively restrict the meaning and applicability of it to concrete social actions. The internal levels of specification progressively narrow the definition of the component, i.e., from broad generalizations to everyday occurrences.

To illustrate, we shall trace the seven *levels of specificity* of values that are shown in Table 6.1. Let us take the value of freedom that is considered to be fundamental to all Western democracies. In order to give the value social meaning we must place restrictions on it (the German sociologist, Niklas Luhmann, would say that we have to reduce its complexity). In the economic area, freedom means free enterprise or *laissez-faire*; in the political sector, it concerns civil and political liberties; in the religious sphere, it means the separation of church and state, and so on. In this sense, freedom is still a general value (first level); we have merely qualified it in reference to various institutional sectors of society (second level). The third level specifies what kinds of activities and rewards are legitimately to be pursued. The fourth level specifies the appropriate type of commitment for the individual actor at the role level (e.g., in business, personal success). At these four levels, commitment to values is rather general. The last three restrict the values to an operative level. Level 5 limits the scope of activity involved by recognizing other competing values as legitimate (e.g., business *vs* religion – in some communities in the US business must close on Sunday though that is unprofitable). Level 6 introduces values that specify the types of commitments which are necessary at the operative organizational level if the higher-level values are to be realized (e.g., efficiency means profit-making). Level 7 involves the commitment to implement, by personal effort, the higher-level values of the organization.

In other words, the higher levels define the general nature of values; the lower levels define the commitments necessary at operative levels if these general values are to be realized. The other components of social action operate on the same basis.

Table 6.1, which summarizes the various levels of specificity in a systematic way, may, according to Smelser, be understood as a map of social action. It indicates the principal transition points as human resources move from general, undefined states to more specific, operative states.

There are several principles to be taken into consideration that facilitate the understanding of Table 6.1:

1 Reading across each row: each transition adds a qualitatively new component of action to values, i.e., first norms, then mobilization, finally facilities.
2 Reading down each column: at each transition a single component is prepared for implementation by the addition of some new restricting condition.
3 Each transition across a row to the right and each transition down a column, then, adds more specific meaning to the process of producing concrete social action.
4 From any given point in the table, any redefinition of the component at this point necessarily requires a corresponding redefinition of all points ('cells') below and to the right. The converse, that is, all 'cells' upward and to the left, does not necessarily follow.[3]

With these categories we have a theoretical framework at hand within which we can trace and define episodes of collective behavior.

6.2.4 Structural strain

Earlier we identified structural strain as one of the major determinants of collective behavior. We will now analyze it in reference to the components of social action (Smelser, 1962: Chapter 3).

Smelser defines strain as an impairment of the relations among, and consequently inadequate functioning of, the components of action. He formulates two propositions:

1 Any kind of strain may be a determinant of any kind of collective behavior; and
2 Strain at any level of any action component will show up first at the lower, more operative levels where the immediate impact of events is most evident and where dissatisfactions accumulate first.

Only as dissatisfaction spreads and attention turns to a search for the source of operative failures are the higher level components activated.

1 Application of strain to lower levels of components of social action implies the following steps:
  (a) Ambiguity as to the adequacy of means for a given goal is the principal strain on situational facilities. It concerns above

all the adequacy of knowledge and skills (e.g., are there unforeseeable financial risks?). Examples of ambiguity at the lower levels of situational facilities are shown in Table 6.1.
(b) Mobilization of motivation includes rewards for fulfillment of role behavior. The strain therefore is actual or potential deprivation of the rewards due. It refers to the balance between motivated activity and its rewards.
(c) In regard to norms the relevant strain involves conflicting roles, regulations, etc. It concerns the integration of human actions.
(d) Strain on values involves discrepancies that may exist between competing values (e.g., personal values *vs* organizational goals). The problem that underlies strain on values is that of obligation or moral commitment.

2 The foci of strain also follow hierarchical principles; i.e.,
(a) strain at any point in the table is a sufficient but not a necessary condition for strain at all points downward and to the right, but
(b) it is neither necessary nor sufficient for strain at points upward and to the left.
When strain is exerted on one or more of these components and when established ways of relieving strain are not available, various kinds of collective behavior tend to arise. Such episodes Smelser interprets as attempts to reconstitute one or more of the above components on which strain has been placed.

3 Strain manifests itself in the lower operative levels as follows:
(a) The general principle for reconstituting social action consists of, when strain exists, attention shifting to higher levels of the components to seek resources to overcome this strain; or in the language of the table, we can define this process by saying that, in the search for solutions to conditions of strain, people turn their attention either upward or to the left, or both. In their attempt to solve the problem of strain, they move toward the more general levels and/or components. They generalize to overcome the strain, and thereby reconstitute that level.
(b) If the process of generalization is successful, i.e., if a level was found that caused strain and was therefore reconstituted to eliminate strain, attempts are made to work back down the levels by reapplying the new level to those below. Attempts are made to generalize, then respecify; the components are first *de*structured, then *re*structured. This is the process by which conventional behavior eliminates strain.

(c) Collective behavior also involves a generalization to a high-level component in search for solutions to strain. The *critical feature* of collective behavior occurs here: Once the generalization has taken place, people do *not* proceed to respecify, step by step, down the line to reconstitute social action.

(d) Instead, they develop a belief that *short-circuits* from a very generalized component directly to the focus of strain. The accompanying belief is that the strain can be relieved by a direct application of a generalized component. This is why collective behavior is irrational, abnormal, and radical. It compresses several levels of the components of action into a *single generalized belief*, from which specific operative solutions are expected to flow.

(e) An episode of collective behavior itself occurs *when people are mobilized for action* on the basis of such a belief.

(f) All collective behavior involves a belief which (i) arises from *strain*, and (ii) *redefines* the situation of strain at which time it selects some aspect of the strained situation and attributes a power or force to it – a force that is sufficiently generalized to guarantee the outcome of the situation.

Collective behavior is therefore distinct from conventional behavioral reactions to strain because, by short-circuiting from high- to low-level components, it bypasses the specifications and controls that are required for society to normally adjust to the redefined component.

6.2.5 *Generalized beliefs*

The three major functions of a generalized belief – identified as a determinant in an episode of collective behavior – are (Smelser, 1962: Chapter 5): (1) reduction of ambiguity in a situation by restructuring, explaining and predicting; (2) reduction of ambiguity by restructuring the situation in a fast, short-circuited manner; (3) preparation of individuals for collective action by creating a common culture within which leadership, mobilization, and concerted action can take place.

Each of the major types of generalized beliefs may restructure a specific component of social action under strain and may also produce a certain kind of collective behavior *if* the other determinants permit action to flow.

1 The first major type is *hysteria*. It transforms an ambiguous situation into an absolutely potent, generalized threat.

Hysterical beliefs restructure the Facilities Series, and, if they give rise to action, lead to *panic*.

2 *Wish-fulfillment* reduces ambiguity by positing absolutely efficacious generalized facilities. Wish-fulfillment beliefs also restructure the Facilities Series and can give rise to the *craze* in the sense of being crazy about novelties (e.g., fashion).

3 *Hostility* involves removing some agent or object perceived as a generalized threat or obstacle. Hostile beliefs restructure the mobilization component and may give rise to such hostile outbursts as scapegoating, even mob violence.

4 *Norm-oriented beliefs*, envisioning the reorganization of a threatened normative structure, reconstitute the Normative Series and, in case they lead to action, give rise to reform movements and counter-movements.

5 *Value-oriented* beliefs envision the reconstitution of a threatened value system, reorganize the Values Series, and can lead to political and religious revolutions, nationalistic movements, secessions, and the formation of cults.

We must now examine the ways in which the six determinants of collective behavior combine in a value-added order within the framework of action components in order to determine what kind of collective behavior will occur. Of the major types of collective behavior, we shall use the *panic*, the simplest type, for the purpose of illustration. The basis for choosing the panic is that the major types of collective behavior are related to one another in a hierarchy, namely, in the sense of value-oriented mobilization > norm-oriented mobilization > hostile outburst > craze > panic. Each of the higher types contains the main elements of the preceding types, in addition to elements characteristic of the particular type. Structural conduciveness is related to the four components in that they indicate the four major types of structural conduciveness (cf. Smelser, 1962: Chapters 6–10).

6.2.6 Panic and other kinds of collective behavior

As mentioned, panic is a type of collective behavior that involves the restructuring of the Facilities Series. This is because the unstructured situation to which panic is a reaction is characterized by lack of knowledge of, or information about, the environmental conditions. It does not directly involve agents, norms, or values.

Structural conduciveness is the first condition that must exist if a panic is to result. In relation to panic, it refers to the (1) degree to which danger, (2) communication of danger, and (3) restricted opportunity to escape can arise at all. To illustrate with an example, in financial panic the question pops up (1) to what degree the dangers of economic fluctuation exist, that is, how effective the institutional controls are (e.g., unemployment insurance, price and wage controls, state investments, anticyclic budget policy); (2) whether news about economic crises can be rapidly communicated; (3) whether people – in the event of a financial panic – have only restricted means of disposing of their assets.

The second necessary condition is structural *strain*. The relevant type of strain here is ambiguity that refers to the perceived presence of some immediate danger of unknown and uncontrollable proportions. Such strain must appear in the context of the structurally conducive features in order to take on meaning as a determinant.

Before the third determinant can appear, *anxiety*, caused by perception of an ambiguous and threatening danger, must develop. This anxiety is converted by the precipitating factor into the next condition, namely, generalized belief. The generalized belief relevant to panic is the *hysterical belief*, or simply fear. This results when a precipitating factor confirms the generalized anxiety of the group and transforms the vague threat into fear of a specific, threatening agent. These events (e.g., presumable or factual bankruptcies of companies in the wake of solvency crises of American banks preceding the 'black Friday' in 1929) serve anxious people as proof that the forces underlying their anxiety are effectively at work. The fifth determinant, namely, *mobilization* for flight, may now be realized, usually under a primitive form of leadership, for the identified destructive agent provides something from which to flee.

In regard to the sixth determinant, *social control*, we can view the stages leading to panic as a series of equilibrium states. At each stage we can assess the balance between forces making for panic and those making for panic control. We may define types of control in terms of the components of social action. For example, values such as faith can act as preventives or as controls in the early stages of panic. Norms may act as preventives (e.g., fire drills tell us how to act in such a situation) or as controls, directing behavior toward some other kind of activity than panic (e.g., saving loved or helpless ones). Organization (Mobilization Series) or simply the structure of roles can control panic (e.g., a soldier does not panic, a leader controls). Facilities, especially information that attempts to explain or dispel the fear, may act as control mechanisms.

In sum, we may define *panic* as a collective flight based on a hysterical belief and postulate that panic will occur if the appropriate conditions of conduciveness are present, if a hysterical belief develops, if mobilization occurs, and if social controls fail to operate.

The other major types of collective behavior are all related to panic and the determinants operate in much the same way. However, as we move on to the more complex types, the main difference between each is the introduction of some new element which makes this type distinct from the others. We will briefly summarize the new elements that are added to the craze, the hostile outburst, the norm-oriented movement, and the value-oriented movement.

Using the increasing degree of complexity as criterion, the second type of collective behavior is *craze*. Like panic, it is also related to the Facilities Series and its relevant strain is also ambiguity. It involves all of the basic elements of the panic but adds, as its defining characteristic, a positive generalized belief which counters the negative, hysterical fear. This is the *wish-fulfillment* belief that guarantees a positive outcome in an uncertain situation by empowering some force with generalized potency to overcome the possibly frustrating, harmful, or even destructive possibilities. The *hostile outburst* may take the form of scapegoating, or, in extreme cases, mob violence. It is more complex than the panic or the craze and contains the major elements of both of these. The hostile outburst differs in that it not only involves a redefinition of the Facilities Series, but also of the mobilization component. The relevant strain is deprivation, i.e., anxiety arises here because of the actual or potential threat of deprivation of rewards which are involved in the mobilization level. Therefore, this anxiety is identified with some responsible agent and a hostile belief develops with the desire to mobilize for an attack on that agent. This identification of, and attack on, a specific agent constitutes the episode's attempt to redefine the mobilization component which is the major difference between it and panic as well as craze.

Norm-oriented movements differ from the previous ones in that they involve an attempt to reconstitute one or more norms. Because of the hierarchy governing the components of action, they necessarily also affect the Mobilization and Facilities Series. The strain here is conflict concerning the integration of human action, while the generalized belief is that of the norm-oriented belief. This goes one step further than the hostile belief. After it has identified the agent responsible for the anxiety, it assumes that regulation of the agents is inadequate and that a normative reorganization is necessary to deal with them. It is, therefore, a movement oriented toward change in the normative structure. By comparison, the *value-oriented movement* involves the redefinition of the Value Series on the basis of a value-oriented belief which was created to explain the relevant strain, namely, discrepancy between competing values. The main difference between the value-oriented movement and the others is that its generalized belief attributes the anxiety and general social disharmony to a degeneration of values. It envisions a *regeneration* of values that will cure all social ills.

In summary, all types of collective behavior are related to one another in that:

1   all must have the six general *determinants* combined in a definitive value-added pattern;
2   all involve the *reconstitution* of a component of social action and their major differences stem from the particular components which each attempts to reconstitute; and
3   the five types of collective behavior stand in a *hierarchy* of increasing complexity and inclusiveness.

6.2.7   Application of Smelser's theory of collective behavior to the Nazi revolution

In his attempt to explain the political change in the wake of modernization in agriculture, industry, and commerce, Moore (1966) made us especially aware of the role of the landed aristocracy and the peasants, on the one hand, and the bourgeoisie's capacity and willingness to form coalitions, on the other. Smelser (1962) also shows that only certain types of society are 'structurally conducive' to revolution. He points to the example of the French Revolution which was preceded by a situation that had been structurally conducive in so far as the bourgeoisie, the peasantry, and the rising proletariat had no access to the omnipotent centralized government (Smelser, 1962: Chapter 10). Under the condition of structural conduciveness the various tensions called for serious consequences. These tensions concerned the aristocracy which fought for its privileges and against the staggering costs of living, the bourgeois middle class which strove for influence and privileges, the peasantry which suffered most under the burden of taxes (although it increasingly acquired property), as well as the clergy and the military in the membership of which ideological and power cleavages came into being.

Using the structural conduciveness and these strains as historico-empirical background, Smelser takes the change of value orientations in the sense of generalized beliefs about reason, individualism, freedom and equality. He shows how these beliefs accounted for the transformations in the wake of the French Revolution in that they were first accepted by the most important groupings of French society and eventually translated into societal change via the mechanisms of mobilization and social control (cf. Smith, 1973: 101–11).

While, for Moore, social classes, their interests and relationships, make political history, value-oriented beliefs represent, for Smelser, the stronghold for social stability at one time and the center of crystallization for long-term changes at another time, of course depending on the degree of structural conduciveness and strain. Smelser follows his teacher, Talcott Parsons, for whom values are not only the fundamental components of action situations but also in control of the other components such as norms, organization of roles, motivation, and environmental conditions. In this sense, as we know from Chapter 4 of the present volume, social change in the structural sense is equated with change of the value system. This aspect will also be elaborated upon in the following case study of the revolution of National Socialism.

Since Smelser subsumes under the notion of value-oriented movements such divergent phenomena as 'messianic movement,' 'millenarian movement,' 'sect formation,' and 'nationalistic movement,' the Nazi revolution seems to be an excellent example for what he means by a value-oriented political revolution, namely, 'a combination of a [secular] value-oriented belief with a hostile outburst' (Smelser, 1962: 367). It was 'a collective attempt to restore [. . . allegedly traditional German] values in the name of a generalized belief' (Smelser, 1962: 313). Involved in the restoration of these values was, necessarily, the restructuring of all other relevant components of action: norms, motivation of individuals, and situational facilities.

In the following discussion we draw on Smelser's model of value-added process of the six determinants of collective behavior in order to trace the development of Germany's National Socialism in the direction of a full-fledged, value-oriented, political movement culminating in a successful revolution. We can clearly see that Smelser (1962: 313–19) views value-oriented revolutions neither as palace revolutions nor necessarily violent revolutions or rapid social change of any kind (e.g., industrial, scientific revolutions). Rather, it has to do with the result of a series of movements and changes characterized by a wide scope, penetrating all segments of society, and in any case focusing not just on single norms but on the reconstitution of values and the social structure.

6.2.7.1 *Structural conduciveness*
According to Smelser's theory, certain structural arrangements must exist in order for a value-oriented movement, rather than another form of collective behavior, to occur.

ANALYSIS OF CHANGE ON DIFFERENT LEVELS OF SOCIETY

1 DIFFERENTIATION OF THE VALUE-SYSTEM FROM OTHER COMPONENTS OF ACTION

> When values are not differentiated from norms, breaking a norm means more than merely trespassing on property, divorcing a spouse, or failing to display proper deference; it also involves defiance of a *general value*. . . . Because of this lack of differentiation, specific dissatisfactions with any social arrangements eventually become . . . protests against values (Smelser, 1962: 320).[4]

Hitler and his disgruntled companions who helped found the Nazi movement did not perceive a distinction between their ultimate values and proposed ways in which these values might be put into effect. They fused all of their complaints against the Weimar regime – political, economic, social organizational, etc. – into one value-oriented belief that viewed the complete overthrow of the system as the only solution to the evils which plagued the government and the nation. In addition, many of the old elites from the monarchy, discontented with their loss of status and influence under the Republic, similarly couched their grievances in value terms and saw a chance to regain their positions through a revolution.

2 AVAILABILITY OF MEANS TO EXPRESS GRIEVANCES

> If a social situation is defined entirely in value-oriented terms, every protest is necessarily value-oriented. This kind of conduciveness, however, never exists in pure form; other conditions of conduciveness also determine in part why a value-oriented movement arises, rather than some other type of outburst. Among the most important of these conditions is the availability of means to express protest or grievances among a population suffering from any kind of strain (Smelser, 1962: 324).

In the Weimar regime, all channels of expression other than value-oriented ones were unavailable to protest groups. The government, split as it was with internal dissension,[5] was incapable of taking reformative action demanded by aggrieved groups, thus precluding the channeling of grievances into norm-oriented agitation which focused on single aspects rather than on the system as a whole. In addition, it was able to put down hostile outbursts effectively (e.g., Hitler's *Putsch* of 1923).

> If a government merely refuses to listen to demands for reform without being willing or able to back this refusal by using force,

the government is likely to topple through palace revolution, *coup d'état*, insurrection, or other revolutionary movements without a value-oriented base (Smelser, 1962: 332).

> Value-oriented beliefs . . . arise when alternative means for reconstituting the social situation are perceived as unavailable. . . . Under such conditions – combined with other determinants – people begin to redefine the fundamental values of the entire system in which they find themselves (Smelser, 1962: 325, 333).

3 INSULATION OF VALUE-ORIENTED MOVEMENTS

Smelser discusses two forms of societal accommodation to value-oriented movements: isolation and insulation. 'Isolation' – especially in the geographical sense – of the movement's adherents may successfully block the spread of a value-oriented movement. 'Insulation,' on the other hand, refers to institutionalized tolerance for the dissidents and their cause, a condition much more conducive to the movement gaining an established foothold within the existing structure from which to continue its campaign.

The Weimar Republic, composed as it was of many greatly dissimilar factions (e.g., Communist Party, Nazi Party) was too weak to isolate dissident groups effectively. Instead, they were often institutionally insulated within the political system, creating conditions amenable to the rise of a value-oriented movement (cf. Smelser, 1962: 336).

4 COMMUNICATION

> As in all collective behavior, the spread of a value-oriented movement depends on the possibility of disseminating a generalized belief (Smelser, 1962: 337).

As the early Nazi Party had no access to the mass media, first communication was by word of mouth and infiltration into schools, unions, etc. Later, the party published its own newspaper and gained access to other channels through influential sympathizers. Communication was generally facilitated by a common language and cultural background.

6.2.7.2 Strain

The conditions of structural conduciveness are a framework within which the remaining conditions rise to significance as determinants of the value-oriented movement. Without conditions of conduciveness, that is, the conditions of strain . . . may be determinants of some other kind of outburst (e.g., a norm-oriented movement, a craze) but not determinants of a value-oriented movement (Smelser, 1962: 338).

1 STRAIN AND FACILITIES

Inadequacy of knowledge or techniques to grapple with new situations sets the stage for value-oriented movements (Smelser, 1962: 338).

The old German elite and other discontents were faced with the defeat and near-destruction of their nation in the First World War and with a new form of government imposed upon them. Neither traditional patterns of reactions nor the weak democratic political structure superimposed on the old order were able to provide successful means for coping with the enormous changes Germany was undergoing.

2 STRAIN AND ORGANIZATION

Two types of relevant strain given by Smelser (1962: 339) were present during the rise of the Nazi movement: deprivation and frustration caused by the failure of the country in the First World War and economic hardship in the early and late 1920s (cf. Abel, 1938). Without denying his sympathy for the thesis of the 'revolution of rising expectations' and the consequences of status inconsistency for change activities, Smelser (1962: 340) notes:

Such deprivations are relative to expectations. By an absolute measure, groups which are drawn into value-oriented movements may be improving. This seems to be the case in connection with the major Western revolutions; 'they took place in societies economically progressive,' and they drew in part upon those classes which were advancing most rapidly. Again, in many colonial countries it is those people who have recently received higher education – i.e., have 'improved' fastest culturally – that lead and join militant nationalist movements. In both cases this improvement on absolute grounds involves deprivation on relative grounds; for the same groups, with their new gains in one sphere (e.g., economic, cultural) often are held back in another (e.g., political).

3 STRAIN AND NORMS

The normative disorganization that war occasions accounts in part for the frequent rise of revolutionary movements during and after wars (Smelser, 1962: 340).

Such strain was felt throughout Germany when normative disorganization, occasioned by the defeat in the First World War, resulted in the traditional institutional framework being rapidly and forcefully replaced by a newly organized one – that of the Weimar parliamentary regime. The transition, however, was far from complete, resulting in a number of institutional anomalies and anachronisms, a state of anomie.

4 STRAIN AND VALUES

This type of strain may take the form of radical schisms. In Germany, after the war, anti-Semitism flourished, especially during the economic crisis when the Jews were one of the few groups who were not greatly affected. This anti-Semitism had its roots far back in Germany's history; the frustrations and deprivations felt by many Germans brought it to the fore, and it formed one of the major themes of the value-oriented belief discussed below.

6.2.7.3 Crystallization of the value-oriented beliefs

Value-oriented beliefs serve a number of different functions within the context of structural conduciveness and strain in a social order. One of the most important functions of such beliefs is to provide an 'explanation' of the strains from which people suffer, an explanation that includes both someone/something to blame for the multitude of problems plus a positive vision of a new and/or regenerated social order. Smelser examines the value-oriented belief associated with German Nazism within the framework of the components of social action:

> Under this umbrella (+ Values), all institutions were to be subordinated – the arts, the press, the army, the family, the economy, and so on (+ Norms). Each was to maintain a separate existence but because all were to be engulfed in unity and national purpose, all bases of conflict were to disappear; correspondingly a state of social stability would ensue. As for the means (+ Facilities) of attaining this broad national regeneration, Nazism laid particular stress on the principle of

leadership under Hitler himself. Finally, millenarian visions – such as the Thousand-Year Reich – completed the utopian picture of the national socialist ideology.

Corresponding to these positive visions were the gloom and despair about contemporary Germany – the decay of the Aryan race, the feebleness of social and political life (− Values, − Norms), and so on. These themes of pessimism were traced to a number of threats – communism, urbanism, industrialization, the Treaty of Versailles, the foreign powers – but in the end all of these rested on an international Jewish conspiracy (− Mobilization) with enormous power and insidiousness (− Facilities). One of the major objectives, moreover, of the gigantic national regeneration prophesied by the Nazis was to obliterate the Jews and thus remove the multi-sided threat to German national life (+ Mobilization) (Smelser, 1962: 128–9).

6.2.7.4 *Precipitating factors*

A precipitating factor for value-oriented movement 'is an event that creates, sharpens, or exaggerates a condition of strain or conduciveness' (Smelser, 1962: 352). A major event that served as an early catalyst for the development of National Socialist sentiment was the harsh Treaty of Versailles which followed Germany's defeat. A later catalyst for more revolutionary sentiment was the Great Depression (e.g., support for the Nazi Party increased dramatically in the elections following the onset of the depression). Hitler, himself, also served as a precipitating factor. With the advent of a charismatic leader, 'there is a telescoping of several determinants of the value-added process – crystallization of belief, precipitating factor, and mobilization – into a single empirical phenomenon, leadership' (Smelser, 1962: 355).

6.2.7.5 *Mobilization for action*

Once the determinants just reviewed have been established, the only necessary condition that remains is to bring the affected group into action. [. . . However,] the determinant of mobilization is linked closely to the determinant of social control. Whether a value-oriented movement becomes a passive cult, a sect, an isolated community experiment, or a revolutionary movement, depends largely on the conditions of conduciveness and on the way the parent society receives the movement once it has arisen (Smelser, 1962: 17, 355).

Smelser discusses four components of the mobilization process, the most important for value-oriented movement being appropriate leadership.

1 LEADERSHIP

Value-oriented movements are characterized by the most generalized form of leadership – charismatic. Smelser attributes this to the character of such movements themselves which requires the type of leader who can generate a total, diffuse sort of commitment and who can symbolize the hopes for a complete restructuring of the social order. Such leadership was truly provided by Adolf Hitler (cf. Abel, 1938; Heiden, 1935). Despite the great power and importance of such leaders, however, Smelser explicitly rejects a 'great man' theory of revolution. '[. . . A] charismatic leader – like all other leaders in collective outbursts – occupies a place in a value-added process. He cannot become a leader until the prior stages are established' (Smelser, 1962: 356).

2 REAL AND DERIVED ASPECTS OF VALUE-ORIENTED MOVEMENTS

In order to be successful, value-oriented movements cannot rely solely on the small core of 'real' devotees but must also be able to engender support from a wider base ('derived' supporters). Hitler was able to do this for the promises he offered were so vague, the discontent so widespread, that the National Socialists attracted numerous adherents who joined for reasons quite unrelated to Hitler's objectives. Such derivative support can, however, be dangerous to the movement if the derived members are strong enough to divert the movement from its goals. Hitler, though, appears to have been strong enough to avoid any major diversions of effort.

3 STRATEGY AND TACTICS

> The success of revolutionary movements – e.g., the Bolshevik movement in Russia and the Nazi movement in Germany – depends largely on the choice of appropriate tactics at the right time by the leaders (Smelser, 1962: 359).

Hitler was a 'tactical genius' (cf. e.g., Bullock, 1958) adept both at playing opponents off against one another and at coordinating his power plays with the fluctuations in strength and weakness of the government and its agencies of social control. So skillful was he that few realized the true extent of his influence until after he had already consolidated his power and rendered the Weimar regime impotent.

4 INSTITUTIONALIZATION OF VALUE-ORIENTED MOVEMENTS

One of the most difficult tasks for a value-oriented movement comes after it has finally won the struggle, for now it must face the multitude of problems encountered by the previous regime. In addition, it must undergo a process of routinization and legitimation. When it has become responsible for the political integration of a society, the movement must: 'generate new types of leadership to sustain the organization of the movement itself; it must seek permanent bases of financing; it must accommodate new and more specialized activities within the movement; it must routinize its modes of recruitment' (Smelser, 1962: 359).

When Hitler seized power, he took over almost complete control of the nation's economy; he set up an intricate party apparatus to oversee specific activities in all spheres of life; he made the youth groups the main sources of recruitment of new members. Hitler rapidly and successfully accommodated his movement to a multitude of other exigencies in all spheres of German society, thereby preventing the rise of counter-revolutionary or new revolutionary movements.

6.2.7.6 Social control

Social control refers to the minimization of the effects of *any* of the stages of value-added process. . . . A major determinant of the course of the movement lies in the behavior of agencies of social control in response to the movement (Smelser, 1962: 364).

In Weimarian Germany, the agencies of social control dealt with dissident groups in a manner that Smelser sees as most conducive to the rise of a value-oriented movement. That is, they displayed unresponsiveness, inflexibility and, for a time, effectiveness (e.g., in dealing with the 1923 Beer Hall-*Putsch*). Toward the end of the 1920s, however, the government's effectiveness was weakened while it remained inflexible and unresponsive to the demands of dissidents. Smelser (1962: 365) says that such a pattern of reaction 'tends to drive the movement underground, or at least into an extreme value-oriented position, and then permits it to rise as a full-scale, and frequently bloody value-oriented revolutionary movement.'

The Republican government was perceived as inflexible, relative to the aggrieved's desires and expectations, in that its weak and cumbersome structure made channels for peaceful agitation as normative change appeared virtually useless. Because the government was so disunified, dissatisfied groups could not focus their grievances on a particular governmental organ considered responsible for hearing their complaints. And, as grievances could not be properly channeled or heard, authorities failed to make attempts at reducing the sources of strain (discussed above) that gave rise to the dissatisfactions. Such failure Smelser refers to as 'unresponsiveness.'

During the early part of the Weimar Republic, the authorities were effective only in the sense that through application of social controls they were able to suppress direct, hostile challenges to their legitimacy. However, this effectiveness was eventually undermined by such factors as the proliferation of factions and parties which virtually paralyzed the governmental apparatus as well as the extreme financial crisis that befell the country in 1929. Governmental control over the army was weakened as was the Nazi's belief in the regime's power to prevent their gaining control.

Smelser (1962: 375–6) describes this situation of decreasing political effectiveness:

> With the crash of 1929, however, a new balance of forces emerged in Germany. The extremist parties, greatly swollen by the ranks of unemployed and others, entered the political party scene, and their obstructiveness, combined with the weakness of the Social Democrats, created a situation of political paralysis. . . . Under such circumstances, the extremist groups . . . were able to marshal private armies to perpetrate illegal violence on mass meetings of other extremist groups, to bully vendors of newspapers and party publications, and to engage in street brawls with opposing parties. The government's response to this outlawry and brigandry – which it permitted with increasing laxness between 1930 and 1932 – displayed an ineffectiveness that contributed greatly to the growth of revolutionary movements.

6.2.8 Summary

As in section 6.1 we have attempted here to explicate the consequences of modernization for the structure of society and the political order, especially as these consequences manifested themselves in different kinds of strain and outbursts of collective behavior. For Smelser, collective behavior must be understood not only in terms of collective outbursts such as panic, craze, and hostilities which are, but not exclusively, frequently of an explosive nature, but also in terms of collective movements which are collective attempts to change norms and values that – as in the case of value-oriented movements – develop mostly over longer periods of time. At any rate, collective behavior refers to the mobilization of *role and organizational performances* on the basis of a belief which *redefines* social action.

As a case in point we have chosen Germany under the Weimar Republic which was characterized by structural conditions conducive to the rise of a value-oriented movement along with severe strains on the society's values and norms. Hitler, we stated, appeared as the charismatic leader who succeeded in formulating and symbolizing a value-oriented belief within which the foci of strain could be interpreted. Precipitating factors fixed this belief to concrete events, thus readying the adherents for collective action. In other words, Hitler was able to mobilize his followers for collective action and to maintain stability and unity within the movement and his new government. Finally, the responses of German institutions of social control – repression followed by a weakening of its effectiveness – allowed the value-oriented movement to become a revolution.

The concepts of strain and value are central to Smelser's theory. *Strain*, conflict, lacking integration are viewed as consequences of modernization as shown by Smelser (1959a) in his earlier study on the British cotton industry. Any social system is characterized by such strains even though the impulse often originates outside the system. Most obvious are strains that manifest themselves as *role* conflicts as a result of structural differentiation, socialization deficits, change of role incumbents, etc., or as *status* conflicts on the basis of distributive effects on the industrial and societal levels. In both cases a decisive role must be ascribed to the psychological assumption that, on the one hand, individuals are frustrated by inadequate role performances and status inconsistencies and, on the other hand, such strains come to be expressed first in anxiety and phantasies and then, under certain circumstances, in various forms of collective behavior (Smelser, 1968). In this sense, strain must be regarded as an *intervening* variable whose causal factors originate elsewhere. It leads above all to changes in the area of *interhuman relations* as well as *role and organizational structures* in different sections of society.

The extent to which strains do have consequences on the societal level depends on the values – the second concept central to Smelser's analysis. *Values*, encompassing moral and political principles just as much as attitudes toward sex, television, and health, represent the fundamental and most general components of each action system including society, thus defining the boundaries of sets of action and whole societies. As stabilizing elements they change only slowly, especially as far as the so-called central values are concerned. If they do change, they not only control the change of other components, but also the range within which an action system can change without losing its identity. The question of whether a change of roles, norms, technologies, and organizations or a value-oriented movement will lead to an alteration *of* society depends a great deal on how *generally* values are defined. To end with the conclusion of one of Smelser's critics:

> since it is the central values of a society in terms of which the revolutionaries formulate their value demands, they are invisibly bound to those values or assumptions. This is partly a function of the power of socialisation experiences; but it also results from the generality of the values themselves. They can be used to legitimate many alternative norms or organisations, while remaining unchanged themselves. What Smelser appears to be saying is that, since adaptation of values to different situations is much easier than discarding them for radically new ones, 'central values' tend to persist as guides to action, and therefore change is limited. The revolutionaries find themselves merely completing what their predecessors had halfheartedly begun (Smith, 1973: 109).

In sum, Germany, under the Weimar Republic, was characterized by structural conditions conducive to the rise of a value-oriented movement along with severe strains on the society's values, norms, etc. Hitler appeared as a charismatic leader who formulated and symbolized a value-oriented belief within which the foci of strain could be interpreted. Precipitating factors fixed this belief on concrete events, thus readying the adherents for collective action. Hitler was able to mobilize his supporters for action and maintain stability and unity within the movement and his new government. Finally, the responses of German agencies of social control – repression followed by a weakening of effectiveness – allowed the value-oriented movement to become a revolution.

6.3 Individual reactions to status inconsistency: theories about social status and change of social relationships

6.3.1 Social identity, mobility, and status consistency

In pre-industrial society and far into the industrializing societies of the nineteenth century the social rank of a person could usually be perceived unequivocally by others. This was possible because of the relatively low degree of division of labor and institutional differentiation as well as the dominant mode of status allocation on the basis of ascribed (i.e., inherited) characteristics. The low extent of specialization hardly allowed institutional niches into which one could seek social refuge at will, enabling the withdrawing individual to hide his status. However, not only was the visibility of status on all dimensions by and large a matter of fact; the allocation of status in terms of ascribed criteria determined beforehand everybody's station in life, his life-style, his occupational chances, his worldview, and his self value. Mobility was very limited, mostly within prescribed avenues, thus avoiding problems with respect to personal and occupational identity. Identity crises for members of society arose only with the extension of the industrial order accompanied by a widening of the social division of labor, institutional differentiation, individualistic achievement orientation, opportunities for social mobility, and, above all, anchoring the achievement principle as the model of status allocation (cf. e.g., Luckmann and Berger, 1964).

Identity crises come to the fore whenever opportunities to demonstrate identity are blocked. This is precisely what happened as individuals and their families, groups from one generation to the next, or simply individuals within one occupational career were increasingly faced with the situation of being able to move up or down the social ladder. For example, upwardly mobile workers do change their economic position measured in terms of income and conspicuous consumption, but not as fast as the social circle they belong to, that is, their friends and acquaintances. The same is true for the downwardly mobile aristocrat who is suddenly forced to curtail himself economically and/or to step into the sphere of a common occupation although he still associates with his noble peers (cf. Blau, 1956). If it is correct that man primarily constructs his reality by communicating with other humans and that it is men themselves who mutually hold the key to gaining identity in their hands (Cooley, 1922); if, furthermore, it is correct to assume that everybody tends to maximize his status according to the resources available to him and his competitors, we can view human life and the association of humans basically as a struggle for status in which deference by others as well as power over others and social resources play the decisive role (Collins, 1975: 59–60). 'To the extent that he has the resources, each individual gravitates toward that world where he shines brightest' (Collins, 1975: 83).

On a macrosociological level this is to mean that human action will be evaluated and subsequently sanctioned according to its functionality for the maintenance of *some* value system. Similar to previous types of social order, in an achievement-oriented society an approximate *correspondence* of social evaluation and reward is regarded as an important presupposition to social stability. In a society under ascriptive auspices, this congruence was automatically given and not in question even when extensive mobility processes did occur. The functional theory of social stratification consequently assumes that equilibrating processes (controlled by so-called congruence rules) take place which operate to align an individual's position on various scales of qualification and reward with criteria of social evaluation (cf. Davis and Moore, 1945; Broom and Jones, 1974; Slomczynski and Wesolowski, 1974; Kimberly, 1966). However, functional theory has maneuvered itself into a dilemma: On the one hand, it presupposes a system of privileges based on socially useful talent whereby the ranks of actors on such status attributes as income, prestige, and power are expected to be congruent in order to be of maximal value in solving the *motivational* problem of social recruitment. On the other hand, several mechanisms operate in social reality that make structured social inequality a less effective device to meet society's recruitment requirements. Melvin M. Tumin (1953; 1963) has aptly shown that the organization of the family and the structure of social inequality itself tend to contribute to the inheritance of status dimensions, thus favoring ascription of positions in society and limiting the possibility of recruiting the most talented persons.

In such a conception social *mobility* constitutes a functional requisite for economic development as it is supposed to warrant that the intellectual and motivational potential of a population will be exploited most effectively. Not least, the various processes of horizontal and vertical mobility lead to imbalanced status dimensions such that the individual is evaluated highly in one respect and less favorably in another. The high-salaried but low-educated athlete may serve as an illustrative example. Of course, the reverse has been suggested as well, namely, that mobility with respect to different status aspects may lead to an equilibration of inconsistent status dimensions (cf. Hartman, 1974).

We define social mobility as improvement or loss of a given rank on one or more status dimensions within a given period of time. We can thus clearly recognize that there is no mobility as such but a number of mobilities. Because of the various kinds of mobility we are faced with the *problem of status inconsistency*.

6.3.2 *Status inconsistency and the processes of status equilibration*

The theory of status inconsistency (and consistency respectively) is based on the proposition that an individual's position in a social system – mainly with respect to the distribution of social rewards and responsibilities – is defined in terms of a multi-dimensional system of social ranking. In other words, one's social status is determined by one's position on a number of status dimensions or status hierarchies, not on a single vertical dimension from high to low.

However, the historical, ideal-typical distinction between ascriptive and achievement-based models of status attainment, referring as they do to historical formations of society (e.g., agrarian *vs* industrial society), must not be confused with the concrete status dimensions of an individual based upon ascription and/or achievement and found in contemporary society. The definition and measurement of social status includes an individual's position on both ascribed and achieved status dimensions. Ascribed or ascriptive status refers to those status characteristics that are not subject to change through personal effort. Only a change in the *social* evaluation of an ascribed characteristic can effect an alteration in its ranking on a continuum from high to low. Ascribed status attributes most commonly used in measuring social status are:

1 racial–ethnic membership;
2 age;
3 sex;
(and often)
4 religion.

Achieved status variables are characterized in that they may be changed by *individual* efforts, although their ranking, as we shall argue below, is also a matter of social evaluation. Achieved status criteria frequently employed in measuring social status are:

1 income;
2 occupational prestige; and
3 education.

However, the classification of status variables into achieved–ascribed criteria does not always reflect their actual efficacy in concrete instances. For example, often schooling takes on the quality of an ascribed status variable, for one can most of the time not make up for it and once attained it can hardly be reversed; however, it is subject to a process of revision in the sense that, if recurrent education is not provided, it may become obsolete as time goes by. In other cases, education, income, and occupation may be practically ascriptive, as shown by innumerable examples of children who stem from urban areas in decay and are born into families with dim prospects in realizing life chances. Their status dimensions are largely fixed according to the social class the child happens to grow up in (cf. Rush, 1967: 87; Galtung, 1971: 277; Zimmermann, 1973: 89–90).

Status equilibrium refers to the social and psychological condition resulting from congruent rankings on all status dimensions measured. Conversely, status disequilibrium, discrepancy or inconsistency refers to the condition resulting from an imbalance of an actor's position on various status characteristics that are associated with his over-all social rank. We may represent the phenomenon on a continuum from perfect status equilibrium (e.g., a WASP, Episcopalian, male, middle-aged MD earning $200,000 per year, or a Mexican-American, Catholic, young, female clerk earning some $5,000 annually) to totally inconsistent status characteristics as exemplified by the incumbent of a low-paying position with high educational prerequisites and relatively low occupational prestige (e.g., some categories of highly trained personnel in research institutions, writers, musicians, and nurses in a few countries).

Central to status inconsistency theory is therefore the idea that consistency in the sense of congruent ranks on salient status dimensions of an individual or social group is normatively expected although it may not often occur in reality. The degree and type of status inconsistency (i.e., which status variables are to what extent inconsistent) may be regarded as decisive for the ensuing attitude toward social changes. The relationship presumed to exist between social status and attitude toward social change is thus based on the psychological effect social evaluation has on the individual's self-evaluation. If an individual's social ranking on all status dimensions relevant to his over-all social status is consistent (i.e., largely on the same level), it is likely that he will be evaluated and ranked in a similar manner in all social spheres, and his self-image – seen here as reflecting the evaluation of 'significant others' – will be free of contradictions. If, however, an individual's positions on various status dimensions are inconsistent, he was and continually will likely be subject to conflicting evaluations by others and perhaps have inconsistent views of himself, depending on which status variable is made salient at the time (cf. Sampson, 1966: 220; Malewski, 1966).

The literature on status inconsistency suggests that such a condition is disturbing to the individual and often produces frustration and insecurity. According to Gerhard Lenski's initial thesis, status inconsistency is stressful because it is more rewarding to the individual to consider himself in view of his highest status dimension(s) while it is more rewarding to others to confront him in terms of his lowest status dimension(s) (Lenski, 1956; 1967; Meyer and

Hammond, 1971; Randall and Strasser, 1976a).[6] The tension between congruence expectations and discrepancy experiences is what may be frustrating for the individual or whole social groups. The so affected individuals may be expected to try – individually or collectively – to alleviate the situation through conventional or unconventional means. The possible or assumed responses of individuals to the condition of status inconsistency productive of stress is the basis for relating it to attitudes and activities involving social change.

If we were to follow Erving Goffman (1959), who compares life with a theatre and social relationships with a performance of role players, we would have to look for the solution of the problem of status inconsistency on the level of the individual in terms of successful *impression management*. Whenever actions of the individual become meaningful for others in that they correspond to certain intentions and also ideals, he must then avoid or hide such activities as do not coincide with those intentions (Goffman, 1959: 30, 41). The prostitute, for example, will try to shield her friends at home from her sphere of work, just as much as some hosts place the *New York Times* and *Saturday Review* on the couch table while hiding the *Daily News* and *Penthouse* in the bedroom. The strategy of impression management is suggested for the mastery of such problems as status inconsistency in the sense that the individual is offered opportunities of selectively mediating meaning and *making visible* status relevant situations.

Following Merton (1968: Chapters 6 and 7) and Edward Sampson (1966), we may think of *role adaptation* as a second strategy, meaning that members of society opt for different ways of adjusting to the desired goals and values depending on their social position. The role adaptations open for an individual in a given situation may be categorized according to his commitment to social goals and access to institutionalized means for attaining those goals:

1 the conformist reaction aiming at the improvement of the low-ranking status dimensions (i.e., in the case of achieved characteristics);
2 the ritualistic response in that lower status dimensions are hidden (i.e., segregation of the audience);
3 the compensatory strategy through innovation, which essentially means improvement of the higher rank dimensions, although it is doubtful as to whether conflicting expectations can be eliminated by an increase of inconsistencies (e.g., through compensatory rewards such as further increase in income with constantly low educational status);

4 the disengagement strategy implies the withdrawal from those social relationships that produce uneasiness (e.g., by renouncing membership in certain organizations); and
5 the rebellious strategy that refers to the active rejection of the evaluative system of the interaction partner (or even of the entire society) and at the same time of the attempt to replace it by another, i.e., acceptable, system of evaluation (i.e., the strategy of system change as exemplified by the active engagement for political parties of the extreme right or left).

The strategy of role adaptation, to be sure, does not take the concrete action of the individual as its point of departure but rather the question as to how the social structure – defined as a context of values and institutionalized avenues to their realization – is reflected in individual role behavior, namely, in the choice of alternative strategies of action assumed to be particularly effective in dealing with specific situations.

We can therefore state that the theory of status inconsistency is based on the assumption that the status inconsistent individual is exposed to various kinds of social pressure:

1 status aspiration, that is, the pressure to maximize one's status position;
2 relative deprivation, that is, the feeling resulting from the disadvantage of one's position compared with that of others; and
3 status equilibration, that is, the pressure to equilibrate a position unequal on various status dimensions.

Although the first two influences are not limited to status inconsistent individuals, they are related to their endeavor to arrive at an equilibration of the status dimensions. We may expect that the tendency to strive for status will render the status inconsistent person to improve his lower status rank, rather than to reduce his higher status dimension or to set in motion corresponding compensatory mechanisms. Relative deprivation, in turn, comes into existence if rank disequilibria make a person feel disadvantaged in so far as the rewards connected with the low-status dimension(s) do not correspond with those of the high-status dimension(s) and the person may expect, on the basis of convention and interaction with others, that the ranks of the various status dimensions are positively related to each other.

However, it is not sufficient to state that consistency of hierarchically ordered status dimensions are normatively expected if, at the same time, the mechanism is not understood by which rewards are related to the formation of *expectations* of the position of the individual on various *criteria* of evaluation which, in turn, constitute the foundation for the *allocation* of rewards in social systems (Cook, 1975). In order to determine the relationship between status allocation and the extent of status inconsistency, we need

1   a distribution rule that specifies how rewards are to be *allocated*;
2   a congruence rule which is closely linked to the distribution rule as it defines the *consistent* relations between status dimensions; and
3   more or less well defined situations of expectation which refer to the state of *knowledge* of the individuals about the relevant criteria of evaluation necessary for explicating what level of rewards to expect.

Before discussing the various ways in which an individual can alter the effects of status discrepancy, we should briefly *summarize* what we have said thus far:

1   We assumed that there is a *multi-dimensional* system of social ranking that determines the social status of a person in a social system.
2   Furthermore, we assumed that the expectation states surrounding various status dimensions operate analogous to the 'law of the communicating pipes' in a *complementary* fashion.
3   The ranks on the various status dimensions cannot be averaged out in a 'mean status' that determines the social position and social treatment but rather must be evaluated and responded to as *discrete* dimensions.
4   The social evaluation of status dimensions that determines the level of *expectable* rewards (that is, how distribution and congruence rules are transformed into social reality) presupposes certain states of individual knowledge about relevant criteria of evaluation, on the one hand, and the social status of individuals with similar ranks on significant status dimensions, on the other hand.
5   The *extent of visibility* is an important, if not the most important, aspect of knowledge about status dimensions on which the status inconsistent's audience bases its status evaluation. As the fact of status inconsistency can be established only in relation to relevant audiences, the degree of visibility, that is, the ease with which some substatuses can be concealed (or especially emphasized) is of great practical, empirical, and theoretical significance (cf. e.g., Box and Ford, 1969; Hyman, 1967; March and Simon, 1958; Randall and Strasser, 1976a: 34, 40).

6   Individuals tend above all to strive for, and to maintain, a favorable *self-image* and correspondence with social expectations. Precisely because of these needs, status disequilibrium may be frustrating as it causes the individual to be confronted with conflicting evaluations that divide his expectations concerning treatment by others and encroach upon his self-image. Such frustrating conditions come potentially into existence if a person is part of a milieu in which other members are not characterized by the same status configuration.

In general, we conclude that the relative deprivation of a person will be the greater the more individuals are oriented toward a reference group that shows a higher rank than that of the person's low-status dimension. The (subjective) meaning of (objective) status disequilibrium may also be influenced by his/her identification with a given system of evaluation and by the perceived persistence of his/her low-status dimension or by the extent of normative and material investment which he/she has undertaken in order to realize his/her higher status dimension(s).

6.3.3   Strategies of changing status inconsistency

If an individual is objectively characterized by inconsistent status dimensions and if he or she *subjectively* attributes meaning in the sense that frustration is the consequence, we may expect that he or she will try to remedy the grievances. We did already hint at two general strategies: impression management and role adaptation. We shall now pursue, illustrating systematically and empirically, the question of which possibilities individuals have to mitigate or to do away with the (negative) effects of status inconsistency. We shall begin with three cases that should lead us to some conclusive statements. This discussion should enable us to develop a typology of reactions toward status inconsistencies.

1   A status inconsistent person may seek to raise his lower status characteristic(s) to the level of his highest one. Naturally, it is hardly conceivable, though not impossible, that somebody opts for the reverse, that is, for lowering his highest status dimension to correspond with his lowest (cf. Benoit-Smullyan, 1944: 151).
   (a) If his lowest status dimension is an achieved variable, he may attempt to raise it by:
      (i) personal effort (e.g., going back to school; training for a 'better' job; moving geographically);
      (ii) attempting to effect change in the social evaluation of the position of his lowest status characteristic (cf.

Malewski, 1966: 304). For example, to advocate a societal order in which all occupations are seen as equally necessary and important to the system of reference; (iii) attempting to (re)institute a system of evaluation in which his lowest status dimension is not a salient feature of social ranking (e.g., when high ethnic status overshadows high achievement status, or simpler: when father's fame has a halo effect on son's accomplishments).

If this person chooses the first alternative, his actions will be system supportive. If he opts for the second or third possibility, it may be expected that he advocates changes of those aspects of the social order that he believes to be responsible for his frustration by supporting a political party that promises such changes (cf. Goffman, 1957: 275). The second alternative would most likely lead to support of a leftist political party, while the third possibility would probably result in an orientation toward a reactionary movement.

(b) If an individual's lowest status dimension is *ascribed*, the only way that he can raise it to the level of his higher ones is to effect a change in the system of evaluation. Such an attempt would most likely lead to affiliation with liberal groups advocating such policies of system change as Black Power, Red Power, Women's Liberation, and Gays' Liberation (cf. Jackson, 1962: 479). The phenomenon of 'agism', that is, discrimination against the aged, may provide an interesting exception to the prediction that low ascribed status (dimensions), when translated into political attitudes and activities, will lead to liberalism. Traditionally one's status increases with one's age. Not only in the US but also in other countries there seems to be a trend toward a reversal of this, at least at some point in the aging process. Therefore, we might expect among the elderly the development and induration of reactionary attitudes, desiring a return to 'the good old days' when age commanded respect, privilege, and honor.

2 If an individual perceives the possibilities of equilibrating his status dimensions or of changing the system of evaluation as negligible, he may react by turning his frustration inward. This reaction represents an alternative for those whose lowest status dimension is ascribed as well as for those it is achieved. However, it is a much more common reaction among those characterized by a configuration of high ascribed-low achieved status variables

than among those with the opposite configuration (Jackson, 1962: 479; Lenski, 1967: 298). Presumably this is the case because the person who fails to attain high status in areas that involve personal effort has only himself to blame for his low position whereas a person with low ascribed status characteristics cannot raise this status through any amount of individual effort – it is a system-imposed criterion of evaluation. However, according to Goffman (1957), even those whose lowest status dimension is in the achievement category may advocate system change rather than reacting with self-blame if the perceived opportunity for upward mobility is low.

3   If an individual regards opportunities of raising his low status dimensions to the level of his higher ones, either through personal effort or system change as negligible, he may try to avoid those who react to him in terms of his lowest status characteristics or may withdraw from all but the essential social contacts (Lenski, 1956: 480; 1967; Malewski, 1966).

In order to be able to predict which alternative a status inconsistent person will choose, we have to take into consideration the factual availability and the subjective perception of possible action strategies. For example, the question may be raised as to whether a movement or social grouping exists which offers a program relevant to the concerned individual's frustrations and, if so, whether joining it would be feasible given the individual's social situation (e.g., would he be likely to lose his job, his wife, his friends, etc., if he were to join a particular movement or political party?). Or, does an education or job training program exist which the individual would have time and money to participate in? If not, then self-blame and/or withdrawal may be the only feasible alternatives open to him.

The three examples suggest that two *general* strategies to eliminate status inconsistency should be distinguished:

1   the lower status characteristics will be brought in line with the higher ones through, if possible, personal effort, or the attempt to change the system of evaluation through reactionary or progressive changes in the social system;
2   withdrawal from society or avoidance of situations in which one's lower status dimensions are made salient.

In order to arrive at a *systematic* survey of the kinds of status inconsistency management, it is useful to differentiate between ascribed and achieved status dimensions as well as between forms of self-blame and system-blame as far as the mechanisms of reaction are concerned.

Taking into consideration the relevant literature we are able to offer the *hypothesis* that status inconsistent individuals with a configuration of *high/ascribed-low/achieved* status characteristics are expected to choose one of the following three change strategies:

1 Raising the low achievement variable through personal effort;
2 Turning frustrations inward;
3 Advocating a reactionary program involving a desire to return to past systems of evaluation in which ascriptive or simply other criteria were more important.

Individuals with *high/achieved-low/ascribed* status dimensions may be expected to turn to the following alternatives or combined responses:

1 Advocating conceptions of change designed to alter the system of evaluation so that either achieved status characteristic(s) become more salient than ascriptive ones or the 'low' evaluation of their ascribed status dimension(s) will be changed;
2 Withdrawing from contacts and organizations in which their ascribed status variables are emphasized.

As already mentioned, achieved status variables such as education and income can be distinguished in terms of their degree of reversibility. In extreme cases they may even take on ascriptive quality (e.g., years of schooling with increasing age). For example, Gary Rush (1967) studied configurations of achieved status characteristics in relation to both right- and left-wing political attitudes.[7] Using the variables of education, income, and occupation, he succeeds in indicating tentatively the type of combination of status characteristics, differentiated in terms of degree of achievement quality and degree of reversibility which leads to alternative extremist responses. He found that (high or low) educational status was the most important among the variables he used if an inconsistent relationship with other variables is shown in the first place. Table 6.2 illustrates the findings of Rush's study.

Eugen Lupri (1972), by contrast, did not find any relationship between characteristics of status inconsistency and voting preference for the right-wing NPD in the 1969 Bundestag election in West Germany. Moreover, NPD supporters showed a significantly higher extent of status consistency than any other group of voters or non-voters. However, almost two-thirds of the status inconsistent individuals who voted for the NPD were characterized by a single type of status inconsistency, namely, high income, low education, and either high or low occupational status. As similar findings by Stanley D. Eitzen (1970), Fred W. Grupp (1969), and Ira Rohter (1969) have shown, such a status configuration clearly indicates that a status *over*evaluation exists. Hence, following Lupri's (1972: 274) concluding remarks, it is to be expected that a social status complex such as this will be defended, for example, by joining a political party that promises to stick with the *status quo* or to establish the *status quo ante*.

TABLE 6.2 *Right-wing extremism by low and high status consistency, controlled for status differences in occupation, income, and education*

1. Types	Occupation	Income	Education
High	a	b	c
Low	d	e	f

2. *Implications*
(1) a + b + c = 'Higher' status consistency
(2) a + b + f = Status inconsistency which is more likely to lead to right-wing extremism than left-wing
(3) a + c + e = Status inconsistency more likely to lead to left-wing extremism
(4) a + e + f = Status inconsistency more likely to lead to right-wing extremism
(5) d + b + c = Status inconsistency more likely to lead to left-wing extremism
(6) d + b + f = Status inconsistency more likely to lead to right-wing extremism
(7) d + e + c = Status inconsistency more likely to lead to left-wing extremism
(8) d + e + f = 'Lower' status consistency

Source: Adapted from Rush, 1967: 87.

These rather randomly selected examples reveal that it is the type of the *low* status characteristic which decisively influences the reactions of the individuals. The distinction between ascribed and achieved status dimensions is thus further specified. The central argument is the following: The perception of deprivation produced by inconsistent ranks on various status dimensions is frustrating, although different consequences may ensue depending on the *kind of inconsistency* and which strategies the individuals concerned regard as feasible for themselves. In other words, we can expect a series of similar reactions for persons with high/ascribed-low/

achieved and for high/achieved-low/ascribed status inconsistency, though for different reasons.

In relation to the mechanisms of reaction we formulate the *hypothesis* that *system-blame* is typical for low/achieved-high/ascribed status inconsistency, while *self-blame* is characteristic of individuals with high/achieved-low/ascribed status configuration (Jackson, 1962). Blaming oneself or blaming the system can therefore be understood as a function of the degree of legitimacy attributed to the system.

> We would like to suggest two situational variables that seem to us rewarding approaches to an investigation of the social conditions that produce external attributions of blame for failure:
> (1) the relative discrepancy between institutionally induced expectations (as distinct from aspirations) and possibilities of achievement, which produces a sense of unjust deprivation; and
> (2) highly visible barriers to the achievement of aspirations, which give rise to feelings of discrimination (Cloward and Ohlin, 1960: 113).

Thus high/ascribed-low/achieved inconsistents (e.g., poor rural WASPs in the US) who feel that their failure to achieve is due to systemic exigencies rather than to personal failure, may well experience a sense of injustice rather than guilt. Richard Cloward and Lloyd Ohlin (1960: 116) also suggest that: 'Those who appraise themselves as better equipped than their fellows according to the formal criteria of advancement seem inclined to blame the system rather than themselves when their expectations of achievement are not met.'

This applies both

1 to those with low ascribed status (dimensions) who have fulfilled the formal criteria for advancement (e.g., education, job experience) and have not been rewarded (e.g., with income, positional promotions); and
2 to those with 'achieved' status inconsistencies of the high/education-low/occupation or income and high/occupation-low/income type.

If we relate to each other the variables of self-blame and system-blame as well as perception of the extent of change strategies as mechanisms of reaction, on the one hand, and the kind of the lowest status dimension, on the other hand, we obtain a scheme of possible reactions to status disequilibrium. This is shown in Table 6.3, which has above all illustrative and heuristic value. Therefore, it does not include a series of considerations relevant in other contexts. For

CHANGE OF THE SOCIAL SYSTEM, GROUPS AND RELATIONSHIPS

TABLE 6.3 *Responses to status disequilibrium*

Lowest status characteristic:	*Self-blame*		*Response mechanisms*: *Perception of change strategies**	*System-blame*
	OPEN	CLOSED	OPEN	CLOSED
Ascribed	1 Over-conformity	1 Intra-punitive response (e.g., psychological stress, suicide) 2 Rationalization ———→	1 Political expression 2 Collective mobility ———→	1 Avoidance/withdrawal 2 Extra-punitivity (e.g., aggressive behavior) 3 Resignation
Achieved	1 Individual mobility striving	1 Intra-punitivity 2 Rationalization	1 Political expression 2 Innovation (Merton's) ———————→	1 Avoidance/withdrawal 2 Extra-punitivity 3 Resignation

* Perception of opportunities/change strategies refers to the belief in the possibility of effecting a change in the position of one's lower substatus. Such perception is seen as affected not only by the objective existence of legitimate and illegitimate opportunity structures, but also by internalized prohibitions, reference group opinion, age, perception of reward, cost ratio, feasibility, etc.

example, the selection of means in order to improve a low status dimension may be determined by the apprehension that one's high status dimension suffers a loss. The means adopted, say, to raise one's lower status dimension may also be affected by fear of losing one's already high status characteristic(s). Of course, some status dimensions are more vulnerable to loss than others (e.g., income and occupation are less 'protected' than education and ascribed dimensions). However, as mentioned before, the latter are indirectly vulnerable, namely, through changing criteria of social evaluation. The individual's over-all position also seems to be relevant here as exemplified by a person with a status configuration of HHHHL who has more to lose by adopting socially unacceptable responses than a person with a LLLLH status position.[8] High risk, though, may color the perception of which alternatives are really possible. Similar considerations will be made if status inconsistency leads to conflicting expectations of different membership groups which, in turn, can influence political attitudes and patterns of social action of the individuals concerned (e.g., the black doctor who feels attached to his racial peers, his co-inhabitants in the neighborhood *and* his professional colleagues).

In short, we can state that status inconsistency results in conflicting expectations and corresponding implications for social action. Regardless on which aspect of evaluated status characteristics the inconsistent individual bases his behavioral strategies, he will always be defined as *deviant*, at least by a part of his audience. These kinds of expectational, behavioral, and situational ambiguities connected with the inconsistent's life-world may ultimately be referred to as *the* reason why status inconsistencies – though depending on their intensity, duration, and extent – are stressful. The significance of the theory of status (in)consistency for explaining social change does not only lie in the analysis of *individual* strategies for mastering status inconsistency. It would be an error to see status inconsistency only in terms of negative consequences inflicted upon the individuals and the social system concerned. It is easily imaginable that whole groups of a society such as age cohorts, members of professions, or races suffer from status inconsistency. What does it mean for the stability of a society? Lenski and others have hypothesized that the more status inconsistents there are in a society, the less stable the society will be. In the following section we shall argue that this hypothesis does not hold water.

6.3.4 Status politics and status inconsistency

The concept of status politics involves politically oriented attitudes and activities that may result from feelings of status insecurity. The underlying idea has been developed by Richard Hofstadter (1964) and elaborated upon by S. M. Lipset (1964), David Schweitzer (1974), and others. Although originally used to explain the tension of status striving and status insecurity in American society, the notion of status politics may well be applicable to the conditions arising in any country undergoing changes in its criteria for according status and other rewards (e.g., societies changing from a feudal to an industrial economy, from a caste to a class system). Status politics

> refers to the . . . resentments of individuals or groups who desire to maintain or improve their social status. . . . The groups which are receptive to status oriented appeals are not only those which have risen in their economic structure and who may be frustrated in their desire to be accepted socially by those who already hold status, but also those groups already possessing status who feel that the rapid social change threatens their own claims to high social position, or enables previously lower status groups to claim equal status with their own (Lipset, 1964: 309).[9]

In contrast to status politics exists the phenomenon of class or interest politics. It is based upon political division in regard to material, economic matters, that is to say, it usually refers to the clash between those who favor redistribution of income and those who favor maintenance of the *status quo*. Following Max Weber (1964), Hofstadter and Lipset argue that interest politics predominate during times of depression, economic discontent, and national emergencies, while status politics become salient in times of economic prosperity, that is, if many individuals can improve their economic lot. The instability of social evaluation of roles and of the distributive system as a whole generated by economic and technological change as well as social mobility tends to be accompanied by more or less successful attempts to counteract this insecurity through status differentiations. This can contribute to the maintenance of the economic privileges they have acquired in the course of these social transformations (Bendix, 1974: 153).

On the other hand, status anxieties are rarely expressed in a clear-cut political program for there are no simple policy solutions. What makes solutions so difficult, is the fact that the entire structure of society would have to be included.

Hofstadter and Lipset agree that the two groups most likely to suffer status insecurity and support right-wing programs are the old-family WASPs and the minority ethnics who have risen to middle and upper-class positions in the economic structure.[10] The former suffer from status anxiety because they see their old claims to status slipping. This group often has little other claim to status than its high ethnic rating (high/ascribed-low/achieved). 'They may be members of families that once were important but whose present position is such that on the basis of personal achievement alone they would have little right to social prestige' (Lipset, 1964: 338). Lipset comments on the interest of upwardly mobile members of the ethnic minority in right-wing programs, which can also be claimed to be relevant for the relationship between the 'old' and 'new' families in many European societies:

> While the old American desires to maintain his status, the new American wishes to obtain it, to become accepted. . . . They believe that one need only move up the economic scale to obtain the good things of the society. But, as they move up economically, they encounter social resistance. . . . One of the major reactions to such discriminations . . . is to become overconformist to an assumed American tradition (Lipset, 1964: 339; cf. also Blau, 1956).

Although Hofstadter and Lipset were writing about the American scene, their concept of status politics is applicable to any social system that is undergoing extensive structural changes. Wherever the foundations and rationales for allocating rewards, prestige, and power are changed, status insecurity may be expected among those individuals and groups who were the recipients under the old system and among those who are seeking to establish their positions on the basis of the new evaluations. Status politics and status (in)consistency are not at all antithetically related; on the contrary, the characterization of the old elite (high/ascribed-low/achieved) whose status foundation is shrinking confirms our earlier statements about reactionary attitudes. If we are taken to the task to integrate the phenomenon of a low/ascribed-high/achieved status configuration leading to reactionary attitudes, into our earlier explanatory scheme, it is necessary, though, to find out other possible reactions for those who seek to alleviate low/ascribed-high/achieved status inconsistencies.

For example, an alternative reaction may consist in making the low/ascribed status characteristic as little visible as possible by withdrawing from contacts with those who show the same status characteristic, and by demonstrating overconformity with the standards of high ascribed groups. Let us consider the example of the economically successful Italian Catholic in the US who may avoid association with members of ethnic groups in low repute, may repudiate ethnic traditions and habits, may terminate open affiliation with his religion, and may even attempt to join voluntary associations and the denomination associated with the majority group. 'Conformity is a way of guaranteeing and manifesting respectability among those who are not sure that they are respectable enough' (Hofstadter, 1964: 93).

There is a whole range of motives underlying conformity with the expectations of others, thus rendering social order problematic and social change its corollary. The preceding discussion testified to the fact that we should not necessarily expect internalized social norms to be expressed in actual behavior; that values men learn in society may be in conflict with each other; and that, 'while men may generally seek approval, they may also be more concerned with the approval of certain types of men than of others and be prepared to offend the latter in the hope of satisfying the former' (Silverman, 1970: 137). The theory of status inconsistency and status politics teaches us not only the lesson that men continually redefine and thus reshape social reality as experienced by themselves and others by seeking differential approval, but also that we should pay attention to the role of the various forms of coercion in imposing a normative definition of the situation on others.

Thus, we may expect that, beyond *individual* rank inconsistency, *systematically* induced status inconsistencies occur when certain kinds of status attributes are in general over- or undersupply, even though at the initial point in time all status dimensions in a given system are regarded as balanced. John Meyer and Phillip Hammond (1971: 95) refer to Frank Cancian (1965) as stating that in a rapidly growing economy new rewards and market needs may be generated more quickly than institutions of education and rules of allocating prestige and deference can respond to. As a consequence, a number of individuals will become status inconsistent. This should be understood as a dynamic process of producing a distributive lag which represents an important preparatory stage toward a system of status politics.

Recent developments in so-called post-capitalistic societies seem to indicate that status politics – in connection with the institutionalization of *non-competitive* strategies in political decision-making processes ('consociational democracy') – is becoming the most salient feature of these societies (cf. Lijphart, 1968/9; Randall and Strasser, 1976b). These societies are above all geared toward securing stability by emphasizing their capacity to react effectively to persisting problems and to adjust to changing conditions.[11] Consociational societies foster 'sponsored' career mobility produced by the far-reaching influence and the protective function of political parties, consociational institutions (often councils in more or less close affiliation with government agencies and consisting of representatives from major social groups), the state, and the bureaucracy in practically all areas of social life. Status politics, which will be defined here as continually making opportunities available to improve single dimensions of the social status of different groups (above all income and participatory rights of any kind), seems to provide normative power for the factually existing chances to be socially mobile in the particular society. This is so although mobility in the sense of changes in the global status of an individual does perhaps occur less frequently than would be the case under different conditions. Status politics in a consociational framework virtually *minimizes* system-threatening conflicts of distribution hence contributing to the *maintenance* of the existing structure of social inequality.

In summary, we should keep in mind that in a consociational society status politics represents an effective instrument for eliminating the potential 'clash of material aims and needs among various groups and blocs' and for institutionalizing instead the 'clash of various projective rationalizations arising out of status aspirations and other personal motives' (Hofstadter, 1964: 83). In a sense, what we are dealing with here is the strategy of modern industrialized societies to conceal the contradiction of declared equality in the face of apparent inequalities. This is accomplished by, among other things, a relatively high degree of artificial mobility: low-ranked members of society are assured of their social value; the passing nature of existing inequalities is emphasized; diffuse, vague and often 'extra-functional' standards as opposed to clearly defined criteria of social ranking are stressed; the attainment of cheap status symbols is facilitated; and opportunities for 'true' upward mobility are more likely reduced, thus increasing the frustration of individuals by continually producing status inconsistencies and at the same time strengthening the stability of society (cf. Tumin, 1963; Offe, 1975).

Thus, status politics does not contribute to the reduction of status inconsistency although its institutionalization may effect a decrease in status insecurity. Status striving triggered and kept going by status inconsistency can explain a number of changes on the level of interpersonal and group relationships. The phenomenon of status inconsistency is, however, the product of factors that originate *elsewhere*, as pointed out in section 6.3.1. Status inconsistency as a problem of individual frustration is thus analytically to be understood as an intervening variable and accordingly to be evaluated for the explanation of social change.

6.3.5 *Application of the theory of status inconsistency to the Nazi revolution*

Similar to Barrington Moore's theory of modernization (section 6.1) and Neil J. Smelser's theory of collective behavior (section 6.2), the theory of status inconsistency is, though on a different level of society, most appropriate in attempting to explain why major groups that supported the Nazi movement were willing to do so.

Three groups were significantly over-represented in the Nazi Party's membership: (1) the upper class, composed of the old elites, i.e., Junkers, wealthy industrialists, and military leaders; (2) the lower middle class, i.e., white-collar workers; (3) youth (Cantril, 1941: 264–6; Conway, 1966: Appendix B).

1 *Status inconsistency of the old elite*: Status should be considered again as synonymous with social recognition and this recognition being relative to the particular norms found in a culture at a given time.

For a long period prior to the Weimar Republic, social recognition was mainly accorded on the basis of ascribed status characteristics passed down on hereditary grounds. The upper class, with its high/ascribed status dimension was, then, by and large characterized by status consistency. However, the establishment of the democratic Weimar Republic brought with it a redefinition of social values and thus of social recognition (cf. e.g., Dahrendorf, 1968: Chapters 5 and 6). Achieved rather than ascribed status criteria became important, although those who were formerly evaluated on an ascriptive basis were unwilling to define others in those new terms.

In terms of these revised grounds for granting social recognition, the status dimensions of the old elites became inconsistent, for they now had high ascribed and, often if not generally, low/achieved status characteristics. As has been mentioned, such inconsistency is likely to lead to reactionary political attitudes and activity.

Another explanation for the behavior of the old elites may be related to the concept of incongruent role status. The old elite believed that it was their 'duty and proper privilege to continue to supply Germany with persons who were, by breeding and tradition, capable of running the state' (Cantril, 1941: 224). But they detested the Weimar regime and its manifest principles and parts of the governing elite that 'obviously did not recognize the superiority of certain types of people and because the tenuous, implicit recognition of [their] value . . . might at any moment be jeopardized' (Cantril, 1941: 224–5). Thus, the old elite felt that their role made a significant contribution to the functioning of German society and that their responsibility to the state was enormous. They perceived that, although proper rewards and prestige used to be accorded to them, the new regime was now allocating to them less rewards and hence much lower status than was consistent with their alleged contribution.

2 *Status inconsistency and the lower middle class*: Owing to conditions under the new economic and political system brought about by the Weimar regime, the lower middle class felt its status threatened by the rapid increase in 'lower class' members being recruited into white-collar positions. On the other hand, manual workers' wages had been increasing at a higher rate than those of the salaried employees.

Incongruent role status may serve to explain the anxieties and behavior of this group.

> These people felt themselves superior to manual workers . . . they were accustomed to receiving more prestige, more respect, more privileges, more social deference than members of less elite groups. They regarded their work as somehow important to the state . . . necessary helpers of their employers. [. . . Now, due to the changes in the economic sphere,] there was every reason for

the white-collar worker, the member of the lower middle class, to feel that this status was threatened, that he would soon be indistinguishable from a member of the proletariat (Cantril, 1941: 227).

Thus, this group perceived that the rewards and prestige usually accorded the contributions and responsibility of their status-role set was fast becoming incongruent and, in an effort to halt this loss, they turned toward right-wing action.

3 *Status inconsistency and German youth*: After the First World War, German 'youth flocked to the universities and technical schools . . . producing a terrific oversupply of lawyers, doctors, teachers, and technical experts.' However, 'comparatively few jobs were available' (Cantril, 1941: 229). That is, much of German youth was characterized by high/achieved education status and low/achieved occupational and income status as well as low/ascribed age status.

The reaction of a considerable part of German youth – joining a right-wing extremist movement – is only at first sight contradictory to the outcome that the theory of status inconsistency would predict. Earlier we have stated that both the educational status and the type of the low(est) status dimensions are predictive of an individual's change strategies. Most of them saw in becoming members of the Nazi Party an opportunity to step into an avenue toward occupational success measured in terms of prestige, power, and income. The Nazi Party and its youth organization, the *Hitler Jugend*, soon permeated all spheres of social life, thus advancing to the central agency for recruiting society's members into jobs and for allocating rewards according to the social values propagated by the NSDAP. Party membership thus represented for these youths an institutionalized means for reaching out for the desired goals offered by the regime and for closing the gap between one's high educational status dimension and one's lower prestige and income dimensions (cf. e.g., Schoenbaum, 1967).

6.4 Summary and comparison of the three theoretical approaches

The theories presented in sections 6.1, 6.2 and 6.3 (as well as Chapter 7) are designed to lay bare to the student of social change the considerable variations in asking questions and finding answers depending on whether he focuses on the global social system, a social organization, a social group, or interpersonal relationships. Many differences between these approaches are obvious. Yet, some concluding remarks are called for in order to, on the one hand, stress significant differences as well as similarities and, on the other hand, relate these perspectives to problems of constructing change theories (assumptions, causes, levels, etc.), as discussed in Part I of this volume.

6.4.1 Differences of assumptions and variables in the analysis of change

Barrington Moore's theory of social change is drawn from an extensive analysis of historical case studies. The theoretical propositions that he develops are not held to be *universally* applicable; in fact, he does little toward generalizing the applicability of his hypotheses to other situations. The dependent variables that he is interested in explaining refer to the three major politico-economic outcomes of the transition from agrarian to industrial society: democratic capitalism, reactionary capitalism (fascism), and communism. He uses six structural relationships as independent variables to explain these outcomes (relationship of central authority to landed aristocracy, etc.).

With respect to the *types* of change theory as discussed in Chapter 2, Moore's theory seems to fit best into the conflict approach within a neo-evolutionary framework. The 'driving force' behind the transition from agrarian to industrial society is the pressure to commercialize. Social evolution may lead to different forms of society (i.e., democracy, fascism, communism) which depend above all upon the cultural tradition of the country, the existing power relations, the reaction of its power elite to the pressures of economic and technological modernization, etc.

In direct contrast to Moore, Smelser developed an *ahistorical* model of social action and organized the determinants (of collective behavior) into an explanatory scheme of *universal* applicability. Smelser's theory is built on an equilibrium model of society, not incompatible with Moore's rather static view of traditional society, pressured into change by the exogenous force of commercializing agriculture. His 'flow chart' of social action is based on identifiable patterns of relation among the components of social action so that change in one initiates predictable changes in others. Collective behavior is seen as a reaction to, and an attempt to reconstitute, a disequilibrated social order.

Smelser seeks to explain how and why episodes of collective behavior occur and the types of change such behavior may bring about. More specifically, he explains why particular types of collective behavior (panic, craze, etc.) occur, according to unique combinations of six independent variables (structural conduciveness, strain, generalized belief, etc.) and how each type affects specific aspects of the social order.

The theory of status inconsistency was initially formulated to explain extremist political responses within US society. However, there seems to be no reason why this approach could not be applied to other societies as well, with some modification according to the type of stratification, value, and norm system.

The package of theories about social status, social mobility, status inconsistency, and status politics appears to be also operating from an *equilibrium model*. The motivation attributed to individuals by these theories is to bring one's lowest status dimension(s) into line with the higher one(s). Discrepancies between status attributes are seen as creating frustration (or disequilibrium at the personality level) and a desire to ameliorate this condition. The dependent variable is political extremism; the independent variables are the various status attributes such as education and income, as well as their composite product: status inconsistency.

6.4.2 *Differences in terms of level of analysis and explanatory claims*

Another major difference between these theories involves the empirical *level* of analysis used. Broadly speaking, all three of these theories are dealing with a similar problem – how stressful situations are produced and what kinds of reaction to stress are employed – but on different levels of society. More specifically, Moore's theory deals with strain and conflict on a societal level; that is, strain placed on existing power relations by economic pressures is of central concern. Propositions about the effects of this strain on social relationships, and possible structural responses to it, form the core of this theory. Smelser's focus is primarily on the subsocietal, or group level. He is concerned with collective reactions to the strains that arise when actors are confronted with unstructured situations which cannot be adequately dealt with by conventional means. The theory of status inconsistency is primarily concerned with the individual or interpersonal level. It aims at explaining the effects of strain and stress on an individual's self-concept which result from discrepancies between status dimensions or threats to his social status in general.

All three approaches try to explain the source, process, and motivation to engage in the change process, though on different levels of society. For Moore, the cause is the pressure to commercialize; the process is the type of reaction to these pressures evoked by the various factions and classes; the motivation implied is the desire for economic and political power. In Smelser's theory, unstructured situations are the cause, the proper combination of his six determinants constitutes the process by which change takes place and the desire to restructure, or reduce the strain of, an unstructured situation is the motivation implicit in his theory. For status inconsistency theory, imbalanced status characteristics create frustration; a desire to alleviate the frustrating condition is the motivation, and attempts to do so may lead to change. From this perspective, all three theories are merely explaining different kinds of change.

Although, on a very general level, each of these theories deals with the same broad categories of problems, the main emphasis of each theory is placed primarily (although not exclusively) on a single, distinctive aspect of change: For Moore it is the cause or source, for Smelser concrete process, while for the status inconsistency theory the motivation to participate optimally in the social system represents the central issue. In other words, Moore's chief concern is with the question of *why* social change occurs and the direction it takes. He designates (1) the pressures that economic modernization places on traditional social structures as the broad structural source of change; and (2) the reactions of various social classes to modernization as more specific sources of change and as determinants of the direction the changes will take. However, he does not offer a theoretical framework for explaining the processes by which change takes place.

Smelser is mainly interested in the question of *how* change occurs. Although he posits the existence of some cause of change (i.e., 'unstructured situations'), he is principally concerned with group responses to a situation, not the source of change. Smelser's theory is also narrower in scope than Moore's. For example, he can explain the reaction of a group to certain stressful conditions or how a particular revolution took place, but not the structural conditions that created the stress or which made a revolution possible. In short, Smelser's theory is geared to examining the development of a particular movement and its outcome but not to interpreting it within a larger context; Moore's theory provides us with an overview of the society-wide preconditions for, and results of, a general upheaval of institutional arrangements but not the mechanics involved. However, neither Smelser nor Moore explains how strains impinge directly on individuals.

The status inconsistency theory is mainly concerned with the question of *why* particular individuals and groups are motivated to engage in actions directed toward bringing about certain types of social change. This theoretical approach describes a type of system-produced stress which manifests itself as strain on one's self-concept allowing the prediction of types of behavior which individuals may be motivated to engage in in order to reduce or do away with the strain. Discrepancy between status attributes is presented as the immediate source of motivation to seek change, but the theory (with the exception of Hofstadter's version of status politics) generally does not explore the broader sources of strain (e.g., changes in the stratification system) nor does it outline the means by which change may take place. A few aspects of the theory seem to indicate that availability, and the perception of availability, of means for enacting change are important in determining which type of behavior may be adopted to alleviate the status inconsistency problem, but none specifies how changes (e.g., in the social evaluation of a status characteristic) are actually brought about. The main contribution of this theory to the study of social change lies in its explanation of the effects of a certain type of stress on individuals and how this stress may motivate them to initiate, or participate in, a change process.

In sum, each of these three theories may be seen as focusing not only on a different level of social analysis but also on distinctive problems in the explanation of social change.

6.4.3 *The complementarity of the explanatory schemes*

In spite of the considerable differences between these theoretical approaches, it is also possible to see them in some respects as complementary in the sense that one theory closes the gap resulting from the particular *level* of explanation of the other theory. In order to illustrate this thesis, we shall examine the most general theory, i.e., that of Barrington Moore, and pose the question as to how the other theories can be used to complement the explanatory potential of the former.

As mentioned, Moore intends above all to explain the sources of change, that is, to answer the question of what the forces are that produce the pressures toward change. The priority to commercialize, to modernize the economic system, and enter the world market, introduced pressures for change, not only in the economic sphere but also in the entire 'superstructure' of traditional society. Moore also explains the probable direction of change which depends on the existing structural relationships (e.g., on how independent the landed aristocracy is in relation to the central authority). In other words, depending on the configuration of his major structural variables, we can predict whether change will take place via a bourgeois revolution leading to capitalist democracy; an abortive bourgeois revolution followed by a revolution from above and culminating in reactionary capitalism, i.e., fascism; or, finally, a peasant revolution leading to communism.

It should be clear by now that Moore's theory focuses on a source of change, namely, economic pressure, and explains three major directions in which change may take place, i.e., democracy, fascism, and communism. What Moore's theory lacks, however, is the specification of a clear-cut mechanism by which actual change takes place. That is, given the pressures set up by an agrarian social structure faced with the problem of commercialization and industrialization, and given the relationships between the major social classes, what is it that transforms the pressure toward change into the actual process of change? What does the revolution, of whatever type, set in motion? Moore's theory simply does not answer this question, except by referring to descriptions of historical cases. And this is where Smelser's theory may prove a fruitful addition.

Smelser's scheme does not overlap Moore's. He is not concerned with the cause of change (except in so far as it represents an 'unstructured situation' to be dealt with by social actors) nor can he explain the direction of change. His theory does not tell us why a peasant revolution occurred rather than a bourgeois or fascist revolution. The macro-structural relationships that are the focus of Moore's theory, Smelser treats as given or non-problematic. However, Smelser can explain, *within the limits of structural conduciveness* set by Moore (i.e., the configuration of his structural variables), how the pressures that created strains in the existing social order led to revolution (or failed to, as in the case of abortive bourgeois revolutions preceding fascism). But Smelser fails to explain one important aspect of the change process, namely, how these strains affect concrete individuals and groups, motivating them to seek change.

The theory of status inconsistency is, in turn, well suited to explain how the type of social change that Moore deals with affects *individuals* and status groups. A society undergoing the transformation from the agrarian to the modern type renders the social status of many of its members insecure. The shift in criteria of evaluation (from ascriptive to achievement) that accompanies economic rationalization is quite uneven, giving rise to frustrations within the old elite who find their basis for status slipping, and within the new elite who find acceptance on achievement alone difficult. The evaluation of the functional importance of different roles also changes radically with the goals of the society, giving rise to role incongruence. The various elements of status inconsistency theory provide us with an explanation of the effect that the changes

Moore discusses have on individuals and status groups and why those so affected are motivated to engage in change-related activities. This approach tells us, in Smelser's terms, who the participants are who will be mobilized for action.

Finally, if we look at the rise of German National Socialism in relation to the theories of Moore, Smelser, and status inconsistency, we arrive at the following conclusions: Moore explains why the structural arrangements of the Weimar Republic were conducive to fascism and why attempts to modernize the German economy without changing the social structure created enormous strains. Smelser explains how these strains were translated by Hitler and his NSDAP into an ideology with massive appeal and how the Nazi movement grew into a revolution, sweeping Hitler to power. The status inconsistency theory contributes to an understanding as to why certain individuals and groups were particularly affected by the strains, conflicts, and contradictions placed on German society and why they were most susceptible to the appeals of National Socialism.

The further utility of employing these three theories in combination is limited, principally by Moore's scheme. However, they could prove useful in predicting the social-structural outcomes of the many countries now undergoing modernization. But such a task would require an entirely new, more comprehensive study which would have to clarify not only future limiting conditions but also the 'age' of certain trends in the past.

Notes

1 That is to say, that of capitalistic democracy with the help of a capitalistic–bourgeois revolution from below, that of fascism through a capitalistic–reactionary revolution from above, and that of communism through a peasant revolution. According to Moore (1966: xvi, Chapter 6), India represents a fourth pattern as there has been neither a capitalistic revolution from below or from above nor a peasant revolution which, not least, should explain the weak impulse toward modernization in this country.

2 As discussed in section 4.3 of this volume, Parsons and Smelser (1956) argue that societies and their subsystems change most likely in the area of the A-function (i.e., the economy) and least likely in the area of the L-function (i.e., the socialization system). The condition hierarchy reads AGIL, while the control hierarchy functions according to the scheme LIGA (cf. section 4.2).

3 Smelser (1962: 43–5) comments on these relations as follows:

> a reallocation of trained personnel to a certain industrial sector (Mobilization Level 5) necessarily involves a reallocation to specific

organizations (Mobilization Level 6) and a reallocation of roles and tasks within these organizations (Mobilization Level 7). Furthermore, the initial reallocation, by definition, redefines the allocation of technological know-how (Facilities Level 5), and this in turn is reflected in the reallocation of know-how to organizations (Facilities Level 6) and within organizations (Facilities Level 7). If these redefinitions of Level 6 and 7 of the Mobilization Series and Levels 5, 6, and 7 of the Facilities Series did not occur, moreover, it would not be possible to produce effective changes in production by means of the original reallocation at Level 5 of the Mobilization Series. The initial reallocation, however, does not necessarily involve a redefinition of either the normative structure or the value system *at any level*; nor does it necessarily involve a redefinition of the Mobilization and Facilities Series above Level 5. *Empirically* the resulting redefinitions at Levels 5–7 of the Mobilization and Facilities Series (if we stay with the same example) *may* set up structural imbalances in the system which may eventually give rise to widespread redefinitions in the normative structure and the value system, as well as the higher levels of the Mobilization and Facilities Series.

4 For further discussion, see Gillin (1910: 246) and Bellah (1958).
5 For example, in Germany of the declining Weimar Republic there were thirty-eight political parties.
6 However, while it is probably true that it is more rewarding to consider oneself in terms of one's highest status dimension, it is not at all plausible that the audience finds it necessarily rewarding to view Ego in terms of the latter's lowest status characteristic(s). In other words, the second proposition simply does not follow from Ego and Alter's attempt to maximize their self-interest. If this were true, one would have to agree with the opinion that man's desire for high status always ranked above all his other goals. The truth is that man's self-interest leads him to order his objectives in hierarchies and priorities, so that in *some*, perhaps in most, situations high status may indeed turn out to be the dominant goal that guides his behavior.
7 Similar to S. M. Lipset (1964), Rush assumes that status inconsistent individuals tend toward extremist political attitudes (either right or left of center, or both, depending on the issue involved) more than individuals whose status configuration is consistent.
8 Status configuration refers here to a continuum from ascribed to achieved status characteristics which can be either high (H) or low (L).
9 As pointed out by Charles A. Reich (1971), the 'green revolution' heralded in the late 1960s and early 1970s was undertaken by the newly greened sons of the affluent. Their alleged denial of the power of work had, according to such commentators as Peter L. and Brigitte Berger (1971), the consequence that social mobility in the US accelerated in the sense that especially children from less well-to-do circles found more opportunities, thus launching a new era of status politics.
10 For the purpose of illustration we refer here to the US situation of the WASP, i.e., the white-Anglo-Saxon Protestant, as the traditionally

dominant ethic group, while members of ethnic minorities who moved up into higher positions in economic terms are the black pro-football player, the black doctor, the dentist stemming from Cuba, or the Chinese businessman in the US.
11 We dealt with these ideas more extensively in Randall and Strasser (1976a: Chapter 7; 1976b); cf. also Pelinka, 1974.

Suggested Reading

Introductory reading

MOORE, BARRINGTON (1966), *Social Origins of Dictatorship and Democracy*, Boston, Mass.: Beacon Press.
This study is an attempt to account for three types of societal formation, namely, democracy, fascism, and communism, in terms of the role the land-owning upper classes and the peasantry play, particularly in commercializing agriculture. The change of the entire social system is of central interest. The author supports his theses by referring to a number of case studies.

SMELSER, NEIL J. (1962), *Theory of Collective Behavior*, New York: Free Press.
Smelser aims at an explanation as to why and how episodes of collective behavior occur which, in turn, lead to changes in interpersonal and group relationships, in role and organizational structures. Such concepts as strain and value as well as the level of social groups, organizations, and subsystems are central to his analysis.

RANDALL, SUSAN C. and STRASSER, HERMANN (1976), *Status Inconsistency Reconsidered: Theoretical Problems and Neglected Consequences*, Research Memorandum Nr. 97, Vienna: Institute for Advanced Studies.
The authors' goal is to uncover the assumptions on which the theory of status inconsistency is built, to systematize the findings in the area of status inconsistency research, and to elaborate upon neglected problems and new research strategies in this area.

LIPSET, SEYMOUR MARTIN and BENDIX, REINHARD (1959), *Social Mobility in Industrial Society*, Berkeley, Cal.: University of California Press.
The causes and consequences of social mobility are explored and discussed on all levels of industrial society.

Further reading

General

WIENER, JONATHAN (1975), 'The Barrington Moore Thesis and Its Critics,' *Theory and Society*, 2: 301–30.
This essay reviews the findings of Moore's analysis of societal change and confronts them with the critiques brought forward against them.

SMELSER, NEIL J. (1968), *Essays in Social Explanation*, Englewood Cliffs, N.J.: Prentice-Hall.
The chapter 'Toward a General Theory of Social Change' merits especial

attention, for the author tries to integrate not only collective behavior, strains, and values but also different levels of society into a theory of change.

JACKSON, ELTON F. and CURTIS, RICHARD F. (1972), 'Effects of Vertical Mobility and Status Inconsistency: A Body of Negative Evidence,' *American Sociological Review*, 37: 701–13.

This study reports findings from empirical research carried out in six American cities and casts doubt on the thesis that status inconsistency has any specifiable effects on the behavior of the individuals concerned.

COSER, LEWIS A. (1967), 'Social Conflict and the Theory of Social Change,' pp. 17–35 in COSER, LEWIS A., *Continuities in the Study of Social Conflict*, New York: Free Press.

Using Karl Marx's conflict and change theory as a point of departure, the author elaborates upon the relationship between social conflict and changes in and of social systems.

NISBET, ROBERT A. (1970), *The Social Bond: An Introduction to the Study of Society*, New York: Alfred A. Knopf: Part III.

In Part III of this introduction, several aspects of the concept of change are dealt with and a conception of social change as crisis and event is developed and typical processes of change are discussed.

Problem-related

DAVIES, JAMES C. (1962), 'Toward a Theory of Revolution,' *American Sociological Review*, 27: 5–19.

The theme is that revolution does not occur because of some pressure to commercialize agriculture or the position of peasantry and landed nobility, but rather because of short-term changes for the worse in times of rising expectations. May be taken as a kind of counter-position to Barrington Moore.

SMELSER, NEIL J. (1959), *Social Change in the Industrial Revolution*, London: Routledge & Kegan Paul.

This study conveys systematic insight into the social conditions that led to the Industrial Revolution in England of the eighteenth century. Smelser uses the example of the British cotton industry to show how the process of modernization generates strains through social differentiation as mechanisms of integration cannot follow suit.

SCHOENBAUM, DAVID (1967), *Hitler's Social Revolution: Class and Status in Nazi Germany 1933–1939*, Garden City, New York: Doubleday Anchor Books.

In this book not only the conservative–bourgeois revolution is traced but also its anchorage in social classes and status groups as well as its impact on interpersonal relationships and the structure of society itself.

GURR, ROBERT TED (1970), *Why Men Rebel*, Princeton, N.J.: Princeton University Press.

The author examines psychological evidence that suggests that man has a capacity for aggression; other evidence is given about the patterns of social conditions in which men exercise that capacity collectively. The concept of deprivation is central to this approach.

7 Organizations and social change

Karl Gabriel

7.1 Introduction*

Social change at the level of complex organizations can be examined in two ways. First, organizations can be looked at as a product of social change in terms of their distinctive characteristics, including their number, size, and significance. Sociologists suggest this approach in their frequent references to modern society as an 'organizational society,' in order to distinguish it from pre-modern societies (Presthus, 1962). It makes no difference which characteristics we select in order to define organizations. We can, for example, conceive of organizations as 'partial social systems' (Mayntz, 1964: 100) and emphasize the specification of their goals and their patterns of behavior, as most sociologists do, or we can focus on such features as recruitment and dismissal of members (Luhmann, 1964: 29ff.; 1973: 339). In either case, complex organizations with specific goals and mobile members have never before existed in such great number or had more importance than at the present time. Thus, organizations may be viewed as a *product* of social change.

Second, if we look into the process of change within modern society, organizations can be considered as the *motor* of social change (Mayntz, 1963: 7). Organizations are capable of adjusting to internal and/or external requirements through changes in their programs, their structure of authority and communication, and their personnel structure. This distinguishes organizations from primary groups such as dyads, families, and peer groups as well as

---

* I am grateful to Lolit Mondal and Linda Rouse for their help in producing the English version of this chapter.

from society as a whole. Organizational change will be shown to tell us a great deal about over-all change in society.

In addition to the processes of change *per se*, the social problems of rapid and continual change are manifested in organizations. As social change is an ambiguous phenomenon with respect to the good or ill of its consequences, so too are the organizational structures identified with it.

These, in brief, are the ideas that will be developed in the following chapter on the subject of organizations and social change. We will first look at some classical and modern theories of social change, focusing on their statements about the development of organizational phenomena. Then we will examine in some detail the structure and processes of complex organizations as they are related to social change. Finally, we will discuss some social problems of rapid social change in and by organizations.

7.2 Social change and organizational development

7.2.1 *Classical approaches: Durkheim, Weber, and Marx*

The origin and classical period[1] of sociology indicates that the discipline was essentially an attempt to explain scientifically the processes of social change in modern times, to understand them, and to contribute actively to the solution of problems associated with social change. Whatever their differences, in comprehension of and critical attitude toward social change, sociologists like Durkheim, Weber, and Marx – among others – all emphasized the structural change of society in the direction of an increasing complexity of organization. (We are thinking of organization here not as strictly defined by the still young sociology of organizations,[2] but rather in the broader sense referred to earlier.)

One searches in vain for a definition of organization in the works of Durkheim; yet if the structural characteristics of the two types of societies that Durkheim compares in his analysis of the division of labor are considered, one finds the idea advanced that the difference between these two types is related to the growing organization of social structure (Durkheim, 1964). Societies with 'organic solidarity' (Durkheim, 1964: 70ff.), in contrast to those with 'mechanical solidarity' (Durkheim, 1964: 111ff.), are distinguished by a new principle of differentiation: the segmental structure consisting of respectively equal units will be replaced on a large scale in an evolutionary process by a functional specificity of units, and multifunctional patterns of behavior will be gradually displaced by specialized patterns with particular functions and goals. The mode of social integration has a new character: functional dependence and interdependence takes the place of a 'collective conscience' (Durkheim, 1964: 129ff.) perpetuated by repressive social controls as the basis for social coherence is transferred from collective values to the specialized requirements of professional and organizational roles.

These processes of structural change are inseparably connected with increasing mobility of social relations and group memberships:

> In effect, individuals are here grouped, no longer according to their relations of lineage, but according to the particular nature of the social activity to which they consecrate themselves. Their natural milieu is no longer the natal milieu, but the occupational milieu. It is no longer real or fictitious consanguinity that marks the place of each one, but the function which he fills (Durkheim, 1964: 182).

Durkheim is also of the opinion that pathological consequences of the division of labor can only be avoided if the affiliation of membership is not based on compulsion but on the principle of individual selection (Durkheim, 1964: 374ff.).

We may state, then, that Durkheim conceives of social change as the development of the following two structural characteristics which will have central significance for the degree of organizational complexity: functional differentiation and specification of roles and patterns of behavior as well as the mobility and accessibility of memberships without compulsion. Nevertheless, Durkheim might be considered only a precursor of the modern sociology of organizations (Mayntz, 1963: 26) by reason of his emphasis on 'occupational groups' and corresponding lack of attention to structural principles and the importance of organizations *per se*.[3]

Unlike Durkheim, Max Weber is recognized as a founder of the modern sociology of organizations (Mayntz, 1964: 97). His conception of bureaucracy has retained the status of a paradigm within the sociology of organizations in spite of its controversial and questionable interpretations.[4] All too often the context of Weber's conception of bureaucracy is ignored; especially, in discussions of his contribution to the sociology of organizations (Mayntz, 1963: 32ff.). Weber considers bureaucracy as part of a universal process of rationalization, which climaxes in its occidental development. He expresses this position most pointedly just before his death in his 'Collected Essays of Sociology of Religion:'

> The inescapable fascination of our existence and also the fundamental conditions of our political, technical, and economic

existence is an organization of qualified officials – the technically, commercially, and, most of all, juridically qualified public official as a bearer of all important functions of every-day life had never been known in a country nor at a time like the modern occident (Weber, 1969: 11).

Weber considers the capitalistic organization of work as well as the governmental bureaucracy with its rational–legal authority, instead of traditional or charismatic legitimation, as an expression of the universal process of rationalization.[5] The separation of household and enterprise, formally free labor, and rational 'capital-accounting' in order to realize a steady profit had never existed before.

In his numerous structural and historical comparative studies Weber researches the origin and development of bureaucratic structures in various social arenas. He considers, for example, the differentiation and functional specification of occupational roles, and, in the political sphere, the establishment of continuing offices and the shift toward the rational–legal type of legitimation.[6] Weber considers the process of bureaucratization irreversible – i.e., too closely tied to the occidental 'culture of world domination' to be revised by socialism for instance.[7] Weber stresses the ambiguity of this development for the life circumstances of people; resignation is mixed with hope for new prophets.

No one knows who will live in this cage in the future, or whether at the end of this tremendous development entirely new prophets will arise, or whether there will be a great rebirth of old ideas and ideals, or, if neither, only mechanized petrifications, embellished with a sort of convulsive self-importance will remain. Of the last stage of this cultural development it might well be truly said: Specialists without spirit, sensualists without heart; this nullity imagines that it has attained a level of civilization never before achieved (Weber, 1930: 183).

The ambiguity of increasing organizational complexity as an aspect of social change was a central subject for Marx even before Weber.

For Marx, the primary organizational phenomenon of interest is the increasing degree of organizational 'cooperation.' Cooperation is understood by Marx to be 'the labor of many people, working systematically together, side by side, in the same production process' (Marx, 1969b: 288). Marx considers cooperation itself a 'productive force,' and describes it in economic and social-psychological terms. It calls forth 'its own arousal of vital spirits to raise individual efficiency' (Marx, 1969b: 291). Even in the case of similar tasks it permits their combination into a quicker and more effective over-all performance, and in critical moments of the production-process releases a lot of labor in less time. Cooperation 'economizes the means of production through their common use' (Marx, 1969b: 291) and 'characterizes individual labor as an average social labor' (Marx, 1969b: 292).

According to Marx, cooperation is dependent on organization and direction in groups above a certain size:

> All direct associative and communal labor more or less requires direction, to arrange the harmony of individual works and perform the general functions, which originate from the mobility of the productive totality rather than the mobility of its individual organs (Marx, 1969b: 293).

Marx analyzes cooperation and its growing organization as a part of the over-all development of the means of production. Simple cooperation on a large scale, mainly based on slavery, is found sporadically in the pre-capitalist era, but in its most familiar form cooperation presumes the capitalistic system of production: 'Its assumption, the simultaneous employment of a large number of workers in the same working-process, constitutes the initial-point of capitalistic production' (Marx, 1969b: 297).

From its simple beginning, the degree of organized cooperation in the labor-divided manufactory is raised by the specification of working tools and the formation, grouping, and combination of partial-labor into a total mechanism (Marx, 1969b: 325). Though at this stage of cooperation, characterized by the division of labor in manufacturing, the substitution of team-work for the individual worker still has a certain degree of casualness, 'the cooperative character of the working process . . . is going to be dictated as a technical necessity by the nature of the working means themselves' (Marx, 1969b: 344) at the stage of 'large machinery.'

Marx is of the opinion that increasing organization is necessary, yet it is connected with the ambiguity of the capitalistic system of production, a system that signifies the emergence of capital as a ruling instrument over the workers:

> If, therefore, the direction of organization under capitalism is ambiguous because of the ambiguity of the directed production process itself, which is both the social working process of production and the realization process of capital, it is, according to its form, despotic. With the development of cooperation on a large scale, this despotism develops its peculiar forms. As the capitalist will be released from manual work as soon as his capital comes up to the minimum amount that will allow him to start

actual capitalistic production, he now delegates the function of direct and continuous control over the individual worker as well as over working groups to a special kind of wage earner. Just like an army with strict hierarchy, the mass of wage earners – working under the commands of the same capital – require industrial officers . . . and non-commissioned officers . . . who command during the working process on behalf of capital. The work of supervision constitutes itself as an exclusive function (Marx, 1969b: 294).

In the category 'organization,' 'means of production' are merged with 'relations of production.' This point, previously overlooked, speaks for the importance of organizational phenomena within the Marxian approach (Grunow and Hegner, 1974: 84). Further, the level of organization represents a significant area of social change – one in which 'relations of production' react rapidly and flexibly to changes in 'means of production' (Grunow and Hegner, 1974: 84). Regarding the dialectical crisis in socio-economic development brought on by capitalism, Marxian theory suggests that the 'only historical way of its solution and new formation' (Marx, 1969b: 242) is the complete development of the capitalistic form of production – including its organizational features. In contrast to Weber, Marx finds the motive power for revolutionizing the relations of imperative control and liberating organization from capitalistic ambiguity in the continued development of production means. Durkheim, however, expects that only from a building-in of structural counter-principles will the anomic tendencies of social change be overcome.

Though an extended comparison of the three classical viewpoints might be interesting and worth while, it would exceed the scope and aim of this article. What should already be clear is that although each has a different perspective and definition, all three writers consider the emergence of complex organizations a late product of the process of social change which has central relevance for further social development.

7.2.2 Organizational development in neo-evolutionary approaches

It is only recently that sociology has again taken up the concerns of the classical writers with respect to theories of development. Modern statements overcome the earlier tendencies toward the idea of mechanical change and dichotomous conceptualizations of industrial and pre-industrial societies. Generally, an emphasis on 'stages' of development takes the place of these ideas. Stages of development are characterized by new levels of adaptive capacity and control of social systems (Eisenstadt, 1964a: 375).

In the following remarks we will try to integrate three different theoretical conceptions of the relationship between organization and social change that continue in the classic tradition.

Parsons, the first author to be considered, has returned to the problem of social and cultural evolution (Parsons, 1967).[8] Central to Parsons's approach is the idea of evolutionary universals:

> An evolutionary universal, then, is a complex of structures and associated processes the development of which so increases the long-run adaptive capacity of living systems in a given class that only systems that develop the complex can attain certain higher levels of general adaptive capacity (Parsons, 1967: 493).

Among the universals of social and cultural evolution Parsons includes 'bureaucratic organization,' assigning it a special place in the evolutionary process (Parsons, 1967: 503–7). From a certain level of development societies can only achieve a higher degree of long-term adaptability if bureaucratic structures are institutionalized.

Parsons considers religion, language, kinship, and technology as the prerequisites for socio-cultural evolution which appear in so-called primitive societies. Only if the static condition of these societies is broken out of by the emergence of a stratification system will there be further pressure in the direction of developing bureaucratic structures. Differentiation of ruling institutions and of special instances of legitimation makes possible the necessary concentration of power to stabilize the bureaucratic structure. The introduction and building-in of bureaucratic elements signals a new level of adaptive capacity.

Parsons emphasizes the general importance of bureaucratic characteristics for adaptation and change of social systems. Like Weber, Parsons regards the institutionalization of the authority of office as a crucial feature of bureaucracy. This enables the organization to act and decide 'in the name of' all members. The principle of office also institutionalizes 'the differentiation of the role of incumbent from a person's other role involvements' (Parsons, 1967: 504).

We may summarize by saying that Parsons considers bureaucracy an evolutionary universal, which places the adaptive capacity of a social system on a new level when it appears at a certain point in socio-cultural evolution. Yet Parsons uncritically accepts Weber's conception of bureaucracy in connection with his theory of evolution and fails to connect the concepts of evolution and bureaucracy with his essays in organizational theory (Parsons, 1960: 16). It seems to us that the relatedness of organization and social change in Parsons's approach is accidental and not sufficiently elaborated. The connection between social differentiation as a formation of partial systems of society and the development of organizational phenomena was no more precisely and explicitly made by Parsons than by classical sociologists.

In contrast, Luhmann's approach to the theory of society and organization may be considered as an innovative extension of the whole previous discussion.[9] He distinguishes between various levels of system building and discusses 'system differentiation' as a formation of partial systems on different levels (Luhmann, 1975a: 38).

Luhmann looks at three different types of system building, the reciprocal relations of which are part of an evolutionary process. These are interaction systems, organizational social systems, and societal systems. The differences between these types are based on different solutions to a problem of system building and maintenance: the constitution and stabilization of meaning boundaries and the regulation of environmental conditions. Systems of interaction are based on presence and selective agreement of people's mutually recognized expectations (Luhmann, 1972). Organizations do not rely on presence but upon membership, and members are connected in the system by formal expectations. Organizations regulate their relation to environment through a combination of changeable expectations of member behavior and mobile memberships (Luhmann, 1964: 59). Society is the most comprehensive social system composed of all events and actions potentially linked to one another (Luhmann, 1975a: 11).

Luhmann describes the gradual separation of these three analytically distinguishable types of system building as a process of 'level differentiation' (Luhmann, 1975a). Historically, the organizational level is interposed more and more between interaction and society, until it obtains its present established prominence. Primitive societies show traces in their total structure of the characteristics of more complex organization. For example, members of these societies will be sanctioned if they offend fundamental normative expectations, and their participation in common undertakings will be restricted.

Functional differentiation of political, religious, and economic systems at the 'high cultural' stage leads to formation of the first large-scale organizations. Rationalized connection of mobile memberships with variable expectations of member behavior is thereby permitted, but only in an incomplete way. Recruitment will still be restricted in keeping with the stratification system and variability of expectations will be limited by the barrier of a 'cosmic moral world-view.'

Luhmann regards two unique constellations in the religious and economic system as a 'take-off' point for more autonomy within the organizational level. Early Christianity combines the confession of faith with a certain mobility of entering and leaving and establishes a high level of organization in the religious system by the institutionalization of the church. The peculiar 'breakthrough' to modern complex organizations, however, occurs in the economic system in early modern times. In the civil society, organization intervenes between society and interaction in nearly all functional spheres (Luhmann, 1975a: 12). According to their complexity, modern societies are more and more characterized by a large number of formal organizations.

Luhmann considers organizations a special type of system which will be very restrictive for the sake of efficiency. In thinking about this efficiency one is reminded of the special affinity of organizational social systems for adaptation and change. By their very structure and processes – this will be elaborated below – organizations are particularly well suited for continual change; they are, so to speak, prototypes of changeable and adaptive social systems.

Both Luhmann and Parsons consider evolution only in terms of the rising adaptive and controlling capacity of social systems. The ambiguity of organizational phenomena, which was noticed by classical writers, has not been sufficiently dealt with by either. Habermas criticizes Parsons and Luhmann on this reduction of socio-cultural evolution to the rising capacity of social systems for self-regulation, and reaffirms the 'ambiguity thesis' regarding organizations in industrially developed capitalistic societies (Habermas, 1969; 1971; 1974b).

Referring to Hegel, he distinguishes two basic types of social action: instrumental action directed by technical rules and symbolic interaction on the basis of shared norms (Habermas, 1969: 62). In the opinion of Habermas, instrumental action objectifies itself in organizations as 'subsystems of purposively rational action.'[10] In contrast, normatively directed symbolic interaction constitutes the 'institutional frame of society' or the 'socio-cultural life sphere' (Habermas, 1969: 62).

> As far as actions are determined by institutions they will be directed and enforced by sanctioned and reciprocal expectations of behavior. As far as they are determined by 'subsystems of purposively rational action' they follow the pattern of instrumental or strategic action (Habermas, 1969: 65).

Habermas views organizational development in the context of the extension of 'subsystems of purposively rational (*zweckrational*) action'[11] and the technical system of means. This extension follows an internal logic first noticed by Arnold Gehlen.

> It seems as if the history of technics would be a continuing projection of purposively rational and efficiency-controlled action onto self-produced objects. Gradually we have imitated the circulous process of instrumental action by machines: at first the performance of the executive organs (hand and foot), then the performance of the sense-organs (eye and ear), and finally the performance of the regulative organ (brain) (Habermas, 1974a: 337).

With the establishment of self-regulated organizations, this progressive objectification of instrumental and efficient, rationally controlled action is complete and definitive.[12] The human behavior element is only partly introduced in organizational systems equipped with mechanisms of self-regulation. Their rationality cannot be understood as the rationality of individual action, but rather as the 'rationality of systems.'[13] In this sense organizations are instruments of environmental control that imitate efficient, rationally-controlled action on a new, reflexive level.

Habermas understands social development as essentially a shifting of the relation between the 'socio-cultural life-sphere' and 'subsystems of purposively rational action.' In all pre-capitalistic societies – from primitive to 'high cultures' – the institutional frame dominates the 'purposively rational action subsystems.' In contrast to traditional societies modern ones are characterized by the freeing of 'purposively rational action subsystems' from the normative limits of institutions. The organizational mechanisms of rational self-regulation have expanded in all partial systems of society, especially within the sphere of labor and administration, liberating people from physical work and material deprivation. The ambiguity of this development within highly developed industrial societies is a result of the following circumstance: 'The man-machine systems which guarantee maximal reliability in the area of societal labor and viable self-maintenance become the model for organizing social relations at large' (Habermas, 1974a: 335).

The expansive 'subsystems of purposively rational action' enter all spheres of daily life and threaten to overwhelm them. Only in the private sphere is human behavior regulated by internalized norms. Other areas of human action will be controlled by organizational programs or stimulated by external stimuli. Sociology – in so far as it stands for social technology – also serves to further the domination of 'subsystems of purposively rational action' over the institutional frame.[14] Institutions lack a counterbalancing force against rationalization stemming from the 'purposively rational action subsystems.' Such a force is needed to rebind technical and organizational development to human needs and interests.

Although the subject of organization is pursued somewhat differently by Habermas, Luhmann, and Parsons, we may nevertheless recognize common elements in their ideas about the organizational aspects of social change. All three theorists see the expansion of goal-oriented, organizational-type social systems as a basic dimension of social change. Differences are related to their evaluation of this process with regard to its results for the life circumstances of modern man.

Taken together, classical and modern theories urge a similar conclusion: organizations – according to their quantitative diffusion as well as their qualitative structure – are a late product of over-all social change and a very important dimension of that same process.

In the next section we will shift our frame of reference and begin to examine the structural and processual aspects of social change within organizations. We will confront such questions as: Which structural characteristics especially fit organizations for social change? Which internal and external conditions are responsible for a high rate of social change in organizations? What stages characterize the organizational change process?

7.3 Social change in organizations

7.3.1 Organization and structural variation

Social action systems may be differentiated by a number of criteria: the degree to which their patterns of behavior are diffuse or specific (Parsons, 1966: 36); whether their system-building behavioral expectations evolve 'naturally' or are consciously created at a certain point in time; the extent to which the system is biologically based or 'culturally fabricated' (Katz and Kahn, 1966: 34); and so on.

In contrast to other types of social systems – small groups or whole societies – organizations exhibit characteristic extremes on all three dimensions mentioned above. 'They are consciously created at an ascertainable point in time' (Silverman, 1970: 147), and their legitimated expectations of member behavior are clearly and rationally defined. 'Organizations have an elaborated formal role pattern in which the division of labor results in a functional specificity of roles' (Katz and Kahn, 1966: 47). They are further defined by 'primacy of orientation to the attainment of specific goals' (Parsons, 1960: 17).

We may now ask how organizational patterns of behavior are stabilized considering their extremely 'contrived' nature. First, it seems important that organizations distinguish more sharply than other social systems between members and non-members. Organizations also regard membership as achieved and not as ascribed. An acquired and losable membership can be connected with well defined basic expectations of behavior.[15]

> Only those who accept certain special, qualified expectations can become and remain members in a formally organized social system. Such systems motivate membership by encouraging the acceptance of a role in the system and broader acknowledgment of all expectations of behavior which have been formalized according to legitimated rules (Luhmann, 1973: 339).

Thus the stability of organizations is secured despite their conditional expectations of behavior and highly specified role patterns. The basis for the special capacity of organizations for structural variability is also thereby created: 'Such a connection of membership with (changeable) expectations is a very elastic mechanism which is able to establish systems of very high complexity and variability' (Luhmann, 1973: 339).

Luhmann develops elements of a theory of structural variation of organizations with the help of the concept of the 'organizational role' (*Stelle*) (Luhmann, 1964: 141; 1975d: 100).[16] The connection of changeable expectations of behavior and membership contingent upon continuing appropriate performance carries over to the internal organization of formal social systems, and may be understood using the concept of 'organizational role' as a point of reference. Three reciprocally variable dimensions of organizational structure are pertinent: changeable programs as conditions of regular action in the organization; a variable communication and authority structure; and contingent personnel resources. Yet organizational roles do not allow boundless variation 'because not every person and not every communication-net are compatible with every task' (Luhmann, 1975d: 100). This idea of the 'limited compatibility' (Luhmann, 1969: 6) of organizational structural dimensions may be used as a theoretical frame of reference for further analysis of structural conditions of social change in organizations. The following supposition may be taken as a starting point:

> Certain solutions of organizational problems obstruct some solutions of other problems; say, of program and personnel

respectively. Solutions in one area make subsequent solutions in another area more or less suitable and vice versa. In other words: The structural decisions in one area limit the possibilities of choice in the others (Luhmann, 1969: 6).

In the following section we will analyze the conditions and limits of structural change in organizations. For this purpose we will deal with the organizational dimensions of program, communication and authority, and personnel. Treating each in turn as a dependent variable, we will illustrate the effect on change in one dimension of decision made in others.

7.3.2 Change of organizational programs

Organizations give their goals the shape of programed working tasks. Generally, organizational programs may be considered the conditions of regular action in organizations. Underlying programs is the supposition that with their accomplishment the crucial problems of the organization have been solved, and its maintenance secured (Luhmann, 1973: 257); hence the central importance of program change in organizations, as seen from the perspective of the organization itself and also with respect to societal interests in certain organizational outputs.

In the long run we may take for granted a minimum of program change for every organization. Yet the rate of program change varies considerably. In this section we will examine the structural conditions and limits of program change that result from decisions regarding organizational rules and personnel. As a theoretical frame of reference we will use the above mentioned thesis of 'limited compatibility.' This concept will be elaborated as we review a number of pertinent research hypotheses and empirical findings.

Jerald Hage and Michael Aiken have developed some hypotheses regarding the rate of program change as dependent upon organizational and personnel factors, and this may serve as a starting point for further considerations: 'The higher the centralization, the lower the rate of program change' (Hage and Aiken, 1970: 38).[17] The authors mention three arguments for the plausibility of this hypothesis. The change process will be blocked by a highly centralized structure of authority because the top administrators perceive change as threatening to the *status quo* and their own positions. By contrast, a more decentralized structure allows the representation of different perspectives and orientations, which leads to a higher rate of program change. In addition, a centralized structure stresses communication at the top thereby limiting the organization's capacity to make adaptive decisions by restricting the flow of information from lower levels.

Hage and Aiken find this hypothesis supported by François Cillié and Joseph Ben-David; the former researched centralized and decentralized school organizations (Cillié, 1940), and the latter medical research organizations (Ben-David, 1962). Hage and Aiken got further evidence from their own research on sixteen welfare organizations (Hage and Aiken, 1967). Organizations with a less centralized power and authority structure have shown a higher rate of program change. In the case of high centralization the 'agents of the organization who are at the level where the necessity of . . . changes is more obvious are less able to introduce the wanted innovations' (Crozier, 1964: 195).[18] Correspondingly, highly centralized organizations have their own peculiar pattern of change: 'The essential rhythm prevalent in such organizations is, . . . an alternation of long periods of stability with very short periods of crisis and change' (Crozier, 1964: 196).

Following Hage and Aiken we can develop another hypothesis, about the interdependence of program change and organizational rules: 'The greater the formalization, the lower the rate of program change' (Hage and Aiken, 1970: 43).[19] Robert K. Merton was the first to refer to this interdependence in his criticism of the Weberian bureaucratic model:

1 An effective bureaucracy demands reliability of response and strict devotion to regulations.
2 Such devotion to the rules leads to their transformation into absolutes.
3 This interferes with ready adaptation under special conditions not clearly envisaged by those who drew up the general rules.
4 Thus, the very elements which conduce toward efficiency in general produce inefficiency in specific instances (Merton, 1960: 366).

Hage and Aiken emphasize that in the case of highly formalized and well-defined organizational rules there is no place for considering alternatives, whereas ambiguously defined rules encourage the search for new directions of action (Hage and Aiken, 1970: 43). According to Luhmann, a certain deformalization effects a higher receptivity to new behavior (Luhmann, 1964: 152). In the above mentioned study in which Hage and Aiken followed up the program changes of sixteen welfare agencies over a period of three years, they found job codification to have a negative correlation with the rate of successful implementation of new programs (Hage and Aiken, 1970: 45).

Not only in the area of organizational rules but also in the personnel dimension, decisions are made that limit the rate of program change in organizations. Professionalization is a relevant, essential aspect of the personnel dimension. 'Professionals' possess training and qualifications outside of the employing organization. This endows 'professionals' with a systematically collected theoretical knowledge of a specific field of inquiry together with a normative orientation which regulates the application of that knowledge (Vollmer and Mills, 1966; Jackson, 1970; Kairat, 1969; Wilensky, 1964).

Besides having specialized, and frequently monopolized, technical knowledge, 'professionals' in organizations are likely to be cosmopolitan rather than local in orientation. Gouldner and Newcomb have adopted this categorization from Merton's research on primary orientations within communities and made it useful for the sociology of organizations (Gouldner, 1957/8; Gouldner and Newcomb, 1968). Unlike 'cosmopolitans,' 'locals' are oriented towards internal organizational reference groups and career opportunities and have a correspondingly narrow relation to the organization's rules.

Both characteristics of professionalization – systematic, complex knowledge and external orientation – increase the possibility and likelihood of program change. Systematic training and accumulated knowledge enable the 'professional' to keep up with developments in the field of his or her professional knowledge outside the organization and to work toward equivalent program changes within the organization.

Moreover, systematic learning favors a cognitive environmental orientation and structures of personality congruent with an 'open mind' rather than a 'closed mind' (Rokeach, 1960; Kahn *et al.*, 1964: 283). A cognitive orientation in lieu of a normative one facilitates perception of the necessities and possibilities for changing programs; more flexible personality structures in place of rigid ones increases the capacity 'to entertain new ideas and new experiences, and to drop old beliefs and preferences' (Kahn *et al.*, 1964: 283).

For the actual implementation of new programs the above mentioned distance of 'professionals' from organizational rules is crucial. It prevents the 'sanctification' of rules described by Merton (Merton, 1960: 368), and permits an orientation that includes consideration of alternatives. In addition, occupational career opportunities outside the employing organization enable 'professionals' to express opposition to existing organizational programs or plans and follow through on their own viewpoints.

ORGANIZATIONS AND SOCIAL CHANGE

The dependence of program change on the degree of professionalization of personnel has been empirically confirmed by Hage and Aiken (Hage and Aiken, 1967). An earlier study about different 'innovative capacities' of schools also pointed to this connection (Ross, 1958). The increase of program change with the growth of specialized professional positions in an organization has been observed by Burns and Stalker in a number of industrial electronics firms in Scotland (Burns and Stalker, 1961), and by Pelz in research organizations (Pelz, 1956).

In the preceding section we considered the organizational program as a dependent variable and explained the dependence of the rate of program change on organizational rules and personnel. Next we will treat organizational rules as a dependent variable, and will describe the conditions and limitations of change in organizational rules imposed by the type of program and the personnel resources of the organization.

7.3.3 Change of organizational rules

Organizations restrict a fundamental condition of human interaction: 'That everyone may communicate always with everybody about all' (Luhmann, 1969: 7). They establish communication networks by fixing formal communication channels and limiting the number of meaningful communication partners. They equip the positions of the system with certain competences and powers, and regulate their exercise. Rules of authority and communication are another fundamental dimension of organizations and of organizational change.

Again we will start with the supposition that organizations cannot survive without a certain degree of adaptability in the area of organizational rules. The rate of change in this area, however, will be limited by decisions concerning programs and personnel.

The organization can solve the problem of programming in two ways: either it takes its output as a basis for shaping a 'purposive program' and searches for suitable means in a certain period; or the organization has to orient itself with respect to its input and programs on an 'if-then-relation' basis. In the latter case, certain information coming to the system produces definite actions in the system (Luhmann, 1971b: 118). In reality, organizations cannot rely solely upon 'purposive programs' or 'conditional programs' but use both types.[20] Organizations can be categorized, then, according to their dominant type of program.

'Purposive programs' are characterized by open selection of suitable means; they therefore require some flexibility of the system. By contrast, 'conditional programs' allow only limited elbow-room for different interpretations of input information. Decisions regarding the dominant program type affect the change-rate of organizational rules. Where 'purposive programs' prevail, a more abstract and flexible system of organizational rules will predominate. 'Conditional programs' are more compatible with well-defined communication and authority structures that stay unchanged over a long term. All information that might suggest a change of organizational structure will be defined as non-relevant for the system and thus deflected by the conditional scheme of the program.

The choice of program type mainly depends on the task structure. Only in the case of relatively homogeneous tasks will conditional programing be possible. Heterogeneous tasks can only be programed by using abstract purposes, with limits of means and a long space of time relatively unimportant. Organizations with heterogeneous tasks and 'purposive programs' tend to have variable communication structures so as to accommodate situational requirements. Horizontal communication channels supplement vertical communications and the division of competence follows the functional requirements of changing tasks.

Empirical support for the expected relationships is provided by Burns and Stalker, who observed an 'adjustment and continual redefinition of individual tasks' and a 'network structure of control, authority, and communication' when 'changing conditions constantly give rise to fresh problems and unforeseen requirements for action' (Burns and Stalker, 1961: 121). Along these lines, we might also mention a number of studies that argue against the rationality of bureaucratic rules in the case of heterogeneous tasks (Stinchcombe, 1959/60; Litwak, 1961/2; Blau, 1955).

Change in authority and communication structure also depends on the personnel of organizations. We have already discussed various aspects of the professionalization of organizational personnel. Now we will refer to characteristics of 'professionals' that render unnecessary and less meaningful a rigid structure of authority and communication. Rigidity of an organizational rule system is an attempt to guarantee that the will of management is transformed into action at lower echelons. If the system of organizational rules cannot fulfill this function, some functional equivalent will be necessary to ensure the desired regularity of action. Professional norms oriented toward technical requirements appear partially to substitute inner controls for external, organizational rules. The increasing presence of professional specialists within organizations necessitates more abstract formulation and more flexible interpretation of organizational rules than might otherwise be required.

The hypothesis that the rate of change of organizational rules increases with growing professionalization of personnel is confirmed by the observation that increased demand for professional autonomy is not compatible with rigid regulation of action (Toffler, 1973: 346). Also, in a study of craft administration Stinchcombe finds professional norms substituted for bureaucratic rules (Stinchcombe, 1959/60). Further support comes from numerous studies concerning the conflict between 'professional' and bureaucratic organizations (Wilensky, 1956; Scott, 1966).

7.3.4 Change of organizational personnel

Organizations require human resources in order to attain their goals. When we consider personnel as a structural dimension of organizations, we think of organizational members not as individuals *per se* but as those who hold certain orientations and have a certain theoretical and practical knowledge (Luhmann, 1969: 9). For an operational definition of this dimension we have previously referred to the 'professionalization-syndrome,' which involves both orientations and knowledge.

Generally, personnel change may take place in two ways: It can be brought about by recruitment and internal redistribution or by education and socialization. Starting from the assumption of at least minimal change, we will outline the structural prerequisites of personnel change associated with programs and organizational rules.

After the dominant program type is established, possibilities are limited in the area of personnel. A 'conditional program' with an elaborate division of labor minimizes the influence of personnel elements in the organization as a whole; consequently, one does not expect much impetus for personnel change. If 'purposive programs' prevail in an organization, however, personnel capacities – which are related to the selection of means – are essential. Professional orientation and technical knowledge here may become crucial for the organization as a whole in so far as they can lead to serious internal conflicts as well as encouraging change. In this context, it seems appropriate that the literature on organizational change focuses a great deal of attention on changing personnel through individual and group counseling, sensitivity training, and group therapy (Schein and Bennis, 1965; Bennis, 1966; Dunette and Campbell, 1970). This suggests that change in the personnel dimension increasingly becomes the bottle-neck of organizational adaptive capacity. These studies, however, do not adequately consider the influence of the dimension of programs or the dimension of authority and communication on personnel change (Katz and Kahn, 1966: 390). Only when there is a decentralized communication structure and distribution of competence along with a flexible rule system will a high rate of personnel change be possible. Empirical studies reporting an inverse relation between centralization and professionalization supply evidence for this contention (Blau *et al.*, 1966; Scott, 1966).

Our previous analysis of social change in the program, authority and communications, and personnel dimensions of complex organizations proceeded from very simple premises. We began with the proposition that decisions in one dimension will place limitations on future decisions in the others. Then we reviewed plausible hypotheses and pertinent empirical studies related to social change in these three dimensions.

Already, we have gained the conviction that there are more complex interdependencies than might be expressed by relations between two variables only. Recent organizational models try to meet this criticism; they introduce the supposition that there is a tendency toward certain configurations of organizational characteristics which constitute different organizational types (Hage and Aiken, 1970: 62). Following this approach, some authors make a distinction between the static and the dynamic type of complex organization.[21] We will discuss these two organizational types in the next section of this chapter.

Also in the next section, we will need to drop a simplification introduced above. We have previously isolated the organization from its environment and treated organizations as if they were able to change their structure along various dimensions limited only by their own previous decisions. Actually, the rate of social change in all dimensions also depends upon the environment of the organization.[22]

7.3.5 *Static and dynamic organization and environment*

The hypothesis of 'limited compatibility' of organizational dimensions suggests a possible extension of the concept to cover the configurations of particular dimensional values that appear as different organizational types. Reciprocal limitations make the occurrence of certain dimensional formations more probable than any others.

The discussion of Weber's concept of bureaucracy in modern sociology of organizations has already produced a similar conclusion. Criticism of Weber, both theoretical and empirical, led to a new interpretation of his concept of bureaucracy. Bureaucratic organization is no longer considered the most efficient organizational mode in all situations; it is simply one typical formation of structural dimensions of organization (Mayntz, 1964: 98; 1968: 27). Bureaucracy is a model of static organization, which is now compared to another organizational type characterized by higher rates of change in all dimensions (Mayntz, 1964: 99; Litwak, 1961/2: 177; Burns and Stalker, 1961: 96). Bureaucratic organizations are distinguished by a strict hierarchy of authority, with emphasis on vertical communication, a strict regulation of competence, a comprehensive orientation of action by rules, and a prevalence of 'conditional programs' based on a homogeneous task structure (Weber, 1947: 329ff.).

The alternative models of dynamic organization proposed by various authors are essentially analogous, in spite of enormous differences in emphasis and definition. Based on their previously mentioned research, Burns and Stalker have developed one such alternative model. Borrowing Durkheim's concept of 'organic solidarity,' they call it an 'organic system of management' in contrast with a 'mechanical system of management' – the latter basically agreeing with the bureaucratic model (Burns and Stalker, 1961: 96). The 'organic management system' is characterized by the following features:

1 'the adjustment and continual re-definition of individual tasks through interaction with others';
2 'a network structure of control, authority, and communication';
3 'a lateral rather than vertical direction of communication through the organization; communication between people of different rank; also, communication resembling consultation rather than command';
4 'commitment to the concern's tasks and to the "technological ethos" of material progress and expansion is more highly valued than loyalty and obedience';
5 'importance and prestige attached to affiliations and expertise valid in the industrial and technical and commercial milieux external to the firm' (Burns and Stalker, 1961: 121–2).

Other authors lay more stress upon the central role of 'professionals,' and define the alternative organizational type as a 'professional model' (Litwak, 1961/2: 182; Scott, 1966: 266; Mayntz, 1964: 99). Altogether, the alternative models propose a high degree of social change in all three structural dimensions:

continuous alterations of programs – due to tasks that are not suited to routine performance or standardization; continual adaptation of authority and communication structures according to the functional requirements of the situation; and a high degree of 'professional' orientation, skills, and knowledge – which allow adjustment to rapid change.

Discussion of 'alternative models' often includes consideration of the organization's relation to the environment; e.g., whether it is more prescriptively oriented to the 'one right way' to organize or more analytically oriented (Luhmann, 1964: 46).[23] The thesis presented in the relevant literature may be summarized as follows: Bureaucratic characteristics tend to develop when the external environment is relatively stable. The organization is mainly confronted with slow, predictable changes that can be planned for over the long run. In this situation bureaucracy is the most efficient type of organization. By contrast, if the organization is confronted with a 'turbulent environment' it will tend to be structured more along the lines of the 'organic' or 'professional' model – which proves more efficient than bureaucratic organization under these circumstances (Emery and Trist, 1965: 21; Hage and Aiken, 1970: 62; Mayntz, 1964: 99).

Both organizational types are to be understood as extreme values of a continuum of structural possibilities:

> Finally, the two forms of system represent a polarity, not a dichotomy; there are, as we have tried to show, intermediate stages between the extremities empirically known to us. Also, the relation of one form to another is elastic, so that a concern oscillating between relative stability and relative change may also oscillate between the two forms. A concern may (and frequently does) operate with a management system which includes both types (Burns and Stalker, 1961: 122).

Litwak discusses the structural problems of such 'mixed models.' He proposes 'mechanisms of segregation' like 'physical distance' and 'role separation' (Litwak, 1961/2: 182).

Mayntz believes that criticism of the bureaucratic model and the present stress on flexibility, adaptability, and innovative change in modern organizational theory 'to a certain extent . . . reflect a concrete historical change' (Mayntz, 1964: 104). The environmental conditions of organizations have changed generally in the direction of greater instability and turbulence. The mastering of rapid environmental change may correspondingly be considered a crucial problem for the majority of modern organizations. In reaction to their environmental situation they are constrained to realize a higher rate of social change in all structural dimensions than was necessary for bureaucracies as Weber described them (Emery and Trist, 1965; Terryberry, 1968).

Until now we have considered organizational change from a structural perspective, describing the dependencies and limitations of structural change with respect to internal decisions and external, environmental conditions. But every change in an organization may also be conceptualized as a process. In the next section we will analyze the process of change in organizations by examining stages in the change process and specific problems associated with each stage.

7.4 Organizational change as a process

Our previous consideration of structural variation in organizations identified only the possibilities, compatibilities, and limits. Every alteration in organizations, however, involves a process of decision making and a series of events over a particular period. The process of organizational change can be divided into certain stages for a detailed recognition of specific problems associated with change. The decision to initiate change, for example, involves complications for the organization different from those connected with efforts to stabilize the innovation once introduced. One must, of course, remain conscious of the 'ideal-typical' character of stage models of organizational change. Numerous statements in the organizational literature urge caution here (Schienstock, 1974: 195). It may be especially difficult to distinguish clearly the beginning of one stage from the end of another stage. Moreover, one has to bear in mind the possibility that in real change processes a stage may be bypassed or exchanged with another.

Granting the 'ideal-typical' character of the stage model, it might nevertheless be useful to distinguish different periods in the organizational change process in practice, and for the purpose of analysis. Table 7.1 shows different proposals for distinguishing stages in the process of organizational change.

In our further exposition we will follow the stage model of Hage and Aiken; a similar proposal is made by Schienstock in an attempt to make the stage model more theoretically convincing by combining it with functional analysis (Schienstock, 1974: 199). Parsons has outlined four essential system problems to be considered in the functional analysis of social systems: pattern maintenance and tension management, goal attainment, adaptation, and integration (Parsons, 1961: 30). Relating this theoretical framework to the idea of stages in the organizational change process allows a theoretical

TABLE 7.1 Several approaches to stages of organizational change

Authors	Shepard (1967: 470ff.)	Hage/Aiken (1970: 92ff.)	Schienstock (1974: 195ff.)	Greiner/Barnes (1970: 10ff.)	Mann/Neff[24] (1961)
Stages of change in organizations	(1) Search for new ideas (2) Acceptance (3) Implementation	(1) Evaluation (2) Initiation (3) Implementation (4) Routinization	(1) Problem perception and search for new ideas (goal attainment) (2) Concretization (adaptation) (3) Implementation (integration) (4) Stabilization (pattern maintenance and tension management)	(1) Diagnosing organization problems (2) Planning of change (3) Launching organization change (4) Following up on organization change	(1) State of organization before change (2) Recognition of need for change (3) Planning change (4) Taking steps to make change (5) Stabilizing change

elaboration of the stage model in which the phases of the change process are connected with basic social system problems.

7.4.1 Evaluation stage

The change process in organizations generally starts with dissatisfaction concerning the efficiency of the organization (Hage and Aiken, 1970: 94). If those in positions of control believe that the organization is not satisfactorily accomplishing its goals, or if it happens as a result of environmental alterations that stated purposes do not secure its maintenance any more,[25] the top management will be pressed for changes. Those in appropriate organizational positions will have to diagnose the changed situation of the organization, discuss solution alternatives, and elaborate solution possibilities.[26] The quality of the problem solution will be dependent on the information and communication system, the qualifications of involved personnel, and on the time available to search for new ideas and solutions.

Management is confronted with a dilemma in making a decision with respect to solving any given problem: too modest a change may prove insufficient for solution of the problem; too disruptive a change may overtax the adaptability of the organization and risk disintegration of the system. This potential risk makes the evaluation phase one of conflict and competition over defining the nature of the organization and the appropriateness of its course.

A decision, made in favor of a certain innovation, completes the first phase of the change process and leads to the second stage in which the preparation of means for the implementation of innovation will be central.

7.4.2 Initiation stage

At the initiation stage of organizational change the social system problem of adaptation is crucial. Following Parsons, it involves procurement of suitable means and techniques for attaining goals. In our terms, the problem may be described as concerning the preparation of means by which the decision made in the evaluation period will be realized.

Hage and Aiken stress two problems confronting the organization in this phase. Change in personnel resources is a means of organizational change; one that can be accomplished either by recruiting from the outside or by internal training. When more rapid and/or dramatic change is desired, the recruitment of external personnel seems more suitable because established attitudes and patterns of relation prevent radical alteration of extant personnel through training. But recruiting new members increases the risk of opposition to the innovation among the other personnel. Without adequate mechanisms of conflict resolution, change impulses threaten to be checked at the outset by the struggle for power and prestige. On the other hand, the innovation is already in danger of being absorbed by the established routine when internal personnel are involved, for 'in every individual situation there is a natural descent to the existing and authorized programs' (Luhmann, 1971b: 133).

A second problem of the initiation stage concerns the procurement of financial resources needed to implement the change. The initiators of the change find themselves confronted here, too, with a dilemma. A change considered necessary may exceed the organization's own financial resources so that help from other institutions must be sought. The resultant cooperative and cooptative relations with other organizations involve the risk of narrowing the sphere of autonomous decisions for the organizations (Thompson and McEwen, 1958: 23).

Nor is the success of organizational change secured simply by making available sufficient personnel and financial resources. The greatest disturbance of organizational equilibrium and, correspondingly, the most difficult conflicts are encountered in the third stage of the change process.

7.4.3 Implementation stage

During the implementation stage the process of change arrives at a critical period characterized by high conflict potential.

The number of participants in the alteration increases compared with the previous stages because now the lower echelons concerned are immediately confronted with the alterations planned. A number of characteristic dilemmas follow, which threaten the proposed organizational change from several directions.

For implementation of an innovation new positions will be required; positions that must be integrated into the existing authority structure. The new occupants of posts normally try to achieve the most favorable position possible within the power, prestige, and reward system of the organization by appealing to the importance of the new programs. Complying with their demand the top management may, for the time being, create good conditions for the installation of the new programs. The established power structure, however, will probably be so little changed that the alteration may be resisted after all by opposition to the new distribution of power and competence.

A second dilemma refers to the problem of transforming a change from the realm of planning and control to lower organizational members concerned with the actual execution. In this situation, the cooperation of participants immediately and intermediately involved becomes a crucial bottle-neck for the success of the change process. The probability of cooperation increases with the amount of information possessed by those involved about the planned alteration, and with the possibility of their participation in making relevant decisions. From this perspective, democratic processes of consensus shaping are viewed as prerequisites for successful change; and they require overriding the strict separation of planning, performance, and control. While successful change thus implies the participation of all concerned members during the period of evaluation and implementation, the manifold interests and lack of competence of these members may impair the quality of the decision to change and prevent alterations being made to the extent necessary.[27]

The limits of organizational adaptability that are evident in this situation may be differently overcome according to the organizational structure. It should be clear that organizations with highly professionalized personnel and a network structure of communication escape the dilemma of necessary participation of concerned organizational members versus maintenance of a satisfactory level of rationality more so than bureaucratic organizations.

The new distribution of power and competence and the dissolution of existing routines of action effect an enduring disturbance of the equilibrium of the organization. The conflicts always connected with organizational change culminate during this stage of organizational change.[28]

Whether the experiment is terminated due to the vehemence of the ensuing conflict or the innovation is retained, after a period of conflict and dissolution there will be a certain return to routine. If the process of change succeeds, routine is settled into at a new level.

7.4.4 Routinization stage

The implementation stage of organizational change ends with the integration of the new activities into the program structure, and the re-attainment of a certain degree of standardization. Hage and Aiken consider the replacement of those persons who were especially involved in implementing the change, and the development of job training programs for the new positions as indicators of the attainment of the routinization stage (Hage and Aiken, 1970: 106).

The transition to the period of routinization confronts top management with problems of evaluation similar to those that appeared during the first period of the change process. Does the alteration solve the problem for which it was designed? The answer of top management will again depend on the quality of the information and control instruments.

The choice of the right moment for decision represents a problem too. The chances of an innovation being adopted increase, the longer the experimental period continues. On the other hand, the period of trial and error is always burdened with conflict and uncertainty. If the innovation survives long enough to be gradually incorporated into the existing organizational structure, the power and reward structure of the organization is also stabilized and the severity of conflicts diminishes. At a new level, however, the organization continues to be confronted by the dilemma posed by the necessity of change versus the avoidance of conflict threatening organizational integration.

7.5 Outlook: from bureaucracy to Ad-Hocracy?

In the last two sections we have tried to summarize the structural and processual aspects of social change in complex organizations. Though a complete statement seems to be impossible due to the magnitude of the theme, some final comments are in order. We may proceed from the concept of 'Ad-Hocracy' forwarded by Alvin

Toffler (1973: 333). He uses this term to describe the coming organizational model of a post-bureaucratic era. Toffler summarizes the essential elements of his dynamic organization model as follows: flexible programs in response to short-term problems; substitution of lateral communication systems for vertical ones; and an increasing number of professionally oriented specialists.

Taking his cue from Warren G. Bennis, he predicts the fall of the hierarchic–bureaucratic form of organization. On this point, as well as in his general explanations, Toffler exaggerates cautious trend statements of social scientists for the sake of 'shock value'. The tendency of complex organizations to include associative and professional elements in their hierarchical frameworks has been empirically verified. Whether this will lead to a general collapse of bureaucratic structures or not – as Toffler and Bennis suggest – remains a moot point.[29]

Finally, we return to the issue of the social situation of people in modern 'organizational society.' Both the structural and processual aspects of organizational change show the extent and importance of conflict within modern organizations. The coexistence of contrary structural principles within one organizational system implies a permanent source of tensions and conflict. These structural conflicts are superimposed on the manifold organizational strains which the process of social change necessarily involves. At the level of the individual organizational member conflict and change are experienced as continual tension and psychological stress.

Organizations today are characteristically confronted with problems of both extremes: monotony and rigid bureaucratic regularity in many spheres but also the burden of persistent alterations, tensions, and ambiguities. Besides the threat of 'bureaucratic petrification' which Weber foresaw as the fate of mankind, there appears an opposite form of alienation: the permanent revolutionizing of social relations and behavioral patterns according to the requirements of organizational adaptation to a turbulent environment. The central social problem set forth by Durkheim has new relevance: How can socially secured meaning, legitimation, and motivation be maintained in spite of rapid change?

According to the diagnoses of opposing theorists – here they agree – the resources of legitimacy and motivation run short in the industrially developed and highly organized societies (Habermas, 1973; 1974b; Luhmann, 1975a). From this perspective, the issue of the democratization of complex organizations assumes added importance. Far-reaching member participation in all organizational activities opens new possibilities for personal meaning, realization, and legitimation. The increase of motivation by participation is among the basic principles of modern personnel management (Maslow, 1970; Herzberg *et al.*, 1959).

Besides increased democratization of member participation, continued expansion of professional training and orientation may help counteract organizational alienation. In general, we suggest that just coping with a high rate of social change requires a new equilibrium between 'organizational rationalization' in order to increase adaptability and 'social rationalization' in order to maintain organizations as a sphere of meaningful human action.

Notes

1 Generally, the origin of sociology is traced to Henri de Saint-Simon and Auguste Comte (Strasser, 1975). Comte first used the concept of 'sociology' with regard to the new science.
2 For a summary of the origin and development of the sociology of organizations, see Mayntz (1964).
3 This is noticeable in the preface to the second edition of the *Division of Labor*, which was written after his work on suicide (Durkheim, 1964: 1ff.).
4 For Weber's significance in regard to the study of bureaucracy, see Merton (1960).
5 Weber develops his analysis of bureaucracy within his sociology of 'imperative control,' in which he distinguishes three types of authority regarding the respectively claimed type of legitimacy: rational–legal, traditional, and charismatic authority (Weber, 1947: 136ff.).
6 Weber tries to explain the formative context of occidental rationalism in his writings on the sociology of religion, whereas his political works are focused on the further developmental tendencies of the process of rationalization (Schluchter, 1972).
7 I.e, in his criticism of Marx, whom he reproaches for belief in a 'primitive democratism' (Schluchter, 1972: 62).
8 In keeping with this contribution of Parsons, two other articles were published in 1964 in the *American Sociological Review* that document a return to the theory of evolution (Eisenstadt, 1964a; Bellah, 1964).
9 For the theory of organization, see Luhmann (1964; 1969); for the theory of society, see Luhmann (1971a; 1975a).
10 The translation of the German term *zweckrational* presents some problems, as has already been noticed by Parsons in his translation of Weber (Weber, 1947: 116).
11 A. Gehlen already developed this idea (Gehlen, 1957: 36ff.).
12 Luhmann elaborates on this consequence in his criticism of the concept of goal (Luhmann, 1973).
13 Habermas himself fails to develop further the concept of a 'subsystem of purposively rational action' as an organizational concept.

14 Habermas tries to explain this in his criticism of structural-functional theory and especially in his discussion with Luhmann (Habermas, 1971).
15 Here as in the following material we are oriented to the organizational theory of Luhmann which focuses on the mechanism of system building typical for organizations. Luhmann's organizational theory is partly based on Chester Barnard (1938) and James G. March and Herbert A. Simon (1958).
16 The translation of the German term *Stelle* is very difficult; Luhmann understands by this special kinds of expectations of behavior which are changeable according to the requirements of social systems. We have chosen the translation 'organizational role,' for organizations especially use such behavioral expectations (Luhmann, 1964: 142–3).
17 Hage and Aiken define program change 'as the addition of new services or products' (Hage and Aiken, 1970: 13) and use a more general conceptualization of program than Luhmann.
18 Crozier develops this thesis in the context of analyses of the 'bureaucratic vicious circle' based on two case studies: a French clerical agency and an industrial monopoly belonging to the French state.
19 By formalization Hage and Aiken mean the degree of codification of the rules of action in the organization; in contrast to Luhmann, who understands formalization as the reference of the organizational expectations of behavior to the membership (Luhmann, 1964: 38).
20 As a rule it happens by 'telescoping' of programs, for example by controlling a 'conditional program' by a 'purposive program' (Luhmann, 1971b: 121).
21 The two 'organizational models' are differently termed by various authors: 'mechanistic' and 'organic systems of management' (Burns and Stalker, 1961: 96ff.); 'bureaucratic' and 'professional model' (Litwak, 1961/2; Scott, 1966); 'bureaucratic' and 'associative organization' (Bosetzky, 1970: 292ff.).
22 The articulation of the 'environment' as a crucial organizational variable more or less characterizes the whole modern sociology of organization oriented to a system approach. See especially Luhmann (1971b: 104ff.); especially regarding organizational change: Burns and Stalker (1961); Emery and Trist (1965); Terryberry (1968); Hage and Aiken (1970); Lipp (1971).
23 The 'prescriptive' criticism confronts the bureaucratic model with a new model more efficient in case of certain environmental conditions (Litwak, 1961/2); the descriptively and analytically oriented criticisms search for empirical deviations from the bureaucratic model (Hall, 1963/4; Pugh and Hickson, 1968).
24 Here cited according to Hage and Aiken (1970: 113) who include a number of other proposals which do not concern organizations.
25 Luhmann distinguishes three sub-functions of the permanent control within organizational social systems: 'It supervises (1) the reinterpretation of the problem of maintenance in goals, (2) the transformation of the system goals into ultimately operational sub-goals,

and, finally, (3) the realization of the operationally defined sub-goals as the strategy to solve problems made soluble' (Luhmann, 1973: 326).
26 In establishing central 'Management Information Systems' the function of control and regulation seems to concentrate again more at the top nowadays, after a phase of 'fictive centralism' (Lipp, 1971).
27 The TVA study by Philip Selznick may be considered a nearly 'classical' study of this dilemma of change and planning (Selznick, 1949).
28 The sociological approach of 'conflict theory' stresses the connection between change and conflict (Dahrendorf, 1968); specifically related to plant organizations, see Dahrendorf (1959b: 45ff.).
29 For an opposite position to Bennis and Toffler, see Robert D. Miewald (1973).

Suggested reading

Introductory reading

HAGE, GERALD and AIKEN, MICHAEL (1970), *Social Change in Complex Organizations*, New York: Random House.
   Hage and Aiken give a synopsis very suitable for introducing the student into the multifaceted problems of social change in organizations. They deal especially with program change, styles of organizational change, and the problems of the change process.

THOMPSON, VICTOR A. (1965), 'Bureaucracy and Innovation,' *Administrative Science Quarterly*, 10: 1–20.
   Thompson tries to develop a catalogue of general and structural requirements for innovative organizational change. At the same time he draws attention to the absence of these requirements in bureaucratic–monocratic organizations.

BENNIS, WARREN G. (1966), 'Changing Organizations,' *Journal of Applied Behavioral Science*, 2: 247–63.
   Bennis forecasts the replacement of bureaucracy by an organic–adaptive organizational structure in the future. It is characterized by adaptive, temporary systems of specialists, linked together by coordinating and task-evaluation experts.

BURNS, TOM and STALKER, G. M. (1961), *The Management of Innovation*, London: Tavistock.
   Based on empirical research, Burns and Stalker develop two different management systems which, following Durkheim, they call mechanistic and organic systems of management. They point out that the mechanistic system, which corresponds to the principles of bureaucratic organization, is suitable only in cases of static environments, whereas under unstable conditions the organic systems appear more efficient.

TOFFLER, ALVIN (1973), 'Organizations: The Coming Ad-Hocracy,' pp. 333–49 in ROWE, LLOYD A., and BOISE, WILLIAM B. (eds), *Organizational and Managerial Innovation: A Reader*, Pacific Palisades, Cal.: Goodyear Publishing Co. (reprinted from Toffler, 1970).
   Toffler assumes that we are witnessing the breakdown of bureaucracy and

the arrival of a new organizational system which he calls 'Ad-Hocracy.' The new 'Ad-Hocracy' is characterized by 'task-force management' to solve short-term problems; an increasing number of professional specialists; and lateral communication systems. He stresses the emergence of a new kind of 'organization man' who is committed to his own self-fulfillment instead of commitment to the organization.

Further reading

General

KATZ, DANIEL and KAHN, R. L. (1966), *The Social Psychology of Organizations*, New York: Wiley.
In their fundamental work on the social psychology of complex organizations, Katz and Kahn deal with organizational change based on 'open-system theory.' They argue critically with several approaches to organizational change, especially with the assumption that individual change will generate organizational change; in contrast, they refer to the importance of structural change.

BLAU, PETER M. (1955), *The Dynamics of Bureaucracy: A Study of Interpersonal Relations in Two Government Agencies*, Chicago: Chicago University Press.
In case studies of a state employment agency and a federal enforcement agency, Blau states that bureaucratic structures continually create conditions that serve to change them. He suggests prerequisites of an adjustive organizational development like professional orientation of the personnel, established work groups, and organizational needs that are experienced as disturbing.

CROZIER, MICHEL (1964), *The Bureaucratic Phenomenon*, London: Tavistock.
Based on two case studies of a French clerical agency and a state-owned enterprise, Crozier scrutinizes the problems of change in bureaucratic organizations. Bureaucratic organizations resist changes as long as possible because of their structural conditions. If there are no other alternatives, disruptive change will occur – introduced by the top. Long periods of stability alternate with short periods of crisis and change.

LEAVITT, HAROLD (1970), 'Applied Organization Change in Industry: Structural, Technical and Human Approaches,' pp. 198–212 in DALTON, G. W. and LAWRENCE, P. R. (eds), *Organizational Change and Development*, Homewood, Ill.: Dorsey.
Leavitt classifies several major approaches to organizational change which focus on structural, technological, or human variables respectively, whereas they neglect the other respective variables.

Problem-related

LITWAK, EUGENE (1961/2), 'Models of Bureaucracy which Permit Conflict,' *American Journal of Sociology*, 67: 177–84.
This article represents one of those approaches that restrict the efficiency of the bureaucratic model to uniform events. When dealing with non-

uniform events, he considers the human relation model more efficient, while the third mixed model (professional model) is regarded as applicable to the bulk of organizations in contemporary society.

SCOTT, W. RICHARD (1966), 'Professionals in Bureaucracies: Areas of Conflict,' pp. 265–75 in VOLLMER, HOWARD M., and MILLS, DONALD L. (eds), *Professionalization*, Englewood Cliffs, N.J.: Prentice-Hall.

Scott contrasts the bureaucratic model, characterized by partial skills of the personnel and organizational controls, with a professional model, characterized by comprehensive skills of the personnel and internalized standards. He discusses areas of conflict and whether these two different principles of organization may be fused.

EMERY, F. E. and TRIST, H. L. (1965), 'The Causal Texture of Organizational Environments,' *Human Relations*, 18: 21–31.

Emery and Trist are the first to develop instruments for the study of the organizational environment as a crucial factor in organizational change and arrive at a typology of static and dynamic environments.

TERRYBERRY, SHIRLEY (1968), 'The Evolution of Organizational Environments,' *Administrative Science Quarterly*, 12: 590–613.

Using the 'open-system theory,' Terryberry develops two hypotheses regarding organizational change:

(1) organizational change is largely externally induced;
(2) organizational adaptability is a function of the capacity to learn and to perform according to changing environmental contingencies.

Select bibliography

ABEL, T. (1938), *Why Hitler Came to Power*, New York: Prentice-Hall.
ABERLE, D. F. *et al.* (1950), 'The Functional Prerequisites of Society,' *Ethics*, 60: 100–11.
ADORNO, T. (1976), *The Positivist Dispute in German Sociology*, New York: Harper & Row.
ALMOND, G. (1967), Review of Moore's *Social Origins*, *American Political Science Review*, 61: 768–70.
ALTVATER, E. (1972), 'Thesen zum Staatsinterventionismus,' in *Probleme des Klassenkampfes*, Erlangen: Polit-Laden.
ANDERSON, P. (1976), *Considerations on Western Marxism*, London: NLB.
APPELBAUM, R. P. (1970), *Theories of Social Change*, Chicago: Markham Publishing Co.
ARON, R. (1950), 'Social Structure and the Ruling Class,' *British Journal of Sociology*, 1: 1–17; 126–44.
ARON, R. (1963), *Frieden und Krieg*, Frankfurt a.M.: Fischer.
ARON, R. (1970), *Main Currents in Sociological Thought*, 2 vols, Garden City, New York: Doubleday Anchor Books.
AUTORENKOLLEKTIV (1972), *Die gegenwärtige wissenschaftlich-technische Revolution*, Berlin: Akademie-Verlag.
AUTORENKOLLEKTIV (1974), *Klassenkampf, Tradition, Sozialismus*, Berlin: Akademie-Verlag.
BAIER, H. (1969), 'Soziale Technologie oder soziale Emanzipation? Zum Streit zwischen Positivisten und Dialektikern über die Aufgaben der Soziologie,' in B. SCHÄFERS (ed.), *Thesen zur Kritik der Soziologie*, Frankfurt a.M.: Suhrkamp.
BALES, ROBERT F. (1950), *Interaction Process Analysis*, Cambridge, Mass.: Addison-Wesley.
BARAN, PAUL A. and SWEEZY, PAUL M. (1968), *Monopoly Capital: An Essay on the American Economic and Social Order*, New York: Monthly Review.
BARDIS, P. D. (1962), 'Synopsis of Theories of Social Change,' *Social Science*, 37: 181–8.

SELECT BIBLIOGRAPHY

BARNARD, C. I. (1938), *The Functions of the Executive*, Cambridge, Mass.: Harvard University Press.
BARNETT, H. G. (1953), *Innovation: The Basis of Cultural Change*, New York: McGraw-Hill.
BARTSCH, G. and CRÜGER, H. (1976), *Geschichte als gesetzmäßiger Prozeß*, Berlin: Dietz.
BEATTIE, J. H. M. (1964), *Other Cultures: Aims, Methods and Achievements in Social Anthropology*, New York: Free Press.
BECKER, H. and BARNES, H. (1961), *Social Thought from Lore to Science*, vol. 3, New York: Dover Publications.
BELL, D. (1965), *The End of Ideology*, New York: Free Press.
BELL, D. (1973), *The Coming of Post-Industrial Society: A Venture in Social Forecasting*, New York: Basic Books.
BELLAH, R. N. (1958), 'Religious Aspects of Modernization in Turkey and Japan,' *American Journal of Sociology*, 64: 1–5.
BELLAH, R. N. (1964), 'Religious Evolution,' *American Sociological Review*, 29: 358–74.
BEN-DAVID, J. (1962), 'Scientific Productivity and Academic Organization in Nineteenth-Century Medicine,' in B. BARBER and W. HIRSCH (eds), *The Sociology of Science*, New York: Free Press.
BENDIX, R. (1974), 'Inequality and Social Structure: A Comparison of Marx and Weber,' *American Sociological Review*, 39: 149–61.
BENDIX, R. and LIPSET, S. M. (eds) (1966), *Class, Status and Power*, 2nd ed., New York: Free Press.
BENNIS, W. G. (1966), 'Changing Organizations,' *Journal of Applied Behavioral Science*, 2: 247–363.
BENNIS, W. G. and SLATER, P. E. (1969), *The Temporary Society*, New York: Harper & Row.
BENOIT-SMULLYAN, E. (1944), 'Status, Status Types and Status Interrelations,' *American Sociological Review*, 9: 151–61.
BENSON, L. (1972), *Toward the Scientific Study of History*, Philadelphia: Lippincott.
BERELSON, B. and STEINER, G. A. (1964), *Human Behavior: An Inventory of Scientific Findings*, New York: Harcourt, Brace & World.
BERGER, PETER L. (1963), Invitation to Sociology: A Humanistic Perspective, Garden City, New York: Doubleday Anchor.
BERGER, PETER L. (1967), *The Sacred Canopy: Elements of a Sociological Theory of Religion*, Garden City, New York: Doubleday Anchor.
BERGER, P. L. and BERGER, B. (1971), 'The Blueing of America,' *Intellectual Digest*, September.
BERGER, P. L. and LUCKMANN, T. (1966), *The Social Construction of Reality*, Garden City, New York: Doubleday Anchor.
BERGHE, P. L. van den (1963), 'Dialectic and Functionalism: Toward a Theoretical Synthesis,' *American Sociological Review*, 28: 695–705.
BERTALANFFY, LUDWIG von (1968), *General System Theory*, New York: George Braziller.
BERTRAND, A. L. (1967), *Basic Sociology: An Introduction to Theory and Method*, New York: Appleton-Century-Crofts.

SELECT BIBLIOGRAPHY

BESHERS, J. C. (1964), 'Mathematical Models of Social Change,' in G. K. ZOLLSCHAN and W. HIRSCH (eds), *Explorations in Social Change*, London: Routledge & Kegan Paul.

BEYME, K. von (1973), *Empirische Revolutionsforschung*, Opladen: Westdeutscher Verlag.

BLACK, C. E. (1967), Review of Moore's *Social Origins*, *American Historical Review*, 72: 1338.

BLAU, P. M. (1955), *The Dynamics of Bureaucracy*, Chicago and London: University of Chicago Press.

BLAU, P. M. (1956), 'Social Mobility and Interpersonal Relations,' *American Sociological Review*, 21: 290–5.

BLAU, P. M., HEYDEBRAND, W. V., and STAUFFER, R. E. (1966), 'The Structure of Small Bureaucracies,' *American Sociological Review*, 31: 179–91.

BLUMER, H. (1969), 'The Methodological Position of Symbolic Interactionism,' in H. BLUMER, *Symbolic Interactionism: Perspective and Method*, Englewood Cliffs, N.J.: Prentice-Hall.

BOCCARA, P. et al. (1972), *Der staatsmonopolistische Kapitalismus*, Frankfurt a.M.: Verlag Marxistische Blätter.

BOCK, K. E. (1963a), *The Acceptance of Histories*, Berkeley and Los Angeles: University of California Press.

BOCK, K. E. (1963b), 'Evolution, Function and Change,' *American Sociological Review*, 28: 229–37.

BÖHRET, C. (ed.) (1972), *Simulation innenpolitischer Konflikte*, Opladen: Westdeutscher Verlag.

BOLLHAGEN, P. (1967), *Gesetzmäßigkeit und Gesellschaft*, Berlin: Deutscher Verlag der Wissenschaften.

BOSETZKY, H. (1970), *Grundzüge einer Soziologie der Industrieverwaltung. Möglichkeiten und Grenzen der Betrachtung des industriellen Großbetriebes als bürokratische Organisation*, Stuttgart: Enke.

BOTTOMORE, T. B. (1974), *Sociology as Social Criticism*, New York: Pantheon Books.

BOX, S. and FORD, J. (1969), 'Some Questionable Assumptions in the Theory of Status Inconsistency,' *Sociological Review*, 17: 187–202.

BRAUNMÜHL, C. V. et al. (1973), *Probleme einer materialistischen Staatstheorie*, Frankfurt a.M.: Suhrkamp.

BRINTON, C. (1965), *The Anatomy of Revolution*, revised and expanded ed., New York: Vintage Books.

BRODBECK, M. (1959), 'Models, Meaning and Theories,' in L. GROSS (ed.), *Symposium on Sociological Theory*, New York: Harper.

BRONFENBRENNER, M. (1955), 'The Appeal of Confiscation in Economic Development,' *Economic Development and Cultural Change*, 3: 201–18.

BROOM L. and JONES, L. F. (1974), 'Problematics in the Study of Stratum Consistency,' Paper presented at the 8th World Congress of Sociology, Toronto.

BUCKINGHAM, W. (1961), *Automation: Its Impact on Business and People*, New York: Harper & Row.

BUCKLEY, W. (1957), 'Structural-Functional Analysis in Modern Sociology,'

SELECT BIBLIOGRAPHY

in H. BECKER and A. BOSKOFF (eds), *Modern Sociological Theory in Continuity and Change*, New York: Rinehart & Winston.

BUCKLEY, W. (1967), *Sociology and Modern Systems Theory*, Englewood Cliffs, N.J.: Prentice-Hall.

BÜHL, W. L. (1970), *Evolution und Revolution*, Munich: Goldmann.

BÜHL, W. L. (ed.) (1975), *Funktion und Struktur. Soziologie vor der Geschichte*, Munich: Nymphenburger.

BULLOCK, A. (1958), *Hitler: A Story in Tyranny*, New York: Bantam Books.

BURNS, T. and STALKER, G. M. (1961), *The Management of Innovation*, London: Tavistock.

CANCIAN, F. (1960), 'Functional Analysis of Change,' *American Sociological Review*, 25: 818–27.

CANCIAN, F. (1965), *Economics and Prestige in a Maya Community*, Stanford, Cal.: Stanford University Press.

CANTRIL, H. (1941), *The Psychology of Social Movements*, New York: Wiley.

CHAMBLISS, W. J. (ed.) (1973), *Sociological Readings in the Conflict Perspective*, Reading, Mass.: Addison-Wesley.

CHODAK, S. (1973), *Societal Development: Five Approaches with Conclusions from Comparative Analysis*, New York: Oxford University Press.

CHILDE, V. G. (1952), *Man Makes Himself*, New York: NAL.

CHILDE, V. G. (1951), *Sociale Evolution*, New York: Schuman.

CILLIÉ, F. (1940), *Centralization or Decentralization: A Study in Educational Adaptation*, New York: Teachers College, Columbia University Press.

CLARKE, B. R. (1962), *Educating the Expert Society*, San Francisco: Cal.: Chandler.

CLOWARD, R. and OHLIN, L. (1960), *Delinquency and Opportunity*, New York: Free Press.

COHEN, P. S. (1968), *Modern Social Theory*, New York: Basic Books.

COLEMAN, J., KATZ, E., and MENZEL, H. (1966), *Medical Innovation*, Indianapolis: Bobbs-Merrill.

COLLINS, R. (1975), *Conflict Sociology: Toward an Explanatory Science*, New York: Academic Press.

COMTE, A. (1855), *The Positive Philosophy*, freely translated and condensed by HARRIET MARTINEAU, New York: Calvin Blanchard.

COMTE, A. (1875), *System of Positive Polity*, vol. 2, London: Longmans, Green & Co.

COMTE, A. (1877), *System of Positive Polity*, vol. 4, London: Longmans, Green & Co.

CONWAY, J. (transl.) (1966), *The Path to Dictatorship: 1918–1933*, New York: Doubleday Anchor.

COOK, K. S. (1975), 'Expectation, Evaluations and Equity,' *American Sociological Review*, 40: 372–88.

COOLEY, C. H. (1922), *Human Nature and the Social Order*, revised ed., New York: Charles Scribner's Sons.

COSER, L. A. (1956), *The Functions of Social Conflict*, New York: Free Press.

SELECT BIBLIOGRAPHY

COSER, L. A. (1967), *Continuities in the Study of Social Conflict*, New York: Free Press.
CROZIER, M. (1964), *The Bureaucratic Phenomenon*, London: Tavistock.
DAHRENDORF, R. (1958), 'Toward a Theory of Social Conflict,' *Journal of Conflict Resolution*, 2: 170–83.
DAHRENDORF, R. (1959a), *Class and Class Conflict in Industrial Society*, Stanford, Cal.: Stanford University Press.
DAHRENDORF, R. (1959b), *Sozialstruktur des Betriebes – Betriebssoziologie*, Wiesbaden: Gabler.
DAHRENDORF, R. (1964), 'Toward a Theory of Social Conflict,' in A. and E. ETZIONI (eds), *Social Change*, New York: Basic Books.
DAHRENDORF, R. (1967), *Pfade aus Utopia. Zur Theorie und Methode der Soziologie*, Munich: Piper.
DAHRENDORF, R. (1968), *Essays in the Theory of Society*, Stanford, Cal.: Stanford University Press.
DAHRENDORF, R. (1979), *Lebenschancen*, Frankfurt a.M.: Suhrkamp.
DAVIES, J. C. (1962), 'Toward a Theory of Revolution,' *American Sociological Review*, 27: 5–19.
DAVIS, K. (1950), *Human Society*, New York: Macmillan.
DAVIS, K. (1959), 'The Myth of Functional Analysis as a Special Method in Sociology and Anthropology,' *American Sociological Review*, 24: 757–73.
DAVIS, K. and MOORE, W. E. (1945), 'Some Principles of Stratification,' *American Sociological Review*, 10: 242–9.
DEMERATH, N. J. III and PETERSON, R. A. (eds) (1967), *System, Change and Conflict*, New York: Free Press.
DEUTSCH, K. W. (1961), 'Social Mobilization and Political Development,' *American Political Science Review*, 55: 493–514.
DEVEREUX, E. C. Jr. (1961), 'Parsons' Sociological Theory,' in M. BLACK (ed.), *The Social Theories of Talcott Parsons*, Englewood Cliffs, N.J.: Prentice-Hall.
DOBB, M. (1937), *Political Economy and Capitalism*, London: Routledge & Kegan Paul.
DOBB, M. (1948), *Soviet Economic Development Since 1917*, New York: International Publ.
DOBB, M. (1963), *Studies in the Development of Capitalism*, New York: International Publ.
DREITZEL, H. P. (1967a), 'Problemgeschichtliche Einleitung,' in H. P. DREITZEL (ed.), *Sozialer Wandel: Zivilisation und Fortschritt als Kategorien der soziologischen Theorie*, Neuwied: Luchterhand.
DREITZEL, H. P. (1967b), 'Nachwort: Uber die historische Methode in der Soziologie,' in H. P. DREITZEL (ed.), *Sozialer Wandel: Zivilisation und Fortschritt als Kategorien der soziologischen Theorie*, Neuwied: Luchterhand.
DUNETTE, M. D. and CAMPBELL, J. P. (1970), 'Laboratory Education: Impact on People and Organization,' in G. W. DALTON and P. R. LAWRENCE (eds), *Organizational Change and Development*, Homewood, Ill.: Irwin Dorsey Press.

DURKHEIM, E. (1928), *Le Socialisme*, Paris: Felix Alcan.
DURKHEIM, E. (1947), *The Elementary Forms of Religious Life*, Glencoe, Ill.: Free Press.
DURKHEIM, E. (1950), *The Rules of Sociological Method*, Glencoe, Ill.: Free Press.
DURKHEIM, E. (1951), *Suicide*, Glencoe, Ill.: Free Press.
DURKHEIM, E. (1964), *The Division of Labor in Society*, New York: Free Press.
EISENSTADT, S. N. (1963), *The Political System of Empires*, New York: Free Press.
EISENSTADT, S. N. (1964a), 'Social Change, Differentiation and Evolution,' *American Sociological Review*, 29: 375–86.
EISENSTADT, S. N. (1964b), 'Institutionalization and Change,' *American Sociological Review*, 29: 235–47.
EISENSTADT, S. N. (1970), *Readings in Social Evolution and Development*, Oxford: Pergamon Press.
EITZEN, S. D. (1970), 'Status Inconsistency and Wallace Supporters in a Midwestern City,' *Social Forces*, 48: 493–8.
ELIAS, N. (1976), *Über den Prozeß der Zivilisation: Soziogenetische und psychogenetische Untersuchungen*, 2 vols, Frankfurt a.M.: Suhrkamp.
ELLUL, J. (1964), *The Technological Society*, New York: Vintage Books.
EMERY, F. E. and TRIST, H. L. (1965), 'The Causal Texture of Organizational Environments,' *Human Relations*, 18: 21–31.
ENGELGERG, E. (1974), 'Probleme der gesetzmäßigen Abfolge der Gesellschaftsformation,' *Zeitschrift für Geschichtswissenschaft*, 2: 145–73.
ENGELS, F. (1962), 'Der Ursprung der Familie, des Privateigentums und des Staats,' *MEW*, vol. 21, Berlin: Dietz.
ENGELS, F. (1968a), 'Anteil der Arbeit an der Menschwerdung des Affen,' *MEW*, vol. 20, Berlin: Dietz.
ENGELS, F. (1968b), 'Biologie,' *MEW*, vol. 20, Berlin: Dietz.
ERIKSON, K. T. (1976), *Everything in Its Path*, New York: Simon & Schuster.
ETZIONI, A. (1964), *Modern Organizations*, Englewood Cliffs, N.J.: Prentice-Hall.
FALLERS, L. A. (1973), *Inequality: Social Stratification Reconsidered*, Chicago: University of Chicago Press.
FELDMANN, G. A. (1969), *Zur Wachstumstheorie des Nationaleinkommens*, Berlin: Akademie-Verlag.
FEUSTEL, R. (1973a), *Technik der Steinzeit*, Weimar: Böhlau.
FEUSTEL, R. (1973b), 'Zum Problem der Evolution und Revolution in urgeschichtlicher Zeit,' *Ethnographisch-Archäologische Zeitschrift*, 1: 55–133.
FLORA, P. (1974), *Modernisierungsforschung*, Opladen: Westdeutscher Verlag.
FOURASTIÉ, J. (1949), *Le grand espoir de la XXe siècle*, Paris: Seuil.
FREIBURGHAUS, D. and MÜLLER, H. P. (1973), 'Zur Struktur des Krisenproblems bei Marx,' *Mehrwert*, 5: 1–187.
FUCHS, V. (1968), *The Service Economy*, New York: Columbia University Press.

SELECT BIBLIOGRAPHY

GALTUNG, J. (1971), 'A Structural Theory of Aggression,' in C. SMITH (ed.), *Conflict Resolution*, Notre Dame, Indiana: University of Notre Dame Press.

GALTUNG, J. (1977), 'Functionalism in a New Key,' in J. GALTUNG, *Essays in Methodology. Vol. 1: Methodology and Ideology*, Atlantic Highlands, N.J.: Humanities Press.

GARTNER, A. and RIESSMAN, F. (1974), *The Service Society and the Consumer Vanguard*, New York: Harper & Row.

GEHLEN, A. (1957), *Die Seele im technischen Zeitalter*, Reinbek: Rowohlt.

GERSCHENKRON, A. (1962), *Economic Backwardness in Historical Perspective*, Cambridge, Mass.: Harvard University Press.

GIDDENS, A. (1973), *The Class Structure of the Advanced Societies*, London: Hutchinson.

GILLIN, J. L. (1910), 'A Contribution to the Sociology of Sects,' *American Journal of Sociology*, 16: 236–52.

GILLMANN, J. M. (1968), *Prosperität in der Krise*, Frankfurt a.M.: Europäische Verlagsanstalt.

GINSBERG, M. (1970), 'Social Change,' in S. N. EISENSTADT (ed.), *Readings in Evolution and Development*, Oxford: Pergamon Press.

GLUCKMAN, M. (1956), *Custom and Conflict in Africa*, Glencoe, Ill.: Free Press.

GLUCKMAN, M. (1968), 'The Utility of the Equilibrium Model in the Study of Social Change,' *American Anthropologist*, 70: 219–37.

GODELIER, M. (1970), *System, Struktur und Widerspruch im 'Kapital'*, Berlin: Merve Verlag.

GODELIER, M. (1973), *Ökonomische Anthropologie*, Reinbek: Rowohlt.

GOFFMAN, E. (1957), 'Status Consistency and Preference for Change in Power Distribution,' *American Sociological Review*, 22: 275–81.

GOFFMAN, E. (1959), *Asylums*, Harmondsworth, England: Penguin.

GOODE, W. J. (1951), *Religion Among the Primitives*, Glencoe, Ill.: Free Press.

GORZ, ANDRÉ (1967), *Zur Strategie der Arbeiterbewegung im Neokapitalismus*, Frankfurt a.M.: Europäische Verlagsanstalt.

GOULD, J. and KOLB, W. L. (eds) (1964), *Dictionary of the Social Sciences*, New York: Free Press.

GOULDNER, A. W. (1954), *Patterns of Industrial Bureaucracy*, Glencoe, Ill.: Free Press.

GOULDNER, A. W. (1957/8), 'Cosmopolitans and Locals: Toward an Analysis of Latent Social Roles,' *Administrative Science Quarterly*, 2: 281–306.

GOULDNER, A. W. (1959), 'Reciprocity and Autonomy in Functional Theory,' in L. GROSS (ed.), *Symposium on Sociological Theory*, New York: Harper & Row.

GOULDNER, A. W. (1970), *The Coming Crisis of Western Sociology*, New York: Basic Books.

GOULDNER, A. W. and NEWCOMB, E. R. (1968), 'Eine Untersuchung über administrative Rollen,' in R. MAYNTZ (ed.), *Bürokratische Organisation*, Cologne: Kiepenheuer & Witsch.

SELECT BIBLIOGRAPHY

GOULDNER, A. and SPREHE, T. (1965), 'The Study of Man, 4: Sociologists Look at Themselves,' *Transaction*, 2: 42–4.

GREINER, L. E. and BARNES, L. B. (1970), 'Organization Change and Development,' in G. W. DALTON and P. R. LAWRENCE (eds), *Organizational Change and Development*, Homewood, Ill.: Irwin Dorsey Press.

GRIESE, A. (1971), 'Philosophischer Gesetzesbegriff und dialektisch-materialistische Entwicklungstheorie,' *Deutsche Zeitschrift für Philosophie*, 10: 1181–91.

GROSSMANN, H. (1929), *Das Akkumulations- und Zusammenbruchsgesetz des kapitalistischen Systems*, Leipzig: Hirschfeld.

GROSSMANN, H. (1969), *Marx, die klassische Nationalökonomie und das Problem der Dynamik*, Frankfurt a.M.: Europäische Verlagsanstalt.

GRUNOW, D. and HEGNER, F. (1974), 'Dimensionen staatlicher Handlungsspielräume: Organisationstheorie als Voraussetzung von Krisenanalysen,' in P. GROTTIAN and M. MURSWIECK (eds), *Handlungsspielräume der Staatsadministration*, Hamburg: Hoffmann & Campe.

GRUPP, F. W. (1969), 'The Political Perspective of Birch Society Members,' in R. A. SCHOENBERGER (ed.), *The American Right-Wing: Readings in Political Behavior*, New York: Holt, Rinehart & Winston.

GUESSOUS, M. (1967), 'A General Critique of Equilibrium Theory,' in W. E. MOORE and R. COOK (eds), *Readings on Social Change*, Englewood Cliffs, N.J.: Prentice-Hall.

GUHR, G. (1969a), 'Ur- und Frühgeschichte und ökonomische Gesellschaftsformation,' *Ethnographisch-Archäologische Zeitschrift*, 2: 167–212.

GUHR, G. (1969b), *Karl Marx und theoretische Probleme der Ethnographie*, Berlin: Akademie-Verlag.

GUMPLOWICZ, L. (1885/1926), *Grundriß der Soziologie*, Innsbruck: Universitätsverlag Wagner.

GÜNDEL, R. et al. (1967), *Zur Theorie des staatsmonopolistischen Kapitalismus*, Berlin: Akademie-Verlag.

GURR, R. (1970), *Why Men Rebel*, Princeton, N.J.: Princeton University Press.

HABERMAS, J. (1967), *Theorie und Praxis*, Frankfurt a.M.: Suhrkamp.

HABERMAS, J. (1969), *Technik und Wissenschaft als Ideologie*, Frankfurt a.M.: Suhrkamp.

HABERMAS, J. (1971), 'Theorie der Gesellschaft oder Sozialtechnologie? Eine Auseinandersetzung mit Niklas Luhmann,' in J. HABERMAS and N. LUHMANN, *Theorie der Gesellschaft oder Sozialtechnologie – Was leistet die Systemforschung?* Frankfurt a.M.: Suhrkamp.

HABERMAS, J. (1973), *Legitimationsprobleme im Spätkapitalismus*, Frankfurt a.M.: Suhrkamp.

HABERMAS, J. (1974), 'Können komplexe Gesellschaften eine vernünftige Identität ausbilden?' in J. HABERMAS and D. HENRICH, *Zwei Reden*, Frankfurt a.M.: Suhrkamp.

HABERMAS, J. (1975), 'Towards a Reconstruction of Historical Materialism,' *Theory and Society*, 2: 287–300.

HABERMAS, J. (1976), *Zur Rekonstruktion des historischen Materialismus*, Frankfurt a.M.: Suhrkamp.

HAGE, J. and AIKEN, M. (1967), 'Program Change and Organizational Properties: A Comparative Analysis,' *American Journal of Sociology*, 72: 503–19.

HAGE, J. and AIKEN, M. (1970), *Social Change in Complex Organizations*, New York: Random House.

HAHN, E. (1968), *Historischer Materialismus und marxistische Soziologie*, Berlin: Dietz.

HALL, R. H. (1963/4), 'The Concept of Bureaucracy: An Empirical Assessment,' *American Journal of Sociology*, 69: 32–40.

HARTMAN, M. (1974), 'On the Definition of Status Inconsistency,' *American Journal of Sociology*, 80: 706–20.

HEIDEN, K. (1935), *A History of National Socialism*, New York: Alfred A. Knopf.

HEIDER, F. (1958), *The Psychology of Interpersonal Relations*, New York: Wiley.

HEMPEL, C. G. (1959), 'The Logic of Functional Analysis,' in L. GROSS (ed.), *Symposium on Sociological Theory*, New York: Harper & Row.

HERZBERG, F., MAUSNER, B., and BLOCH SNYDERMAN, B. (1959), *The Motivation to Work*, 2nd ed., New York: Wiley.

HILFERDING, R. (1968), *Das Finanzkapital*, Frankfurt a.M.: Europäische Verlagsanstalt.

HINDESS, B. and HIRST, P. Q. (1975), *Pre-Capitalist Modes of Production*, London and Boston: Routledge & Kegan Paul.

HINDESS, B. and HIRST, P. Q. (1977), *Mode of Production and Social Formation. An Auto-Critique of Pre-Capitalist Modes of Production*, London: Macmillan.

HIRSCH, J. (1973), 'Elemente einer materialistischen Staatstheorie,' in C. VON BRAUNMÜHL et al. (eds), *Probleme einer materialistischen Staatstheorie*, Frankfurt a.M.: Suhrkamp.

HOBSBAWN, E. J. (ed.) (1964), *K. Marx: Pre-Capitalist Economic Formations*, London: Lawrence & Wishart.

HOFFMANN, E. (1972), 'Über die Dorfgemeinde und ihre Stellung im Übergangsprozeß von der Urgesellschaft zur Klassengesellschaft,' *Ethnographisch-Archäologische Zeitschrift*, 2: 71–143.

HOFSTADTER, R. (1964), 'The Pseudo-Conservative Revolt,' in D. BELL (ed.), *The Radical Right*, Garden City, New York: Doubleday Anchor Books.

HOMANS, G. C. (1950), *The Human Group*, New York: Harcourt, Brace & World.

HOMANS, G. C. (1967), 'Fundamental Social Processes,' in N. J. SMELSER (ed.), *Sociology: An Introduction*, New York: Wiley.

HOMANS, G. C. (1971), 'Bringing Men Back In,' in H. TURK and R. L. SIMPSON (eds), *Institutions and Social Exchange: The Sociologies of Talcott Parsons and George C. Homans*, Indianapolis: Bobbs-Merrill.

HORNEY, K. (1937), *The Neurotic Personality of Our Time*, New York: W. W. Norton.

HOSELITZ, B. F. and MERRILL, R. S. (1969), 'Sozialer Wandel in unterentwickelten Ländern,' *Handbuch der empirischen Sozialforschung*, vol. 2, ed. by R. KÖNIG, Stuttgart: Enke.

HYMAN, D. (1967), 'The Unpleasant Consequences of Rank Inconsistency: Suggestions for a Reorientation of Theory and Research,' *The Sociological Quarterly*, 8: 383–96.

INKELES, A. (1964), *What Is Sociology?*, Englewood Cliffs, N.J.: Prentice-Hall.

INSTITUT FÜR WELTWIRTSCHAFT UND INTERNATIONALE BEZIEHUNGEN DER AKADEMIE DER WISSENSCHAFTEN DER UdSSR (1972), *Politische Ökonomie des heutigen Monopolkapitalismus*, Frankfurt a.M.: Verlag Marxistische Blätter.

ISAJIW, W. W. (1968), *Causation and Functionalism in Sociology*, New York: Schocken Books.

JACKSON, E. F. (1962), 'Status Consistency and Symptoms of Stress,' *American Sociological Review*, 27: 469–80.

JACKSON, J. A. (1970), *Professions and Professionalization*, Cambridge: Cambridge University Press.

JAEGGI, U. and HONNETH, A. (eds) (1977), *Theorien des Historischen Materialismus*, Frankfurt a.M.: Suhrkamp.

JAFFE, A. J. (1968), 'Ogburn, William Fielding,' *International Encyclopedia of the Social Sciences*, vol. 11, ed. by D. L. SILLS, New York: Macmillan.

JOHNSON, H. M. (1960), *Sociology: A Systematic Introduction*, New York: Harcourt, Brace & World.

JONAS, F. (1968), *Geschichte der Soziologie*, vols 1 and 2, Reinbek: Rowohlt.

KAHN, R. L., WOLFE, D. M., QUINN, R. P., and SNOEK, J. D. (1964), *Organizational Stress: Studies in Role Conflict and Ambiguity*, New York: Wiley.

KAIRAT, H. (1969), *'Profession' oder 'Freie Berufe'?*, Berlin: Duncker & Humblot.

KATZ, D. and KAHN, R. L. (1966), *The Social Psychology of Organizations*, New York: Wiley.

KERR, C., DUNLAP, J., HARBISON, F., and MEYERS, C. A. (1960), *Industrialism and Industrial Man*, Cambridge, Mass.: Harvard University Press.

KIEVENHEIM, C. and LEISEWITZ, A. (eds) (1973), *Soziale Stellung und Bewußtsein der Intelligenz*, Cologne: Pahl-Rugenstein.

KIMBERLY, J. C. (1966), 'A Theory of Status Equilibrium,' *Sociological Theories in Progress*, vol. 1, ed. by J. BERGER, M. ZELDITCH jr and B. ANDERSON, Boston: Houghton Mifflin.

KISS, G. (1973), *Einführung in die soziologischen Theorien*, vol. 2, Opladen: Westdeutscher Verlag.

KLAGES, H. (1974), *Die mobile Gesellschaft*, Munich: C. H. Beck.

KRIPPENDORFF, E. (ed.) (1968), *Friedensforschung*, Cologne: Kiepenheuer & Witsch.

KROEBER, A. L. (1944), *Configurations and Culture Growth*, Berkeley and Los Angeles: University of California Press.

KRYSMANSKI, H. J. (1971), *Soziologie des Konflikts*, Reinbek: Rowohlt.

KUHN, T. S. (1970), *The Structure of Scientific Revolutions*, 2nd ed., Chicago:

University of Chicago Press.
KUSHNER, G. et al. (1962), *What Accounts for Sociocultural Change? A Propositional Inventory*, Chapel Hill, N.C.: Institute for Research in Social Science.
KÜTTLER, W. (1976), 'Theoretische Grundlagen und Methoden historischer Analyse von Gesellschaftsformationen,' *Deutsche Zeitschrift für Philosophie*, 24: 1079–93.
LANGE, O. and TAYLOR, F. M. (1948), *On the Economic Theory of Socialism*, ed. by B. E. LIPPINCOTT, Minneapolis: University of Minnesota Press.
LAPIERE, R. (1938), *Collective Behavior*, New York: McGraw-Hill.
LAUER, R. H. (1973), *Perspectives on Social Change*, Boston: Allyn & Bacon.
LEAVITT, H. J. (1970), 'Applied Organization Change in Industry: Structural, Technical and Human Approaches,' in G. W. DALTON and P. R. LAWRENCE (eds), *Organizational Change and Development*, Homewood, Ill.: Irwin Dorsey Press.
LE BON, G. (1896/1952), *The Crowd*, New York: Free Press.
LEFÈBVRE, H. (1972), *Soziologie nach Marx*, Frankfurt a.M.: Suhrkamp.
LENIN, W. I. (1971a), 'Was sind die "Volksfreunde" und wie kämpfen sie gegen die Sozialdemokraten?' *Lenin-Werke*, vol. 1, Berlin: Dietz.
LENIN, W. I. (1971b), 'Der Imperialismus als höchstes Stadium des Kapitalismus,' *Lenin-Werke*, vol. 22, Berlin: Dietz.
LENK, K. (1973), *Theorien der Revolution*, Munich: Fink-Verlag.
LENSKI, G. (1956), 'Social Participation and Status Crystalization,' *American Sociological Review*, 21: 458–64.
LENSKI, G. (1966), *Power and Privilege*, New York: McGraw-Hill.
LENSKI, G. (1967), 'Status Inconsistency and the Vote: A Four-Nation Study,' *American Sociological Review*, 32: 298–301.
LEVIN, N. G. (1967), 'Paths to Industrial Modernity,' *Dissent*, 14: 239–44.
LEVY, M. J. (1952), *The Structure of Society*, Princeton, N.J.: Princeton University Press.
LEVY, M. J. (1967), 'Social Patterns and Problems of Modernization,' in W. E. MOORE and R. COOK (eds), *Readings on Social Change*, Englewood Cliffs, N.J.: Prentice-Hall.
LEWIS, O. (1951), *Life in a Mexican Village: Tepoztlán Restudied*, Urbana, Ill.: University of Illinois Press.
LIJPHART, A. (1968/9), 'Typologies of Democratic Systems,' *Comparative Political Studies*, 1: 3–44.
LIPP, W. (1971), 'Innovationsprozesse im industriellen Großbetrieb. Technologischer Wandel und sozialer Konflikt,' *Die Unternehmung*, 25: 313–27.
LIPSET, S. M. (1964), 'The Sources of the "Radical Right",' in D. BELL (ed.), *The Radical Right*, Garden City, New York: Doubleday Anchor Books.
LIPSET, S. M. (1975), 'Social Structure and Social Change,' in P. M. BLAU (ed.), *Approaches to the Study of Social Structure*, New York: Free Press.
LIPSET, S. M. and BENDIX, R. (1959), *Social Mobility in Industrial Society*, Berkeley and Los Angeles: University of California Press.

LITWAK, E. (1961/2), 'Models of Bureaucracy Which Permit Conflict,' *American Journal of Sociology*, 67: 177–84.
LOCKWOOD, D. (1956), 'Some Remarks on the "Social System",' *British Journal of Sociology*, 7: 134–46.
LOCKWOOD, D. (1964), 'Social Integration and System Integration,' in G. K. ZOLLSCHAN and W. HIRSCH (eds), *Explorations in Social Change*, London: Routledge & Kegan Paul.
LOWENTHAL, D. (1968), Review of Moore's *Social Origins, History and Theory*, 7: 257–78.
LÖWITH, K. (1960), *Gesammelte Abhandlungen: Zur Kritik der geschichtlichen Existenz*, Stuttgart: Kohlhammer.
LUCKMANN, T. and BERGER, P. L. (1964), 'Social Mobility and Personal Identity,' *European Journal of Sociology*, 5: 331–44.
LUHMANN, N. (1964), *Funktionen und Folgen formaler Organisation*, Berlin: Duncker & Humblot.
LUHMANN, N. (1969), 'Allgemeines Modell organisierter Sozialsysteme,' unpubl. ms, Bielefeld.
LUHMANN, N. (1971a), *Soziologische Aufklärung*, 2nd ed., Opladen: Westdeutscher Verlag.
LUHMANN, N. (1971b), *Politische Planung*, Opladen: Westdeutscher Verlag.
LUHMANN, N. (1972), 'Einfache Sozialsysteme,' *Zeitschrift für Soziologie*, 1: 51–65.
LUHMANN, N. (1973), *Zweckbegriff und Systemrationalität*, Frankfurt a.M.: Suhrkamp.
LUHMANN, N. (1975a), 'Interaktion, Organisation, Gesellschaft,' in N. LUHMANN, *Soziologische Aufklärung 2*, Opladen: Westdeutscher Verlag.
LUHMANN, N. (1975b), 'Allgemeine Theorie organisierter Sozialsysteme,' in N. LUHMANN, *Soziologische Aufklärung 2*, Opladen: Westdeutscher Verlag.
LUHMANN, N. (1975c), 'Die Weltgesellschaft,' in N. LUHMANN, *Soziologische Aufklärung 2*, Opladen: Westdeutscher Verlag.
LUHMANN, N. (1975d), *Macht*, Stuttgart: Enke.
LUHMANN, N. (1975e), 'Weltzeit und Systemgeschichte,' in N. LUHMANN, *Soziologische Aufklärung 2: Aufsätze zur Theorie der Gesellschaft*, Opladen: Westdeutscher Verlag.
LUHMANN, N. (1975f), 'Evolution und Geschichte,' in N. LUHMANN, *Soziologische Aufklärung 2: Aufsätze zur Theorie der Gesellschaft*, Opladen: Westdeutscher Verlag.
LUHMANN, N. (1975g), 'Systemtheorie, Evolutionstheorie und Kommunikationstheorie,' in N. LUHMANN, *Soziologische Aufklärung 2: Aufsätze zur Theorie der Gesellschaft*, Opladen: Westdeutscher Verlag.
LUHMANN, N. (1975h), 'Einführende Bemerkungen zu einer Theorie symbolisch generalisierter Kommunikationsmedien,' in N. LUHMANN, *Soziologische Aufklärung 2*, Opladen: Westdeutscher Verlag.
LUHMANN, N. (1975i), *Soziologische Aufklärung 2*, Opladen: Westdeutscher Verlag.

LUPRI, E. (1972), 'Statuskonsistenz und Rechtsradikalismus in der Bundesrepublik,' *Kölner Zeitschrift für Soziologie und Sozialpsychologie*, 24: 265–81.
LUXEMBURG, R. (1913), *Die Akkumulation des Kapitals*, Berlin: Vorwärts.
MAINE, H. (1907), *Ancient Law*, London: John Murray.
MALEWSKI, A. (1966), 'The Degree of Status Incongruence and Its Effects,' in R. BENDIX and S. M. LIPSET (eds), *Class, Status, and Power*, 2nd ed., New York: Free Press.
MALINOWSKI, B. (1926), *Crime and Customs in Savage Society*, New York: Dutton.
MALINOWSKI, B. (1945), *The Dynamics of Culture Change: An Inquiry into Race Relations in Africa*, New Haven: Yale University Press.
MALINOWSKI, B. (1969), *A Scientific Theory of Culture and Other Essays*, New York: Oxford University Press.
MANDEL, E. (1969), *Marxist Economic Theory*, 2 vols, New York: Monthly Review.
MANDEL, E. (1978), *Late Capitalism*, Boston: Schocken.
MANN, F. C. and NEFF, F. W. (1961), *Managing Major Change in Organizations*, Ann Arbor, Mich.: Foundation for Research on Human Behavior.
MARCH, J. G. and SIMON, H. A. (1958), *Organizations*, New York: Wiley.
MARTINDALE, D. (1960), *The Nature and Types of Sociological Theory*, Boston: Houghton Mifflin.
MARTINDALE, D. (1964), 'Introduction,' in G. K. ZOLLSCHAN and W. HIRSCH (eds), *Explorations in Social Change*, London: Routledge & Kegan Paul.
MARTINDALE, D. (ed.) (1965), *Functionalism in the Social Sciences*, Philadelphia: American Academy of Political and Social Sciences.
MARWEDEL, P. (1976), *Theorie und Herrschaft. Zur Entwicklung des Funktionalismus von Malinowski zu Luhmann*, Cologne: Pahl-Rugenstein.
MARX, K. (1953), *Grundrisse der Kritik der Politischen Ökonomie*, Berlin: Dietz.
MARX, K. (1962–4), *Das Kapital, MEW*, vols 23–5, Berlin: Dietz.
MARX, K. (1962a), *Das Kapital, MEW*, vol. 23, Berlin: Dietz.
MARX, K. (1962b), 'Entwürfe einer Antwort auf den Brief von V. I. Sassulitsch,' *MEW*, vol. 19, Berlin: Dietz.
MARX, K. (1964a), 'Einleitung zur Kritik der politischen Ökonomie,' *MEW*, vol. 13, Berlin: Dietz.
MARX, K. (1964b), *Das Kapital, MEW*, vol. 25, Berlin: Dietz.
MARX, K. (1964c), 'Zur Kritik der politischen Okonomie,' *MEW*, vol. 13, Berlin: Dietz.
MARX, K. (1965), 'Theorien über den Mehrwert,' *MEW*, vol. 26, 1–3, Berlin: Dietz.
MARX, K. (1968a), 'Lohnarbeit und Kapital,' *MEW*, vol. 6, Berlin: Dietz.
MARX, K. (1969a), 'Thesen über Feuerbach,' *MEW*, vol. 3, Berlin: Dietz.
MARX, K. (1969b), *Das Kapital*, vol. 1, Frankfurt a.M.: Ullstein.
MARX, K. (1971), *Das Kapital*, vol. 3, Frankfurt a.M.: Ullstein.
MARX, K. and ENGELS, F. (1961), 'Lohnarbeit und Kapital,' *MEW*, vol. 6, Berlin: Dietz.

MARX, K. and ENGELS, F. (1969a), 'Die deutsche Ideologie,' *MEW*, vol. 3, Berlin: Dietz.
MARX, K. and ENGELS, F. (1969b), 'Manifest der Kommunistischen Partei,' *MEW*, vol. 4, Berlin: Dietz.
MASLOW, A. H. (1970), *Motivation and Personality*, 2nd ed., New York: Harper & Row.
MATTICK, P. (1971), *Marx and Keynes*, Frankfurt a.M.: Europäische Verlagsanstalt.
MAYNTZ, R. (1963), *Soziologie der Organisation*, Reinbek: Rowohlt.
MAYNTZ, R. (1964), 'The Study of Organizations,' *Current Sociology*, 13: 95–119.
MAYNTZ, R. (1968), 'Max Webers Idealtypus der Bürokratie und die Organisationssoziologie,' in R. MAYNTZ (ed.), *Bürokratische Organisation*, Cologne: Kiepenheuer & Witsch.
McCLELLAND, D. (1961), *The Achieving Society*, New York: Free Press.
McCLELLAND, D., ATKINSON, J. W., CLARK, R. A., and LOWELL, E. L. (1953), *The Achievement Motive*, New York: Appleton-Century-Crofts.
MEAD, G. H. (1964), *On Social Psychology*, ed. by A. Strauss, Chicago, Ill.: University of Chicago Press.
MEAD, M. (ed.) (1953), *Cultural Patterns and Technical Change*, Paris: UNESCO.
MENDER, J. H. (1975), *Technologische Entwicklung und Arbeitsprozeß*, Frankfurt a.M.: Fischer.
MERTON, R. K. (1960), 'Bureaucratic Structure and Personality,' in R. K. MERTON, A. P. GRAY, B. HOCKLEY, and H. C. SELVIN (eds), *Reader in Bureaucracy*, Glencoe, Ill.: Free Press.
MERTON, R. K. (1968), *Social Theory and Social Structure*, enlarged ed., New York: Free Press.
MEYER, J. W. and HAMMOND, P. E. (1971), 'Forms of Status Inconsistency,' *Social Forces*, 50: 91–101.
MIEWALD, R. D. (1973), 'The Greatly Exaggerated Death of Bureaucracy,' in L. A. ROWE and W. B. BOISE (eds), *Organization and Managerial Innovation: A Reader*, Pacific Palisades, Cal.: Goodyear Publishing Co.
MILLS, C. W. (1956), *The Power Elite*, New York: Oxford University Press.
MILLS, C. W. (1959), *The Sociological Imagination*, New York: Oxford University Press.
MITCHELL, G. D. (1968), *A Hundred Years of Sociology*, Chicago: Aldine.
MOORE, B. (1966), *Social Origins of Dictatorship and Democracy*, Boston, Mass.: Beacon Press.
MOORE, B. (1978), *Injustice: The Social Bases of Obedience and Revolt*, White Plains, New York: M. E. Sharpe.
MOORE, W. E. (1960), 'A Reconsideration of Theories of Social Change,' *American Sociological Review*, 25: 810–18.
MOORE, W. E. (1963), *Social Change*, Englewood Cliffs, N.J.: Prentice-Hall.
MOORE, W. E. (1968), 'Social Change,' *International Encyclopedia of the Social Sciences*, ed. by D. L. SILLS, vol. 14, New York: Macmillan.
MOORE, W. E. and COOK, R. (eds) (1967), *Readings on Social Change*, Englewood Cliffs, N.J.: Prentice-Hall.

SELECT BIBLIOGRAPHY

MOSZKOWSKA, N. (1943), *Zur Dynamik des Spätkapitalismus*, Zürich and New York: Aufbruch.
MÜLLER, W. and NEUSÜSS, C. (1970), 'Die Sozialstaatsillusion und der Widerspruch von Lohnarbeit und Kapital,' *Sozialistische Politik*, 2: 4–67.
MULLINS, N. C. (1975), 'A Sociological Theory of Scientific Revolution,' in K. D. KNORR, H. STRASSER, and H. G. ZILIAN (eds), *Determinants and Controls of Scientific Development*, Dordrecht: Reidel Publ. Co.
MÜNCH, R. (1973), 'Soziologische Theorie und historische Erklärung,' *Zeitschrift für Soziologie*, 2: 163–81.
MYRDAL, G. (1974), *Ökonomische Theorie und unterentwickelte Regionen*, Frankfurt a.m.: Fischer.
MYRDAL, G., STERNER, R., and ROSE, A. (1944), *An American Dilemma*, 2 vols, New York: Harper & Row.
NADEL, S. F. (1957), *The Theory of Social Structure*, London: Cohen & West.
NAGEL, E. (1956), *Logic Without Metaphysics*, Glencoe, Ill.: Free Press.
NAGEL, E. (1961), *The Structure of Science: Problems in the Logic of Scientific Explanation*, New York: Harcourt, Brace & World.
NISBET, R. A. (1969), *Social Change and History*, New York: Oxford University Press.
NISBET, R. A. (1970), *The Social Bond*, New York: Alfred A. Knopf.
O'CONNOR, J. (1973), *The Fiscal Crisis of the State*, New York: St Martin's Press.
OECD (1975), 'Working Paper of the Manpower and Social Affairs Division,' Unpub. ms, Paris.
OFFE, C. (1972), 'Politische Herrschaft und Klassenstruktur: Zur Analyse spätkapitalistischer Gesellschaftssysteme,' in G. KRESS and D. SENGHAAS (eds), *Politikwissenschaft – Eine Einführung in ihre Probleme*, Frankfurt a.M.: Europäische Verlagsanstalt.
OFFE, C. (1975), *Leistungsprinzip und industrielle Arbeit*, 4th ed., Frankfurt a.M.: Europäische Verlagsanstalt.
OFFE, C. (1977), *Strukturprobleme des kapitalistischen Staates*, 4th ed., Frankfurt a.M.: Suhrkamp.
OGBURN, W. F. (1946), *The Social Effects of Aviation*, Boston: Houghton Mifflin.
OGBURN, W. F. (1947), 'How Technology Changes Society,' *Annals of the American Academy of Political and Social Science*, 249: 81–8.
OGBURN, W. F. (1964), *Culture and Social Change*, ed. by O. D. Duncan, Chicago: University of Chicago Press.
OGBURN, W. F. (1966), *Social Change*, New York: Dell.
ORTEGA Y GASSET, J. (1951), *The Revolt of the Masses*, London: Allen & Unwin.
ORTEGA Y GASSET, J. (1978), *Gesammelte Werke in sechs Bänden*, Stuttgart: Deutsche Verlags-Anstalt.
PACKARD, VANCE (1972), *A Nation of Strangers*, New York: David McKay.
PARETO, V. (1966), *Sociological Writings*, selected and introduced by S. E. FINER, New York: Praeger.
PARKIN, F. (1971), *Class Inequality and Political Order*, New York: Praeger.

PARSONS, T. (1945), 'Racial and Religious Differences as Factors in Group Tensions,' in L. FINKELSTEIN et al. (eds), *Approaches to National Unity*, New York: Harper.
PARSONS, T. (1949), *Essays in Sociological Theory*, 1st ed., Glencoe, Ill.: Free Press.
PARSONS, T. (1951), *The Social System*, Glencoe, Ill.: Free Press.
PARSONS, T. (1953), 'A Revised Analytical Approach to the Theory of Social Stratification,' in R. BENDIX and S. M. LIPSET (eds), *Class, Status and Power*, 1st ed., Glencoe, Ill.: Free Press.
PARSONS, T. (1954a), 'Propaganda and Social Control,' in T. PARSONS, *Essays in Sociological Theory*, revised ed., Glencoe, Ill.: Free Press.
PARSONS, T. (1954b), 'The Present Position and Prospects of Systematic Theory in Sociology,' in T. PARSONS, *Essays in Sociological Theory*, revised ed., Glencoe, Ill.: Free Press.
PARSONS, T. (1954c), 'Democracy and Social Structure in Pre-Nazi Germany,' in T. PARSONS, *Essays in Sociological Theory*, revised ed., Glencoe, Ill.: Free Press.
PARSONS, T. (1957), 'The Distribution of Power in American Society,' *World Politics*, 10: 123–43.
PARSONS, T. (1960), 'A Sociological Approach to the Theory of Organizations,' in T. PARSONS, *Structure and Process in Modern Societies*, New York: Free Press.
PARSONS, T. (1961), 'An Outline of the Social System,' in T. PARSONS, E. A. SHILS, K. NAEGELE, and J. PITTS (eds), *Theories of Society*, New York: Free Press.
PARSONS, T. (1964a), 'A Functional Theory of Change,' in A. and E. ETZIONI (eds), *Social Change*, New York: Basic Books.
PARSONS, T. (1964b), *Structure and Process in Modern Societies*, New York: Free Press.
PARSONS, T. (1966), *Societies: Evolutionary and Comparative Perspectives*, Englewood Cliffs, N.J.: Prentice-Hall.
PARSONS, T. (1967), 'Evolutionary Universals in Society,' in T. PARSONS, *Sociological Theory and Modern Society*, New York: Free Press.
PARSONS, T. (1968), *The Structure of Social Action*, paperback ed., 2 vols, New York: Free Press.
PARSONS, T. (1970), 'On Building Social System Theory: A Personal History,' *Daedalus*, 99: 826–81.
PARSONS, T. (1971), *The System of Modern Societies*, Englewood Cliffs, N.J.: Prentice-Hall.
PARSONS, T., BALES, R. F., and SHILS, E. A. (1953), *Working Papers in the Theory of Action*, Glencoe, Ill.: Free Press.
PARSONS, T. and SHILS, E. A. (eds) (1951), *Toward a General Theory of Action*, Cambridge, Mass: Harvard University Press.
PARSONS, T. and SMELSER, N. J. (1956), *Economy and Society*, New York: Free Press.
PELINKA, A. (1974), 'Postklassischer Parlamentarismus und Sozialpartnerschaft,' *Österreichische Zeitschrift für Politikwissenschaft*, 3: 333–45.

PELZ, D. C. (1956), 'Some Social Factors Related to Performance in a Research Organization,' *Administrative Science Quarterly*, 1: 310–25.
PHILLIPS, B. S. (1969), *Sociology: Social Structure and Change*, London: Macmillan.
PIGOU, A. C. (1935), *The Economics of Stationary States*, London: Macmillan.
PLESSNER, H. (1959), *Die verspätete Nation*, 2nd enlarged ed., Stuttgart: Kohlhammer.
POULANTZAS, N. (1974), *Les Classes sociales dans le capitalisme aujourd'hui*, Paris: Seuil.
POWICKE, F. (1956), *Modern Historians and the Study of History*, reprint, London: Odhams Press.
PRESTHUS, R. (1962), *The Organizational Society*, New York: Alfred A. Knopf.
PUGH, D. S. and HICKSON, D. J. (1968), 'Eine dimensionale Analyse bürokratischer Strukturen,' in R. MAYNTZ (ed.), *Bürokratische Organisation*, Köln/Berlin: Kiepenheuer & Witsch.
RADCLIFFE-BROWN, A. R. (1935), 'On the Concept of Function in Social Science,' *American Anthropologist N.S.*, 37: 394–402.
RADCLIFFE-BROWN, A. R. (1952), *Structure and Function in Primitive Society*, Glencoe, Ill.: Free Press.
RADCLIFFE-BROWN, A. R. (1957), *A Natural Science of Society*, Glencoe, Ill.: Free Press.
RANDALL, S. C. and STRASSER, H. (1976a), *Status Inconsistency Reconsidered: Theoretical Problems and Neglected Consequences*, research memorandum no. 97, Vienna: Institute for Advanced Studies.
RANDALL, S. C. and STRASSER, H. (1976b), 'The Social Functions of Status Inconsistency,' paper presented at the annual meeting of the American Sociological Association, New York.
RAPOPORT, A. (1968), 'Tolstoi und Clausewitz,' in E. KRIPPENDORF (ed.), *Friedensforschung*, Cologne: Kiepenheuer & Witsch.
RATZENHOFER, G. (1907), *Soziologie. Positive Lehre von den menschlichen Wechselbeziehungen*, Leipzig: F. A. Brockhaus.
RAWLS, J. (1972), *A Theory of Justice*, New York: Oxford University Press.
REDFIELD, R. (1930), *Tepoztlán: A Mexican Village*, Chicago: University of Chicago Press.
REICH, C. A. (1971), *The Greening of America*, New York: Bantam Books.
REX, J. (1961), *Key Problems of Sociological Theory*, London: Routledge & Kegan Paul.
RICHTA, R. et al. (1971), *Politische Ökonomie des 20. Jahrhunderts*, Frankfurt a.M.: Makol.
RIDDER, P. (1972), 'Historischer Funktionalismus,' *Zeitschrift für Soziologie*, 1: 333–52.
RIDDER, P. (1974), 'Bewegung sozialer Systeme: Über die endogene Erzeugung von Veränderungen,' *Kölner Zeitschrift für Soziologie und Sozialpsychologie*, 26: 1–28.
RITSERT, J. (1973), *Probleme politisch-ökonomischer Theoriebildung*, Frankfurt a.M.: Athenäum.

SELECT BIBLIOGRAPHY

RITZER, G. (1975), *Sociology: A Multiple Paradigm Science*, Boston: Allyn & Bacon.
RÖDEL, U. (1972), *Forschungsprioritäten und technologische Entwicklung*, Frankfurt a.M.: Suhrkamp.
ROGERS, E. M. (1962), *Diffusion of Innovations*, New York: Free Press.
ROHTER, I. (1969), 'Social Psychological Determinants of Radical Rightism,' in R. A. SCHOENBERGER (ed.), *The American Right-Wing: Readings in Political Behavior*, New York: Holt, Rinehart & Winston.
ROKEACH, M. (1960), *The Open and Closed Mind*, New York: Basic Books.
ROLSHAUSEN, C. (ed.) (1970), *Kapitalismus und Krise*, Frankfurt a.M.: Europäische Verlagsanstalt.
RÖMER, P. (1973), 'Funktions- oder Formwandel des Eigentums?,' *Demokratie und Recht*, 1: 48–64.
ROSDOLSKY, R. (1969), *Zur Entstehungsgeschichte des Marxschen 'Kapital'*, Frankfurt a.M.: Europäische Verlagsanstalt.
ROSS, D. (ed.) (1958), *Administration for Adaptability*, New York: Metropolitan School Study Council.
ROSTOW, W. W. (1960), *The Stages of Economic Growth*, New York: Cambridge University Press.
ROTHMAN, J. (1974), *Planning and Organization for Social Change*, New York: Columbia University Press.
ROTHMAN, S. (1970), 'Barrington Moore and the Dialectics of Revolution: An Essay Review,' *American Political Science Review*, 64: 61–82.
RUNCIMAN, W. G. (1966), *Relative Deprivation and Social Justice*, London: Routledge & Kegan Paul.
RUSH, G. (1967), 'Status Consistency and Right-Wing Extremism,' *American Sociological Review*, 32: 89–92.
SAHLINS, M. D. (1960), 'Evolution: Specific and General,' in M. D. SAHLINS and E. R. SERVICE (eds), *Evolution and Culture*, Ann Arbor, Mich.: University of Michigan Press.
SAMPSON, E. (1966), 'Status Congruence and Cognitive Consistency,' in C. W. BACKMAN and P. F. SECORD (eds), *Problems in Social Psychology*, New York: McGraw-Hill.
SCHEIN, E. H. and BENNIS, W. G. (1965), *Personal and Organizational Change Through Group Methods: The Laboratory Approach*, New York: Wiley.
SCHELSKY, H. (1975), *Die Arbeit tun die anderen*, 2nd ed., Opladen: Westdeutscher Verlag.
SCHIEDER, T. (ed.) (1973), *Revolution und Gesellschaft. Theorie und Praxis der Systemveränderung*, Freiburg i.Brsg.: Herder.
SCHIENSTOCK, G. (1974), 'Organisation innovativer Rollen,' dissertation, Technische Universität Berlin.
SCHLUCHTER, W. (1972), *Aspekte bürokratischer Herrschaft*, Munich: List.
SCHMIDT, A. (ed.) (1969), *Beiträge zur marxistischen Erkenntnistheorie*, Frankfurt a.M.: Suhrkamp.
SCHMIEDE, R. (1973), *Grundprobleme der Marx'schen Akkumulations- und Krisentheorie*, Frankfurt a.M.: Athenäum.
SCHNEIDER, L. (1976), *Classical Theories of Social Change*, Morristown, N. J.: General Learning Press.

SCHOENBAUM, D. (1967), *Hitler's Social Revolution: Class and Status in Nazi Germany 1933–1939*, Garden City, New York: Doubleday Anchor Books.
SCHON, D. A. (1971), *Beyond the Stable State*, Harmondsworth, England: Penguin.
SCHUMPETER, J. A. (1927), 'Die sozialen Klassen im ethnisch homogenen Milieu,' *Archiv für Sozialwissenschaft und Sozialpolitik*, 57: 1–67 (abgedruckt in J. A. SCHUMPETER, *Aufsätze zur Soziologie*, Tübingen: Mohr, 1953).
SCHUMPETER, J. A. (1951), *The Theory of Economic Development*, Cambridge, Mass.: Harvard University Press.
SCHWEITZER, D. R. (1974), *Status Frustration and Conservatism in Comparative Perspective: The Swiss Case*, Beverly Hills and London: Sage.
SCOTT, W. R. (1966), 'Professionals in Bureaucracies: Areas of Conflict,' in H. M. VOLLMER and D. L. MILLS (eds), *Professionalization*, Englewood Cliffs, N.J.: Prentice-Hall.
SELLNOW, I. (1961), *Grundprinzipien einer Periodisierung der Urgeschichte*, Berlin: Akademie-Verlag.
SELZNICK, P. (1949), *TVA and the Grass Roots*, New York: Harper.
SEMJONOW, J. I. (1974), 'Zur Diskussion über die ökonomische Gesellschaftsformation als historisches Entwicklungsstadium,' *Sowjetwissenschaft-Gesellschaftswissenschaftliche Beiträge*, 2: 161–6.
SERVICE, E. R. (1960), 'The Law of Evolutionary Potential,' in M. D. SAHLINS and E. R. SERVICE (eds), *Evolution and Culture*, Ann Arbor, Mich.: University of Michigan Press.
SERVICE, E. R. (1971), *Primitive Social Organization: An Evolutionary Perspective*, 2nd ed., New York: Harper & Row.
SERVICE, E. R. (1975), *Origins of the State and Civilization*, New York: W. W. Norton.
SHAPIRO, J. J. (1976), 'Critical Theory and Social Evolution,' paper presented at the Annual Meeting of the American Sociological Association, New York.
SHEPARD, H. A. (1967), 'Innovation Resisting and Innovation Producing Organizations,' *Journal of Business*, 40: 470–81.
SHILS, E. A. (1960), *Political Development in the New States*, The Hague: Mouton.
SHILS, E. A. (1963), 'On the Comparative Study of the New States,' in C. GEERTZ (ed.), *Old Societies and New States*, New York: Free Press.
SILVERMAN, D. (1970), *The Theory of Organizations*, London: Heinemann.
SIMMEL, G. (1964), *Conflict and the Web of Group Affiliations*, New York: Free Press.
SLOMCZYNSKI, K. and WESOLOWSKI, W. (1974), 'Reduction of Inequalities and Status Inconsistency,' paper presented at the 8th World Congress of Sociology, Toronto.
SMELSER, N. J. (1959a), *Social Change in the Industrial Revolution*, London: Routledge & Kegan Paul.
SMELSER, N. J. (1959b), 'A Comparative View of Exchange Systems,' *Economic Development and Cultural Change*, 8: 173–82.

SELECT BIBLIOGRAPHY

SMELSER, N. J. (1962), *Theory of Collective Behavior*, New York: Free Press.
SMELSER, N. J. (1966), 'The Modernization of Social Relations,' M. WEINER (ed.), *Modernization*, New York: Basic Books.
SMELSER, N. J. (ed.) (1967), *Sociology*, New York: Wiley.
SMELSER, N. J. (1968), *Essays in Sociological Explanation*, Englewood Cliffs, N.J.: Prentice-Hall.
SMITH, A. D. (1973), *The Concept of Social Change: A Critique of Functionalist Theory of Social Change*, London: Routledge & Kegan Paul.
SOFRI, G. (1969), *Über asiatische Produktionsweise*, Frankfurt a.M.: Europäische Verlagsanstalt.
SOLLOWAY, O. and STRASSER, H. (1977), 'Zur soziologischen Theorie von Entfremdung und Anomie,' in M. BRENNER and H. STRASSER (eds), *Die gesellschaftliche Konstruktion der Entfremdung*, Frankfurt a.M.: Campus Verlag.
SOROKIN, P. A. (1937–41), *Social and Cultural Dynamics*, 4 vols, New York: American Book Co.
SOROKIN, P. A. (1947), *Society, Culture, and Personality*, New York: Harper & Row.
SOROKIN, P. A. (1966), *Sociological Theories of Today*, New York: Harper & Row.
SPENCER, H. (1898–9), *The Principles of Sociology*, 3 vols, New York: Appleton.
SPENCER, H. (1958), *First Principles of a New System of Philosophy*, New York: DeWitt Revolving Fund.
SPENGLER, O. (1926), *The Decline of the West*, New York: Alfred A. Knopf.
SPICER, E. H. (ed.) (1952), *Human Problems in Technological Change*, New York: Russell Sage Foundation.
SPIEGEL-RÖSING, I. S. (1973), *Wissenschaftsentwicklung und Wissenschaftssteuerung*, Frankfurt a.M.: Athenäum-Verlag.
STALIN, J. (1955), *Fragen des Leninismus*, Berlin: Dietz.
STINCHCOMBE, A. L. (1959/60), 'Bureaucratic and Craft Administration: A Comparative Study,' *Administrative Science Quarterly*, 4: 168–87.
STINCHCOMBE, A. L. (1968), *Constructing Social Theories*, New York: Harcourt, Brace & World.
STÖLTING, E. (1974), *Wissenschaft als Produktivkraft*, Munich: List.
STONE, L. (1972), *Causes of the English Revolution*, New York: Harper & Row.
STRASSER, H. (1975), 'Social Technologists and Social Emancipists: Factors in the Development of Sociology,' in K. D. KNORR, H. STRASSER, and H. G. ZILIAN (eds), *Determinants and Controls of Scientific Development*, Dordrecht, Holland: D. Reidel Publishing Co.
STRASSER, H. (1976), *The Normative Structure of Sociology*, London and Boston: Routledge & Kegan Paul.
STRASSER, H. (1977), 'Discovering the Paradigmatic Structure of Sociology,' in K. H. FERGUSON *et al.* (eds), *Proceedings of the Sociological Research Symposium VII*, Richmond, Virginia: Virginia Commonwealth University.

SELECT BIBLIOGRAPHY

STRASSER, H. (1980), 'Stratum and Class Formation: Principles of a Theory of Social Inequality,' *Canadian Journal of Sociology*, 5: 103–20.
SUMNER, W. G. (1913), *War and Other Essays*, New Haven, Conn.: Yale University Press.
SWANSON, G. (1971), *Social Change*, Glenview, Ill.: Scott, Foresman & Co.
SWEEZY, P. M. (1956), *Theory of Capitalist Development*, New York: Monthly Review.
SZTOMPKA, P. (1974), *System and Function: Toward a Theory of Society*, New York: Academic Press.
TANTER, R. and MIDLARSKY, M. (1967), 'A Theory of Revolution,' *Journal of Conflict Resolution*, 11: 264–80.
TERRYBERRY, S. (1968), 'The Evolution of Organizational Environments,' *Administrative Science Quarterly*, 12: 590–613.
THOMAS, W. I. (1909), *Source Book of Social Origins*, Chicago, Ill.: University of Chicago Press.
THOMPSON, J. D. and McEWEN, W. J. (1958), 'Goals and Environments: Goal-Setting as an Interaction Process,' *American Sociological Review*, 23: 23–31.
THOMPSON, V. A. (1961), 'Hierarchy, Specialization, and Organizational Conflict,' *Administrative Science Quarterly*, 5: 458–521.
THOMPSON, V. A. (1965), 'Bureaucracy and Innovation,' *Administrative Science Quarterly*, 10: 1–20.
THRALL, C. A. and STARR, J. M. (eds) (1972), *Technology, Power, and Social Change*, Lexington, Mass.: D. C. Heath & Co.
TIMASHEFF, N. S. (1967), *Sociological Theory: Its Nature and Growth*, 3rd ed., New York: Random House.
TJADEN, K. H. (ed.) (1971), *Soziale Systeme*, Neuwied: Luchterhand.
TJADEN, K. H. (1972), *Soziales System und sozialer Wandel*, Stuttgart: Enke.
TJADEN, K. H. (1973), 'Soziale Systeme und gesellschaftliche Totalität,' in D. HÜLST et al., *Methodenfragen der Gesellschaftsanalyse*, Frankfurt a.M.: Athenäum.
TJADEN, K. H. (1977), 'Naturevolution, Gesellschaftsformation, Weltgeschichte. Gesellschaftswissenschaftliche Entwicklungstheorie,' *Das Argument*, 19: 8–55.
TJADEN-STEINHAUER, M., HÜLST, D., and TJADEN, K. H. (1973), *Methodenfragen der Gesellschaftsanalyse*, Frankfurt a.M.: Athenäum.
TJADEN-STEINHAUER, M. and TJADEN, K. H. (1973), *Klassenverhältnisse im Spätkapitalismus*, Stuttgart: Enke.
TOCH, H. (1965), *The Social Psychology of Social Movements*, Indianapolis: Bobbs-Merrill.
TOCQUEVILLE, A. de (1856), *The Old Regime and the French Revolution*, New York: Harper & Bros.
TOFFLER, A. (1970), *Future Shock*, New York: Random House.
TOFFLER, A. (1973), 'Organizations: The Coming Ad-Hocracy,' in L. A. ROWE, and W. B. BOISE (eds), *Organization and Managerial Innovation: A Reader*, Pacific Palisades, Cal.: Goodyear Publishing Co.
TOMBERG, F. (1974), *Basis und Überbau*, Darmstadt: Luchterhand.
TÖNNIES, F. (1887), *Gemeinschaft und Gesellschaft*, Leipzig: Fues.

TÖPFER, B. (1967), 'Zur Problematik der vorkapitalistischen Klassengesellschaften,' *Jahrbuch für Wirtschaftsgeschichte*, 4: 259–86.

TÖPFER, B. (1971), 'Zur Frage der gemeinsamen Wesensmerkmale der vorkapitalistischen Klassengesellschaften und der Anwendungsmöglichkeit des Revolutionsbegriffs für die Zeit des Bestehens dieser Gesellschaften,' *Ethnographisch-Archäologische Zeitschrift*, 2: 221–30.

TOURAINE, A. (1971), *The Post-Industrial Society*, New York: Random House.

TOURAINE, A. (1974), *Soziologie als Handlungswissenschaft*, Darmstadt: Luchterhand.

TOYNBEE, ARNOLD (1947), *A Study of History*, abridged by D. C. SOMERVELL, New York: Oxford University Press.

TROTTER, W. (1916), *Instincts of the Herd in Peace and War*, New York: Free Press.

TUMIN, M. M. (1953), 'Some Principles of Stratification: A Critical Analysis,' *American Sociological Review*, 18: 387–93.

TUMIN, M. M. (1963), 'On Social Inequality,' *American Sociological Review*, 28: 19–26.

TURNER, R. and KILLIAN, L. (1957), *Collective Behavior*, Englewood Cliffs, N.J.: Prentice-Hall.

VARGA, E. (1934), *Die große Krise und ihre politischen Folgen*, Moscow and Leningrad: Verlagsgen. ausl. Arbeiter i.d. UdSSR.

VEBLEN, T. (1899), *The Theory of the Leisure Class*, New York: Macmillan.

VOLLMER, H. M. and MILLS, D. L. (1966), *Professionalization*, Englewood Cliffs, N.J.: Prentice-Hall.

WALDMANN, P. (1975), 'Zeit und Wandel als Grundbestandteile sozialer Systeme,' in W. L. BÜHL (ed.), *Funktion und Struktur: Soziologie vor der Geschichte*, Munich: Nymphenburger.

WALLACE, W. L. (ed.), *Sociological Theory: An Introduction*, Chicago: Aldine.

WALLERSTEIN, I. (1974), *The Modern World System: Capitalist Agriculture and the Origins of the European World Economy in the Sixteenth Century*, New York: Academic Press.

WEBER, A. (1950), *Kulturgeschichte als Kultursoziologie*, 2nd enlarged ed., Munich: Piper.

WEBER, M. (1930), *The Protestant Ethic and the Spirit of Capitalism*, trans. by T. PARSONS, New York: Charles Scribner's Sons.

WEBER, M. (1947), *The Theory of Social and Economic Organization*, trans. by A. H. HENDERSON and TALCOTT PARSONS, Glencoe, Ill.: Free Press.

WEBER, M. (1964), *Wirtschaft und Gesellschaft*, Cologne: Kiepenheuer & Witsch.

WEBER, M. (1969), *Die protestantische Ethik I*, ed. by J. WINCKELMANN, Munich and Hamburg: Siebenstern.

WIENER, J. (1975), 'The Barrington Moore Thesis and Its Critics,' *Theory and Society*, 2: 301–30.

WILENSKY, H. L. (1956), *Intellectuals in Labor Unions: Organizational Pressures on Professional Roles*, Glencoe, Ill.: Free Press.

WILENSKY, H. L. (1964), 'The Professionalization of Everyone?' *American Journal of Sociology*, 70: 137–58.

WIRTH, M. (1972), *Kapitalismustheorie in der DDR: Entstehung und Entwicklung der Theorie des staatsmonopolistischen Kapitalismus*, Frankfurt a.M.: Suhrkamp.

WISWEDE, G. and KUTSCH, T. (1978), *Sozialer Wandel: Zur Erklärungskraft neuerer Entwicklungs- und Modernisierungstheorien*, Darmstadt: Wissenschaftliche Buchgesellschaft.

WITTFOGEL, K. A. (1957), *Oriental Despotism*, New Haven, Conn.: Yale University Press.

WRIGHT, E. O. (1976), 'Class Boundaries in Advanced Capitalist Societies,' *New Left Review*, 98: 3–41.

WYGODSKI, S. L. (1972), *Der gegenwärtige Kapitalismus*, Cologne: Pahl-Rugenstein.

YOUNG, F. W. and YOUNG, R. C. (1962), 'The Sequence and Direction of Community Growth: A Cross-Cultural Generalization,' *Rural Sociology*, 27: 374–86.

ZAGALOW, N. N. et al. (1970), *Lehrbuch Politische Ökonomie*, Frankfurt a.M.: Verlag Marxistischer Blätter.

ZAPF, W. (ed.) (1969), *Theorien des sozialen Wandels*, Cologne: Kiepenheuer & Witsch.

ZELENÝ, J. (1973), *Die Wissenschaftslogik bei Marx und 'Das Kapital'*, Frankfurt a.M.: Europäische Verlagsanstalt.

ZETTERBERG, H. (1963), *On Theory and Verification in Sociology*, Totowa, N.J.: Bedminster Press.

ZIMMERMAN, C. C. (1961), 'Contemporary Trends in Sociology in America and Abroad,' in J. S. ROUCEK (ed.), *Readings in Contemporary American Sociology*, Paterson, N.J.: Littlefield, Adams.

ZIMMERMANN, E. (1973), 'Fragen zur Theorie der Statusinkonsistenz: Auf dem Wege zu einer Neuorientierung?' *Zeitschrift für Soziologie*, 2: 83–100.

Index

Abel, T., 238, 241
Aberle, D. F., 136, 139, 157
accumulation, 70–1; capital, 107
achievement criteria, 58
achievement motivation, 30
action system, 185–7n
adaptability, 65–6
adaptation, 175, 182n, 297
adaptive upgrading, 56, 159–61
Ad-Hocracy, 301–2
adjustment, 70, 182n
Adorno, T., 45
agrarian revolution, neolithic, 100
Aiken, M., 288–91, 294–301 *passim*, 304n, 305n
alienation, 39, 45
Allen, F. R., 86
Almond, G., 215
Altvater, E., 38
ambiguity (strain), 228–9, 230
Anderson, P., 38
anxiety, 232
Appelbaum, R., 16, 22, 26, 65, 152, 158, 159
aristocracy, 200, 234; bourgeoisie and, 207–9; capitalists and, 216–17; commercialization and, 203–5, 212; peasantry and, 216; relations with authority, 200, 202–3, 213
Aron, R., 36, 47, 55, 57, 63; conflict theory, 52–3
Ashgarner, R., 35
Asiatic mode of production, 95
assumptions, 5, 23–6; background and domain, 181–2n
authority, 146–7, 211; conflict theory and, 47–8; aristocracy and, 202–3; Royal, 201
authority structure, 289, 292, 294, 305n; change and, 300
autonomic dimensions, 23
autonomy: functional, 148, 180; institutional, 58

Autorenkollektiv, 127n

Baier, H., 19
Bales, R. F., 177
Baran, P. A., 95, 109
Bardis, P. D., 62
Barnard, C., 304n
Barnes, H., 59, 62
Barnes, L. B., 298
Barnett, H. G., 77, 87n
Beattie, J. H. M., 135
Becker, H., 59, 62
behavior patterns, 13
behaviorist theories, 21–2
beliefs, 169; norm-oriented, 231; value-oriented, 231, 234–5, 239–40
Bell, D., 2, 35n, 36, 37, 38
Bellah, R. N., 182n, 273n, 303n
Ben-David, J., 289
Bendix, R., 14, 51, 261, 274n
Bennis, W. G., 2, 293, 302, 305n
Benoit-Smullyan, E., 253
Benson, L., 215
Berelson, B., 77
Berger, B., 273n
Berger, P. L., 22, 86n, 246, 273n
Berghe, P. L. van den, 143
Bertalanffy, L. von, 143
Bertrand, A. L., 76–7
Beshers, J. C., 56
Beyme, K. von, 219
Black, C. E., 215, 219
Blau, P. M., 246, 261, 292, 294, 306n
Blumer, H., 22, 25
Boccara, P., 95, 127n
Bock, K. E., 155, 156, 157, 175
Böhret, C., 152
Bollhagen, P., 96, 103, 114, 128
Bosetzky, H., 304n

331

INDEX

Boskoff, A., 191n
Bottomore, T. B., 51, 84n
boundary maintenance, 81, 149–50, 162
boundary positions, 167
bourgeoisie, 151, 200, 205, 212, 234; aristocracy and, 207–9
Box, S., 252
Brinton, C., 179
Brodbeck, M., 132
Broom, L., 247
Buckingham, W., 84n
Buckley, W., 23, 178, 188n
Bühl, W. L., 39, 40, 47, 69, 148, 152, 188n
Bullock, A., 35n, 241
bureaucracy, 83; agrarian, 211; repressive, 215; *see also* organizations
bureaucratization, 15, 60, 64
Burns, T., 291–305 *passim*

Campbell, J. P., 293
Cancian, F., 190, 263
Cantril, H., 30, 216, 219, 265, 266
capital: accumulation, 107, 108–10, 111, 121, 124; augmentation of, 106–7, 112, 124; constant, 115; ownership and function, 111
capitalism, 15, 56, 106–16, 121–3; democratic, 199, 202, 205, 211–13; development of, 45; in conflict theory, 42; late, 37–8, 95; mode of production in, 113–16; organizations under, 280–1; reactionary, 199; relations with socialism, 125; self-negatory tendencies, 45; transformation of, 85; transition from feudalism to, 46
capitalistic reproduction, 38
catastrophe, 124
cause and causation, 1–2, 26–33, 195; defined, 27; latent, 146, 174; multiple, 150
centralization, oligarchic, 149
Chambliss, W. J., 47, 51
change *see* social change
change of system, 12–13, 28; from outside, 27
change within systems, 12–13, 28
charisma, 30, 64, 241, 244, 245
Childe, V. G., 96, 100, 101, 129n
China, 201–20 *passim*
Chirot, D., 35n
Chodak, S., 33, 87n, 158
choice, 49
Cillié, F., 289
civil liberties, 85n
civilization, 60; stages of, 160; Western, 162–3, 182n
Clarke, B., 2
class and classes: coalitions between, 200, 208–9, 212–13; delineation of, 51; 'in itself and for itself', 44–5
class conflict, 100, 111–13; economic and political, 51; fragmentation of, 46; in industrial society, 37; institutionalization of, 85n; land ownership and, 102; Marxist view of, 38; reproduction and, 45–6
class consciousness, 112; conflict theory and, 44; formation of, 44–5
class contradiction, 44
class relations, pluralization of, 48
class struggle, 56; conflict theory and, 44; diminishing, 45; functionalist view of, 51; Marxist concept of, 94; revolution and, 39
classical evolutionary theory, 54–9
classless society, 52
classlessness, 37
climatic theories, 21, 78, 101
Cloward, R., 258
coercion, 183n; consensus and, 144; status and, 262
cognitive interest, 18–19
cognitive orientation, 290
Cohen, P. S., 142
Coleman, J., 77
collective bargaining, 37
collective behavior theory, 220–45, 267–72; defined, 220–1; determinants of, 222–3; types of, 221
collectivism, 101, 133, 153–4; consensus within, 141; subcollectivities, 164
Collins, R., 47, 53, 135, 246
commercialization, 203–5, 210, 212, 217–19, 268–9
commodity exchange, 121
commodity production, 121
communication, 237
communicative-constructive dimension, 23
communism, 56, 272n; in Barrington Moore's theory, 199–213 *passim*
compatibility in organizations, 287–8
compensatory mechanisms, 147–8
competition, 110
complexity, degree of, 164
Comte, A., 15, 54, 55, 150–9 *passim*, 175, 303n
concentration, 109, 111, 121; of industrial labor, 114
concepts, 1
conflict, 132, 181; alternative views of, 38; antagonistic and non-antagonistic, 124; as (the medium of) change, 51–2; consensual nature of, 53; endogeneous change and, 169; in functionalist theory, 146–7, 150–1, 154–5, 173, 178; in historic-materialist theory, 119–20; caused by incompatibility, 146; between individuals and groups, 29; normalization of, 162–3; organizational change and, 301, 302, 305n; societalization and, 124–5; typology of, 50; *see also* strain
conflict theory, 13, 26, 183n, 267; cyclical, 53; definition of change, 14–15; dynamic-evolutionary, 53; inequality and, 172; Marxist, 41–7; non-Marxist, 47–53; variants of, 41–53
consensus, 141; for change, 300; coercion and,

INDEX

144; equilibrium and, 180; of values, 150, 180
consociational societies, 263
constancy, pattern, 183n
constraint, 154, 183–4n
contradictions, 73, 183n; solution structures and, 123
convergence, 40
Conway, J., 264
Cook, R., 16, 17, 34, 252
Cooley, C. H., 246
co-operation, 110–20
Coser, L. A., 12–13, 14, 16, 17, 47, 52, 86n, 172, 178, 187n, 275n; on conflict theory, 49–51
craze, 233
crises, 78–80; capitalist, 95, 97, 108
Crozier, M., 289, 304n, 306n
cultural change, 70; distinguished from social change, 17
cultural diffusion, 169, 175, 179
cultural lag, theory of, 44, 56, 69–73
cultural orientation systems, 141
cultural system, 185n
culture, 59–60, 84n
culture contact theory, 74–8
Curtis, R. F., 275n
cybernetic control, 168, 185n
cyclical change, 19–20, 136; *see also* rise and fall theories

Dahrendorf, R., 14, 24, 25, 33, 36, 47, 51, 52, 64, 85n, 87n, 135, 141, 142, 172, 178, 183n, 189n, 265, 305n; on conflict theory, 47–9
Darwin, C., 69, 70
Davies, J. C., 196, 220, 275n
Davis, K., 16, 19–20, 75, 80–1, 131, 142, 172, 174, 175, 247
Demerath, N. J., 131, 132
democracy: in Barrington Moore's theory, 199, 202, 205, 211–13, 215, 272n; institutionalization of, 42
demographic factors, 3, 179
deprivation, 50; *see also* relative deprivation
de Tocqueville, A., 220
development, 15
Devereux, E. C., 173, 181n
dialectic relations, 1, 22, 41; in conflict theory, 42
dialectic sociology, 25
differentiation, 24, 55–8, 64; equated with change, 156; evolution and, 158–63; in functionalist theory, 73–4, 81–2, 134, 154, 155, 157; in historic-materialist theory, 105; interdependence and, 57; level, 283–4; segmental, 185n, 187n, 277–8; stabilization and, 185; structural, 68, 177; of the working class, 38, 85
diffusion theory, 66, 74–8, 169
directionality, 18–19

disequilibrium, 180
division of labor: conflict and, 43–4, 46; in evolutionary change, 59, 153–4; in historic-materialist theory, 98; solidarity and, 184n, 278
Dobb, M., 95, 127n
domination and dominance, 38, 41, 49, 50, 64; conflict theory and, 41, 49, 50, 53; roles, 48
Dreitzel, H. P., 23, 50, 57, 60, 66, 154, 155
Duncan, O. D., 70
Dunette, M. D., 293
Durkheim, E., 15, 21, 36, 54–8 *passim*, 83, 130, 150, 173, 175, 183–4n, 277–8, 281, 303n; evolutionary theory and, 153–6, 159; modernization theory and, 68
dynamic analysis, 138–42, 172
dysfunctionality, 84, 137–8, 150–1, 182n, 184n

economic factors, 3, 72, 84n, 270–1
economic growth, 108
economic necessity, 100–4
economic society formations, 96
'educated society', 2
efficiency, 284
Eisenstadt, S. N., 54, 58, 68, 87n, 141, 169, 171, 175, 182n, 282, 303n
Eitzen, S. D., 257
Elias, N., 4, 60, 87, 149, 151
elites, 30; circulation of, theory, 62–3; formation of, 68–9; lack of, 85n; status of, 264–6
Ellul, J., 2
embourgeoisement, 39, 40
Emery, F. E., 296, 297, 304n
empirical data, 24
empirical levels, 31–2
endogenous change, 33, 40–73, 168, 170, 175
energy transformations, 66
Engelberg, E., 102, 104, 128
Engels, F., 43, 47, 91–6 *passim*, 127n, 220
England, 201–20 *passim*; Civil War, 202–3, 210
environment, 21, 164; control over, 136; history and, 125–6; organizations and, 296–7, 304n; system and, 168
epoch, 55; Marxist theory of, 56; movement from one to another, 15
equilibrium, 132, 134, 137, 141, 150; changing, 163–72; moving, 141, 167, 169–70, 173, 177; old to new, 179; stable, 167
equilibrium theories, 13, 26, 73–4, 80–4, 152–74, 267, 268; critique of, 174–81; view of what is not change, 14; view of small scale change, 16; *see also* functionalist theory
equivalence functionalism, 137
Erikson, K. T., 78
ethnic minorities, 261, 274n
ethnomethodology, 86n
events, 78–80
evolution, 15, 126, 146; biological, 69–70; specific and general, 65

333

INDEX

evolutionary theories, 13, 26, 153–8; functionalist critique of, 156–7
evolutionary universal, 182n
exchange, 70; generalized, 148; mutual, 147
exogenous change, 33, 73–84, 168, 175, 179–80
expectations, 145, 170–1, 251–2; conflicting, 259–60; institutionally induced, 258; of others, 262; rising, 220
'expert society', 2
exploitation, 39
external influences *see* exogenous change

Fallers, L. A., 43
family structure, 11–12
fascism, 199, 203–13 *passim*, 272n; revolution and, 210–11
fear, 232
Feldmann, G. A., 95
feudalism, 15, 56, 201; transition from, to capitalism, 46, 100–1
Feustel, R., 100
Flora, P., 67
forces of production, 43–4, 47
Ford, J., 252
formalization, 289
formative laws, 100–4
Fourastié, J., 2
France, 201–20 *passim*
Freiburghaus, D., 127n
French Revolution, 179, 234–5
Freud, S., 21
Fuchs, V., 2
function: concepts of, 140; defined, 136–7
functional alternatives, 146, 180
functional equivalence, 145, 173
functional imperativism, 137
functional requisites, 64, 139, 157, 166, 172
functionalist theory, 130–91; conflict theory and, 51; conservative bias of, 174; dynamic analysis, 138–42; historical, 187n; organismic model, 133–8; processnal, 187–8n; subjective, 187n; systems analysis, 142–7; types of change explained by, 175–6; *see also* equilibrium theories
functionality, 182n
'future shock', 3, 18
futurology, 28

Gabriel, K., 7
Galtung, J., 182n, 249
Gartner, A., 2
Gasset, J. O. y, 40, 85n
Gehlen, A., 285, 303n
Gemeinschaft, 57
generalized belief, 223, 230–1
genetic-diachronic dimension, 23, 25, 175
genetic-structural laws, 126
geographical theories, 21, 78, 101
Germany, 204–20 *passim*; Nazi revolution, 213–18

Gerschenkron, A., 68
Gesellschaft, 57
Gandhi, M., 64
Giddens, A., 45, 46, 85n
Gillin, J. L., 273n
Gillmann, J. M., 127n
Ginsberg, M., 13, 28, 29–30, 34n
Gluckman, M., 52, 157, 190n
goal orientation, 21, 29, 117, 188–9n; of organizations, 286, 287, 297
goal state, 166–7
Godelier, M., 46, 96, 127n
Goffman, E., 250, 254, 255
Gorz, A., 38, 46
Gould, J., 27
Gouldner, A., 47, 131, 143–52 *passim*, 165, 172, 175, 181n–3n, 190n, 290
'great man', role of, 30–1
Greiner, L. E., 298
grievances, expression of, 236–7
Griese, A., 127n
Grossmann, H., 107, 127n
group mind, 29–30
groups, 21, 22, 29–30, 268, 271–2; individuals and, 29; social conditions and, 195; *see also* collective behavior theory
Grunow, D., 281
Grupp, F. W., 257
Gündel, R., 95
Guessous, M., 81, 174, 179, 180, 188n
Guhr, G., 105, 127n
Gumplowicz, L., 47
Gurr, R. T., 219, 220, 275n

Habermas, J., 37–46 *passim*, 84n, 284–5, 302, 303–4n
Hage, J., 288–91, 294–301 *passim*, 304n, 305n
Hahn, E., 38, 129n
Hall, R. H., 304n
Hammond, P. E., 249–50, 263
Hartman, M., 247
Hegel, G. W. F., 2, 284
Hegner, F., 281
Heiden, K. A., 241
Heider, F., 139
Hempel, C. G., 137, 188n
Herzberg, F., 303
Hickson, D. J., 304n
Hilferding, R., 95
Hindenburg, O. von, 214
Hindess, B., 127n
Hirsch, J., 38, 128n
Hirst, P. Q., 127n
historic materialism, 38, 84n, 91–126; approach of, 94–6; conflict theory and, 42; critique of, 125–6; defined, 91; developmental characteristics of, 93; human societalization, 96–106
historical chance, 100
historicism, 25

INDEX

history, 23; desire for an interpretation of, 3–4; environment and, 125–6; social-psychological view of, 29–30
Hitler, A., 64, 236, 240–2, 244–5, 255, 272
Hobsbawm, E. J., 102
Hoffmann, E., 127n
Hofstadter, R., 260–2, 263, 270
Homans, G. C., 21–2, 135, 174, 188n
homeostatic-synchronic dimension, 23, 25
Horney, K., 21, 29
Hoselitz, B. F., 77
hostility, 231, 233
Hull, L., 21
Hyman, D., 252
hysteria, 230–1

idealistic system, 61
ideational system, 61
ideology, 82; conflict and, 124
immanence, 156, 157
imperialism, 114, 122
impression management, 250
India, 272
individualism, 133
individualization, 80, 153–4; of conflict, 178
individuals, 21, 195, 268, 271–2; social environment and, 30
Industrial Revolution, 1, 100
industrial society, 5, 36–40; Marxist view of, 37, 38–9
industrialization, 15, 60, 67, 68, 158, 210; in historic-materialist theory, 109
inequality, 147–8, 263–4; functionalist view of, 172; maintenance of, 263; structured, 247
Inkeles, A., 25, 133
innovation, 67–8, 80, 162; in organizations, 291, 299; transfer, 84n
input-output-exchanges, 164–5
institutionalization: of value-oriented movements, 242; organizations and, 282; role of, 170–1
institutions, 1; change in, 137; democratic, 83; system survival and, 83; *see also* organizations
integration, 132, 150, 173, 178, 297; functional autonomy and, 147–51; mechanisms of, 68, 146–7, 173; moral aspects of, 146, 180; societal, 66
intelligentsia, 112
interaction: conflict as, 120; systems, 283
interest politics, 260–1
interdependence, 22, 132, 141–50 *passim*, 158, 165, 174
interest situations, 1
interest groups and interests: conflict between, 48; formation of, 52; pluralization of, 48, 51; status quo and, 50; vested, 170–2
internalization, 183n
international relations, 117, 122, 124
intersystem relations, 116–25

invention, 70–1
Isajiw, W. W., 132, 133, 183n
isomorphism, 132

Jackson, E. F., 254, 255, 258, 275n
Jackson, J. A., 290
Jaffe, A. J., 69
Japan, 201–20 *passim*
John XXIII, Pope, 64
Johnson, H. M., 13
Jones, L. F., 247

Kahn, R. L., 286, 290, 294, 306n
Kairat, H., 290
Katz, D., 286, 294, 306n
Kennedy, J. F., 64
Kerr, C., 68
Kievenheim, C., 112
Killian, L., 75, 78, 79, 85n
Kimberly, J. C., 247
kinship, 126
King, M. L., 64
Kiss, G., 40, 63
Klages, H., 2
knowledge, 71; transmission of, 42
Kolb, W. L., 27
Kroeber, A. L., 64
Krysmanski, H. J., 5, 94, 116, 128n
Kushner, G., 77
Kutsch, T., 25, 27, 28, 74

labor, social organization of, 96
labor power, 106, 110, 115
land ownership, 102
Lange, O., 95
language, 184–5n
LaPiere, R., 174
large scale change, 16, 168–9
late capitalism, 37–8, 95
Lauer, R. H., 34–5, 177
law of movement, 106–10
leadership, 145, 241; *see also* charisma
learning, 42–3
Leavitt, H., 306n
Le Bon, G., 40, 195
Lefèbvre, H., 45
legal system, 83
legitimation and legitimacy, 83; change and, 302; in functionalist theory, 144, 146, 179; of inequality, 50; Marxist view of, 38–9; status inconsistency and, 258; of value-oriented movements, 242
Leisewitz, A., 112
Lenin, W. J., 64, 95, 127n
Lenk, K., 219
Lenski, G., 147, 191n, 249, 255, 260
Levin, G., 219
Levy, M., 33, 67, 139, 153, 156, 166, 178
Lewis, O., 137
liberation movements, 95, 115

335

INDEX

life chances, 49
Lijphart, A., 263
linear change, 19–20
Lipp, W., 304n, 305n
Lipset, S. M., 14, 36, 51, 172, 260–2, 273, 274n
Litwak, E., 292, 295, 296, 304n
Lockwood, D., 36, 47, 52, 135, 146, 178, 183n, 190–1n
long-term change, 5
Löwith, K., 63
Lowenthal, D., 215
Luckmann, T., 246
Luhmann, N., 56, 137, 144–6, 151, 152, 161–3, 164, 174, 176, 177, 185n, 187n, 188n, 227, 276; theory of organization, 283–4, 287–8, 289, 291, 293, 296, 299, 302, 304n
Lupri, E., 256–7
Luxemburg, R., 95

McClelland, D., 30, 35n
McEwen, W. J., 299, 305n
McLuhan, M., 18
macrofunctionalism, 143
macrosociological strategy, 25, 86, 199–220
Maine, H., 56–7
Malewski, A., 249, 254, 255
Malinowski, B., 75, 80, 136–7, 147, 166, 173
Man, H. de, 40
management, organic and mechanical systems of, 295, 304n
managerial positions, 112
Mandel, E., 95, 127n, 129
Mann, F. C., 298
Mao, 64
March, J. G., 252, 304n
market, 83
Martindale, D., 4, 131, 143
Marwedel, P., 146
Marx, K., 2, 14, 21, 41–3, 46–50, 55, 63, 72, 73, 91–5, 97, 99, 100, 102, 108–10, 114, 115, 127n, 128n, 129n, 211, 220, 277, 279–81; on change within systems, 13; compared with Ogburn, 72–3; concept of epochs, 56; concept of power, 14; functionalist theory and, 150, 151, 155, 156
Marxist theory, 130–1; of conflict, 41–7; of organizations, 279–81; *see also* historic-materialism
Maslow, A., 303
mass society, 40
Mattick, P., 127n
mature society, 85n
Mayntz, R., 276, 278, 295, 296, 303n
Mead, G. H., 21, 22
Mead, M., 77
meaning, 22
means of production: expansion of, 121; new, 44; reproduction of, 98
Mender, J. H., 108, 127
Merrill, R. S., 77

Merton, R., 29, 83–4, 137–58 *passim*, 169, 171, 174, 175, 178, 181n, 184n, 189n, 250; on bureaucracy, 289, 290, 303n
method and methodology, 181n
Meyer, J. W., 249–50, 263
microfunctionalism, 143
microsociological strategy, 24–5
Midlarsky, M., 220
Miewald, R. D., 305n
militarism, 218
Mills, C. W., 47, 172
Mills, D. L., 290
Mitchell, G. D., 56, 62
'mobile society', 2
mobilization, 223, 232, 240–2, 244; of motivation, 225, 229, 230, 272–3n
mode of production, 97, 101; capitalist, 113–16; class antagonistic, 102, 103; pre-socialist, 104–6; primitive, 103; revolutionizing, 103; socialist, 103; super-structures and, 113; types of, 102
models, 132–3
modernization, 15, 40, 269; Barrington Moore's theory of, 199, 206, 208–11, 219; fascist, 217–18; social structure prior to, 201–2; theories, 67–9, 158
money system, 83
monopoly, 114
Moore, B. *Social Origins of Dictatorship and Democracy*, 6, 7, 196–8, 199–220, 234–5, 264, 267–72; his thesis, 199–201
Moore, W. E., 12, 16, 17, 19, 34n, 67, 83–4, 86n, 138, 157–78 *passim*, 247; on cultural contact, 76
moral beliefs, 175
moral density, 153
moral requirements, 57
Morgan, L. H., 155
Moszkowska, N., 127n
motivation, 269–70; mobilization of, 225, 229
motivational structures, 170–1
movement, 15
movements: norm-oriented, 233; value-oriented, 233–4, 237, 241–4
Müller, H. P., 127n
Müller, W., 38
Mullins, N. C., 33n
multilinear evolution theory, 65–7
multilinearity, 104
Münch, R., 82, 152, 182n
Myrdal, G., 174, 220

Nadel, S. F., 187n
Nagel, E., 133, 134, 138, 152, 183, 187n
nationalism, 220
natural disasters, 78
natural sciences, 125; models, 133
Nazi revolution, 272; Barrington Moore's theory of, 213–18; collective behavior theory and, 234–43; status inconsistency

INDEX

theory and, 264–6
Neff, F. W., 298
neo-evolutionary theory, 65–73; organizations in, 281–6
Neusüss, C., 38
Newcomb, E. R., 290, 314
Newton, J., 24
Nisbet, R. A., 11–12, 13, 31, 34n, 37, 55, 65, 86n, 141, 156, 157, 159, 275n; theory of crisis, 79–80
normative codes, 160
normative functionalism, 183n
normative specification, 163–4
norms, 12, 148; conflict and, 41, 171; defined by authority, 48–9; in functionalist theory, 144, 165; in social action, 225; strain and, 229, 233–4, 239; values and, 236

occupational decentralization, 155
occupational structure, 3
O'Connor, J., 84n
OECD, 3
Offe, C., 37, 38, 45, 46, 264
Ogburn, W. F., 44, 56, 69–73, 87n
Ohlin, L., 258
opportunity, 119
order, 132, 133, 153, 154
orderly persistence, 2
organizational change: evaluation of, 298n–9, 301; finance of, 299; implementation of, 300–1; initiation of, 299; routinization of, 301
organizational development, 277–86
organizations, 197–8, 276–307; change in, 286–97; change as process in, 297–301; environment and, 296–7; formal, 284; Marx's theory of, 279–81; membership of, 287; personnel, 292–4, 299; program changes in, 288–91; program types, 291–2, 293, 304n; rule changes in, 291–2; social action and, 224; static and dynamic, 294–7
organismic model, 133–8, 152

Packard, V., 2
panic behavior, 231–4
Pareto, V., 15, 62, 63, 81, 130
Parkin, F., 45
Parsons, T., 12, 21, 25, 36, 37, 56, 69, 132, 137, 166–7, 173–91 *passim*, 235, 272n, 286, 297, 299; AGIL scheme, 73, 185–8n, 225, 272n; analysis of Nazi Germany, 189n; concept of process, 182n; on differentiation, 163–72; functionalist theory, 81, 82, 139–42, 141–59 *passim*; neo-evolutionary theory, 159–63, 177; view of bureaucracy, 282–3
participation and, 302–3
pattern maintenance, 297
pauperization, 39, 45
Pavlov, J. P., 21
peaceful change, 20

peasantry, 199, 200, 205–7, 212, 234; aristocracy and, 206; in Nazi Germany, 215–17; revolution and, 211
Pelinka, A., 274n
Pelz, D. C., 291
personality *see* individuals
Peterson, R. A., 131, 132
petty bourgeoisie, 112
phase-movement, 177
phenomenological perspective, 22
Phillips, B. S., 21
Pigou, A. C., 179
Plessner, H., 41
pluralistic society, 52
political factors, 3
politicization, 80
post-industrial society, 3, 37
positivistic organization, 85n
Poulantzas, N., 38, 45
power, 64; balance of, 211; different concepts of, 14; differentials, 148; distribution of, 53; in functionalist theory, 144; mobilization of, 149; pluralization of, 48
power relations, 14
Powicke, F., 4
pre-capitalist societies, 95
precipitating factors, 223, 240
prediction, 4, 28
Presthus, R., 276
primitive societies, 283
problem solving, 69, 141–2; activities, 117–20; capitalist, 113, 121–3; institutionalized, 118–19; potential, 101, 103; results of, 117; socialist, 121–3; strategy, 116; structures, 120–3
process, 15, 26–33, 182n; defined, 27
productivity, 107–8, 110, 115
professionalization, 290–1, 294, 295, 300
progress, 15, 151–2, 153
proletarianization, 40
proletariat: Barrington Moore's view of, 220; in conflict theory, 42; embourgeoisement of, 39, 45
property, 15
Prussia, 201–20 *passim*
psychological factors, 179, 195
psychological perspective, 21, 28–9
Pugh, D. S., 304n
purposively rational action, 285–6

Radcliffe-Brown, A. R., 80, 130, 133–5, 136–7, 138, 140, 156–7, 173
radical change, 180
radical sociology, 84n
Randall, S. C., 147, 250, 252, 263, 274n
Rapoport, A., 123
rate of change, 18
rate of profit, 109–10, 115–16
rationalization, 64, 279, 303
Ratzenhofer, G., 47

337

INDEX

Rawls, J., 49
reciprocity, 147, 180
recruitment requirements, 247, 283–4
Redfield, R., 137
reference points, 173
Reich, C. A., 273n
reification, 135
reintegration, 83
relative deprivation, 220, 251, 253, 257
religion, 220
reproduction: capitalist, 95, 97, 127n; production and, 118–19
'restless society', 2
revolution, 15; in Barrington Moore's theory, 200, 209–11, 213; in elite theory, 63; in industrial society theory, 39
rewards, allocation of, 252
Rex, J., 47, 87n, 135, 138, 142, 178, 183n
Richta, R., 84n
Ridder, P., 77, 165, 173, 187n
Riessman, F., 2
'rise and fall' theories, 15, 26, 59–64
Ritsert, J., 127
Ritzer, G., 23–4
Rödel, V., 84n
Rogers, E. M., 35n
Rohter, I., 257
Rokeach, M., 290
role adaptation, 250–1
role strain, 183n
roles, 12; organizational, 287; in social action, 224; specification of, 278
Rolshausen, C., 127n
Rosdolsky, R., 127n
Ross, D., 291
Rostow, W. W., 220
Rothman, J., 77
Rothman, S., 214
routinization, 80, 242
Runciman, W. G., 220
Rush, G., 249, 256, 273n
Russia, 201, 205
Russian Revolution (1917), 95

Sahlins, M. D., 65, 66
Saint-Simon, H. de, 36, 151, 252, 303n, 304n
Sampson, E., 249, 250
scarce resources, allocation of, 41; conflict over, 153, 154
Schein, E. H., 293
Schelsky, H., 3, 37–8
Schieder, T., 219
Schienstock, G., 297, 298
Schluchter, W., 303n
Schmiede, R., 108
Schmidt, A., 127n
Schneider, L., 86, 159
Schoenbaum, D., 266, 275n
Schon, D. A., 3
Schumpeter, J. A., 80, 179, 220

Schweitzer, D., 260
Scott, W. R., 293, 294, 295, 304n
secularization, 15, 80
segmentation, 163–4, 185n
self-image, 253
self-interest, 273
self-regulation, 138, 140–1, 285
Sellnow, I., 96, 98, 129n
Selznick, P., 305n
Semjonow, J. I., 104
sensate system, 6, 62
Service, E. R., 65–7
'service society', 2
Shapiro, J. J., 43
Shepard, H. A., 298
Shils, E., 68, 69, 141, 147–51, 183n, 220
short term change, 5
Silverman, D., 262, 286
Simmel, Georg, 21, 22
Simon, H. A., 252
situational facilities, 225
Skinner, B. F., 21
Slater, P. E., 2
slavery, 56
Slomczynski, K., 247
small scale change, 16–17, 168–9; defined, 17; stability and, 2
Smelser, N. J., 7, 54, 55, 60, 70, 136, 139, 158, 166–9, 184n, 188n; *Theory of Collective Behavior*, 196–8, 220–45, 265, 267–72
Smith, A. D., 55, 130, 141, 142, 152–65 *passim*, 171, 180, 181n, 182n, 190n, 235, 245
social action, 224–45, 267, 286; components of, 224–8; instrumental and symbolic, 284
social behaviorism, 133
social change: absence of, 11–12; by adjustment, 134; bourgeois theory of, 94; compatible, 176; conditions for, to occur, 82; deduced from properties of systems, 141; defining, 11–16; describing, 16–20; direction of, 39–40, 156; distinguished from cultural change, 16; distinguished from societal change, 137; explanation of, 4; factors of, 27–8; gradual, 156; historical materialism's view of, 93–4; inevitability of, 59; inherent, 141–2; initial occurrence of, 188; levels of, 20–3; means for enacting, 270; motivation sources of, 169; oscillatory, 176; possibility of understanding, 25; range of, 168–9; as a response to external stimuli, 21; significance of amounts of, 13; structural and substructural, 168, 173, 178–9, 185–7n; types of, 2, 5
social character, 182n
social class, 118; *see also* class
social control, 165; collective behavior and, 223, 232, 242–3
Social Darwinism, 21, 47, 124
social development, 97–100

social evaluation, 246–7, 249; changing system of, 256; criteria of, 251, 254, 256
social factors, 3
social gross product, 98
social history, 105
social interaction, 12, 21–2
social maladjustment, 71–2
social mobility, 85n, 246, 273n; opportunity for, 264
social praxis, 92–3, 117, 120
social problems *see* problem-solving
social-psychological perspective, 21, 29–30
social ranking, 252
social reality, 1; cognitive image of, 24; empirical data for, 24; reshaping, 262
social relations, mobility of, 278
social scientists and sciences: interests of, 23–6; natural sciences and, 125; ruling class perspective and, 124
social structure: recognition of, 135; stabilization of, 118–19
social system: flexibility of, 53; organic systems and, 135; organizational, 282; perpetuation of, 134
social withdrawal, 255, 256, 262
socialism, 15, 56, 95, 115, 121–3; relations with capitalism, 125; transition to, 46
socialization, 42, 165, 183n
societal change: distinguished from social, 137
societal development, 25
societal organization, 25
societal persistence, 166
societal systems, 283
societalization, 96–106; conflict and, 124–5; global, 99–104; intersystem, 123; social developments and, 97–100; trans-system, 119–20
society: growth of, 58; nature of, 23–6; nineteenth-century concepts of, 151
sociological perspectives, 21
sociological theory, 23–6; paradigmatic types of, 24; stability and change in, 4
sociology, 181n, 303n; multiparadigmatic nature of, 23–4
Sofri, G., 127n
solidarity, 155; conservative, 206, 215; division of labour and, 184; maintaining, 167; mechanical organic, 15, 57, 277–8; radical, 207, 211
Solloway, O., 146
solution structures *see* problem solving
Sorokin, P. A., 60–2, 85n
specialization *see* differentiation
Spencer, H., 36, 40, 54, 58–9, 66, 130, 151–9 *passim*
Spengler, O., 40, 54, 56, 60, 64, 130
Spicer, E., 77, 137, 179
Spiegel-Rösing, I. S., 84n
Sprehe, T., 181n
stability: belief in, 3; change necessary for, 176–7; conflict leading to, 53; of organizations, 287; persistence of, 155; small-scale change and, 2; social theories and, 23; value-oriented beliefs and, 235
stabilization, 164, 173, 175, 185n
stages *see* epoch
Stalin, J., 100
Stalker, G. M., 291–305 *passim*
Starr, J. M., 170
state, theory of, 38
state intervention, 113, 116, 121
state monopolistic capitalism, 38, 45, 95
state ownership, 111
status, 12, 245–6; allocation, 83; anxiety, 261; aspiration, 251; attributes, supply of, 263; configuration, 273; equilibration, 247–53; overevaluation, 257; visibility, 252
status attainment: achieved and ascribed, 248, 255–8, 265; barriers to, 258
status discrepancy, 183n
status inconsistency, 197, 245–66; changing, 253–60; congruence and, 253, 265; frustration and, 254–5, 256; meaning of, 253; in Nazi Germany, 264–6; response to, 249–50, 258–60
status politics, 260–4
Steiner, G. A., 77
Stelle, 304n
Steward, J., 65
stimulus-response theories, 21
Stinchcombe, A. R., 37, 139, 292, 293
Stolting, E., 127n
Stone, L., 219
strain, 83, 149, 150–1, 169–70, 173, 271; alternative views of, 38–9; cause of, 188n; defined, 170, 228; failure to contain, 171; norms and, 239; organization and, 238–9; structural, 222, 228–30, 238–9, 244; values and, 239; *see also* conflict
Strasser, H., 6, 19, 24, 33, 36, 45, 50, 131, 146, 151, 153, 174, 179, 250, 252, 263, 274, 303n
strategy, revolutionary, 241–2
stratification: functionalist view of, 172, 247
stress, 268, 270
structural antagonism, 43–4
structural categories, 140
structural conduciveness, 222
structural-functional theory *see* functionalist theory
structural-genetic laws, 103
Sumner, W. G., 2, 58, 59
superstructure, cultural, 126
surplus product, 98; appropriation of, 102–3
surplus value, 45, 106–7, 108, 110, 114–15
survival, 119, 139, 146
Swanson, G., 16, 27, 35n
Sweezy, P. M., 95, 109, 129n
symbolic interactionism, 22, 133
syndicalism, 38
system analysis, 142–7

339

INDEX

system theory, functionalist, 122
Sztompka, P., 131, 135, 136, 144, 166, 168, 169, 175, 181
tactics, revolutionary, 241–2
Tanter, R., 220
task structure, 292
Taylor, F. M., 95
technocrats, 38
technological change, 72, 84; in historic-materialist theory, 108; in primitive communities, 137; levels of, 110–11; transition to capitalism and, 46
'technological society', 2
technology transfer, 75
temporarity, 177
temporary society', 2
tension, 29, 64, 149, 159; racial, 183n
tension-management, 84, 169, 188–9n, 297
Terryberry, S., 297, 304n
Third World countries, 51, 75
Thomas, W. I., 31
Thompson, J. D., 299
Thompson, V. A., 305n
Thrall, C. A., 170
Timasheff, N. S., 62
time span, 17–18, 33n
Tjaden, K. H., 6, 94, 112, 114, 117, 118, 127n, 128n
Tjaden-Steinhauer, M., 112, 114, 127n, 128n
Toch, Hans, 30
Tocqueville, A. de, 220
Tönnies, F., 56–7, 58, 130
Toffler, A., 2, 3, 18, 20, 34n, 293, 301–2, 305–6n
Tomberg, F., 129n
Töpfer, B., 102
Touraine, A., 2, 37–8, 137, 141, 165, 174
Toynbee, A., 64
traditional society, 36–7
transformation, 15
transition, 15
Trist, H. L., 296, 297, 304n
Trotter, W., 195
Tumin, M., 247, 264
Turner, R., 75, 78–9
Tylor, B., 155

underdevelopment, 47
unilinearity, 104, 158

United States, 201–20 *passim*; Civil War, 210
upper classes, 199; modernization and, 206
urbanization, 15, 60

value preferences, 1
value system, 246
values: conflict over, 178; consensus on, 150, 165, 180; cultural, 202; fundamental to change, 235; institutionalized, 169; moral, 181n; norms and, 236; regeneration of, 234; shared, 182; social action and, 224–5, 226–7; strain on, 229, 239, 244–5
Varga, E., 127n
Veblen, T., 36
violence, institutional, 20
violent change, 20
Vollmer, H. M., 290

Waldmann, P., 173
Wallace, W. L., 23, 24
Wallerstein, I., 130
war, 52, 152
Weber, A., 64
Weber, M., 14, 28, 30, 43, 49, 58, 80, 130, 182n, 261; concept of bureaucracy, 278–9, 281, 282–3, 294–5, 297, 303n; theory of social change, 63–4
welfare, indicators of, 28
Wesolowski, W., 247
Western civilization, 162–3, 182n
white collar workers, 45, 85n
Wiener, J., 215, 219, 274n
Wilensky, H. L., 290, 293
Wirth, M., 38
wish-fulfillment, 231, 233
Wiswede, G., 25, 27, 28, 74
Wittfogel, K., 78
working classes, 115, 151
Wright, E. O., 38, 172
writing, 184n
Wygodski, S. L., 109, 127n

Young, F. and R., 137

Zagalow, N. N., 95
Zapf, W., 27, 49
Zelený, J., 103, 127n
Zimmerman, C. C., 2
Zimmermann, E., 249

Routledge Social Science Series

Routledge & Kegan Paul   London, Henley and Boston

39 Store Street,
London WC1E 7DD
Broadway House,
Newtown Road,
Henley-on-Thames,
Oxon RG9 1EN
9 Park Street,
Boston, Mass. 02108

Contents

International Library of Sociology 2
General Sociology 2
Foreign Classics of Sociology 2
Social Structure 3
Sociology and Politics 3
Criminology 4
Social Psychology 4
Sociology of the Family 5
Social Services 5
Sociology of Education 5
Sociology of Culture 6
Sociology of Religion 6
Sociology of Art and Literature 6
Sociology of Knowledge 6
Urban Sociology 7
Rural Sociology 7
Sociology of Industry and Distribution 7
Anthropology 8
Sociology and Philosophy 8
International Library of Anthropology 9
International Library of Phenomenology and Moral Sciences 9
International Library of Social Policy 9
International Library of Welfare and Philosophy 10
Library of Social Work 10
Primary Socialization, Language and Education 12
Reports of the Institute of Community Studies 12
Reports of the Institute for Social Studies in Medical Care 13
Medicine, Illness and Society 13
Monographs in Social Theory 13
Routledge Social Science Journals 13
Social and Psychological Aspects of Medical Practice 14

*Authors wishing to submit manuscripts for any series
in this catalogue should send them to the Social Science Editor,
Routledge & Kegan Paul Ltd, 39 Store Street,
London WC1E 7DD.*
● *Books so marked are available in paperback.*
○ *Books so marked are available in paperback only.*
*All books are in metric Demy 8vo format (216 × 138mm approx.)
unless otherwise stated.*

International Library of Sociology
General Editor John Rex

GENERAL SOCIOLOGY

Barnsley, J. H. The Social Reality of Ethics. *464 pp.*
Brown, Robert. Explanation in Social Science. *208 pp.*
● Rules and Laws in Sociology. *192 pp.*
Bruford, W. H. Chekhov and His Russia. *A Sociological Study. 244 pp.*
Burton, F. and Carlen, P. Official Discourse. *On Discourse Analysis, Government Publications, Ideology. About 140 pp.*
Cain, Maureen E. Society and the Policeman's Role. *326 pp.*
● Fletcher, Colin. Beneath the Surface. *An Account of Three Styles of Sociological Research. 221 pp.*
Gibson, Quentin. The Logic of Social Enquiry. *240 pp.*
Glassner, B. Essential Interactionism. *208 pp.*
Glucksmann, M. Structuralist Analysis in Contemporary Social Thought. *212 pp.*
Gurvitch, Georges. Sociology of Law. *Foreword by Roscoe Pound. 264 pp.*
Hinkle, R. Founding Theory of American Sociology 1881–1913. *About 350 pp.*
Homans, George C. Sentiments and Activities. *336 pp.*
Johnson, Harry M. Sociology: *A Systematic Introduction. Foreword by Robert K. Merton. 710 pp.*
● Keat, Russell and Urry, John. Social Theory as Science. *278 pp.*
Mannheim, Karl. Essays on Sociology and Social Psychology. *Edited by Paul Kecskemeti. With Editorial Note by Adolph Lowe. 344 pp.*
Martindale, Don. The Nature and Types of Sociological Theory. *292 pp.*
● Maus, Heinz. A Short History of Sociology. *234 pp.*
Myrdal, Gunnar. Value in Social Theory: *A Collection of Essays on Methodology. Edited by Paul Streeten. 332 pp.*
Ogburn, William F. and Nimkoff, Meyer F. A Handbook of Sociology. *Preface by Karl Mannheim. 656 pp. 46 figures. 35 tables.*
Parsons, Talcott and Smelser, Neil J. Economy and Society: *A Study in the Integration of Economic and Social Theory. 362 pp.*
Payne, G., Dingwall, R., Payne, J. and Carter, M. Sociology and Social Research. *About 250 pp.*
Podgórecki, A. Practical Social Sciences. *About 200 pp.*
Podgórecki, A. and Łos, M. Multidimensional Sociology. *268 pp.*
Raffel, S. Matters of Fact. *A Sociological Inquiry. 152 pp.*
● Rex, John. Key Problems of Sociological Theory. *220 pp.*
  Sociology and the Demystification of the Modern World. *282 pp.*
● Rex, John. (Ed.) Approaches to Sociology. *Contributions by Peter Abell, Frank Bechhofer, Basil Bernstein, Ronald Fletcher, David Frisby, Miriam Glucksmann, Peter Lassman, Herminio Martins, John Rex, Roland Robertson, John Westergaard and Jock Young. 302 pp.*
Rigby, A. Alternative Realities. *352 pp.*
Roche, M. Phenomenology, Language and the Social Sciences. *374 pp.*
Sahay, A. Sociological Analysis. *220 pp.*
Strasser, Hermann. The Normative Structure of Sociology. *Conservative and Emancipatory Themes in Social Thought. About 340 pp.*
Strong, P. Ceremonial Order of the Clinic. *267 pp.*
Urry, John. Reference Groups and the Theory of Revolution. *244 pp.*
Weinberg, E. Development of Sociology in the Soviet Union. *173 pp.*

FOREIGN CLASSICS OF SOCIOLOGY

● Gerth, H. H. and Mills, C. Wright. From Max Weber: *Essays in Sociology. 502 pp.*

● **Tönnies, Ferdinand.** Community and Association *(Gemeinschaft und Gesellschaft).* |*Translated and Supplemented by Charles P. Loomis. Foreword by Pitirim A. Sorokin. 334 pp.*

SOCIAL STRUCTURE

Andreski, Stanislav. Military Organization and Society. *Foreword by Professor A. R. Radcliffe-Brown. 226 pp. 1 folder.*
Broom, L., Lancaster Jones, F., McDonnell, P. and **Williams, T.** The Inheritance of Inequality. *About 180 pp.*
Carlton, Eric. Ideology and Social Order. *Foreword by Professor Philip Abrahams. About 320 pp.*
Clegg, S. and **Dunkerley, D.** Organization, Class and Control. *614 pp.*
Coontz, Sydney H. Population Theories and the Economic Interpretation. *202 pp.*
Coser, Lewis. The Functions of Social Conflict. *204 pp.*
Crook, I. and **D.** The First Years of the Yangyi Commune. *304 pp., illustrated.*
Dickie-Clark, H. F. Marginal Situation: *A Sociological Study of a Coloured Group. 240 pp. 11 tables.*
Giner, S. and **Archer, M. S.** (Eds) Contemporary Europe: *Social Structures and Cultural Patterns, 336 pp.*
● **Glaser, Barney** and **Strauss, Anselm L.** Status Passage: *A Formal Theory. 212 pp.*
Glass, D. V. (Ed.) Social Mobility in Britain. *Contributions by J. Berent, T. Bottomore, R. C. Chambers, J. Floud, D. V. Glass, J. R. Hall, H. T. Himmelweit, R. K. Kelsall, F. M. Martin, C. A. Moser, R. Mukherjee and W. Ziegel. 420 pp.*
Kelsall, R. K. Higher Civil Servants in Britain: *From 1870 to the Present Day. 268 pp. 31 tables.*
● **Lawton, Denis.** Social Class, Language and Education. *192 pp.*
McLeish, John. The Theory of Social Change: *Four Views Considered. 128 pp.*
● **Marsh, David C.** The Changing Social Structure of England and Wales, 1871–1961. *Revised edition. 288 pp.*
Menzies, Ken. Talcott Parsons and the Social Image of Man. *About 208 pp.*
● **Mouzelis, Nicos.** Organization and Bureaucracy. *An Analysis of Modern Theories. 240 pp.*
● **Ossowski, Stanislaw.** Class Structure in the Social Consciousness. *210 pp.*
● **Podgórecki, Adam.** Law and Society. *302 pp.*
Renner, Karl. Institutions of Private Law and Their Social Functions. *Edited, with an Introduction and Notes, by O. Kahn-Freud. Translated by Agnes Schwarzschild. 316 pp.*
Rex, J. and **Tomlinson, S.** Colonial Immigrants in a British City. *A Class Analysis. 368 pp.*
Smooha, S. Israel: Pluralism and Conflict. *472 pp.*
Wesolowski, W. Class, Strata and Power. *Trans. and with Introduction by G. Kolankiewicz. 160 pp.*
Zureik, E. Palestinians in Israel. *A Study in Internal Colonialism. 264 pp.*

SOCIOLOGY AND POLITICS

Acton, T. A. Gypsy Politics and Social Change. *316 pp.*
Burton, F. Politics of Legitimacy. *Struggles in a Belfast Community. 250 pp.*
Crook, I. and **D.** Revolution in a Chinese Village. *Ten Mile Inn. 216 pp., illustrated.*
Etzioni-Halevy, E. Political Manipulation and Administrative Power. *A Comparative Study. About 200 pp.*
Fielding, N. The National Front. *About 250 pp.*
● **Hechter, Michael.** Internal Colonialism. *The Celtic Fringe in British National Development, 1536–1966. 380 pp.*
Kornhauser, William. The Politics of Mass Society. *272 pp. 20 tables.*

Korpi, W. The Working Class in Welfare Capitalism. *Work, Unions and Politics in Sweden.* 472 pp.
Kroes, R. Soldiers and Students. *A Study of Right- and Left-wing Students.* 174 pp.
Martin, Roderick. Sociology of Power. *About 272 pp.*
Merquior, J. G. Rousseau and Weber. *A Study in the Theory of Legitimacy. About 288 pp.*
Myrdal, Gunnar. The Political Element in the Development of Economic Theory. *Translated from the German by Paul Streeten.* 282 pp.
Varma, B. N. The Sociology and Politics of Development. *A Theoretical Study.* 236 pp.
Wong, S.-L. Sociology and Socialism in Contemporary China. *160 pp.*
Wootton, Graham. Workers, Unions and the State. *188 pp.*

CRIMINOLOGY

Ancel, Marc. Social Defence: *A Modern Approach to Criminal Problems. Foreword by Leon Radzinowicz.* 240 pp.
Athens, L. Violent Criminal Acts and Actors. *104 pp.*
Cain, Maureen E. Society and the Policeman's Role. *326 pp.*
Cloward, Richard A. and Ohlin, Lloyd E. Delinquency and Opportunity: *A Theory of Delinquent Gangs.* 248 pp.
Downes, David M. The Delinquent Solution. *A Study in Subcultural Theory.* 296 pp.
Friedlander, Kate. The Psycho-Analytical Approach to Juvenile Delinquency: *Theory, Case Studies, Treatment.* 320 pp.
Gleuck, Sheldon and Eleanor. Family Environment and Delinquency. *With the statistical assistance of Rose W. Kneznek.* 340 pp.
Lopez-Rey, Manuel. Crime. *An Analytical Appraisal.* 288 pp.
Mannheim, Hermann. Comparative Criminology: *A Text Book. Two volumes.* 442 pp. and 380 pp.
Morris, Terence. The Criminal Area: *A Study in Social Ecology. Foreword by Hermann Mannheim.* 232 pp. 25 tables. 4 maps.
Rock, Paul. Making People Pay. *338 pp.*
● Taylor, Ian, Walton, Paul and Young, Jock. The New Criminology. *For a Social Theory of Deviance.* 325 pp.
● Taylor, Ian, Walton, Paul and Young, Jock. (Eds) Critical Criminology. *268 pp.*

SOCIAL PSYCHOLOGY

Bagley, Christopher. The Social Psychology of the Epileptic Child. *320 pp.*
Brittan, Arthur. Meanings and Situations. *224 pp.*
Carroll, J. Break-Out from the Crystal Palace. *200 pp.*
● Fleming, C. M. Adolescence: Its Social Psychology. *With an Introduction to recent findings from the fields of Anthropology, Physiology, Medicine, Psychometrics and Sociometry.* 288 pp.
● The Social Psychology of Education: *An Introduction and Guide to Its Study.* 136 pp.
Linton, Ralph. The Cultural Background of Personality. *132 pp.*
● Mayo, Elton. The Social Problems of an Industrial Civilization. *With an Appendix on the Political Problem.* 180 pp.
Ottaway, A. K. C. Learning Through Group Experience. *176 pp.*
Plummer, Ken. Sexual Stigma. *An Interactionist Account.* 254 pp.
● Rose, Arnold M. (Ed.) Human Behaviour and Social Processes: *an Interactionist Approach. Contributions by Arnold M. Rose, Ralph H. Turner, Anselm Strauss, Everett C. Hughes, E. Franklin Frazier, Howard S. Becker et al.* 696 pp.
Smelser, Neil J. Theory of Collective Behaviour. *448 pp.*
Stephenson, Geoffrey M. The Development of Conscience. *128 pp.*
Young, Kimball. Handbook of Social Psychology. *658 pp. 16 figures. 10 tables.*

SOCIOLOGY OF THE FAMILY

Bell, Colin R. Middle Class Families: *Social and Geographical Mobility*. *224 pp.*
Burton, Lindy. Vulnerable Children. *272 pp.*
Gavron, Hannah. The Captive Wife: *Conflicts of Household Mothers*. *190 pp.*
George, Victor and **Wilding, Paul.** Motherless Families. *248 pp.*
Klein, Josephine. Samples from English Cultures.
    1. Three Preliminary Studies and Aspects of Adult Life in England. *447 pp.*
    2. Child-Rearing Practices and Index. *247 pp.*
Klein, Viola. The Feminine Character. *History of an Ideology*. *244 pp.*
McWhinnie, Alexina M. Adopted Children. *How They Grow Up*. *304 pp.*
● **Morgan, D. H. J.** Social Theory and the Family. *About 320 pp.*
● **Myrdal, Alva** and **Klein, Viola.** Women's Two Roles: *Home and Work*. *238 pp. 27 tables.*
Parsons, Talcott and **Bales, Robert F.** Family: Socialization and Interaction Process. *In collaboration with James Olds, Morris Zelditch and Philip E. Slater*. *456 pp. 50 figures and tables.*

SOCIAL SERVICES

Bastide, Roger. The Sociology of Mental Disorder. *Translated from the French by Jean McNeil*. *260 pp.*
Carlebach, Julius. Caring For Children in Trouble. *266 pp.*
George, Victor. Foster Care. *Theory and Practice*. *234 pp.*
    Social Security: *Beveridge and After*. *258 pp.*
George, V. and **Wilding, P.** Motherless Families. *248 pp.*
● **Goetschius, George W.** Working with Community Groups. *256 pp.*
Goetschius, George W. and **Tash, Joan.** Working with Unattached Youth. *416 pp.*
Heywood, Jean S. Children in Care. *The Development of the Service for the Deprived Child. Third revised edition*. *284 pp.*
King, Roy D., Ranes, Norma V. and **Tizard, Jack.** Patterns of Residential Care. *356 pp.*
Leigh, John. Young People and Leisure. *256 pp.*
● **Mays, John.** (Ed.) Penelope Hall's Social Services of England and Wales. *368 pp.*
Morris, Mary. Voluntary Work and the Welfare State. *300 pp.*
Nokes, P. L. The Professional Task in Welfare Practice. *152 pp.*
Timms, Noel. Psychiatric Social Work in Great Britain (1939–1962). *280 pp.*
●   Social Casework: *Principles and Practice*. *256 pp.*

SOCIOLOGY OF EDUCATION

Banks, Olive. Parity and Prestige in English Secondary Education: a Study in Educational Sociology. *272 pp.*
● **Blyth, W. A. L.** English Primary Education. *A Sociological Description*.
    2. Background. *168 pp.*
Collier, K. G. The Social Purposes of Education: *Personal and Social Values in Education*. *268 pp.*
Evans, K. M. Sociometry and Education. *158 pp.*
● **Ford, Julienne.** Social Class and the Comprehensive School. *192 pp.*
Foster, P. J. Education and Social Change in Ghana. *336 pp. 3 maps.*
Fraser, W. R. Education and Society in Modern France. *150 pp.*
Grace, Gerald R. Role Conflict and the Teacher. *150 pp.*
Hans, Nicholas. New Trends in Education in the Eighteenth Century. *278 pp. 19 tables.*
●   Comparative Education: *A Study of Educational Factors and Traditions*. *360 pp.*
● **Hargreaves, David.** Interpersonal Relations and Education. *432 pp.*
●   Social Relations in a Secondary School. *240 pp.*
    School Organization and Pupil Involvement. *A Study of Secondary Schools*.

- **Mannheim, Karl** and **Stewart, W. A. C.** An Introduction to the Sociology of Education. *206 pp.*
- **Musgrove, F.** Youth and the Social Order. *176 pp.*
- **Ottaway, A. K. C.** Education and Society: An Introduction to the Sociology of Education. *With an Introduction by W. O. Lester Smith. 212 pp.*

  Peers, Robert. Adult Education: *A Comparative Study. Revised edition. 398 pp.*

  Stratta, Erica. The Education of Borstal Boys. *A Study of their Educational Experiences prior to, and during, Borstal Training. 256 pp.*
- **Taylor, P. H.**, **Reid, W. A.** and **Holley, B. J.** The English Sixth Form. *A Case Study in Curriculum Research. 198 pp.*

SOCIOLOGY OF CULTURE

Eppel, E. M. and **M.** Adolescents and Morality: *A Study of some Moral Values and Dilemmas of Working Adolescents in the Context of a changing Climate of Opinion. Foreword by W. J. H. Sprott. 268 pp. 39 tables.*

- **Fromm, Erich.** The Fear of Freedom. *286 pp.*
- The Sane Society. *400 pp.*

  Johnson, L. The Cultural Critics. *From Matthew Arnold to Raymond Williams. 233 pp.*

  Mannheim, Karl. Essays on the Sociology of Culture. *Edited by Ernst Mannheim in co-operation with Paul Kecskemeti. Editorial Note by Adolph Lowe. 280 pp.*

  Merquior, J. G. The Veil and the Mask. *Essays on Culture and Ideology. Foreword by Ernest Gellner. 140 pp.*

  Zijderfeld, A. C. On Clichés. *The Supersedure of Meaning by Function in Modernity. 150 pp.*

SOCIOLOGY OF RELIGION

Argyle, Michael and **Beit-Hallahmi, Benjamin.** The Social Psychology of Religion. *256 pp.*

Glasner, Peter E. The Sociology of Secularisation. *A Critique of a Concept. 146 pp.*

Hall, J. R. The Ways Out. *Utopian Communal Groups in an Age of Babylon. 280 pp.*

Ranson, S., **Hinings, B.** and **Bryman, A.** Clergy, Ministers and Priests. *216 pp.*

Stark, Werner. The Sociology of Religion. *A Study of Christendom.*
  Volume II. *Sectarian Religion. 368 pp.*
  Volume III. *The Universal Church. 464 pp.*
  Volume IV. *Types of Religious Man. 352 pp.*
  Volume V. *Types of Religious Culture. 464 pp.*

Turner, B. S. Weber and Islam. *216 pp.*

Watt, W. Montgomery. Islam and the Integration of Society. *320 pp.*

SOCIOLOGY OF ART AND LITERATURE

Jarvie, Ian C. Towards a Sociology of the Cinema. *A Comparative Essay on the Structure and Functioning of a Major Entertainment Industry. 405 pp.*

Rust, Frances S. Dance in Society. *An Analysis of the Relationships between the Social Dance and Society in England from the Middle Ages to the Present Day. 256 pp. 8 pp. of plates.*

Schücking, L. L. The Sociology of Literary Taste. *112 pp.*

Wolff, Janet. Hermeneutic Philosophy and the Sociology of Art. *150 pp.*

SOCIOLOGY OF KNOWLEDGE

Diesing, P. Patterns of Discovery in the Social Sciences. *262 pp.*

- **Douglas, J. D.** (Ed.) Understanding Everyday Life. *370 pp.*
- **Hamilton, P.** Knowledge and Social Structure. *174 pp.*
  Jarvie, I. C. Concepts and Society. *232 pp.*
  Mannheim, Karl. Essays on the Sociology of Knowledge. *Edited by Paul Kecskemeti. Editorial Note by Adolph Lowe. 353 pp.*
  Remmling, Gunter W. The Sociology of Karl Mannheim. *With a Bibliographical Guide to the Sociology of Knowledge, Ideological Analysis, and Social Planning. 255 pp.*
  Remmling, Gunter W. (Ed.) Towards the Sociology of Knowledge. *Origin and Development of a Sociological Thought Style. 463 pp.*
  Scheler, M. Problems of a Sociology of Knowledge. *Trans. by M. S. Frings. Edited and with an Introduction by K. Stikkers. 232 pp.*

URBAN SOCIOLOGY

Aldridge, M. The British New Towns. *A Programme Without a Policy. 232 pp.*
Ashworth, William. The Genesis of Modern British Town Planning: *A Study in Economic and Social History of the Nineteenth and Twentieth Centuries. 288 pp.*
Brittan, A. The Privatised World. *196 pp.*
Cullingworth, J. B. Housing Needs and Planning Policy: *A Restatement of the Problems of Housing Need and 'Overspill' in England and Wales. 232 pp. 44 tables. 8 maps.*
Dickinson, Robert E. City and Region: *A Geographical Interpretation. 608 pp. 125 figures.*
   The West European City: *A Geographical Interpretation. 600 pp. 129 maps. 29 plates.*
Humphreys, Alexander J. New Dubliners: *Urbanization and the Irish Family. Foreword by George C. Homans. 304 pp.*
Jackson, Brian. Working Class Community: *Some General Notions raised by a Series of Studies in Northern England. 192 pp.*
- **Mann, P. H.** An Approach to Urban Sociology. *240 pp.*
  Mellor, J. R. Urban Sociology in an Urbanized Society. *326 pp.*
  Morris, R. N. and **Mogey, J.** The Sociology of Housing. *Studies at Berinsfield. 232 pp. 4 pp. plates.*
  Mullan, R. Stevenage Ltd. *About 250 pp.*
  Rex, J. and **Tomlinson, S.** Colonial Immigrants in a British City. *A Class Analysis. 368 pp.*
  Rosser, C. and **Harris, C.** The Family and Social Change. *A Study of Family and Kinship in a South Wales Town. 352 pp. 8 maps.*
- **Stacey, Margaret, Batsone, Eric, Bell, Colin** and **Thurcott, Anne.** Power, Persistence and Change. *A Second Study of Banbury. 196 pp.*

RURAL SOCIOLOGY

Mayer, Adrian C. Peasants in the Pacific. *A Study of Fiji Indian Rural Society. 248 pp. 20 plates.*
Williams, W. M. The Sociology of an English Village: *Gosforth. 272 pp. 12 figures. 13 tables.*

SOCIOLOGY OF INDUSTRY AND DISTRIBUTION

Dunkerley, David. The Foreman. *Aspects of Task and Structure. 192 pp.*
Eldridge, J. E. T. Industrial Disputes. *Essays in the Sociology of Industrial Relations. 288 pp.*
Hollowell, Peter G. The Lorry Driver. *272 pp.*
- **Oxaal, I., Barnett, T.** and **Booth, D.** (Eds) Beyond the Sociology of Development.

Economy and Society in Latin America and Africa. 295 pp.
Smelser, Neil J. Social Change in the Industrial Revolution: *An Application of Theory to the Lancashire Cotton Industry, 1770–1840.* 468 pp. 12 figures. 14 tables.
Watson, T. J. The Personnel Managers. *A Study in the Sociology of Work and Employment,* 262 pp.

ANTHROPOLOGY

Brandel-Syrier, Mia. Reeftown Elite. *A Study of Social Mobility in a Modern African Community on the Reef.* 376 pp.
Dickie-Clark, H. F. The Marginal Situation. *A Sociological Study of a Coloured Group.* 236 pp.
Dube, S. C. Indian Village. Foreword by Morris Edward Opler. 276 pp. 4 plates.
India's Changing Villages: *Human Factors in Community Development.* 260 pp. 8 plates. 1 map.
Fei, H.-T. Peasant Life in China. *A Field Study of Country Life in the Yangtze Valley.* With a foreword by Bronislaw Malinowski. 328 pp. 16 pp. plates.
Firth, Raymond. Malay Fishermen. *Their Peasant Economy.* 420 pp. 17 pp. plates.
Gulliver, P. H. Social Control in an African Society: a Study of the Arusha, Agricultural Masai of Northern Tanganyika. 320 pp. 8 plates. 10 figures.
Family Herds. 288 pp.
Jarvie, Ian C. The Revolution in Anthropology. 268 pp.
Little, Kenneth L. Mende of Sierra Leone. 308 pp. and folder.
Negroes in Britain. *With a New Introduction and Contemporary Study by Leonard Bloom.* 320 pp.
Tambs-Lyche, H. London Patidars. *About 180 pp.*
Madan, G. R. Western Sociologists on Indian Society. *Marx, Spencer, Weber, Durkheim, Pareto.* 384 pp.
Mayer, A. C. Peasants in the Pacific. *A Study of Fiji Indian Rural Society.* 248 pp.
Meer, Fatima. Race and Suicide in South Africa. 325 pp.
Smith, Raymond T. The Negro Family in British Guiana: *Family Structure and Social Status in the Villages.* With a Foreword by Meyer Fortes. 314 pp. 8 plates. 1 figure. 4 maps.

SOCIOLOGY AND PHILOSOPHY

Adriaansens, H. Talcott Parsons and the Conceptual Dilemma. *About 224 pp.*
Barnsley, John H. The Social Reality of Ethics. *A Comparative Analysis of Moral Codes.* 448 pp.
Diesing, Paul. Patterns of Discovery in the Social Sciences. 362 pp.
● **Douglas, Jack D.** (Ed.) Understanding Everyday Life. *Toward the Reconstruction of Sociological Knowledge.* Contributions by Alan F. Blum, Aaron W. Cicourel, Norman K. Denzin, Jack D. Douglas, John Heeren, Peter McHugh, Peter K. Manning, Melvin Power, Matthew Speier, Roy Turner, D. Lawrence Wieder, Thomas P. Wilson and Don H. Zimmerman. 370 pp.
Gorman, Robert A. The Dual Vision. *Alfred Schutz and the Myth of Phenomenological Social Science.* 240 pp.
Jarvie, Ian C. Concepts and Society. 216 pp.
Kilminster, R. Praxis and Method. *A Sociological Dialogue with Lukács, Gramsci and the Early Frankfurt School.* 334 pp.
● **Pelz, Werner.** The Scope of Understanding in Sociology. *Towards a More Radical Reorientation in the Social Humanistic Sciences.* 283 pp.
Roche, Maurice. Phenomenology, Language and the Social Sciences. 371 pp.
Sahay, Arun. Sociological Analysis. 212 pp.
● **Slater, P.** Origin and Significance of the Frankfurt School. *A Marxist Perspective.* 185 pp.

Spurling, L. Phenomenology and the Social World. *The Philosophy of Merleau-Ponty and its Relation to the Social Sciences.* 222 pp.
Wilson, H. T. The American Ideology. *Science, Technology and Organization as Modes of Rationality.* 368 pp.

International Library of Anthropology
General Editor Adam Kuper

● **Ahmed, A. S.** Millennium and Charisma Among Pathans. *A Critical Essay in Social Anthropology.* 192 pp.
Pukhtun Economy and Society. *Traditional Structure and Economic Development.* About 360 pp.
Barth, F. Selected Essays. *Volume I. About 250 pp.* Selected Essays. *Volume II. About 250 pp.*
Brown, Paula. The Chimbu. *A Study of Change in the New Guinea Highlands.* 151 pp.
Foner, N. Jamaica Farewell. 200 pp.
Gudeman, Stephen. Relationships, Residence and the Individual. *A Rural Panamanian Community.* 288 pp. 11 plates, 5 figures, 2 maps, 10 tables.
The Demise of a Rural Economy. *From Subsistence to Capitalism in a Latin American Village.* 160 pp.
Hamnett, Ian. Chieftainship and Legitimacy. *An Anthropological Study of Executive Law in Lesotho.* 163 pp.
Hanson, F. Allan. Meaning in Culture. *127 pp.*
Hazan, H. The Limbo People. *A Study of the Constitution of the Time Universe Among the Aged.* About 192 pp.
Humphreys, S. C. Anthropology and the Greeks. 288 pp.
Karp, I. Fields of Change Among the Iteso of Kenya. *140 pp.*
Lloyd, P. C. Power and Independence. *Urban Africans' Perception of Social Inequality.* 264 pp.
Parry, J. P. Caste and Kinship in Kangra. 352 pp. *Illustrated.*
Pettigrew, Joyce. Robber Noblemen. *A Study of the Political System of the Sikh Jats.* 284 pp.
Street, Brian V. The Savage in Literature. *Representations of 'Primitive' Society in English Fiction, 1858–1920.* 207 pp.
Van Den Berghe, Pierre L. Power and Privilege at an African University. 278 pp.

International Library of Phenomenology and Moral Sciences
General Editor John O'Neill

Apel, K.-O. Towards a Transformation of Philosophy. 308 pp.
Bologh, R. W. Dialectical Phenomenology. *Marx's Method.* 287 pp.
Fekete, J. The Critical Twilight. *Explorations in the Ideology of Anglo-American Literary Theory from Eliot to McLuhan.* 300 pp.
Medina, A. Reflection, Time and the Novel. *Towards a Communicative Theory of Literature.* 143 pp.

International Library of Social Policy
General Editor Kathleen Jones

Bayley, M. Mental Handicap and Community Care. *426 pp.*
Bottoms, A. E. and **McClean, J. D.** Defendants in the Criminal Process. *284 pp.*
Bradshaw, J. The Family Fund. *An Initiative in Social Policy.* About 224 pp.

Butler, J. R. Family Doctors and Public Policy. *208 pp.*
Davies, Martin. Prisoners of Society. *Attitudes and Aftercare. 204 pp.*
Gittus, Elizabeth. Flats, Families and the Under-Fives. *285 pp.*
Holman, Robert. Trading in Children. *A Study of Private Fostering. 355 pp.*
Jeffs, A. Young People and the Youth Service. *160 pp.*
Jones, Howard and Cornes, Paul. Open Prisons. *288 pp.*
Jones, Kathleen. History of the Mental Health Service. *428 pp.*
Jones, Kathleen with **Brown, John, Cunningham, W. J., Roberts, Julian** and **Williams, Peter.** Opening the Door. *A Study of New Policies for the Mentally Handicapped. 278 pp.*
Karn, Valerie. Retiring to the Seaside. *400 pp. 2 maps. Numerous tables.*
King, R. D. and **Elliot, K. W.** Albany: Birth of a Prison—End of an Era. *394 pp.*
Thomas, J. E. The English Prison Officer since 1850: *A Study in Conflict. 258 pp.*
Walton, R. G. Women in Social Work. *303 pp.*
● **Woodward, J.** To Do the Sick No Harm. *A Study of the British Voluntary Hospital System to 1875. 234 pp.*

International Library of Welfare and Philosophy
General Editors   Noel Timms and David Watson

● **McDermott, F. E.** (Ed.) Self-Determination in Social Work. *A Collection of Essays on Self-determination and Related Concepts by Philosophers and Social Work Theorists.* Contributors: F. P. Biestek, S. Bernstein, A. Keith-Lucas, D. Sayer, H. H. Perelman, C. Whittington, R. F. Stalley, F. E. McDermott, I. Berlin, H. J. McCloskey, H. L. A. Hart, J. Wilson, A. I. Melden, S. I. Benn. *254 pp.*
● **Plant, Raymond.** Community and Ideology. *104 pp.*
Ragg, Nicholas M. People Not Cases. *A Philosophical Approach to Social Work. 168 pp.*
● **Timms, Noel** and **Watson, David.** (Eds) Talking About Welfare. *Readings in Philosophy and Social Policy.* Contributors: T. H. Marshall, R. B. Brandt, G. H. von Wright, K. Nielsen, M. Cranston, R. M. Titmuss, R. S. Downie, E. Telfer, D. Donnison, J. Benson, P. Leonard, A. Keith-Lucas, D. Walsh, I. T. Ramsey. *320 pp.*
● Philosophy in Social Work. *250 pp.*
● **Weale, A.** Equality and Social Policy. *164 pp.*

Library of Social Work
General Editor   Noel Timms

● **Baldock, Peter.** Community Work and Social Work. *140 pp.*
○ **Beedell, Christopher.** Residential Life with Children. *210 pp. Crown 8vo.*
● **Berry, Juliet.** Daily Experience in Residential Life. *A Study of Children and their Care-givers. 202 pp.*
○ Social Work with Children. *190 pp. Crown 8vo.*
● **Brearley, C. Paul.** Residential Work with the Elderly. *116 pp.*
● Social Work, Ageing and Society. *126 pp.*
● **Cheetham, Juliet.** Social Work with Immigrants. *240 pp. Crown 8vo.*
● **Cross, Crispin P.** (Ed.) Interviewing and Communication in Social Work. Contributions by C. P. Cross, D. Laurenson, B. Strutt, S. Raven. *192 pp. Crown 8vo.*

- **Curnock, Kathleen** and **Hardiker, Pauline.** Towards Practice Theory. *Skills and Methods in Social Assessments. 208 pp.*
- **Davies, Bernard.** The Use of Groups in Social Work Practice. *158 pp.*
- **Davies, Martin.** Support Systems in Social Work. *144 pp.*
  Ellis, June. (Ed.) West African Families in Britain. *A Meeting of Two Cultures. Contributions by Pat Stapleton, Vivien Biggs. 150 pp. 1 Map.*
- **Hart, John.** Social Work and Sexual Conduct. *230 pp.*
- **Hutten, Joan M.** Short-Term Contracts in Social Work. *Contributions by Stella M. Hall, Elsie Osborne, Mannie Sher, Eva Sternberg, Elizabeth Tuters. 134 pp.*
  Jackson, Michael P. and **Valencia, B. Michael.** Financial Aid Through Social Work. *140 pp.*
- **Jones, Howard.** The Residential Community. *A Setting for Social Work. 150 pp.*
- (Ed.) Towards a New Social Work. *Contributions by Howard Jones, D. A. Fowler, J. R. Cypher, R. G. Walton, Geoffrey Mungham, Philip Priestley, Ian Shaw, M. Bartley, R. Deacon, Irwin Epstein, Geoffrey Pearson. 184 pp.*
  Jones, Ray and **Pritchard, Colin.** (Eds) Social Work With Adolescents. *Contributions by Ray Jones, Colin Pritchard, Jack Dunham, Florence Rossetti, Andrew Kerslake, John Burns, William Gregory, Graham Templeman, Kenneth E. Reid, Audrey Taylor. About 170 pp.*
- ○ **Jordon, William.** The Social Worker in Family Situations. *160 pp. Crown 8vo.*
- **Laycock, A. L.** Adolescents and Social Work. *128 pp. Crown 8vo.*
- **Lees, Ray.** Politics and Social Work. *128 pp. Crown 8vo.*
- Research Strategies for Social Welfare. *112 pp. Tables.*
- ○ **McCullough, M. K.** and **Ely, Peter J.** Social Work with Groups. *127 pp. Crown 8vo.*
- **Moffett, Jonathan.** Concepts in Casework Treatment. *128 pp. Crown 8vo.*
  Parsloe, Phyllida. Juvenile Justice in Britain and the United States. *The Balance of Needs and Rights. 336 pp.*
- **Plant, Raymond.** Social and Moral Theory in Casework. *112 pp. Crown 8vo.*
  Priestley, Philip, Fears, Denise and **Fuller, Roger.** Justice for Juveniles. *The 1969 Children and Young Persons Act: A Case for Reform? 128 pp.*
- **Pritchard, Colin** and **Taylor, Richard.** Social Work: Reform or Revolution? *170 pp.*
- ○ **Pugh, Elisabeth.** Social Work in Child Care. *128 pp. Crown 8vo.*
- **Robinson, Margaret.** Schools and Social Work. *282 pp.*
- ○ **Ruddock, Ralph.** Roles and Relationships. *128 pp. Crown 8vo.*
- **Sainsbury, Eric.** Social Diagnosis in Casework. *118 pp. Crown 8vo.*
- Social Work with Families. *Perceptions of Social Casework among Clients of a Family Service. 188 pp.*
  Seed, Philip. The Expansion of Social Work in Britain. *128 pp. Crown 8vo.*
- **Shaw, John.** The Self in Social Work. *124 pp.*
  Smale, Gerald G. Prophecy, Behaviour and Change. *An Examination of Self-fulfilling Prophecies in Helping Relationships. 116 pp. Crown 8vo.*
  Smith, Gilbert. Social Need. *Policy, Practice and Research. 155 pp.*
- Social Work and the Sociology of Organisations. *124 pp. Revised edition.*
- **Sutton, Carole.** Psychology for Social Workers and Counsellors. *An Introduction. 248 pp.*
- **Timms, Noel.** Language of Social Casework. *122 pp. Crown 8vo.*
- Recording in Social Work. *124 pp. Crown 8vo.*
- **Todd, F. Joan.** Social Work with the Mentally Subnormal. *96 pp. Crown 8vo.*
- **Walrond-Skinner, Sue.** Family Therapy. *The Treatment of Natural Systems. 172 pp.*
- **Warham, Joyce.** An Introduction to Administration for Social Workers. *Revised edition. 112 pp.*
- An Open Case. *The Organisational Context of Social Work. 172 pp.*
- ○ **Wittenberg, Isca Salzberger.** Psycho-Analytic Insight and Relationships. *A Kleinian Approach. 196 pp. Crown 8vo.*

Primary Socialization, Language and Education
General Editor Basil Bernstein

Adlam, Diana S., *with the assistance of Geoffrey Turner and Lesley Lineker.* Code in Context. *272 pp.*
Bernstein, Basil. Class, Codes and Control. *3 volumes.*
● 1. *Theoretical Studies Towards a Sociology of Language. 254 pp.*
2. *Applied Studies Towards a Sociology of Language. 377 pp.*
● 3. *Towards a Theory of Educational Transmission. 167 pp.*
Brandis, W. and **Bernstein, B.** Selection and Control. *176 pp.*
Brandis, Walter and **Henderson, Dorothy.** Social Class, Language and Communication. *288 pp.*
Cook-Gumperz, Jenny. Social Control and Socialization. *A Study of Class Differences in the Language of Maternal Control. 290 pp.*
● **Gahagan, D. M.** and **G. A.** Talk Reform. *Exploration in Language for Infant School Children. 160 pp.*
Hawkins, P. R. Social Class, the Nominal Group and Verbal Strategies. *About 220 pp.*
Robinson, W. P. and **Rackstraw, Susan D. A.** A Question of Answers. *2 volumes. 192 pp. and 180 pp.*
Turner, Geoffrey J. and **Mohan, Bernard A.** A Linguistic Description and Computer Programme for Children's Speech. *208 pp.*

Reports of the Institute of Community Studies

Baker, J. The Neighbourhood Advice Centre. A Community Project in Camden. *320 pp.*
● **Cartwright, Ann.** Patients and their Doctors. *A Study of General Practice. 304 pp.*
Dench, Geoff. Maltese in London. *A Case-study in the Erosion of Ethnic Consciousness. 302 pp.*
Jackson, Brian and **Marsden, Dennis.** Education and the Working Class: *Some General Themes Raised by a Study of 88 Working-class Children in a Northern Industrial City. 268 pp. 2 folders.*
Marris, Peter. The Experience of Higher Education. *232 pp. 27 tables.*
● Loss and Change. *192 pp.*
Marris, Peter and **Rein, Martin.** Dilemmas of Social Reform. *Poverty and Community Action in the United States. 256 pp.*
Marris, Peter and **Somerset, Anthony.** African Businessmen. *A Study of Entrepreneurship and Development in Kenya. 256 pp.*
Mills, Richard. Young Outsiders: *a Study in Alternative Communities. 216 pp.*
Runciman, W. G. Relative Deprivation and Social Justice. *A Study of Attitudes to Social Inequality in Twentieth-Century England. 352 pp.*
Willmott, Peter. Adolescent Boys in East London. *230 pp.*
Willmott, Peter and **Young, Michael.** Family and Class in a London Suburb. *202 pp. 47 tables.*
Young, Michael and **McGeeney, Patrick.** Learning Begins at Home. *A Study of a Junior School and its Parents. 128 pp.*
Young, Michael and **Willmott, Peter.** Family and Kinship in East London. *Foreword by Richard M. Titmuss. 252 pp. 39 tables.*
The Symmetrical Family. *410 pp.*

Reports of the Institute for Social Studies in Medical Care

Cartwright, Ann, Hockey, Lisbeth and **Anderson, John J.** Life Before Death. *310 pp.*
Dunnell, Karen and **Cartwright, Ann.** Medicine Takers, Prescribers and Hoarders. *190 pp.*
Farrell, C. My Mother Said... *A Study of the Way Young People Learned About Sex and Birth Control. 288 pp.*

Medicine, Illness and Society
General Editor W. M. Williams

Hall, David J. Social Relations & Innovation. *Changing the State of Play in Hospitals. 232 pp.*
Hall, David J. and **Stacey, M.** (Eds) Beyond Separation. *234 pp.*
Robinson, David. The Process of Becoming Ill. *142 pp.*
Stacey, Margaret *et al.* Hospitals, Children and Their Families. *The Report of a Pilot Study. 202 pp.*
Stimson, G. V. and **Webb, B.** Going to See the Doctor. *The Consultation Process in General Practice. 155 pp.*

Monographs in Social Theory
General Editor Arthur Brittan

● **Barnes, B.** Scientific Knowledge and Sociological Theory. *192 pp.*
Bauman, Zygmunt. Culture as Praxis. *204 pp.*
● **Dixon, Keith.** Sociological Theory. *Pretence and Possibility. 142 pp.*
   The Sociology of Belief. *Fallacy and Foundation. About 160 pp.*
Goff, T. W. Marx and Mead. *Contributions to a Sociology of Knowledge. 176 pp.*
Meltzer, B. N., Petras, J. W. and **Reynolds, L. T.** Symbolic Interactionism. *Genesis, Varieties and Criticisms. 144 pp.*
● **Smith, Anthony D.** The Concept of Social Change. *A Critique of the Functionalist Theory of Social Change. 208 pp.*

Routledge Social Science Journals

The British Journal of Sociology. *Editor – Angus Stewart; Associate Editor – Leslie Sklair. Vol. 1, No. 1 – March 1950 and Quarterly. Roy. 8vo. All back issues available. An international journal publishing original papers in the field of sociology and related areas.*
Community Work. *Edited by David Jones and Marjorie Mayo. 1973. Published annually.*
Economy and Society. *Vol. 1, No. 1. February 1972 and Quarterly. Metric Roy. 8vo. A journal for all social scientists covering sociology, philosophy, anthropology, economics and history. All back numbers available.*

Ethnic and Racial Studies. *Editor – John Stone. Vol. 1 – 1978. Published quarterly.*
Religion. Journal of Religion and Religions. *Chairman of Editorial Board, Ninian Smart. Vol. 1, No. 1, Spring 1971. A journal with an inter-disciplinary approach to the study of the phenomena of religion. All back numbers available.*
Sociology of Health and Illness. *A Journal of Medical Sociology. Editor – Alan Davies; Associate Editor – Ray Jobling. Vol. 1, Spring 1979. Published 3 times per annum.*
Year Book of Social Policy in Britain. *Edited by Kathleen Jones. 1971. Published annually.*

Social and Psychological Aspects of Medical Practice
Editor   Trevor Silverstone

Lader, Malcolm. Psychophysiology of Mental Illness. *280 pp.*
● **Silverstone, Trevor** and **Turner, Paul.** Drug Treatment in Psychiatry. *Revised edition. 256 pp.*
Whiteley, J. S. and **Gordon, J.** Group Approaches in Psychiatry. *240 pp.*